Personal Finance

Personal Finance

Edited by
George Callaghan
Ian Fribbance and
Martin Higginson

wiley.com

in association with

The Open University

Published by

John Wiley & Sons Ltd, The Atrium, Southern Gate, Chichester,
West Sussex PO19 8SQ, England
Telephone (+44) 1243 779777

in association with

The Open University, Walton Hall, Milton Keynes MK7 6AA
http://www.open.ac.uk

First published 2007

Edited and designed by The Open University.

Typeset in India by Alden Prepress Services, Chennai.

Printed and bound in the United Kingdom by CPI, Bath.

This book forms part of an Open University course DB123 *You and your money: personal finance in
context*. Details of this and other Open University courses can be obtained from the Student
Registration and Enquiry Service, The Open University, PO Box 197, Milton Keynes MK7 6BJ,
United Kingdom: tel. +44 (0)870 333 4340, email general-enquiries@open.ac.uk

A catalogue record of this book is available from the British Library.

Library of Congress Cataloging-in-Publication Data
Personal finance / edited by George Callaghan, Ian Fribbance, and Martin Higginson.
      p. cm.
   Includes bibliographical references and index.
   ISBN-13: 978-0-470-02855-1 (pbk.)
   ISBN-10: 0-470-02855-6 (pbk.)
1. Finance, Personal. 2. Investments. I. Callaghan, George. II. Fribbance, Ian. III. Higginson,
Martin.
   HG179.P3745 2006
   332.024–dc22   2006019155

ISBN-13: 978-0-470-02855-1
ISBN-10: 0-470-02855-6

1.1

Contents

Personal acknowledgements

This book is the result of a genuinely collaborative process and invaluable contributions were made by a number of people. We are grateful to our External Assessor, Mike Danson, Professor of Economics & Management at the University of Paisley, for his helpful feedback as this book was written. Valuable feedback was also received from two critical readers, Ernest Dyer, a Regional Manager of the Openings Programme at The Open University, and Lucy O'Connell, an Open University student.

We would also like to thank Alison Kirkbright for her tireless and enthusiastic project support; Chris Wooldridge for his numerous editorial suggestions; Howie Twiner for his excellent graphics; Diane Mole for her wonderful design; and particularly Jonquil Lowe for her expert guidance and comments throughout the development of the course and this book.

We also wish to express our gratitude to our respective mothers and fathers: Maureen and (the late) Terry Callaghan, June and Bill Fribbance, and Margaret and (the late) Roy Higginson whose commitment to our own well-being helped bring about this publication.

George Callaghan, Ian Fribbance and Martin Higginson
November 2006

Disclaimer

This book does not claim to give specific individual financial advice and nothing contained within it should be interpreted as doing so. If you think you need specific individual financial advice, you should see an authorised financial adviser.

Contributors

Vivienne Brown, Professor of Intellectual History, The Open University

George Callaghan, Lecturer in Economics, The Open University

Ian Fribbance, Lecturer in Economics, The Open University

Martin Higginson, Lecturer in Economics, The Open University

Susan Himmelweit, Professor of Economics, The Open University

Jonquil Lowe, Freelance Financial Researcher and Journalist

Janette Rutterford, Professor of Financial Management,
OU Business School

Martin Upton, Lecturer in Finance, OU Business School

Foreword

In a society in which people are increasingly required to take responsibility for their financial affairs, it's crucial that individuals develop greater 'financial capability'. People now have to take many difficult personal financial decisions – not just about day-to-day budgeting, but also about how to make provision for retirement, how to save for the future, and how to deal with high levels of debt. Taking such decisions is particularly challenging in a society with sophisticated marketing techniques, easy access to credit and an increased acceptance of high levels of personal debt. As individuals become more knowledgeable about personal finance, so they will become better informed about their choices by planning ahead, getting expert advice when they need it, buying products that meet their needs, and being equipped to manage and pay back their debts.

Research carried out on behalf of the Financial Services Authority has shown that the current level of financial capability amongst the population is insufficient and throws up some significant challenges for the future. Financial education has not kept pace with some of the major changes in society, such as changing work and lifestyle patterns, the implications of living longer and the range of financial products on offer. But there is now an increasing recognition – across the financial services industry, the government, education and the voluntary sector – that this needs to change.

The Financial Services Authority aims to be the catalyst for delivering a step change to the level of financial capability amongst UK citizens, by providing leadership to that end and by coordinating the contributions from a wide range of partners. For instance, a programme of financial education in the workplace is being developed, with a plan to deliver seminars to hundreds of thousands of employees across the UK. The education sector also has a major role to play in delivering increased financial capability and the government has embedded financial education in the school curriculum in England by including it in 'functional maths'.

In these circumstances, I warmly welcome the very timely initiative of The Open University in developing an innovative new course and this accompanying textbook on the subject of personal finance. The book not only explores all the key personal finance topics in a systematic and accessible way, it also places these topics within the changing social and economic context.

This development is particularly significant given The Open University's policy of open access to all potential students regardless of educational background, and its presence across the whole of the UK and beyond. Reflecting these educational and social values, *Personal Finance* should appeal to almost anyone wishing to learn about the issues related to financial capability. The Open University also has a record of influencing higher education curricula, and I hope that this publication will lead to an increase in the study of personal finance at introductory higher education level, where the subject can be studied in depth, and enjoyed by many thousands of students.

John Tiner
Chief Executive, Financial Services Authority
July 2006

Introducing personal finance

Ian Fribbance, George Callaghan and Martin Higginson

> ## Financial ignorance has us facing a fall
> (*The Scotsman*, 1 April 2006)

> ## FSA launches new financial education drive
> (Reuters, 28 March 2006)

> ## Money lessons coming to a street near you
> (*The Times*, 1 April 2006)

> ## Study reveals financial crisis of the 18–40s
> (*The Guardian*, 28 March 2006)

> ## Households on 'money knife-edge'
> (BBC Online, 28 March 2006)

There has never been a better time to study or read about the subject matter of *Personal Finance*. Research has shown that many people – especially those under 40 – have a poor knowledge of basic financial matters. For instance, one survey found that approximately 15 per cent of 18- to 24-year-olds mistakenly believed that a major tax-free savings product, an ISA (individual savings account) was in fact an iPod accessory, while another 10 per cent thought it was an energy drink (Credit Action, 2006). Moreover, this lack of knowledge feeds through into some worrying financial behaviour. In research published in 2006, it was estimated that four million people – spread in proportion across high- and low-income earners – *always* run out of money at the end of the week or month. Seven per cent of people had no idea of their current account balance, even to within the nearest £500; nearly 70 per cent of consumers had made no provision to see them through an unexpected event such as a sudden drop in income, and even though 81 per cent of working age adults recognised that the state pension would not be enough for them to enjoy a comfortable retirement, only 37 per cent of them had made any additional provision (FSA, 2006). This mixture of problems was potentially storing up trouble for many UK citizens. Consequently, with the need for financial education at an all-time high, we believe that *Personal Finance* will do much to help meet that need.

There are many reasons for you to read *Personal Finance*. Perhaps it's because you want to have a better understanding of the world of personal finance; or you want to be able to manage your money better; or you want to be able to read the financial press with more critical understanding. Perhaps you are young and haven't had much experience of money matters yet and you want to think ahead and learn about this vital subject. It may be because you are studying the innovative course from The Open University entitled *You and Your Money: Personal Finance in Context*, or you might be studying one of the growing number of other courses, diplomas, certificates and modules in further and higher education that now focus on personal finance. Or perhaps you are one of the hundreds of thousands of people who work in the financial services industry, and you want to have a broader perspective on some of the issues with which you are working.

Whatever your reason, personal finance is an interesting and important subject to learn about. Saving, borrowing, insuring and budgeting are routine activities for most people for much of their lives, they impact on major life decisions they make, and are a major current affairs and news topic. Competence in personal finance – or 'financial capability' as it has come to be called – is an essential skill for all and is increasingly recognised as an important part of 'good citizenship'.

One of the unique things about *Personal Finance* is that this book places the study of personal finance firmly within the broader social and economic background, and we believe that this is the first time that such a project has been attempted. We feel that it is crucial to set personal finance within its proper context because we strongly believe that the study of personal finance has to include the wider picture. Having an understanding of the social and economic background will give you a fuller understanding of the subject matter, and will better prepare you for the real-life version of financial planning that inevitably takes place within a rapidly changing social and economic environment. Another unique feature of this book is that we recognise that financial planning isn't always an individual process – there may be other household members or other relatives who both influence and are affected by financial decisions that are taken. This is often wrongly overlooked in other personal finance material, which usually ignores the fact that individuals are often part of a larger household or have wider family or caring concerns even if they live on their own. Furthermore, we emphasise the question of looking ahead and thinking about changes over a lifetime, including through to retirement.

The combination of these features makes *Personal Finance* a crucial book for developing better and more realistic financial planning. For example, learning the practical skill of how to budget in order to save towards a pension may be a very useful skill in itself. However, it may be of limited value if you don't also understand that, say, a high level of inflation will have a major impact on the value of the pension you hope to receive from those savings, and that the question of who within a household has built up their *individual* pension savings is also an important issue.

Inflation and individual savings are both important issues when considering pensions

Personal Finance is much more than a self-help book about how to manage money. We *do* include all the important practical issues, financial techniques and tips that you might expect, but we also look at the social and economic changes that impact on each personal finance topic. For instance, we will be discussing not just the types of mortgage available to buy a property, or the different types of investment that can be made, but also how changes in economic conditions may affect both. Similarly, our discussions of pensions, insurance and caring also look at the impact of government policy and the population changes that are taking place in our society.

In order to cover both the practical *and* the wider picture, the team that has written this book blends academics and teachers from both an economics and a business studies background, and further complements this with expertise and experience from the practical world of financial research and journalism. We very much hope that you will be getting the best of all worlds.

This has been an ambitious project, and as a result we have restricted ourselves primarily to discussing the UK. Indeed, since the introduction of devolution, there is some divergence even within the UK on a number of issues, such as care for the elderly, and these differences are interesting and important to take into account. In general, when we talk about the actions of 'the government' or look at our 'changing society', we are talking specifically about the UK. Reference is made to other countries, but this is primarily for contrast and comparison with the UK situation.

It's noteworthy that the development of the academic study of personal finance in the UK has somewhat lagged behind that of some other countries, especially the USA. There, many textbooks about personal finance are now available, with the result that many students and teachers of personal finance in the UK are forced to rely on books from a country where some of the social and economic context can be *very* different, for example, the taxation and health care systems. *Personal Finance* should help to redress that deficiency.

This book is written primarily as a distance learning type of textbook. This means that it can be studied independently and that it is written in a style that directly addresses you, a student of personal finance. The chapters proceed logically and are designed to be read in order, but each chapter also provides a handy point of reference for understanding a particular topic. *Personal Finance* covers all the important topic areas, with cross-referencing throughout, and the consistent development of core themes. There are many marginal notes that provide concise explanations of key terms when they are introduced. You'll also see 'Boxes' that explain core concepts, give technical explanations, or introduce articles to enhance your understanding. The book is also liberally illustrated with figures, tables, graphs, photos and cartoons.

Personal Finance includes 'Activities' for you to complete. We suggest that you should stop and carry out these Activities when they are suggested in the text. Some Activities will ask you to pause and think about what you have read; others will ask you to apply concepts and information that the book has covered. Some of the Activities allow you to reflect on your finances or on those of your household, but most will try to get you thinking more generally about financial questions so that you can develop a fuller understanding. We hope you will find this an engaging way of learning, and that it will help you to apply what you learn to your own circumstances. Let's start with an Activity that everyone can do, and is an example of one which focuses on your own finances.

Activity

Do you know exactly what you spend your money on? Many people don't. Try keeping a 'spending diary' as you read *Personal Finance*, and list all of your spending under some different, general headings. A good time period to do this for would be between two and four weeks. As you do this, think about what causes you to spend your money in the way you do.

Comment

Many people find that keeping a spending diary can be an enlightening experience. It's often an essential first step towards developing a cash flow statement, and the budgeting skills that you will develop in Chapter 3. After all, if you don't know where your money actually goes now, it is almost impossible to plan for it to go to where you want. Chapter 3 will also discuss some of the influences on people's spending habits. ■ ■ ■

Chapter 1 focuses on providing the crucial context for the remainder of the book. As well as introducing some key terms and ideas, it carefully explains the four themes that run throughout *Personal Finance*. In discussing the first theme about the social and economic context, the chapter also looks at some of the social changes that have made financial education so important. It then introduces and explains the three other themes: the interrelationship between individuals and their households; change over the life-course; and financial planning.

Chapters 2 and 3 look at the income and expenditure side of personal finances – earning money and spending it, usually with the necessity of deciding how to balance the competing demands on income. Such decisions often involve more than one person, be these partners, other adults or children, and are analysed within the social and economic context, such as the changing world of employment and education, and the changing social pressures on spending, such as advertising. These two chapters also introduce the practical financial skills of cash flow statements, budgeting and financial planning.

Chapters 4 and 5 consider the two sides of the 'financial balance sheet' – debts and borrowings, and savings and investments. Chapter 6 builds on the previous two chapters by examining the specific topic of housing, and also draws together the preceding material by looking at the financial balance sheet in detail, as well as introducing some additional practical financial tools.

Chapters 7, 8 and 9 seek to enhance understanding of the earlier material by exploring other personal finance topics in some detail. Chapter 7 considers planning for later life by focusing on pensions and, after discussing the changing social context, examines different pension types and financial planning for retirement, and questions of inheritance. Chapter 8 explores the 'caring and sharing' aspects of relationships between individuals and their households, and the financial implications of the creation, change and dissolution of households. Chapter 9 looks at life's unexpected events and how to protect against the negative financial consequences of some of these by taking out insurance.

Chapter 10 returns to the four themes of the book, and also looks ahead to see how future economic or social changes may impact on personal finance matters. Financial planning necessarily involves being able to think about what might happen in the future, and how to respond to change.

One of the benefits of placing the study of personal finance within its wider context is that, by introducing you to some economic, social and business analysis, we hope you will have your appetite whetted, and that you will consider further study in these important and thought-provoking subjects. Doing so would certainly further improve your financial planning skills. In the meantime, we very much hope that you enjoy reading *Personal Finance*.

References

Credit Action (2006) 'Debt facts and figures' [online], http://www. creditaction.org.uk/debtstats.htm (Accessed 3 April 2006).

Financial Services Authority (FSA) (2006) *Financial Capability in the UK: Establishing a Baseline* [online], http://www.fsa.gov.uk/pubs/other/fincap_baseline.pdf (Accessed 3 April 2006).

Personal finance: setting the context

Vivienne Brown

Contents

1   Introduction

'All the best things in life are free.' Or so the old saying has it. Since ancient times, philosophers have emphasised that true happiness comes from the goods of the mind: wisdom, love and friendship are more important, they argue, than material goods. On the other hand, economists think that nothing is free. Everything comes with a price, they say, in their less inspirational expression: 'There's no such thing as a free lunch.' According to this point of view, even wisdom, love and friendship have to be worked at. Some people might want to say that some of these can be bought rather than earned. Whatever the truth here, many of the things that people aspire to are not free in a monetary sense, and so questions of money seem impossible to avoid.

Questions about the good life and ultimate values may be timeless, but we live in society, and that is changing all the time. What people aspire to also changes over time. It is easy to overlook the current social and economic context, but when we stand apart from it a little we can see how people's aspirations – such as what they want to buy or do for a living – are influenced by it. This context is also important when studying personal finance. The context in which financial decisions are now made is the result of political, social and economic changes in the past, and as the present unfolds, new financial issues emerge. In *Personal Finance*, we shall examine how personal financial decisions are part of this wider picture. We shall also look at changes in family life and in the ways that people live together in households.

Although sharing this general context, people have different values and ambitions. These may reflect social factors such as different cultural, ethnic, religious or regional backgrounds. Each person's situation is different, with different circumstances and priorities. In spite of these differences, however, there is much that people have in common, and this also holds true when it comes to personal financial planning and looking ahead to what the future might bring. In *Personal Finance*, we shall examine these similarities by exploring personal financial planning and how it relates to a person's **life-course**. Later chapters will explore some of the differences between people by studying various financial 'scenarios' for different individuals and their households.

Life-course
The time profile of various stages in a person's life.

By covering both the wider context and personal financial planning, *Personal Finance* explains how personal financial decisions fit into the broader picture of society. The knowledge and understanding that this provides should help you to understand more about the financial decisions and choices you face. It should also equip you with critical tools for understanding new developments and changes in the world of personal finance.

The material in this chapter will introduce you to the main 'themes' of the book which run through all the chapters. In summary, the main themes of *Personal Finance* are:

1   *The changing social and economic context:* This theme examines how changes in society, politics and the economy impact on financial decision making.

2   *The interrelationship between individuals and households:* This theme looks at the connection between individual and household financial decision making and how an individual's financial decisions can be influenced by, or impact on, other household members.

3   *Change over the life-course:* This theme considers issues such as 'typical' life-courses, and looking ahead to future events.

4   *Financial planning:* This theme explores financial decision making.

The sections of this chapter concentrate on one theme at a time, and by the end of the chapter you will have a good sense of how all the themes are interconnected.

2   The changing social and economic context

2.1   A changing society

Living standards in the UK in the 2000s were higher than in any previous period. As you'll see in Chapter 2, one measure suggests that the overall standard of living has more than doubled between 1971 and 2004. Higher living standards mean that more money than ever before passes through households. Over the same period, however, there was an increase in inequality, which means that living standards did not improve as much for the poor as for the rich (*Social Trends*, 2005).

The way money is handled has been transformed by technological developments in banking and retailing. The weekly 'wage packet' – the little brown envelope with its precise amount of notes and coins – has virtually become a thing of the past, and having a bank account is now considered to be standard. How we use bank accounts has also been transformed with the growth of plastic payment cards – largely debit and credit cards – instead of cash or cheques. According to the Association for Payment Clearing Services (APACS, 2005), approximately 90 per cent of adults in the UK held one plastic card or more in 2005.

By the end of 2004, the total value of cash transactions in the UK was overtaken for the first time by plastic card transactions. In 2004, debit cards accounted for almost two-thirds (65 per cent) of all plastic card use, although for internet shopping credit cards were preferred. Online shopping had also increased: in 2004, 22 million adults made 262 million online transactions totalling £16 billion, and almost three-quarters (72 per cent) of these were credit card transactions (APACS, 2005).

Consumer society
A society in which people place a high value on possessions, and are continually encouraged to purchase more.

As well as this increased affluence, many argue that we now also live in a **consumer society** in which there is great emphasis on buying more, what people buy is seen to shape their identity, and shopping has become a leisure activity. Changes in technology, and sourcing from all over the world have introduced new products and new generations of established products. New tastes, aspirations and patterns of consumption are continually being created. In this, consumers may think they are immune to the power of marketing and advertising, but the effects of advertising suggest otherwise. Moreover, advertisements themselves illustrate social changes over the years, reflecting different gender roles and new attitudes to family life, sex, and career aspirations.

Living in a consumer society implies that there is pressure to buy the latest products, whether they are goods (such as electronic goods) or services (such as leisure activities and holidays). This consumer culture also involves buying more financial products. For example, borrowing money – such as taking out a personal loan – has come to be seen as buying a financial product, much like any other kind of product. More ways of borrowing money have been developed as well as many more inducements to do so. Earlier notions of financial prudence and caution seem to have been replaced by a different approach to spending and indebtedness. Ready access to mortgages, loans, credit cards and other forms of credit helped lead to an increase in personal indebtedness in the early 2000s.

This is clearly seen from the following data. In July 2004, total UK personal debt passed the £1 trillion mark – that is, £1,000,000,000,000. By mid 2005 this had risen to £1.1 trillion, a 10 per cent increase in just one year. Just over four-fifths of this debt was accounted for by

Cash wage packets and lower levels of affluence have been increasingly replaced by a consumer society of 'must have' hi-tech goods and online shopping using plastic cards

mortgages. Just under one-fifth was accounted for by consumer borrowing; this worked out at £4071 of consumer debt on average for each adult in the UK, a 45 per cent increase between 2000 and 2004. (Consumer debt includes credit cards, motor and retail finance, overdrafts and unsecured personal loans.) The increased availability and widespread use of credit cards have contributed to the increase in consumer credit, with nearly one-third of consumer debt accounted for by credit card debt: £56 billion with an average interest rate of 15.18 per cent in mid 2006 (Credit Action, 2006).

Financial products are often sold with heavy advertising, just as consumer products are. In previous centuries, a trip to the local pawn shop was a common way of surviving financial crises, but now there is extensive advertising encouraging people to take out debt. For instance, unsolicited mail through the letter box invites recipients to take out loans so that they can spend more money – whether or not they can afford to do so. Sometimes, as added inducement, this direct mail advertising includes a specimen cheque already made out in the recipient's name.

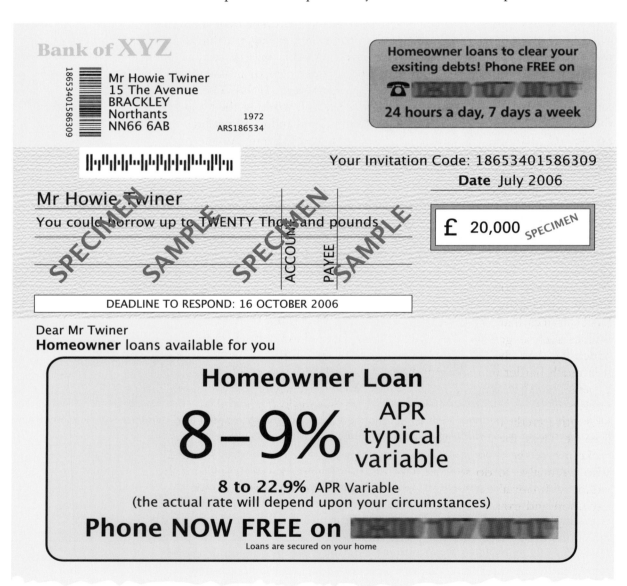

A typical ready-made credit cheque

Many consumers are able to manage their debt and find it a convenient way of planning their purchases. Furthermore, many households live comfortably in a home that they have purchased by using a mortgage to borrow money. Yet there are others who are over-indebted and are struggling to keep afloat. Sometimes, this indebtedness is the result of poverty, in that no amount of economising could pay off all debts or prevent debt in the first place. In other cases, over-indebtedness appears to be the result of poor money management. A survey by the Department for Trade and Industry (DTI) found that, in 2004, 9 per cent of surveyed individuals were spending more than half their income on total credit repayments (DTI, 2005). Other studies suggest that at that time, 18 per cent of households had arrears in paying bills or credit repayments on time, a figure which rose to 30 per cent of families with children and 50 per cent of lone parents (EurekAlert!, 2005). The longer-term effects of this increased indebtedness are still working their way through the economy, but in 2005 the Consumer Credit Counselling Service (CCCS), the UK's largest debt charity, and Citizens Advice both reported that they were dealing with an increased number of debt-related queries (Credit Action, 2005).

As I've just noted, problems of indebtedness are particularly acute for those on low incomes. In addition, those on low incomes are more likely to experience **financial exclusion**: lack of access to mainstream banking and financial services such as bank accounts and low-cost loans. A UK government report on financial exclusion in 2004 stated that one in twelve households in the UK did not have a bank account of any kind (HM Treasury, 2004, Foreword). Without banking facilities for personal financial management, such households end up with higher costs for basic services than those on higher incomes. For example, paying for utilities such as gas and electricity by using cash in meters is more expensive than cheque payment or direct debits; without a bank account it is much harder to make purchases by telephone or computer and it is expensive and inconvenient to cash a cheque; and relying on doorstep lenders or 'loan sharks' (sometimes termed 'non-prime lenders', or the alternative credit market) results in being charged extremely high rates of interest. Thus, there is a marked divide between those who are able to make use of the financial services on offer and the financially excluded who are unable to do so. This has led to government concern about the extent of financial exclusion, particularly as it also feeds into social exclusion and exacerbates problems of poverty.

Financial exclusion
Lack of access to mainstream banking and financial services.

Take a moment to think about your spending behaviour.

Do you find that you rely on credit for a lot of your spending? Do you worry about paying back what you owe?

Do you think this is different from your parents' experience? ■ ■ ■

2.2 Economic and political change

Welfare state
A system whereby the state funds or provides public services and redistributes income to provide a 'safety net' for its citizens.

Liberalisation
Government policy to promote free markets and competition.

Changes in personal finance are linked to changes in the political and economic climate. The post-Second World War political consensus in the UK about the **welfare state** suggested that the state had a recognised responsibility of care 'from the cradle to the grave'. Yet this consensus came under attack particularly after 1979 when the Conservative Government of Margaret Thatcher began to place increased emphasis on free markets and competition – a process sometimes referred to as **liberalisation**. This included the privatisation of nationalised industries such as gas, electricity, and later rail, partly in an attempt to promote competition. Liberalisation also included the introduction of commercial principles into areas of public-sector activity such as health and education. New bodies were set up to regulate the newly liberalised markets, partly to compensate for the limited extent of actual competition in such markets. This emphasis on free markets spread throughout many other areas of government policy. For instance, there were attempts to make the job market more competitive by encouraging employment mobility, and legislation was introduced allowing council tenants to buy their home.

Linked to this changing social and economic environment, characterised by reduced state provision and a focus on markets and competition, has been an increasing emphasis on financial self-reliance for individuals. State financial support still exists in many areas, for example, in the payment of state benefits. However, that state support is also taking new forms which are aimed at helping to promote 'self-reliance', for instance, with the introduction of Tax Credits paid since 1999, and the Child Trust Fund which started in 2005.

The movement towards greater individual responsibility for financial provision is evident in areas such as retirement pensions and student finances. For instance, in 1980 the Conservative Government abolished the link between pensions and earnings so that, instead, annual state pension rises were linked to price inflation. In practice, this means that pensions have risen less than they would have done otherwise, because prices have not risen as fast as wages, and state pensioners have not shared the same growth in standard of living as the working population. Combined with greater life expectancy and a declining proportion of the population who are of working age, an increased emphasis on private provision of pensions has developed. With regard to student finances, the move to a mass higher education system and changes to financial support under both Conservative and Labour governments mean many students now have to take out large loans to finance their studies. The debts of new graduates have been rising, and it was estimated that UK university students who graduated in summer 2004 had an average debt of £13,500, a 12 per cent increase in just one year (Credit Action, 2005).

This greater emphasis on individual responsibility and financial self-reliance means that individuals now, in turn, have to bear increased 'risk' themselves, rather than sharing it collectively through state provision. For example, individuals taking out private pensions have to bear the risks attached to those pension schemes. If a pension scheme does not pay out as much as expected, then the individuals concerned have reduced pensions. Similarly, students taking out loans to finance their studies have to bear the risk that their indebtedness might not be compensated by increased earnings in the future.

Risk derives from the fact that we don't know what the future will bring. As individuals now have to bear increased risk, it has become even more important for individuals to understand the risks involved and be able to make informed financial decisions. The idea of 'risk' is important to financial decision making, and so we shall return to it throughout the book.

2.3 Changes in financial services

The process of liberalisation has also been accompanied by changes in the financial services industry, which provides financial products such as credit, insurance policies, pensions and banking facilities. Before the 1980s, there had been controls on financial activities and movements of money. For instance, lending to consumers was controlled by the government: the terms of hire-purchase agreements for retail credit were subject to government control. The liberalisation of the financial services industry provided incentives for firms to offer a wider range of financial products. This, in turn, helped to lead to an expansion of the financial services industry. Between 1992 and 2003, the contribution to the output of the UK economy from finance and business services increased by nearly 140 per cent, whereas manufacturing increased by less than 30 per cent. This meant that in 2003 business and financial services accounted for 32 per cent of the output of the UK, whereas the manufacturing sector accounted for less than 15 per cent (ONS, 2005).

In some parts of the financial services industry, there was also greater competition to attract customers. The wider range of products that has become available might be thought to make financial planning easier as it provides more options to choose from; but intense competition can lead to aggressive marketing, and consumers are often confused by the array and complexity of financial products on offer. The old adage 'consumer beware' is as true, if not more so, for the financial services industry as it is for any other. (For example, do you know the actual rate of interest you are paying on the last item you bought on credit? Do you know what the **small print** says on the last financial contract you signed?)

Events have underlined the dangers for unsuspecting consumers. The dramatic rise in the value of stocks and shares at the end of the last century seemed to suggest that lucrative financial investments were easily available. With the fall in the stock market in the early part of this century, however, many ordinary investors learned the hard way that the warning that 'the value of investments can go down as well as up' was something to be taken seriously. Moreover, some spectacular financial scandals in the late twentieth century, such as pensions **mis-selling**, and the problems associated with Equitable Life, emphasised the perils involved for ordinary consumers and investors. Closer to home, buying housing at the peak of a property boom has proved a risky strategy for those overstretched with mortgage debt.

Even financial products that seem specifically designed to offer additional security for prudent consumers can sometimes turn out to be hazardous. For example, in 2005, the consumer body Citizens Advice issued a 'super complaint' to the Office of Fair Trading (OFT), a regulatory body, against the sale of payment protection insurance (PPI) policies. PPI policies are meant to provide cover for credit repayments in the event of illness or job loss, but Citizens Advice argued that the policies were failing in this. In their report, *Protection Racket: CAB Evidence on the Cost and Effectiveness of Payment Protection Insurance*, they argued that these policies were a financial 'racket' which brought in profits by being mis-sold to people who would not benefit from them and often could not afford them (Citizens Advice, 2005a). Box 1.1 shows how the Citizens Advice press release worded this.

Small print
A product's terms and conditions, typically written in small letters and/or technical jargon.

Mis-selling
High-pressure or misleading sales techniques inducing people to buy inappropriate financial products.

Box 1.1   Citizens Advice calls for OFT investigation into payment protection insurance

Payment protection insurance is failing many of those who need it most, adding to their debts instead of protecting them against hard times, a new report from national charity Citizens Advice says today.

The report – Protection Racket – says the insurance sold to cover credit payments in the event of illness or job loss is often very expensive, mis-sold to people who cannot possibly claim on it, and designed to exclude many of the most common situations that can lead to debt problems.

Citizens Advice is making a 'super complaint'* to the Office of Fair Trading, calling on them to launch an investigation into the payment protection insurance (PPI) business, which has an estimated 20 million policies in force and produces annual revenue in excess of £5 billion.

As Citizens Advice Chief Executive, David Harker, put it:

'Payment protection insurance is sold to borrowers with the promise of peace of mind and reassurance that credit repayments will be covered if they fall on hard times. People are lulled into a false sense of security, only to find that far from providing protection against an unexpected drop in income, PPI often just adds to their debt problems.

'At best the excessive cost for minimal benefits makes it bad value for many people; at worst mis-selling means the most vulnerable people are parted from large amounts of money under false pretences and left even more exposed to debt. This is particularly worrying at a time when personal debt levels are escalating.

'These problems are not new – we first reported on them ten years ago. It is a scandal that in this time so little has been done to remedy them. Selling PPI is big business, and this insurance does not come cheap, so it is high time the industry developed good minimum standards of cover. We badly need an official investigation of how this market is operating, leading to effective regulation that ensures a fair deal for all consumers, and which also protects the most vulnerable.'

*A 'super complaint' is a request to the OFT (or other specified regulator) to investigate an issue or a market that the consumer body believes is working against the consumer interest. The OFT (or other specified regulator) is required to publicly respond to a super complaint within 90 days.

(adapted from Citizens Advice, 2005b)

Problems such as mis-selling – where high-pressure or misleading sales techniques induce people to buy financial products that do not deliver on their purported benefits or are otherwise inappropriate for them – have highlighted the importance of consumer watchdogs, such as Citizens Advice, and regulatory bodies, such as the OFT. In 1997, the UK Government set up a new watchdog to oversee the financial services industry: the Financial Services Authority (FSA). The FSA is an independent non-governmental body which received its full statutory powers, given by the Financial Services and Markets Act 2000, from 1 December 2001. Its funding comes from the financial services industry, whereby the FSA charges fees to all authorised firms that carry out activities which the FSA regulates (see Box 1.2).

Box 1.2 The Financial Services Authority (FSA)

According to the Financial Services and Markets Act 2000, the FSA has four statutory objectives:

- market confidence: maintaining confidence in the financial system;
- public awareness: promoting public understanding of the financial system;

- consumer protection: securing the appropriate degree of protection for consumers; and
- the reduction of financial crime: reducing the extent to which it is possible for a business to be used for a purpose connected with financial crime.

(Financial Services Authority, 2005a)

The modern day complexity of financial products and the dangers of mis-selling emphasise the importance for consumers of financial products to develop 'financial capability'. The nineteenth century brought with it the need for the working population to have basic literacy associated with the 'three Rs' of reading, writing and arithmetic, rather than for this literacy to be the preserve of the ruling elite and the religious orders. This process of democratising education continued during the twentieth century with the move, first, to mass secondary education, and then to mass higher education. The late twentieth century brought with it the need for the population to have a minimum of computer literacy to equip them for living in a computer age, rather than for this knowledge to be the preserve of high-tech workers. More recently still there has been a move by government and organisations such as the FSA to extend mass literacy to financial issues which were once the preserve, in the UK, of bowler-hatted gentlemen in the City of London. As we have just seen, one of the objectives of the FSA is the promotion of the public understanding of the financial system. This has also included recognition of the problems of financial exclusion for disadvantaged groups. Financial capability now forms part of the basic understanding and skills needed by all citizens.

The precise meaning and definition of financial capability is still evolving and is the subject of research (Financial Services Authority, 2005b). That initial research suggested that there are several aspects of financial capability. These aspects are: managing money (primarily about being able to live within one's means); planning ahead (to cope with unexpected events and to make provision for the long term); making choices (being aware of available products, and being able to choose the most appropriate) and getting help (including both self-reliance and assistance from third parties). By developing your knowledge and understanding of the four themes of *Personal Finance*, and the financial terms and concepts it explains, you should become more financially capable across all these aspects.

There are serious concerns about the level of financial capability among the adult population. For instance, according to research in 2005 (Credit Action, 2005), one-third of adults say they lack confidence in how to handle their financial affairs. One indication of this is that over half

Intestate
Dying without a valid will, meaning that law determines who benefits from the deceased's property.

(57 per cent) of all adults had not drawn up a will, meaning that they would die **intestate**. A further 19 per cent had experienced a change in their circumstances since making their will, meaning that the will may no longer be valid.

Activity 1.2

Think about how confident you are in handling your financial affairs. How comfortable would you feel in answering each of the following questions?

1   Can you explain what 'APR' is?

2   Do you understand:
    (a) the difference between a repayment and an interest-only mortgage?
    (b) what an ISA is?

3   Can you explain what inflation is and why it matters?

4   Can you explain what the principle underlying insurance products is?

5   Can you calculate 4 per cent interest on £2000 over two years?

Comment

Don't worry if you weren't able to answer some or all of the questions in Activity 1.2, because you are in good company! The results of a survey conducted by MORI in 2005 confirmed a widespread lack of financial capability (Credit Action, 2005). In particular, it was found that:

1   Nearly four out of five people do not know that 'APR' refers to the interest and other costs of a loan.

2   Four in ten admit they do not understand mortgages or ISAs (Individual Savings Accounts).

3   One in five did not understand that 'inflation' is an increase in the price level.

4   Nearly one-third did not know that insurance products are designed to protect their owners from losses arising from unforeseen events.

5   Only 30 per cent could calculate 4 per cent interest on £2000 over two years. ■■■

During the course of *Personal Finance* we shall be exploring all these different aspects of financial capability in more detail, and by the end of *Personal Finance* you should be able to answer confidently the questions in Activity 1.2, and thus you will have increased your own financial capability. As part of this, you should also develop a broader social and economic understanding of the need for financial capability in a consumer society such as the UK, as well as a critical awareness of public and policy debate about these issues. Chapter 10 will revisit Activity 1.2 so you can see the difference in your understanding.

3 The interrelationship between individuals and households

Living with other people has a range of financial implications. Individual financial decisions can be affected by other household members, and the impact of these decisions can also have complex consequences for those people. Like many other aspects of UK society, living arrangements have been changing in recent decades, and these changes have financial implications.

3.1 Changing households

One change that has taken place is that there has been an increase in the number of people living on their own. In 1971, 6 per cent of all people lived on their own, whereas by 2005 this had doubled to 12 per cent of people living alone. This increase is partly the result of more people being able to afford to live on their own, and doing so either through choice or circumstances such as marital break-up. It is also the result of greater life expectancy, so that there are more one-person pensioner households (with many more women pensioners living alone than men pensioners). Some of the financial implications of these changes will be considered in Chapters 7 and 8.

A related change is the switch away from the 'traditional' UK family of a couple with children. The proportion of people living in a family household of a couple with children fell from 62 per cent in 1971 to 45 per cent in 2005. This is partly due to the increase in the number of people living alone, but also due to smaller family size; and partly due to more couple households without children, including pensioner couples. It is also the result of an increase in lone-parent families, including those resulting from marital break-up. The percentage of people living in lone-parent households tripled between 1971 and 2005. This information on changes in how people live comes from *Social Trends*, 2006, produced by the Office for National Statistics (ONS). ONS is the UK Government department that provides 'official statistics' on many aspects of social and economic life, including population, work and finance, and you will come across its data throughout *Personal Finance*. ONS also provides statistics on types of household. The data for 2005 is shown in Table 1.1.

Table 1.1 Types of households in Great Britain[1], 2005

Type of household	As a percentage of all households	
One-person households	29	
One-family households	67	
Couple (no children)		29
Couple (with children)		28
Lone parent		10
Two or more unrelated adults	3	
Multi-family households	1	
All households (24.2 million)	100	

[1]excludes Northern Ireland.

Source: data from *Social Trends*, 2006, p. 22, Table 2.2

Table 1.1 shows that two-thirds (67 per cent) of households in 2005 were one-family households and just under one-third (29 per cent) were one-person households. The second column of data gives the percentages for each type of one-family household as a percentage of all households: 29 per cent were couples with no children, 28 per cent were couples with children, and 10 per cent were lone-parent families. Of these lone-parent families, about nine out of ten were headed by mothers (*Social Trends*, 2006, p. 22).

Activity 1.3

According to the data in Table 1.1:

1 What is the (approximate) proportion of all households that include children?

2 What is the proportion of households that include children that are lone-parent households?

Comment

1 Table 1.1 shows that 28 per cent of households comprise a couple with children and 10 per cent comprise lone-parent families. In addition, the 1 per cent of multi-family households probably includes some with children. Adding these together suggests that approximately 39 per cent of all households (nearly four households in ten) include children.

2 As lone-parent families are 10 per cent of all households, it follows that lone-parent households make up just over one-quarter of all households with children. ■■■

Living arrangements impact directly on many other areas of people's lives, including their finances – how they pay their way, meet their everyday needs, and plan for the future. As we saw in Table 1.1, 71 per cent of households have more than one member. Approximately 88 per cent of individuals still live in a multi-person household (*Social Trends*, 2006). In such households, money issues are shared with other members of the household to some degree or other. These households may have complete pooling of finances among adult members and sharing of decisions about money matters, or there may be individual control over money, and perhaps incomplete disclosure of income to other household members. The possibilities here are many and varied, but household finances for these adults are affected by the fact that they live together in the same household. For one-person households, this element of household sharing is absent, but such people may still have financial relationships with others outside the household: perhaps parents, family, friends or partners that they don't live with. Furthermore, different households may help each other financially or send money to relatives living elsewhere. For instance, members of an extended family might give money to relatives living in other households or in another country.

As we can see, households are varied. This makes it difficult to generalise across all households. Later chapters will address this by introducing financial scenarios for different types of households. But what exactly is a household? In financial terms, a **household** is the unit within which people who live together share at least some of their resources, although we have seen that nearly one-third of households comprise only one person. The official definition of household is flexible and is designed to include the many different living arrangements in the UK today. For example, a household may include more than one family.

This raises questions about what 'sharing' means. Sharing relates to what happens within households. Households are affected by events such as marriage, divorce and bereavement, and they are also affected by changing gender roles. Households may also differ according to ethnicity and religious customs, which have implications for the way in which households share resources, and for how people try to earn their living and provide for their dependants (including children, elderly relatives, and the infirm). Relations between individuals and their household are complex. They involve issues of power and responsibility, and these in turn have implications for caring for household members and allocating money between them. Also, households sometimes break up; as a result of separation, divorce and bereavement, households may have a shorter lifespan than the individuals living in them, while some households may continue in spite of individuals entering and leaving. The financial effects of household break-up can be devastating: death and divorce are two of the most distressing events, not only emotionally, but financially too.

Household
A person living alone or a group of people who have the address as their only or main residence and who either share one meal a day or share the living accommodation.

There is a diversity of household types in the twenty-first-century UK

There are many practical implications of the changes in household composition and some of them have significant gender effects too. One implication is the increase in the number of children growing up in lone-parent households. In 1971, about 7 per cent of all dependent children were living in lone-parent families but by 2005 this had increased to 24 per cent; nine-tenths of these were headed by the mother, with 21 per cent of all children living in lone-mother families (*Social Trends*, 2006, Table 2.6, p. 24). There is evidence to suggest that lone parents are more likely to be financially excluded than couples with children. Such evidence was produced in a report by the charity One Parent Families (2004), which is summarised in Box 1.3.

Box 1.3 Personal finance and lone-parent families

Financial exclusion

Lone parents are more likely to be financially excluded than couples with children, and they use fewer financial products such as insurance and bank accounts. For example, while 91 per cent of couple families have a current account, only 72 per cent of one-parent families do so.

Debt

Lone parents have more debts than other family types, with 48 per cent of lone parents having debts in the past year compared with 25 per cent of two-parent families. Lone parents' debts often follow a fall in income after a relationship has broken down. If lone parents had the same material circumstances as other families they would be no more likely to be in debt.

Savings

Lone parents are saving less than couples with children, with only 22 per cent of lone parents saving regularly, compared with 47 per cent of couples with children. The most frequent reason for lone parents not saving is that they can't afford to – one study found that two-thirds of lone parents could not afford to save £10 a month.

Pensions

Lone parents are also less likely to be provided for in old age. Nine out of ten lone parents are women, and as the Pensions Commission recently concluded, women pensioners in the UK are significantly poorer than men due to gaps in their state pension provision. Lone parents are also less likely to have a private or occupational pension – 79 per cent of lone parents have neither.

(adapted from One Parent Families, 2005)

Think about your experience of household living arrangements, and that of your family and friends. Do you find that these correspond to the official picture of what has been happening? Can you see yourself as part of this wider picture?   ■ ■ ■

3.2 Households in the economy

We have seen that changing household composition is important for understanding personal finance. However, households also play a key role in the economy, and so the relationship between households and the rest of the economy is also important. It is necessary to think about the interconnectedness of households and the whole economy because they are *interdependent*: changes in one affect the other. This is important for the study of personal finance because changes in the economy will affect financial planning.

We can think of households as forming a distinct 'sector' of the economy, in contrast to two other sectors of the economy: the government sector and the corporate sector. The government sector comprises central and local government. The corporate sector comprises financial corporations (such as banks and building societies) and non-financial corporations (for example, firms producing goods such as cars, and services such as leisure activities). These three sectors of the economy are linked together by flows of goods and services, and by flows of money. The flows of money between the three sectors are illustrated in Figure 1.1.

Figure 1.1 shows the three sectors of the economy with the money flows between them. The arrows show the direction of the money flows. The arrows on the outside show the direction of money going out of a sector and the arrows on the inside show the direction of money going into a sector. These flows of money illustrate how the sectors are linked together in a continuous process of money flows over time. For simplicity, Figure 1.1 represents what is called the 'domestic economy', ignoring international flows. Therefore, money sent or spent abroad, or spent on goods made abroad by any of the three sectors, and money received from abroad, is not shown.

In Figure 1.1, the category 'households' contains everyone resident in the UK as recipients of income and consumers of products. It thus comprises all households irrespective of size or composition. It also includes those small businesses where household and business accounts can't be separated. In official data, the household sector also includes non-profit institutions such as charities, so we'll note that a donation

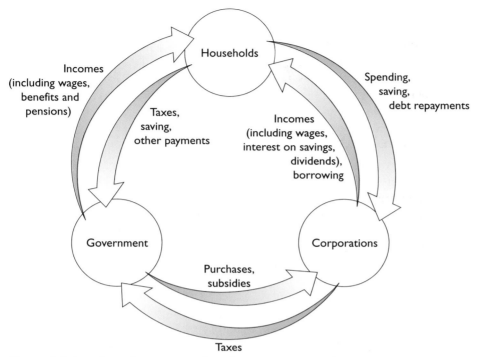

Figure 1.1 *Interdependence: money flows between sectors in the economy*

from a household to a charity is a money flow within the household sector.

To describe the money flows, I will now take each pair of money flows from Figure 1.1 in turn, and describe some examples of the flows between the different sectors. Many of the terms and concepts mentioned as part of these flows will be defined and explored later in the book.

Households and corporations

■ The money flow out of households into corporations comprises mainly spending on goods and services, and savings with and payments to financial corporations. For instance, it includes spending on clothes, food and leisure activities, payments on rent, repayments of debt, and purchase of financial products. It also includes saving in a building society and purchases of stocks and shares.

■ The money flow into households from corporations comprises mainly incomes and loans. For example, it includes income from employment and self-employment, interest on savings accounts, investment income and dividends, and private pensions. It also includes money borrowed using a credit card, and financial pay outs such as insurance.

Council Tax

A domestic property tax collected by local authorities based on the estimated property value so that the bigger the property, the higher the tax. Some adults such as full-time students and carers are 'disregarded' for Council Tax; a 25 per cent discount is applied to households with only one adult who is not disregarded; a 50 per cent discount is applied to households where *all* the residents are disregarded (such as a household consisting only of full-time students).

Households and government

■ The money flow out of households into government comprises mainly taxes, some savings and some payments to the government. For instance, it includes taxes on income, **Council Tax**[1], money saved in National Savings & Investments products, and government bonds. It also includes payments for services such as rental payments for living in council properties.

■ The money flow into households from government includes benefits, tax credits and incomes. For example, it includes retirement pensions and Jobseeker's Allowance, and the income from employment of those working for the government such as civil servants and firefighters.

Corporations and government

■ The money flow out of corporations into government comprises mainly taxes. For instance, this includes Corporation Tax.

■ The money flow into corporations from the government mainly comprises spending on goods and services, and subsidies. For example, it includes purchases on equipment for hospitals, schools and the armed services.

Figure 1.1 shows how the three sectors are linked together by the money flows between them. We can think of the money flowing round and round the economy over time, between the sectors and within them. We saw in Section 2 that social and economic changes over time are important for understanding personal finance. Here we see another dimension of the significance of 'time': money transactions are flows over time. Some money flows come around more quickly than others. Weekly wages are paid more frequently than annual bonuses, and mortgage or home rental payments are made more often than renewing the home contents policy. In the whole economy, all these different flows are taking place continuously.

> ### Activity 1.5
>
> Four arrows in Figure 1.1 show the four money flows into and out of households. Try to think of examples of monetary transactions in which you've been involved recently that match these four money flows.

---

[1] In Northern Ireland, there is a different 'rates' system of local taxation; when Council Tax is referred to later in *Personal Finance*, rates are included too.

Comment

There are many different examples which you might have provided here, but possible illustrations could include:

- Spending on food at the local supermarket would be a money flow from households to corporations.

- Borrowing money on a credit card would be a flow from corporations to households.

- The local doctor's NHS income would be a flow from government to households.

- Income Tax would be a money flow from households to government. ■ ■ ■

In addition to money flows between the sectors, there are also money flows within sectors. For households, this involves flows between members of the same household, flows between different households and some small businesses, as well as donations to charities. Flows within households raise issues of how financial decisions are made, with the possibility of differences of interest and perhaps conflict between household members. Flows between households, and between households and some small businesses, include all manner of small domestic trades, such as building, plumbing and gardening, as well as childminding and babysitting. Therefore, money flows within the household sector include:

- transactions between households; for example, payment for babysitting, childminding and domestic services such as cleaning

- transfers within households; for example, 'housekeeping' allowance, pocket money, financial support for students or elderly members

- transfers between households; for example, money sent to relatives in other households

- household donations to charity.

Figure 1.1 helps you to see how ordinary transactions by individuals and households fit into the wider economy. This illustrates the interdependence of these different sectors, and suggests that changes in one can affect the others. For instance, if households decided to spend less of their income on high street shopping, such a change might have significant economic effects in reducing the profits of corporations. Economic changes in turn impact back on to the household sector. For example, if corporations made people unemployed in response to their falling profits, then some household budgets would be severely affected. This illustrates the fact that financial decisions are not taken in isolation from the economic context, and that those financial decisions in turn affect the economic context. You will come across different examples of this interdependence throughout *Personal Finance*.

Can you think of any ways in which many households taking similar financial decisions might affect the economy? How might such economic changes in turn affect the personal financial decisions of households?

There are many examples you might have thought of, but two possible examples are:

- If many households decide to take out debts in order to increase their spending, that might result in corporations making more profits. They might create jobs and employ more people or pay people higher wages. Either or both of those would benefit household finances.

- If many households decided to stop buying the goods of one corporation and start buying those of another instead, this might not change the overall level of employment, but it would still have an impact. The first corporation might make people redundant, causing unemployment, which would adversely impact on the finances of the specific households affected. Those employed by the second corporation might find that their household finances benefit. ■■■

4 Change over the life-course

So far in this chapter, we have looked at two of the themes of *Personal Finance*: the social and economic context; and the interrelationship between individuals and households. In this section, we look at the theme of change over the life-course. This theme is important because it highlights the need to look and plan ahead in financial decision making.

The idea of an individual's 'life-course' shows us that as mortal beings we are subject to the passage of time. The notion of stages of the life-course provides a means of thinking ahead to future stages in life and seeing them as part of an overall pattern. For many people, a typical pattern of the life-course might start as youth, adolescence, then young adulthood, perhaps going from being single to becoming part of a couple. Adulthood may then entail having dependent children who later on, in turn, become independent. The later part of the life-course is usually marked by retirement. The life-course won't be the same for everyone, as some people won't form part of a couple or have children, whilst others will separate or divorce.

Each of these stages has different financial implications for individuals and their households. The important thing about the idea of the life-course is that it encourages planning ahead for each of these different stages. For example, many people delay thinking about their provision for retirement because they don't want to think about growing older, but they often come to regret this later in life when they realise that they would have benefited from earlier planning. Thinking in terms of stages in the life-course might help to overcome this natural aversion. It provides a framework for thinking about possible life events such as marriage, parenthood, retirement, or even death; and this can make it easier to think ahead constructively.

The idea of the life-course may help make financial planning for the future more realistic

No one can know exactly what will happen in the future. Financial capability involves thinking ahead and planning for what might happen in the future; this not only includes things that we hope for, but also things that we hope will not happen. Sensible planning takes account of the fact that the future may bring events that can be anticipated, and also unexpected events – either welcome or unwelcome – with financial implications. Planning for the unexpected is one important aspect of financial capability.

You will meet different examples of the life-course in later chapters where it provides a framework for thinking about various patterns of income and expenditure in the future. For example, you'll see it again when we look at planning for 'later life' in Chapter 7. This makes it easier to look ahead and plan accordingly. It also helps in understanding the variety of different people's situations.

Try jotting down what you think your personal and financial circumstances might be in ten years' time.

If you had performed a similar exercise ten years ago, what would you have expected your current situation to be? How close would it have been to what has actually happened to you?

Does this lead you to revise what you think your circumstances might be in ten years' time? ■ ■ ■

5   Financial planning

In Section 2, we saw how changes in the social and economic context have implications for personal finance and, in Section 3, we looked at changes in household composition and at how households form one part of the overall economy. It may seem to many people that their own financial concerns are far removed from these larger issues in society and the economy. None the less, it is clear that because of the interdependence between different sectors of the economy, individual financial concerns are part of the wider economic situation.

Section 2 also showed that the wider social and economic context helps to explain why there is a growing need for financial capability – or rather for new forms of financial capability. This wider context also helps to explain why it has become even more important to look ahead and plan for the future. In this section, I am going to take a first step in exploring financial capability. I shall do this by introducing financial planning. This is the fourth theme of *Personal Finance*. Financial planning is a process that should help make financial decision making more systematic.

5.1   Goals

One aspect of planning is that it needs to take into account the end goal which is aimed at. Clearly, people have different goals in life, and not all goals have financial implications, although many do. Goals are affected by individual circumstances and backgrounds, and the kind of society in which the person or household is living. People don't form their goals in life in a social vacuum; they are responsive to the myriad of factors that make up their environment. Many goals in life may be 'self-interested'; others may relate to political, ethical or religious commitments. For example, some people may have a goal of helping achieve social fairness; they might be altruistic with their money and give to charity, or they might buy 'fair trade' products that don't exploit those who produce them. Developments in ethical banking and ethical investment reflect these changes. Increasing awareness of environmental issues has affected some people's goals by changing their pattern of consumption, such as cutting back on unnecessary travelling.

It is very likely that goals will change in the course of a life as events unfold. For instance, goals may have to change as people form or leave relationships, have children, experience illness or disability, learn to cope with bereavement, move in and out of different household or family groupings, or live and work in different countries. It is probable that some goals will relate to stages in a typical life-course, where a person moves from financial dependence in youth, through young adulthood with increasing financial responsibilities, and later adulthood with reduced financial responsibilities, and eventually to retirement. According to this typical life-course, the greatest period of financial strain and indebtedness is during young adulthood when, perhaps, children are being cared for and mortgage repayments on the home have to be met. In later adulthood, the financial strain eases and this makes possible greater saving for retirement. Caring for elderly relatives may become significant at any stage during adulthood. However, this one-size life-course does not fit all cases. Cultural and ethnic diversity and plurality of lifestyles mean that this 'typical' life-course may function as a reference point for some people, but not for all.

Let's look at some typical examples of goals with financial implications that, say, a young, single adult might have:

- take a holiday abroad next year
- buy a flat within ten years
- help the homeless
- get married in three years' time
- have a comfortable retirement.

These goals relate to different time periods. In financial terms, 'short term' is normally taken to be under five years, 'medium term' is around five to ten years, and 'long term' is normally more than ten years. Taking a holiday next year and getting married in three years' time are short-term goals. Buying a flat within ten years is a medium-term goal. Providing for a comfortable retirement is a long-term goal. Helping the homeless is an ongoing goal.

Try noting down a list of your goals.

Keep this list, and I shall ask you to look at it again later. ■ ■ ■

5.2 Prioritising

Financial constraint
Inadequate resources which limit achievable goals.

Thinking about goals is one starting point for financial planning, but the achievement of goals may be constrained by the resources that a household has, together with its commitments. You will look at these resources in detail in later chapters. For most households, achieving their goals is subject to the **financial constraint** of the resources that are available. For some households, their goals may not be much affected by the available resources. In such cases, the resources are not functioning as a constraint on financial plans. This may be because the household is rich; or it may be because the household has goals that are not financially demanding. For other households, the goals are severely constrained by available resources; for these households, money difficulties are a constant source of anxiety and severely inhibit their goals. Here the main goal might be that of basic financial survival.

Trade-off
A sacrifice of something in order to have something else.

Therefore, an important question is whether all the goals can be achieved, given the financial constraints. For instance, whether a person is able to simultaneously take a holiday next year, help the homeless, get married and buy a flat depends on their financial constraints. If the person can't afford to do all these things, then choices have to be made. There is a **trade-off** between using money and resources in some ways rather than in others. A trade-off involves giving up something in order to have something else that is preferred: taking lavish holidays means not being able to buy a flat. Which is more important? It is necessary to prioritise.

Take a look at the list of goals that you made for Activity 1.8.

Have you listed the goals in any particular order?

Try listing the goals in order of priority for you, given your circumstances and resources.

Are there trade-offs between your goals?

Has this exercise prompted you to rethink any of your goals? ■ ■ ■

When doing (or buying) something involves giving up something else, the real cost is what would have been done (or bought) instead. This is called the **opportunity cost**. For example, the opportunity cost of buying a car is what would have been done or bought instead. The money might be spent on other things, or it might be saved or given away; it might be used to reduce or pay off existing debt. The opportunity cost of buying the car is the best alternative that is forgone in order to buy the car, such as buying a holiday with the money instead.

For many people, time as well as money is a scarce resource; they can't do all the things they want to do partly because they don't have the time. To illustrate, the opportunity cost of you spending your time reading this book is the best alternative use of your time, or what you would have done with your time instead of reading it. (If you wouldn't have done anything else, then you're not giving up anything to read it; here the opportunity cost is zero.) This indicates that some busy people are particularly 'time-poor', even though they may be rich in a monetary sense.

Sometimes, too, trade-offs have to be made between doing something now and doing it in the future. This is where time comes in again. Here it involves a trade-off between doing things or having things in the present as opposed to in the future. Financial planning involves making choices for future periods even though no one knows exactly what will happen in the future. In addition, many financial products involve trade-offs of their own. For instance, financial investment tends to involve a trade-off between risk and return, in that the higher the expected return, the higher the risk attached. Which is the right product depends not only on how much risk – if any – can be afforded, but also how risk averse a person is. **Risk-aversion** is the preference for a lower but more certain return rather than a higher but less certain return, **other things being equal**.

Activity 1.10

Do you think you are risk averse? Or are you a risk-taker?

What changes in your circumstances might affect your answer?

Comment

Both Chapter 5 ('Savings and investments') and Chapter 9 ('Insurance and life events') will make you think more about what kinds of risk you might want to take. Some of the circumstances which might affect your attitude to risk include whether or not you have children, your age, and your economic circumstances. ■ ■ ■

Opportunity cost
The cost of doing or having something measured in terms of the best alternative forgone.

Risk-aversion
Preferring a lower but more certain financial return rather than a higher but less certain return.

Other things being equal
A term used by economists and others to indicate that while changing one factor, other factors remain unchanged.

Risk and return

5.3 Goals and a financial planning model

Financial plans are a means of achieving goals. Therefore, being clear about goals helps when working out financial plans. Let's consider the examples shown in Table 1.2 of how goals might be achieved by means of financial plans (these examples are adapted from the FSA website).

Table 1.2 Goals and financial plans

Goal	Financial plan
Help the homeless	Adjust pattern of spending
Reduce debt worries	Improve debt management
Have some money to draw on in a crisis	Build up an emergency fund
Have a lump sum for specific projects	Build up short-term savings
Have a comfortable retirement	Build up long-term savings
Buy flat	Save for a deposit
Protect dependants	Make a will

In each case, the financial plan provides a means of achieving a goal. To illustrate, saving in the short term is a means of achieving a lump sum for specific projects such as taking a holiday next year, and saving for a deposit is a means of buying a flat.

One aspect of financial capability involves being able to work out a financial plan for achieving a goal, given the constraints. For example, if the goal is to reduce debt worries, then financial capability involves better debt management. If someone decides to consolidate their debts into one package and then pay them all off systematically, some of these packages cost less than others (other things being equal). If there are debt problems, it's better to seek advice from a money advice service such as the CCCS or Citizens Advice rather than going to a 'loan shark' who charges extremely high rates of interest. Alternatively, when saving to buy a flat, some savings schemes offer a better return than others (other things being equal), and all of them are likely to be better than stuffing cash under the proverbial mattress. Seeking out well-informed advice and choosing better products, given constraints and goals, would be evidence of greater financial capability.

Financial planning is a process that goes through different stages. Let's look at one way of describing this staged financial process. It is a 'model', or to put it another way, a simplification that is designed to help clarify a more complex process. This model of the financial planning process will be applied to different financial situations at various points in *Personal Finance*.

The model is shown in diagrammatic form in Figure 1.2. It shows a four-stage approach to financial planning. Stage 1 is to *assess* the situation, including the relative importance of different goals. Stage 2 is to *decide* on a financial plan, given goals and constraints. Then, Stage 3 is to *act* on the financial plan, and Stage 4 is to *review* the outcome of the plan.

We can look at each of these stages of the financial planning process in more detail:

- **Stage 1: Assess** the situation

  This involves clarifying and prioritising goals; working out constraints and resources; finding out relevant information; and perhaps seeking out well-informed advice.

- **Stage 2: Decide** on a financial plan

  This entails working out possible actions to take or changes to make, such as deciding on which type of financial product or financial service might be required to achieve a particular goal; or setting a budget to adjust income and/or expenditure.

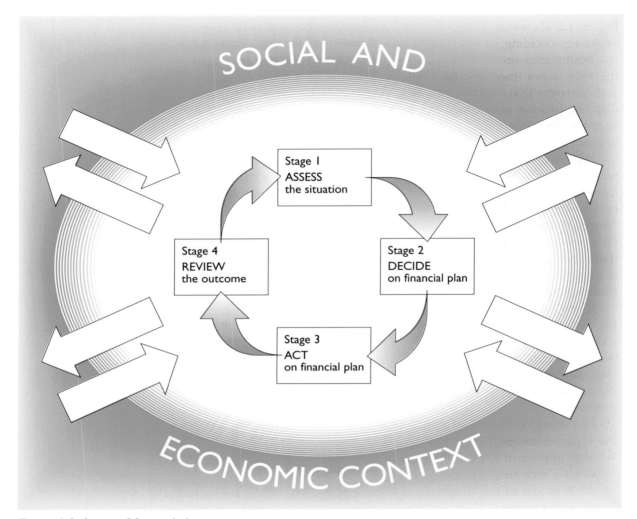

Figure 1.2 *Stages of financial planning*

- **Stage 3: Act** on the financial plan

  This means acting on what has been decided, for example, making the planned changes to income and/or expenditure; shopping around and selecting which financial product is the best buy, given needs and constraints (such as a specific savings account or a specific insurance policy).

- **Stage 4: Review** the outcome

  This involves regularly reviewing the outcome of the action and taking account of recent changes or events – is it still the best option? Does further advice need to be sought? Perhaps moving into a new circle of financial planning is necessary.

Figure 1.2 shows each stage in the planning process and how each one – assessing; deciding; acting; reviewing – leads into the next stage. Planning is a continuous process over time, with one complete sequence through the four stages leading naturally into another such sequence. This demonstrates that financial planning is not a one-off matter but an ongoing process over time. Financial plans need to respond and think ahead to the different stages in a person's life-course, and also to take into account possible future events.

We have seen how goals need to be clarified and prioritised: this is part of Stage 1. We have also seen how deciding on a financial plan aims to fulfil the goals, given the constraints: this is part of Stage 2. Stage 3 entails acting on the financial plan; there's little point in devising brilliant financial plans if they aren't actually acted upon! This stage might involve shopping around for best buys of specific financial products. Stage 4 is the important one of reviewing the outcome and checking progress in the light of changing circumstances. This, in turn, may lead to another round of financial planning.

There may well be some toing and froing between the various stages. For instance, financial plans are worked out on the basis of existing goals, but some goals may have to be revised in view of the financial plans that they turn out to require. Someone might have a goal of climbing Everest, but then they learn that the financial plan required to do it is too demanding, and so the goal is revised. Alternatively, perhaps a financial plan has to be revised when more information is acquired about the actual financial products available. In reality the lines dividing the separate stages of the financial planning process may be blurred. What is important is that this model of the financial planning process provides a structured way of thinking about financial decisions.

This model of financial planning thus provides a flexible framework for thinking systematically about what is involved in planning as an ongoing process throughout life. It helps us to identify goals and resources, and to then act on a plan to advance those goals, given the resources. It is not meant as a rigid or constricting approach, but it is an approach which you will come across again throughout the book as it is applied to various specific areas of financial decision making.

Activity 1.11

Think of a recent financial decision that you have taken and see if you can analyse your own process of financial planning in terms of Figure 1.2. Try to remember each stage of what you did and see if you can analyse these stages in terms of this diagram.

If you were to make a similar financial decision now, would you approach it differently? ■ ■ ■

5.4 Financial planning in context

We have seen that financial planning can be understood in terms of a continuous process involving a sequence of stages: assess, decide, act and review. Yet Figure 1.2 also reminds us that these four stages need to be understood within a broader context; this is shown by the arrows pointing into and out of the four-stage financial planning process.

This context includes both social factors (including values, culture and religion) and economic factors. These factors can play an important role in financial planning because they can influence the goals that people have and also how people go about trying to achieve those goals. This is indicated by the arrows pointing into Figure 1.2. In Section 2, I mentioned how advertising can influence attitudes to debt and spending, and in Section 5.1, I touched upon developments in ethical banking and environmental concerns. Some people have religious values that will affect particular financial practices. For example, the taking or paying of interest is prohibited under shariah law, as it was by the Roman Catholic Church in earlier centuries. Approaches to charitable giving and providing care and financial support for family members are also affected by these contextual factors.

Figure 1.2 also indicates that the planning process impacts on the wider society; this is shown by the arrows pointing out from the diagram. This is another way of illustrating the interdependence I discussed in Section 3.2. For example, individual financial plans may have cumulative effects of their own. If many people decide to buy a flat, there is likely to be a rise in the price of flats which will have knock-on effects. Or, if many people decide to reduce their indebtedness, spending will fall and high-street retailers will face falling profits.

These examples, of increases in property prices and falling retail sales, illustrate the cumulative effect of many individual decisions, and how far the impact of individual decisions can spread. These effects were not an intended consequence of the individuals' decisions at the time, and they can be different from what people individually expect. For instance, if an individual person or household goes on a spending spree, the consequences mainly affect that individual; but if a significant proportion of households go on a spending spree, there will be cumulative effects which impact back throughout the economy. Sometimes the effects of many people doing the same thing can become a 'bubble', and this can impact much more widely: every bubble eventually bursts, and when it does it sends ripples throughout society. For instance, in the late 1980s many people wanted to buy property. Prices rose steeply in 1988 and 1989, but the bubble burst and property prices fell sharply in the early 1990s, and this had severe consequences for some of those who bought when prices were at their peak. In the late 1990s there was a stock market bubble, with many people buying shares, especially in companies related to new technology and the internet. But from 2000 to 2002, the value of many stocks and shares fell dramatically, with negative financial impacts for those holding such stocks and shares.

Consequently, what individuals and households do with their money is not separate from the larger economy; in fact, it helps to define what that larger economy is. We can also see this by relating financial planning back to the money flows in Figure 1.1. Saving (for a holiday, wedding, festival or for retirement) is a transaction that could be conducted with the corporate sector or with the government sector. Giving to charity rather than spending money in the high street will increase money flows within the household sector and reduce flows to the corporate sector. Some financial plans will involve more than one sector. To illustrate, taking out a mortgage to buy a flat involves a sequence of two money flows: one is the money borrowed from the corporate sector which flows to the household sector; and the other is the flow of this borrowed money from the purchaser of the flat to the seller of the flat, who may be in the household sector (if a private owner of the flat), the corporate sector (if a property developer) or the government sector (if the flat is owned by the council).

We have seen that the arrows coming in and going out of Figure 1.2 illustrate the interdependence between financial planning and the wider social and economic context. This context helps to shape goals and the achievement of these goals, but it, in turn, is influenced by the collective impact of millions of individual decisions.

Activity 1.12

Take another look at the goals you listed in Activity 1.8. Think about the social and economic influences on these goals. If these influences had been different, would your goals have been different too?

Comment

It can be hard to imagine having had different influences. But if any of your economic circumstances or your social and cultural background were different, it is likely that your goals would be too. Try to reflect on some specific examples. ■ ■ ■

6 Conclusion

In this chapter, I have concentrated on outlining the main themes of *Personal Finance*. In Section 2, we looked at the changing social and economic context for personal finance. In Section 3, we considered changes in households and ways of living, and how households contribute to the money flows between different sectors in the economy. The importance of the interrelationships between individuals and their households was also explored in Section 3, and we then examined the importance of change over the life-course in Section 4. In Section 5, we started to consider how financial planning can enhance financial capability and how it involves thinking ahead. We have noted that financial issues are affected by a wide range of social and economic factors, and we have looked at issues relating to the financial services industry and changes in the direction of government policy.

Understanding this broader social and economic context will help you to develop an understanding of the role of personal finance in a consumer society such as the UK. It will help to explain why financial capability has become an important issue for government, financial providers, independent regulators and consumer watchdogs. Above all, it should enable you to enhance your own financial capability with a deeper understanding of the implications of your own financial plans and a new appreciation of the role of values and priorities in everyday financial activities.

References

Association for Payment Clearing Services (APACS) (2005) '22 million UK consumers use cards to buy online in 2004' [online], press release, 8 September, http://www.apacs.org.uk (Accessed 28 November 2005).

Citizens Advice (2005a) *Protection Racket: CAB Evidence on the Cost and Effectiveness of Payment Protection Insurance*, London, Citizens Advice; also available online at http://www.citizensadvice.org.uk/ protection_racket_final.pdf (Accessed 16 November 2005).

Citizens Advice (2005b) 'Citizens Advice calls for OFT investigation into payment protection insurance' [online], press release, 13 September, http://www.citizensadvice.org.uk/press-050913 (Accessed 16 November 2005).

Credit Action (2005) 'Debt facts and figures – compiled 4th July 2005' [online], www.creditaction.org.uk/debtstats.htm (Accessed 16 July 2005).

Credit Action (2006) 'Debt facts and figures – compiled 4th May 2006' [online], www.creditaction.org.uk/debtstats.htm (Accessed 30 May 2006).

Department for Trade and Industry (DTI) (2005) 'Over-indebtedness in Britain: a DTI report on the MORI Financial Services survey 2004' [online], http://www.dti.gov.uk/ccp/topics1/pdf1/debtdtionmori.pdf (Accessed 28 November 2005).

EurekAlert! (2005) 'Personal debt: envy, penury or necessity?' [online], press release, 17 June, http://www.eurekalert.org/pub_releases/2005-06/esr-pde061705.php (Accessed 17 November 2005).

Financial Services Authority (FSA) (2005a) 'Statutory objectives' [online], http://www.fsa.gov.uk/Pages/About/Aims/Statutory/index.shtml (Accessed 16 November 2005).

Financial Services Authority (FSA) (2005b) *Measuring Financial Capability: An Exploratory Study*, Consumer Research 37, June, prepared for the Financial Services Authority by Personal Finance Research Centre, University of Bristol; also available online at http://www.fsa.gov.uk/pubs/consumer-research/crpr37.pdf (Accessed 16 November 2005).

HM Treasury (2004) *Promoting Financial Inclusion*, December, London, The Stationery Office; also available online at http://www.hm-treasury.gov.uk/media/8F9/37/pbr04_profininc_complete_394.pdf (Accessed 17 November 2005).

Office for National Statistics (ONS) (2005) 'Input–Output: manufacturing less than 15% of economy' [online], press release, 19 August, http://www.statistics.gov.uk/CCI/nugget.asp?ID=946 (Accessed 16 November 2005).

One Parent Families (2004) *Personal Finance and One Parent Families: The Facts*, London, One Parent Families.

One Parent Families (2005) 'Summary – personal finance and one parent families: the facts' [online], http://www.oneparentfamilies.org.uk/1/lx3x1olx85x1olx-5001x1oix2029x1/0/0/160905/0/0//personal-finance.htm (Accessed 16 November 2005).

Social Trends (2005) no. 35, Basingstoke and New York, Palgrave Macmillan for The Office for National Statistics (ONS); also available online at the ONS website, http://www.statistics.gov.uk/downloads/theme_social/Social_Trends35/Social_Trends_35.pdf (Accessed 14 November 2005).

Social Trends (2006) no. 36, Basingstoke and New York, Palgrave Macmillan for The Office for National Statistics (ONS); also available online at the ONS website, http://www.statistics.gov.uk/downloads/theme_social/Social_Trends36/Social_Trends_36.pdf (Accessed 30 May 2006).

Income

George Callaghan

Chapter 2

Contents

1   Introduction

The basic pay of Jean-Pierre Garnier, Chief Executive of pharmaceutical company GlaxoSmithKline, was $1.73 m. (approximately £920,000) in 2006/07 (GSK, 2005, p. 39) – over thirty times the average UK income – and that was before bonuses and incentives of several millions more. He is one of a number of executives whose level of remuneration has been described satirically as 'fat cat' pay. The purpose of this chapter is not to explain how to jump into that kind of feline pay league but to focus on the issues that affect individual and household incomes for most people. In order to understand personal finance, it's important to appreciate from where and how income is generated *before* considering how it can be spent, supplemented by borrowing, or saved and invested – the subjects of Chapters 3 to 5. Studying income will also begin to develop skills in financial planning and budgeting that are further developed in later chapters; these are important tools for achieving financial capability.

I start this chapter by looking at what income is, and how it is different from wealth and assets. In Section 3, I then examine the social and economic background to income such as how levels of household income have changed in recent years and the different sources of income. As paid employment is by far the largest income source, the world of work and the salaries that different jobs pay are explored and explained in Sections 4 and 5. In this chapter, I also introduce changing income flows over time and the connection this has with household formation and financial planning. In the final sections, I look at the impact of taxes and benefits (including Income Tax calculations) and how to begin making a cash flow statement, one of the first practical tools you will come across in *Personal Finance*.

2   Income, wealth and assets

Income
Money *flows* received over time.

Assets
Everything that a person owns that has a monetary value (e.g. property, investments or cash).

When thinking about personal finance, it is important to make a distinction between income and what is commonly called 'wealth'. This might appear strange because having a high income and being wealthy, for example, are sometimes perceived as being the same thing. In reality, they are two different concepts. **Income** is a flow of money received over time – such as salary or benefit payments. Therefore, an income flow might be, say, £24,000 per year, or the same amount could be expressed as £2000 per month, or £462 per week.

By contrast, wealth is a stock of **assets** owned and valued at a particular point in time. There are several ways of categorising these assets. For example, the Office for National Statistics splits assets into two categories: financial assets and non-financial assets (*Social Trends*, 2005). Financial assets are those assets which are not physical things and are held in order to produce a flow of income and/or a monetary gain, like money held in a savings account (which pays interest) or share holdings (which usually pay dividends). In contrast, non-financial assets are those assets, usually tangible, physical items, which don't normally provide a flow of income, such as a property, jewellery or an expensive work of art. Usually, to obtain money from these assets, they would have to be sold.

Assets can take a variety of different forms

Assets can be categorised in other ways too. A second type of distinction is between marketable assets and non-marketable assets. All of the examples described above are assets for which a market value (or price) can be realised, and so are said to be 'marketable'. However, there are some assets – such as money held in an occupational pension scheme – that generally cannot be sold. Such assets are thus classed as 'non-marketable assets'.

A third way of categorising assets is perhaps the most important for personal finance. This is dividing up assets according to how *liquid* they are. The most liquid asset is cash. Other **liquid assets** can be easily and readily converted into cash, for instance, the balance on a current account or a savings account. There are other assets which cannot be sold or liquidated so easily, such as a house. Chapters 5 and 6 look at these assets in more detail. In Chapter 6, we also explore how they are crucial components of financial balance sheets, an important tool in the study of personal finance. In this chapter, however, I concentrate on income.

Liquid assets
Those assets that can be quickly converted into cash.

Activity 2.1

Categorise each of the following items in terms of income and assets:

1   A regular monthly salary of £1800.
2   One hundred shares in GlaxoSmithKline.
3   An antique clock.
4   Eight years membership of a civil service pension scheme.
5   Child benefit of £17.45 per week for a first child in 2006/07.

Comment

1   This is a flow of income over time.
2   These are assets. They are a form of financial asset because they could provide a flow of income in the form of dividend payments (see Chapter 5). They are also a type of marketable asset as the shares could be sold easily, although their price would vary.
3   This is another asset. It is a non-financial asset, whose value could only be realised if sold. It is a less liquid asset than the shares, which can be bought and sold easily.
4   This is an asset. It is also a financial asset which provides entitlement to a future flow of income. It is also a form of non-marketable asset.
5   This is a flow of income over time. ■ ■ ■

3   The social and economic context

We need to start our focus on income by considering the social and economic context. This means looking at the sources of household income, how levels of household income have changed over time, and how household income is distributed. Let's start with the sources of household income – where does it come from? Figure 1.1 in Chapter 1 provided an overview of income sources by showing money flows between different sectors – illustrating how households receive income from both the corporate and the government sectors, and from other households too. Now we can look at household income sources in another way. Table 2.1 contains information on the components of total weekly household income in the UK in 2003–04 from the *Family Resources Survey* (DWP, 2004).

Table 2.1 Components of total (gross) weekly household income in the UK, 2003–04

Components	%
Pay	65
Self-employment	9
Investments	2
Pensions	13
Social security benefits	7
Tax credits	1
Other	3
Total	**100**

Source: DWP, 2004, Table 3.3

This table shows figures for **gross income**: this means income before any deductions. A total of 74 per cent of weekly household income comes from paid employment (65 per cent from pay received from working for others, plus 9 per cent from self-employment). The expression **paid employment** as opposed to 'working' is used in order to distinguish work that receives financial payment from work which is unpaid such as housework. Thus, overall, paid employment is by far the most important component of UK household income.

The next largest categories of income in Table 2.1 are pensions (which is the subject of Chapter 7) and social security benefits (which will be explored in Section 7 of this chapter, along with tax credits). Of course, these figures mask large differences in the financial circumstances

Gross income
Total income before any deductions have been made.

Paid employment
Work that receives a financial payment.

of particular households; although benefits make up 7 per cent of overall household income, for particular households, benefits could comprise anything from 0 per cent to 100 per cent of income. Similarly, for many households where all the members are over 65, pensions will form a much larger proportion of household income – in many cases it will be 100 per cent of household income. It is noteworthy that only 2 per cent of the overall household income in the UK comes from investments – although *Social Trends* (2005) suggests this figure may be under-reported. These investments are financial assets, such as savings accounts and shares, which were defined in Section 2. We discuss these types of investments in detail in Chapter 5.

Informal economy
Paid employment that is hidden from the state.

There is a source of income which is not included in official statistics like those shown in Table 2.1. This is work in the **informal economy**. Other names for this kind of activity include: the 'underground sector'; the 'black economy'; 'cash-in-hand work'; the 'hidden economy'; and 'informal employment'. A recent report offers this definition: 'Informal work involves the paid production and sale of goods or services which are unregistered by or hidden from, the state, for tax and/or benefit purposes but which are legal in all other respects' (Small Business Council, 2004). It's difficult to calculate the extent of this work, but average estimates show that about 7 per cent of all economic activity in the UK takes place in the informal economy. Research suggests that most of this income is payments for work such as property maintenance and repair, routine housework, gardening and childcare.

Activity 2.2

I've mentioned that sources of income won't be the same for everyone. For example, full-time university students, who will often have very low levels of income, will obtain their income in different ways from most people. Full-time university students in England and Wales had an average income of £5513 in 2002/03. What do you think are the top three sources of their income?

Comment

The top three income sources for these students were: student loans at 49 per cent; money from their family at 24 per cent; and paid work at 20 per cent. This was a big change from the 1990s when student grants were much more widely available. We might expect to see these figures change again in the future as new systems of student finance work through the higher education system. ■ ■ ■

Household income across the UK also changes over time. This might be as a result of the economy (usually) growing and as a result of changes in government policies. To measure such changes in household income, government statisticians use a measure known as disposable income. This is the income that households have after allowing for all payments of Income Tax, National Insurance, Council Tax and pension contributions, and after any social security benefits have been added.

In order to consider changes over time, in income or indeed other financial variables, it's important to know whether figures are in 'real terms'. Figures that are expressed in 'real terms' have been adjusted to take account of inflation, so that we can compare like with like. Box 2.1 explains this in more detail.

Box 2.1   Inflation

Inflation refers to a continual increase in the general level of prices. This means that a given amount of money will buy fewer goods and services.

The rate of inflation is expressed as a percentage figure and measures how much a typical 'basket' of goods changes in price from one year to the next. The UK Government measures the cost of over 600 typical goods and services each year to calculate this annual measure of inflation.

If, for example, the inflation rate was 4 per cent, this would mean that you would need £104 to buy the same goods and services next year that you could buy this year with £100.

Inflation is a concept which is crucial to personal finance, and it appears throughout this book. One common distinction you will come across is between *real* values, which have been adjusted to take account of inflation, and *nominal* values, which have not. Real values are usually expressed in terms of a particular time's or year's prices, such as 'expenditure in today's prices' or 'income at 1999 prices'. When you see such a phrase added to a set of figures or a graph, you can tell the values have been adjusted to take account of inflation.

In real terms, household disposable income per head almost doubled in just over thirty years. In 1971, median income was £180.12 per week, and by 2002 it had reached £311.08 per week (*Social Trends*, 2005). Consequently, the median household had substantially more disposable income in 2002 than it did in 1971, which would appear to suggest that

Standard of living
The quality of life enjoyed by an individual or household, depending on factors such as income, housing condition, the environment, and public services such as health and education.

households in the early twenty-first century could afford a considerably higher **standard of living** than households thirty years earlier.

The *distribution* of that income across households is not equal: indeed, there is considerable income inequality. For example, the 10 per cent of households in Great Britain with the highest income received a 28 per cent share of total income in 2002/03 (*Social Trends*, 2005). Moreover, the gap between the highest and lowest incomes has increased between 1971 and 2002. I used the term 'median' when talking about changes in disposable income above, and in order to examine these changes more closely, you first need to read Box 2.2 to understand what is meant by mean, median and percentiles.

Box 2.2   Mean, median and percentiles

Social scientists, economists and statisticians often want to measure the 'average' of something to get an idea of what the 'central tendency' of a set of numbers is. But there are different ways of measuring that average.

The mean is one type of average which provides a general measure of the size of the values involved. The mean is calculated by adding up all the values in a set of numbers and dividing that total by the number of values in the set.

The median is another, slightly different, measure of average. The median is the middle value of a set of numbers arranged in order. (If the set has an even number of values, the median is the mean of the two middle values.) This indicates that half of the population will have values less than or equal to the median and half of the population will have values equal to or greater than the median.

Let's see why these two different measures might tell us different things by looking at an example.

The following set of data is the different incomes of ten different people.

Person A: £1000
Person B: £1000
Person C: £1000
Person D: £1000
Person E: £2000
Person F: £2000
Person G: £3000
Person H: £3000
Person I: £4000
Person J: £22,000

The mean is £4000 (£40,000 ÷ 10 = £4000).

The median is £2000. (The fifth and sixth values are both £2000, so the mean of them is £2000).

These two measures of average have produced very different results in this case. This is important because incomes vary a great deal, and very few people have extremely high incomes. Thus, the mean can imply that most people's incomes are higher than is in fact the case – or that most people earn less than average. The mean may lead us to believe that most people's incomes are near this number, but in fact the mean income is *higher* than most people's incomes because the high income outliers skew the result. In contrast, the median income resists the effect caused by these extreme values, and might be more informative in the circumstance of a very few people (in this case one person) with very high income.

The idea of a percentile is an extension of the idea of the median. A median divides the values into two equal parts. A percentile is any of the 99 values that divide the sorted data into 100 equal parts, so that each part represents $\frac{1}{100}$ th of the data. So, for example, the 10th percentile cuts off the lowest 10 per cent of data, whereas the 90th percentile cuts off the lowest 90 per cent of data. The median is the 50th percentile, because half of the data will be below it and half above it. Using the data above, the income of the tenth percentile would be £1000.

If you look at Figure 2.1, you can see how household disposable income in the UK has changed since 1971 for different parts of the population. Using the information in Box 2.2, the 90th percentile is the level of income that separates the top 10 per cent with the highest incomes from the 90 per cent with the lowest incomes. The tenth percentile is the level of income that separates the top 90 per cent with the highest incomes from the 10 per cent with the lowest income. Examining how the income levels of those percentiles have moved over time, it seems that during the 1970s the distribution of disposable income remained relatively stable because the percentiles do not diverge significantly. However, in the 1980s there was a significant increase in income inequality, with a much larger increase in income at the 90th percentile than the 10th percentile. The income distribution appeared to stabilise in the early 1990s, but since 2000 there appears to have been a further increase in inequality, with larger income increases at the top, as shown by the increased divergence of the 90th percentile from those lower down.

Income is also distributed unequally between different types of household. For example, in 2003/04, people living in UK households consisting of two adults, without children, who both work full time were twice as likely to be in the group with the top 20 per cent of disposable

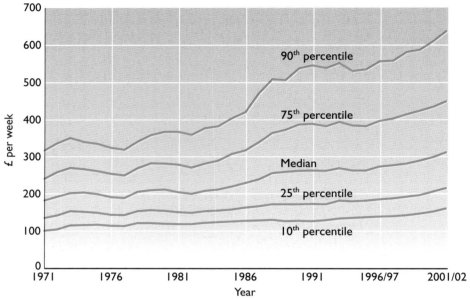

Figure 2.1 *Distribution of real household disposable income*
Source: *Social Trends*, 2005, p. 72, Figure 5.13

income as the population as a whole. Conversely, lone parents had a greater than average risk of being in the bottom 20 per cent (*Social Trends*, 2006). The threshold for low income usually used in the UK is 60 per cent of **equivalised** contemporary median household disposable income. In 2003/04, this threshold was £201 per week for a couple household without children (the equivalent of £10,452 disposable income per annum), so any household with equivalised income below this level would be considered 'low income'. Section 5 of Chapter 3 will show you how to calculate equivalised household incomes.

Equivalised
Household income adjusted to take account of household size and composition. For example, a household of three would require a higher income than a household of one.

Activity 2.3

Figure 2.2 shows the percentage of individuals in different household categories that were below the threshold for low income from 1991 to 2003. What happened to the percentage of each household type that experienced low income over this period? Can you see any patterns?

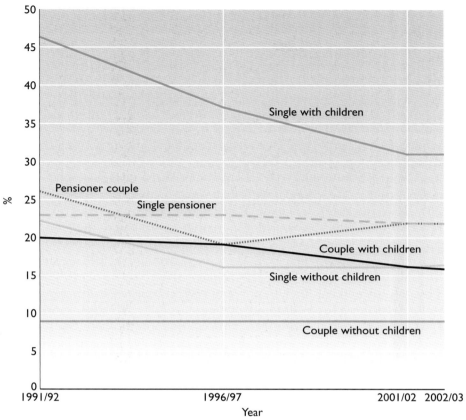

Figure 2.2 *Individuals in households with incomes below low-income threshold, 1991–2003*

Source: *Social Trends*, 2005, p. 77, Table 5.20

Comment

The percentages of individuals living in households below the low-income threshold fell across all but one household category ('couple without children') over the whole period from 1991 to 2003. Two further categories ('pensioner couple' and 'single without children') have had upwards movements over individual time periods. Some of the largest falls are for the 'couple with children' and, especially, the 'single with children' types of household. This reflects recent UK Government policy to focus additional state support on households with children. The forms of that support are discussed further in Section 7 of this chapter and again in Chapter 8. ▪ ▪ ▪

4 Paid employment in the UK labour market

In Section 3, you saw that paid employment is the most important source of overall household income in the UK. This is also true for the majority of individual households, and for the vast majority of households whose members are of pre-retirement age. Therefore, it's important to explore paid employment further, and we'll look at the UK labour market: the arena where employers (who need labour) come together with employees (who supply labour in return for pay).

Let's start by continuing our examination of the changing social and economic context. Chapter 1 noted that some of the main changes in recent years have arisen from the political and policy emphasis on liberalisation and from the increased attention given to competition and market forces. We saw how the need for increased financial capability arises because of these changes. Such forces have also helped to shape the current UK labour market. This process started in the early 1980s with the aim of making the labour force respond more flexibly to changing demand. This meant encouraging flexibility in wages, working time, working practices, and in geographical and job mobility. Some of these changes, particularly around the wage bargaining system, have involved lengthy disputes between the UK Government and the trade union movement. Other changes have included providing skills training to enable people to move into and between jobs, and changing the benefits system to give added incentive for more people to take paid employment.

Accompanying this process of encouraging labour market flexibility have been some major structural changes in the UK economy. First, the number of people in employment has been rising in recent years, but the sectors of the economy that people work in have been changing. There has been a sharp decline in the number of people working in **manufacturing**. However, this has been more than compensated for by an increase in the number of people working in **services**. Figure 2.3 shows changes in jobs defined by sector from 1983 to 2003. You can see that the difference between service sector and manufacturing jobs has increased markedly over the twenty-year period. By 2003, there were nearly 21 million service sector jobs (part time and full time) compared to 15 million in 1983, whereas manufacturing jobs fell from 5.2 million to only 3.5 million over the same period (*Social Trends*, 2004, Table 4.13). The biggest increase over this period has been in financial and business services which, by 2004, accounted for one in five of all jobs (*Social Trends*, 2005). This trend towards the service sector constitutes a major change to the structure of the UK economy, and it is likely that it will continue in the future, with fewer and fewer jobs in manufacturing.

Manufacturing
Manufacturing jobs are those in industries that convert raw materials and components into goods (e.g. textiles, steel, cars).

Services
Service sector jobs include those in business services and finance, education, hotels and restaurants, the health sector and most public sector work.

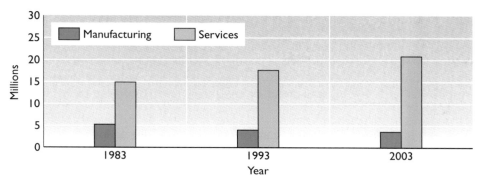

Figure 2.3 *Jobs in manufacturing and service industries, 1983–2003*
Source: *Social Trends*, 2004, p. 59, Table 4.13

A second major structural change has been the increasing number of women in employment. Female employment in the UK grew from 9.9 million in 1983 to 12.8 million in 2003. This represents an employment rate of 70 per cent of women of working age, up from 59 per cent in 1983. During the same period, the employment rate for men rose from 78 per cent to 79 per cent – so the gap between men's and women's employment rates has decreased from 19 per cent to just 9 per cent. In 2003, approximately 91 per cent of women in paid employment worked in the service sector, compared with 70 per cent of men (*Social Trends*, 2004, Table 4.13). Moreover, the 5.2 million women who work part time make up approximately 81 per cent of the part-time workforce (*Social Trends*, 2005).

Writing about Britain's work culture, author Madeleine Bunting demonstrates that one outcome of the growing numbers of women participating in paid employment is an increase in the numbers of women returning to work following childbirth:

> Of all the statistics on women's employment, the most dramatic is the leap in the proportion of mothers returning to work within one year of childbirth from 24 per cent in 1981 to 67 per cent in 2001, while the number of mothers of children under five who are in paid work has increased from 28 per cent to 58 per cent. Most of this work is part-time, and represents women reverting to a pre-industrial pattern of combining some work and some caring.
>
> (Bunting, 2004, p. 220)

In the 2000s, UK Government policy has tried to engage with the issue of combining paid employment and childcare through encouraging flexible working patterns. For example, parents of children under six have a right to request a flexible work pattern. This could be either a change to the hours they work, a change to the times when they are required to work, or the opportunity to work from home.

Activity 2.4

Read the following two extracts from Madeleine Bunting's book *Willing Slaves: How the Overwork Culture is Ruling Our Lives* (2004), which contain descriptions of some of the pressures on women who work and have caring responsibilities. Is your household or any household you know facing similar challenges?

This extract is from Catherine, a single mother, working as a part-time teacher in further education:

> After seven years of it, I'm really tired. The kids are always saying, 'Why can't you be a sandwich-maker so you don't bring your work home with you?' The problem is finding someone to look after the kids. I feel terrible – this isn't good – but I leave them. On Mondays it's only for one hour and twenty minutes; on Saturdays it's a bit longer. They don't go near the stove and usually they have a couple of videos. I was left when my mum went out to work as a cleaner – she left me in charge of my three brothers, and the neighbours would watch out for us. But I haven't got that kind of support network, because I am working. I can't ask people to baby-sit. The family is two buses and one and a half hours away.
>
> (Bunting, 2004, p. 259)

This extract is from a full-time working mother with two children:

> I dread the summer holidays when the kids are off. Holiday clubs cost a fortune. My partner and I do not take holidays at the same time – we need to cover as much of the holiday period ourselves. I am lucky in that I work in local government and my council allows staff to take up to 30 days' unpaid leave a year. I take 10 days – as much as I can afford. We still struggle to cover holidays and days when the kids are off sick. I know I have sent the kids to school when they are feeling ill as neither of us could take the time off. I am just waiting for my son to start senior school and then that will be just one child to pay after-school care for ... life is just one massive juggling game of arrangements of who can pick up who at what time.
>
> (Bunting, 2004, pp. 213–14)

■ ■ ■

In addition to 6.4 million part-time workers, there were also a further 3.6 million people who were self-employed in the UK in 2004. The self-employed represent 13 per cent of all those in paid employment. Work in construction is the most common for self-employed men, and work in community, social and personal services is the most common for self-employed women (*Social Trends*, 2005).

Thus the UK labour market of the mid 2000s is characterised by a predominance of employment in the service sector, high levels of part-time employment, and a concentration of female employees in service sector and part-time jobs. The UK's labour market is also a 'flexible' one; that is, it is distinguished by mobility between types of jobs and their geographical locations (HM Treasury, 2003). Major political and economic ideas underpin the desire for such flexibility: supporters of economic liberalisation believe that it offers employers the chance to respond quickly to changing demand, thus maintaining their competitiveness and the prosperity of the UK economy. They also argue flexibility offers employees the opportunity to mix caring and other responsibilities with paid employment. Nevertheless, the combination of the flexible labour market and the UK benefits system (which I discuss in Section 7) increases incentives on people to take paid employment. In addition, as with some of the people Bunting (2004) interviewed, trying to fit work around other commitments can be very difficult – an issue to which we shall return in Chapter 8. Let's now turn to the salaries that different jobs pay.

5 How much are people paid?

I opened this chapter with a reference to the £920,000 salary of GlaxoSmithKline's Chief Executive. Yet the nurses who administer this company's drugs in National Health Service hospitals are paid on average £25,000 per year, and those who clean the hospitals earn an average of £13,000 per year. Clearly, income from employment varies widely. Consequently, it is interesting to know what is the average level of pay, and how this varies across different jobs.

Table 2.2 contains selected data from the ONS *Annual Survey of Hours and Earnings*, 2005. Across all employees, the mean gross monthly pay in the UK in 2004 was £2188, or £26,256 per year (remember that this is a mean, not the median, so a majority of people earned less than this). This annual ONS survey also classifies jobs into more than 450 different types of **occupation** and shows the average pay for each one. Table 2.2 shows fourteen selected occupations for simplicity. In this case, using the mean will give a better guide to the average because the pay of individuals in each occupation will be less dispersed than that of the whole population. You'll see some very large differences in pay: at the extremes, in 2004, 58,000 directors and chief executives received gross average monthly pay of £8952 (or £107,424 per year), whereas 41,000 waiters and waitresses received an average £984 per month (or £11,808

Occupation
A group of similar jobs found in different industries or organisations.

per year). In between these extremes, in 2004, secondary education teaching professionals received £2667 per month (or £32,004 per year), and nurses received an average £2091 (or £25,092 per year) in 2004.

Table 2.2 Gross monthly pay for full-time employee jobs (selected occupations only) in the UK, 2004

Description	Number of jobs (thousand)	Average (mean) gross monthly pay (£)
Directors and chief executives of major organisations	58	8952
Medical practitioners	122	5245
Police officers (inspectors and above)	19	3892
Marketing and sales managers	489	3829
Secondary education teaching professionals	359	2667
Nurses	366	2091
Plumbers, heating and ventilating engineers	78	2076
Heavy goods vehicle drivers	179	1843
Motor mechanics, auto engineers	112	1762
Food, drink and tobacco process operatives	134	1483
Childcare and related personal services	155	1122
Cleaners, domestics	131	1080
Hairdressers, barbers	19	1075
Waiters, waitresses	41	984
All employees	**161 419**	**2188**

Source: adapted from *Annual Survey of Hours and Earnings*, 2005, Table 14.1a

There are other aspects of remuneration apart from pay, ranging from smaller fringe benefits, such as luncheon vouchers, through to more financially important benefits, such as bonuses and pensions. In particular, the availability – or otherwise – of job-related pensions is likely to be an increasingly important element of remuneration to be considered when choosing occupations or specific jobs. This is because, as Chapter 1 pointed out, changes to pension provision by the UK government and reduction in pension benefits available from some employers imply increasing responsibility for individuals to make their own financial provision for their old age.

Gender matters in pay too, as women in the UK are paid, on average, less than men. This is mostly due to the fact that women are concentrated more in lower paid occupations, which leads to lower relative pay, rather than because of differences in rates of pay for similar jobs. This is especially the case since the Equal Pay Act 1970 and the Sex Discrimination Act 1975 established the principle of equal pay for equal work in the UK. The ONS uses hourly pay for comparisons of men's and women's pay because including overtime would distort the figures as men work relatively more overtime than women. These figures suggest that the gender pay 'gap' is closing. In 1986, the hourly pay of women working full time in Great Britain was 74 per cent that of men, but by 2003 the percentage had risen to 82 per cent (*Social Trends*, 2004). One factor that may shrink the gap further is the National Minimum Wage (NMW), introduced in 1999 in the UK, and increased several times since. The NMW has increased pay in low paid sectors of the labour market, such as retail, hospitality, childcare, and hairdressing, where women tend to predominate. From October 2006, the NMW rate for workers aged twenty-two and over was £5.35 per hour (DTI, 2006). There are not just gender differences in average pay: there is also evidence to suggest that ethnic minority workers have lower earnings than white workers in the UK (Schifferes, 2002).

On average, in the UK, part-time employees receive lower hourly pay than full-time employees, and the gap between women and men who work part time is relatively smaller than between those that work full time. For example, in 2003 the hourly pay of women working part time was 88 per cent of men's (*Social Trends*, 2004). As you saw in Section 4, part-time work is mainly undertaken by women, very often because of caring responsibilities. Indeed, employers may find that offering jobs whose hours are compatible with caring responsibilities is the only way to find a workforce willing to accept the low pay necessary to make their business profitable, and parents (usually women) who can only work limited hours may feel that they have no choice but to accept these jobs.

Human capital
The accumulation of a person's knowledge and skills, built up through formal or informal education and training.

Why do different jobs pay different amounts? One possible explanation is that different pay levels reflect different amounts of what economists describe as **human capital**. The reasoning is that people invest time and money on education and training to increase their skills and knowledge and that this, in turn, improves their performance. This increased skill, knowledge and performance is then rewarded in the labour market through higher pay. Consequently, the argument runs, in the same way that a manufacturer can improve performance by investing in physical capital such as new machines, an individual can improve their performance (and therefore pay) by investing time and money in building on their human capital – so that they can get promoted, or get a new, higher paid job, for example.

There is a substantial amount of UK-based research which suggests that education and training that result in qualifications *do* improve pay levels (McIntosh, 2004). This holds true throughout most of education, from good grades at GCSE level, through obtaining two or more A levels, to being awarded a university degree. A Learning and Skills Council (LSC) report in 2005, which is summarised in Box 2.3, showed the financial benefit of A-level-equivalent and other qualifications.

Studying for qualifications increases human capital and improves pay levels

Box 2.3 Young people set to miss out on £4000 a year by dropping out

Students opening their GCSE results this Thursday (25 August 2005) could see their lifetime earnings increase by up to £4,000 a year, but only if they stay in education and training – which they can now be paid to do with an Education Maintenance Allowance (EMA).

Official figures reveal that staying on to gain A-Levels, GNVQ [General National Vocational Qualification] level 3s, or retaking GCSEs, can increase a person's earning power by up to £4,000 a year or a quarter (24 per cent) more than someone who leaves education without good GCSEs.

This means that over their lifetime, a young person who gains further education qualifications, such as A-Levels, will earn £185,000 more than some of their peers. Those who leave education without good GCSEs can expect to earn £16,739 whereas a young person with FE qualifications can earn on average £20,692 a year.

The findings show that retaking exams to achieve five GCSEs at grade A–C, including English and Maths, can also increase a person's earning power by 9 per cent on average – almost £1,400 a year – more than someone leaving education without key GCSEs.

Employment rate and gross weekly earnings: by highest qualification in the UK, spring 2003

	Employment rate (%)	Gross weekly earnings (£ per week)
No qualification	49.9	297.85
Other qualifications	71.0	345.96
5 GCSE grades A–C or equivalent	75.4	350.19
A-Level/GNVQ level 3 or equivalent	78.0	397.94
Higher education	85.5	475.63
Degree or equivalent	88.0	631.70

(LSC, 24 August 2005)

The improvement in pay also holds true for vocational training qualifications with, for example, HNC/HND (Higher National Certificate/Diploma), ONC/OND (Ordinary National Certificate/Diploma) and City & Guilds qualifications all increasing pay (McIntosh, 2004).There is also evidence that in-work training improves pay, but these rewards tend to be smaller, perhaps because such training usually lasts for a shorter period of time and tends to develop skills specific to a particular job (Elias et al., 2002).

One particular aspect of this issue, which has interested some researchers, is whether there is a financial reward for gaining a university degree. Such a reward is generally known as the **graduate earnings premium**. This measures the difference between what a graduate is paid and what a person similar in other respects, but not having received higher education, would receive. A recent extensive research project into graduate careers in a changing labour market concluded: 'All the evidence suggests that employers continue to pay a premium to degree holders but graduate earnings and career development vary according to sector and region of employment, and to gender and age' (Purcell and Elias, 2004, p. 5).

Graduate earnings premium
The extra earnings received by virtue of having a university degree.

A report from the Department for Education and Skills (DfES) called *Student Loans and the Question of Debt* also concluded that graduates can expect to receive £120,000 more over a lifetime than someone going into work with two A levels (DfES, 2004). Therefore, in general, it would appear that most graduates can expect to receive *some* earnings premium. Typically they do this by taking jobs where the opportunities for promotion and salary increases are much greater. Such jobs are often described as 'career' type employment. The evidence for the existence of this graduate earnings premium was an argument put forward by those who supported the introduction of fees for university students.

There is some evidence which suggests that the jobs market for graduates is split along gender lines, with the graduate earnings premium for women growing for only ten years after graduation as opposed to fifteen years for men (Purcell and Elias, 2004). There is also evidence that the subject studied at university has an effect on the level of financial return. This research shows that those who took an arts degree earn about 20 per cent less than law, social sciences, engineering, business studies or education graduates (Elias and Purcell, 2004). Age at graduation also has an impact on financial rewards and accessing degree-related employment, with those graduating over the age of 30 more likely to have experienced difficulty in obtaining such employment (Purcell and Elias, 2004). It might also be the case that as the number of graduates increases, as has been happening in the UK in recent years, the size of the graduate earnings premium decreases.

There are two other points about human capital that are worth making. First, it is worth emphasising that qualifications are not the only element of human capital, for example, there are famous millionaires with no qualifications. Moreover, in addition to skills and knowledge, human capital may include a broader range of skills such as the social skills to 'get on' at work. Yet qualifications *are* a key determinant of likely future earnings over the life-course. Second, investment in human capital (such as studying towards qualifications) is an example of the trade-offs you saw in Chapter 1. Obtaining a qualification usually has a trade-off in terms of the time given up for studying that could have been used for doing something else. It will also have a financial trade-off in the short term – that of giving up the income that could have been earned during the time spent studying.

Activity 2.5

1   Make a list of the types of human capital you have built up.

2   How might you add to your human capital in the future?

3   What impact might this have on your future earnings potential?

Comment

1   Your human capital might include formal educational qualifications from school, college or university. It might also include informal skills, knowledge and experience built up 'on the job' and through broader life experience.

2   You might hope to add more of any of these forms of human capital in the future. Perhaps you might gain some additional qualifications, such as a degree from The Open University.

3   How these forms of human capital will impact your future earnings will be affected by a number of individual factors such as your age, gender, type of employment, location, your mobility and so on.   ■ ■ ■

It is not clear that the human capital argument is enough to explain differences in pay. For example, can it explain the gender differences in pay? There is an argument that because women expect to take time out of the labour market for caring responsibilities, they invest less – or perhaps their employer invests less – in their human capital. Then, when women are out of the labour market for a time, they also accumulate less human capital. This results in relatively more women in lower skilled, lower paid jobs.

This explanation may seem inadequate, and it would not explain why women tend to receive smaller financial improvements in pay from educational qualifications than men do, such as with the smaller graduate earnings premium. An alternative explanation is offered by something called 'segmented labour market theory' (Gordon et al., 1982; Callaghan, 1996). This argues for a more complex view of the labour market, in which rates of pay and employment opportunities are strongly influenced by factors such as historical patterns, gender and ethnicity. For instance, this theory would suggest that over time certain types of work have become seen as 'men's work' and others as 'women's work' and consequently they are paid differently because 'men's work' is seen as 'more important'. Linked to this is the argument that what counts as 'skilled' work – and hence receives higher pay – is influenced by gender. Pay differences may also be the result of choices, such as the number of hours worked and the type of subject studied at school or university, which are also influenced by gender (Callaghan, 1996; Elias and Purcell, 2004).

6   Income profiles and the life-course

As Chapter 1 pointed out, thinking about *change over the life-course* is a central theme of *Personal Finance*, and it is crucial to financial capability. This is because financial planning necessarily involves thinking ahead. One of the most significant aspects is how income may change over a person's life-course. In this section, I examine how paid employment might change over time – looking first at individuals and then at households. These issues are explored through illustrative fictional lifetime scenarios.

The first scenario involves Sarah Wilson. It's 2004 and Sarah is twenty-eight. She has worked for four years at a banking call centre in Leeds. Before this she was a retail assistant at a large store. She works thirty-seven hours per week and is paid £14,000 per year. Figure 2.4 illustrates Sarah's lifetime pay from 1992 to 2004. We'll record Sarah's pay at 2005 prices – as you saw in Box 2.1, the fact that the figures have been adjusted to take account of inflation is shown by the use of the word 'real' in the figure caption.

Sarah's income has changed quite dramatically since the age of sixteen. As a teenager, she worked part time in a pizza delivery shop, and her pay from this, combined with her pocket money, was £1200 per year. There was a sharp rise in 1996 at the age of twenty when she started working full time as a retail assistant and her pay rose to £11,700. Sarah's salary remained relatively constant until she moved to the call centre in 2000 and earned £14,000 per year. Figures like Figure 2.4 are useful for illustrating such income changes over time. In this case, the time frame

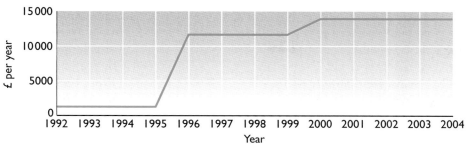

Figure 2.4 *Sarah's real gross income from paid employment*

Sarah works at a customer call centre

was from 1992 to 2004, covering Sarah's income from paid employment from the ages of sixteen to twenty-eight.

Now let's introduce the second scenario, which involves Peter Taylor. In 2004, Peter Taylor is thirty and teaches history at a local high school in Leeds. Figure 2.5 shows his real income from 1996 to 2004 (again adjusted for inflation).

Peter first started teaching in 1996 at the age of twenty-two. He started on £18,105 per year but, unlike Sarah, his pay steadily increased as he moved through the salary scale associated with his job as a teacher, until he was earning £28,668 per year in 2004. Such a salary scale is typical of professional jobs with a career structure. It's common in such jobs that an employee progresses through the salary scale up until a certain point. Pay increases beyond this usually then depend upon promotion. This pattern of pay is shown in Figure 2.5 where Peter's income from paid employment steadily increases.

Peter works as a schoolteacher

By comparing Figures 2.4 and 2.5, it is evident that jobs such as teaching, which offer steady progression through a salary scale, provide an increasing income profile over a working life, whereas jobs such as those in call centres have a relatively flatter income profile. Of course, this is a simplification, as it may be possible for Sarah to gain promotion to call centre team leader and to then build a career with increased pay. Nevertheless, the basic distinction between jobs with a flat pay profile and those with salary progression holds true. This is significant for financial planning where it is important to know realistically how flows of income might change over a lifetime.

Another theme of this book is *the interrelationship between individuals and their households*. In 2004, as Table 1.1 in Chapter 1 showed, over 70 per cent of households were made up of two or more people. Given this, it's often important that financial planning takes account of the income flows coming into the household from different individuals.

Let's explore this using the example of Sarah and Peter coming together to form a household. Figure 2.6 illustrates this by showing

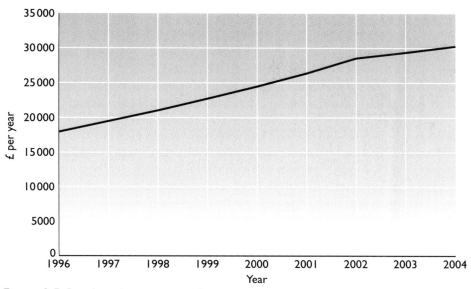

Figure 2.5 *Peter's real gross income from paid employment*

Sarah's and Peter's joint household income after 2004, as well as their individual incomes. Note that the title refers to 'income' as opposed to the 'income from paid employment' in Figures 2.4 and 2.5. This is because it includes income from sources other than paid employment (mainly related to social security benefits associated with having children).

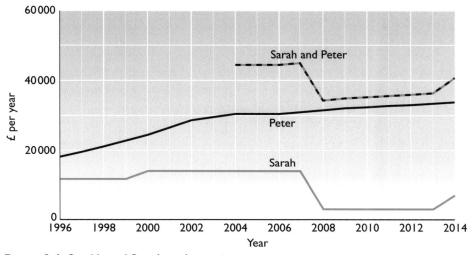

Figure 2.6 *Sarah's and Peter's real gross income*

Of the three separate lines on the graph in Figure 2.6, the two which run from 1996 to 2014 represent Sarah and Peter as individuals, while the line starting in 2004 represents Sarah's and Peter's joint household income. This line could be extended for many years but in this example it is shown for ten years, until 2014.

Sarah's income remains flat until 2008 when she leaves work to look after her and Peter's children, born in 2008 and 2010. Not all women leave work when they have children and, of course, it doesn't have to be Sarah rather than Peter, but for now we'll assume Sarah decides to give up paid employment. This means her pay falls to zero after she finishes her maternity leave, but Sarah still receives some income in the form of child-related benefits. Child and some other benefits are considered in Section 7 and also in Chapter 8. Sarah's income does not begin to recover from its sharp fall until 2014 when she goes back to work part time. Because Peter's income only increases slightly it is the change to Sarah's income that most influences their joint household income, which falls from £44,392 in 2004, and is still only £40,886 by 2014.

Activity 2.6

Think about your own household (or just you if you are a one-person household).

Try sketching your own individual or household income profile for the past and the future. What pattern or shape is it likely to take in the future? How might this impact on your goals? ■ ■ ■

Thinking about flows of income changing over the life-course can help with financial planning. This is because it's possible to anticipate future flows of income. For example, if an individual has the goal of taking a break from paid employment, perhaps to raise children or travel around the world, they can estimate the impact this will have on future income flows. This, in turn, may lead to decisions to change spending and/or saving now. We'll be using these kinds of representations, or models, of income profiles over time when we consider this issue in detail in Chapter 8.

There are many other situations when this idea of income changing over the life-course can be used. For instance, when taking out a mortgage it is important to know likely future household income flows which will influence how much can be borrowed, and when considering insurance it is important to consider how certain events might interrupt or reduce those income flows. We will look at mortgages and insurance in Chapters 6 and 9, respectively. Thinking about how income might change over the life-course, especially in response to events such as setting up a new household or having children, is an important component of financial planning.

Income profiles also raise the question of how to increase income. Section 4 of Chapter 3 will focus on budgeting and the balance between income and expenditure, and you will see that there are ways to change spending. Expenditure, in fact, is often the easier of the two to change, but income is not necessarily fixed. Box 2.4 gives some of the top suggestions for increasing income.

Box 2.4   Options for increasing income

Regardless of current income, there may be options to increase it. Personal finance experts often suggest some of the following are worth considering as potential ways of increasing income:

- Work longer hours or do overtime.
- Take on two paid jobs at the same time (an option currently taken by 4 per cent of those in employment in the UK (*Social Trends*, 2005)).
- Negotiate a pay rise – perhaps through a trade union, and perhaps reflecting improved productivity or profitability of the employer.
- Move jobs – including obtaining promotion, a new, better paid job with a new employer, or perhaps starting up a business.
- Make further investment in human capital for longer-term increases in pay, e.g. by further studying or training.
- Take in a lodger (if there is space) – Section 4 of Chapter 6 provides more details on this.
- Check all benefit entitlements and do not overpay Income Tax.

---

7   Income Tax, National Insurance and state benefits

In this section, I look in more detail at the deductions (for Income Tax and National Insurance) and additions (through benefit payments) that take us from gross to **net income**. Note that for some people another possible deduction from gross income is contributions to their pension scheme: these schemes are discussed separately in Chapter 7.

In terms of the money flows between the household, government and corporate sectors described in Chapter 1, Figure 1.1, Income Tax and National Insurance payments are examples of money flowing from the household to government sector, while benefit payments flow in the opposite direction.

Exploring taxes and benefits is important to personal finance for two reasons. First, taxes and benefits represent an example of the interdependence between the individual and the broader social and

Net income
Income after deductions such as Income Tax and National Insurance.

Income Tax
A tax which is payable on almost all sources of income within a given tax year from 6 April to the following 5 April. There is no minimum age at which a person becomes liable to pay income tax.

HM Revenue & Customs (HMRC)
HMRC is the department responsible for the business of the former Inland Revenue and HM Customs and Excise – and collects the bulk of tax revenue as well as paying tax credits and Child Benefit.

Progressive taxation
A tax whereby the proportion of a person's income paid as tax increases as their income increases.

economic environment in which they live. Taxation funds state benefits, such as state pensions and social security benefits, and pays for public services such as the National Health Service. Second, exploring taxes and benefits helps in financial planning by enabling accurate calculation of the amount of income that is available to spend or save – crucial for budgeting, which will be discussed in Section 4 of Chapter 3.

Income Tax is levied on almost all types of income, including paid employment. When it is collected via one's employer, it is often referred to as a 'pay as you earn' (PAYE) tax. Income Tax is paid on income received within a given tax year, from 6 April to 5 April. Income Tax is the single largest source of government revenue. For example, in 2004/05, **Her Majesty's Revenue & Customs (HMRC)** collected £127 billion in Income Tax – or just under 30 per cent of all government receipts.

In the UK Income Tax system, each person receives an 'allowance' of income that can be earned before Income Tax has to be paid. This 'personal allowance' was £5035 for someone under 65 in 2006/07. The allowances are higher for older people and some others, such as those who are registered blind. Income above this level is then subject to tax at three different standard rates. In 2006/07, the first £2150 of taxable income was taxed at 10 per cent; the next £31,150 at the basic rate of 22 per cent, and income above this at 40 per cent. By taxing additional income slices at higher rates, the proportion of tax increases with income. Therefore, UK Income Tax is an example of **progressive taxation**, meaning that the proportion of a person's income paid as tax increases as their income increases.

HMRC is responsible for Income Tax collection

Activity 2.7

Use the information given above to work out how much Income Tax would be paid by someone under 65 earning £22,000 for 2006/07.

Pay from employment or pension	£22 000
Minus personal allowance	£_____
Leaves taxable pay of	£_____
Starting rate_____% on £_____ is	£_____
Basic rate_____% on £_____ is	£_____
Tax to be paid in the year 2005/06 is	£_____

Comment

The answer to Activity 2.7 is given at the end of the chapter. ■ ■ ■

A second important deduction from gross income is **National Insurance** contributions. National Insurance – which was introduced in 1911 and subsequently expanded, especially in the 1940s – is paid by both employees and employers. Historically, it formed the basis for paying social security benefits related to unemployment, illness and retirement. By the twenty-first century, the receipts from National Insurance contributions were added to those from general taxation. Government's tax and National Insurance receipts fund all benefits as well as other public services and state provision. National Insurance contributions from employers and employees make up the second single largest contribution to UK Government receipts, at £78 billion in 2004/05 or approximately 17 per cent of all government receipts.

The mechanics of collection are that the Department for Work and Pensions issues each person in the UK with a National Insurance account number against which contributions are then recorded. The level of contributions influences entitlement to, and in some cases the level of, certain benefits. As with Income Tax, the rules and regulations surrounding National Insurance change regularly. In 2006/07 there was an 'Employee's Earnings Threshold' of £5035 below which no National Insurance is paid and an 'Upper Earnings Limit' of £33,540. On income between these limits, National Insurance is generally levied at 11 per cent. Any portion of income above the Upper Earnings Limit is subject to only a 1 per cent levy.

National Insurance Contributions from both employees and employers which form the basis for paying state benefits related to unemployment, sick pay and pensions.

Pay Slip

		O/T Hrs Worked	Units Paid	Rate	Credits	Dedits
PAYMENTS(* = tax not deducted)						
Gross Pay					2550.59	
DEDUCTIONS						
P.A.Y.E						411.08
National Insurance						199.32
Pension Scheme Contributions						161.96
	TOTALS				2552.59	772.36

Pay-As-You-Earn Income Tax payments

Taxable Pay		Tax Paid to date	Nat Ins to date	Pension to date (inc. AVCs)
This Period	To Date			
2545.25	4350.00	4937.00	2350.00	1830.00

BANK BRANCH NO   BANK ACCOUNT NO   BANK ACCOUNT TYPE   NET PAY 1778.23

A typical pay slip showing gross pay, deductions and net pay

As I mentioned at the beginning of this section, Income Tax and National Insurance, along with other taxes like VAT, excise duties, Stamp Duty Land Tax and Inheritance Tax, raise revenue which pays for state services such as education, health, defence, the transport infrastructure and the police service. In other words, money raised in taxes goes a substantial way towards paying for the physical and social framework within which citizens live and work. Money raised and spent collectively is also significant in personal finance terms because it reduces the need for private expenditure that would otherwise be needed on health, school education and so on.

Taxation pays for important public services, such as the NHS and care for the elderly

The UK's tax and benefits system also has the effect of some **redistribution of income**. That is to say that some of the taxes raised collectively are transferred back to individuals with particular needs. Think of this in terms of Chapter 1's Figure 1.1, with money flowing from the household to the government sector, which in turn funds benefits which flow back to households. Of course, those receiving benefits will often be different from those paying taxes such as Income Tax, but many people will pay tax and receive benefits at different stages in their life-course. The availability of state benefits is also important as part of the way of coping with unexpected events, which we shall examine later in Chapter 9. An increase in income redistribution since the election of the Labour Government in 1997 helps to explain the trend shown in Figure 2.2: namely, the fall in the number of individuals now living in low-income households.

Let's now turn to look at state benefits, starting with their underlying general principles. One of the backgrounds to the UK's benefits system in the mid 2000s dates from the Labour Government coming to power in 1997. After that time, the primary principles behind the design of benefits became to help people move off welfare and into paid employment, and to tackle child poverty, which is much higher in the UK than in many other European countries. To do this, a new form of payment was introduced called a 'tax credit'. In 2006, these consisted of the Working Tax Credit (WTC) and the Child Tax Credit (CTC). They are called tax credits because they are an attempt to integrate the benefit system with the tax system. This use of benefits links back to my

Redistribution of income
The process of re-allocating income to achieve social objectives, usually the creation of a 'fairer society' through a more equal distribution.

discussion in Section 4 of flexible labour markets where the UK Government uses policy to encourage as many people as possible to obtain paid employment.

Means tested

Means tested refers to payments that are made only to those who are assessed to have a certain level of income or less, and in some cases, a certain level of assets or less.

WTC and CTC are both **means tested** on household income. This means that the amount of WTC or CTC a person receives goes down as their household income goes up. WTC is available to households where at least one adult is in employment and working at least sixteen hours per week (or thirty in some cases) and CTC is available to parents whether or not they are in employment, as long as their income is below £58,175 (or £66,350 if they have a child under 1 year old).

WTC is designed to encourage people into employment by providing financial help to those on low incomes. Before 1999, people who were paid relatively little could be in an 'unemployment trap' in which they would receive no more in a job than they received in benefits when unemployed. This discouraged people from taking employment. The intention of WTC was to change this so that it should always be worth moving from benefits to employment. Since WTC is designed to help the very poorest households into employment, the full amount is paid only if household income is very low (£5220 in 2006/07). Above that minimum, WTC is withdrawn at a rate of 37p for every £1 in gross income. CTC is paid to people who are responsible for at least one child (or qualifying young person), and is paid directly to the person who is mainly responsible for caring for the child or children. Nine out of ten families with children are entitled to CTC and, like WTC, most of it is also withdrawn at a rate of 37p for every £1 in gross income. There are also payments for childcare, and these are explored further in Chapter 8.

One criticism of WTC and CTC is that the link to annual (instead of weekly) income has meant that tax credit claims are initially based on an estimate of income for the year, for which purpose the previous year's income is taken. The award is then confirmed or revised after the end of the year once actual income is known (though in-year adjustments can be made and must be if there is a very large change in income). If estimated income was too low and credits overpaid, then money will be due to HMRC. This inflexibility can lead to severe hardship in low-income households who may have spent the money and have little or no savings. However, the government has attempted to address this problem by raising the level of in-year change in income that can be disregarded from £2500 to, from 2006/07 onwards, £25,000. A further alleged problem has been errors and problems in calculation by the HMRC – see Box 2.5 which reproduces a newspaper article about such problems, and gives some practical advice for anyone who receives WTC or CTC.

Box 2.5   Criticisms of WTC and CTC, and some steps to take to minimise problems

Six million say: it's no credit to the government

Neasa MacErlean finds Gordon Brown's bid to help 'hard working families' is not coming across

Sarah has received 11 different notices of what she is meant to receive in the form of working tax credit (WTC) in the past year – but still has no idea ... fairly typical example of the problems dogging the administration of WTC and child tax credit (CTC), received by an estimated 6 million families.

Chancellor Gordon Brown introduced these benefits to help people (mainly parents, but some non-parents as well) who work – but the administration is putting some people off, according to Citizens Advice.

'The administration needs to be improved,' says the CAB's Katie Lane. 'People need to be confident of what they are going to get, but some people have had bad experiences about going back to work again and not getting the benefits they expected.'

She cites the example of one woman with two children under the age of five who was over-paid WTC, then had the repayment docked over the next few months and ended up working 42 hours a week (far more than she wanted to work) to keep her family going on the reduced WTC income and her earnings.

Citizens Advice, who received 134,000 calls for help on WTC/CTC in 2003–04 suggest some steps you can take to try to minimise the problems:

- Tell the Revenue quickly of any change in circumstance – a new job, increase in hours or new child, for instance. (Remember that a child staying on at school after the age of 16 is regarded as a change in circumstance and your money will fall if you do not notify the Revenue of this.)

- Ensure that all changes in circumstances are responded to by the Revenue. 'If you do not get an award notice,

you should follow up,' says Lane.

- Ask for detailed backing information if you are puzzled by your awards notice. The Revenue is planning to make these more comprehensible (although probably not for at least a year). In the meantime, many families have lost out because they did not pick up strange errors (such as stating their earnings at work as £0.00) on the awards notices.

- Go to a Citizens Advice Bureau, ring the single parents' helpline at Gingerbread (0800 018 4318), ring the Revenue helpline (0845 300 3900), download the free leaflets and get as much help as you need to understand the system.

- Appeal if you believe you are missing out or are suffering hardship because of Revenue maladministration.

(*The Observer*, 5 December 2004)

In addition to WTC and CTC, there are conventional state benefits paid in various circumstances. For example, Jobseeker's Allowance (JSA) is paid to those available and actively looking for employment. It is split into 'contributions-based' JSA and 'income-based' JSA. Under contributions-based JSA those over twenty-five who have paid a certain number of National Insurance contributions are eligible for payments of £57.45 per week in 2006/07 for six months. Under income-based JSA, those on a low income may be eligible for payment even if they have not made National Insurance contributions. Eligibility, and the amount of income-based JSA, depends on a number of factors, including household income and savings.

The government provides a range of state benefits

There are many other types of benefit in the UK, which include the following:

- ***Income Support*** is a means-tested benefit paid to certain groups of people who do not have enough money to live on.
- ***Incapacity Benefit*** is for people who cannot work and do not get Statutory Sick Pay.

- *Disability Living Allowance* is a benefit for people under 65 who have personal care needs or problems with mobility. Chapter 8 discusses this in more detail.

- *Carer's Allowance* is a benefit for people who are giving regular and substantial care to disabled people in their own homes. Chapter 8 discusses this in more detail.

- *Attendance Allowance* is a benefit for people with care needs who are over 65. Chapter 8 discusses this in more detail.

- *Child Benefit* is a tax-free benefit paid to most people with children. This is discussed in more detail in Chapter 8.

- *Pension Credit* is a means tested benefit for people aged 60 or over. Chapter 7 discusses this in detail.

- *Council Tax Benefit* is a benefit for people on low income to help them pay Council Tax.

- *Housing Benefit* is a benefit for people on low income to help them pay their rent.

- *Free and subsidised prescriptions and dental treatment.*

Child Benefit is a good example of what is called a 'universal benefit', namely, one that is paid regardless of the income level of the recipients. Consequently, everyone who has children is entitled to Child Benefit. A major category of state payments which has not been mentioned in detail is pensions: these are dealt with separately in Chapter 7.

In total, during 2005/06, the UK Government spent some £146 billion on state benefits (including pensions), representing around one-third of all government spending and being the largest single direction of government spending (HM Treasury, 2005).

Taxes and benefits are, therefore, important both at the broad level of the economy and society, and also at the level of individuals and households. At the broader level, taxes are the way in which infrastructure, public services and state benefits are funded. At the level of individuals and households, public expenditure on services such as health and education reduces the need for private expenditure on such services. And knowledge of the tax and benefits system is essential in order to be able to calculate net income accurately. Indeed, being able to work out things such as Income Tax liability and any benefit entitlements is an important building block of financial capability.

8 Cash flow statement: the income side

You have seen that households can receive income from a number of different sources. As Figure 1.2 in Chapter 1 showed, assessing is always an important first step in financial planning, and assessing income is often one of the most important factors in financial decision making. One tool which can be used to do this is the **cash flow statement**. This involves recording inflows and outflows of money on a regular basis. In this section, I concentrate on inflows. The spending side – outflows – of the cash flow statement is covered in Section 4 of Chapter 3.

Cash flow statement
A record of income and expenditure over a certain period of time.

There are different issues to be considered in recording the income side of a cash flow statement. First, the statement should record flows of income as they are actually received, for example into a bank account, in the particular time period such as a month or a week. For most people, this will represent their net income: standard rate Income Tax payers whose income consists of pay will already have been taxed via PAYE, and National Insurance contributions (and, for people in occupational pension schemes, pension contributions) will have been paid. However, some people will receive at least some income paid gross, such as some investment returns or state benefits. In this case, the gross income should be recorded in the cash flow statement, but it must be remembered that there may be tax still due on this income at the end of the tax year, and tax payments may be an expense that will need to be factored into the budgeting process.

Second, it is important to include all the different sources of income in the cash flow statement. Using the categorisations from Table 2.1, this means including income from paid employment, self-employment, savings and investments, pensions and social security benefits. Any additional income is recorded under the 'other' category.

Third, it is important to think about how frequently different types of income are received. For instance, a household may receive a combination of weekly benefits *and* monthly pay. In order to standardise these different frequencies of income, the most common technique is to calculate an equivalent annual income first (for example, by multiplying a weekly income by fifty-two) and then estimate a monthly income equivalent by dividing this figure by twelve.

Fourth, the cash flow statement can be drawn up at the level of the household or individual. Which is chosen will depend on household composition, but to get an accurate figure of total household income it is necessary to include all income earners.

Complete the income part of the cash flow statement below for your household or for just yourself if you are in a one-person household. If you are in a multi-person household, the normal assumption would be that the income of other household members would be recorded. However, if this is not possible, simply complete this using your own income.

Your household cash flow statement (income side), current week/month

Person	Component of income						Total
	Pay	Self-employment	Savings and investments	Pension	Social security benefits	Other	
Total							

Comment

You can check the internal consistency of the table by ensuring that the overall total in the box at the bottom right of the table equals the sum of column and row totals. ■ ■ ■

9 Conclusion

This chapter has focused on various aspects of income such as its different sources, including paid employment and state benefits. It has also helped to develop the four themes of *Personal Finance*. For example, Sections 3, 4 and 5 showed how the changing social and economic context impacted upon paid employment, the most important component of household income. In addition, the interrelationship between individuals and households and how income flow changes over time were examined in Section 6. Section 7 returned to the economic context, explaining the tax and benefits system in the UK and applying this knowledge at the level of the individual. Finally, Section 8 introduced the cash flow statement, a crucial first step in financial planning.

Thus, taking these aspects together, this chapter represents some important early steps in building financial capability. Having established where income comes from, the following chapters explore how it can be spent, supplemented by borrowing, or saved and invested. Chapter 3 starts this process by looking at expenditure.

Answer to Activity

Answer to Activity 2.7

Pay from employment or pension	£22 000
Minus personal allowance	£5035
Taxable pay	£16 965
Starting rate 10% on £2150 is	£215
Basic rate 22% on £14,815 is	£3259
Tax to be paid in the year 2005/06 is	£3474

£3474 of tax would be paid. This is calculated in four stages:

1 Subtract the tax-free amount of £5035 from £22,000 to give £16,965 of taxable income.
2 The next £2150 of income is taxed at 10 per cent giving £215 of tax.
3 The next £14,815 is taxed at 22 per cent. To work out how much this means in this example, subtract £2150 from the taxable income figure of £16,965 to give £14,815. Twenty-two per cent of this is £3259.
4 Add £215 and £3259 to give £3474 of tax. ■ ■ ■

References

Annual Survey of Hours and Earnings (2005) Table 14.1a [online], Office for National Statistics (ONS), http://www.statistics.gov.uk/downloads/theme_labour/ASHE_2004_exc/tab14_1a.xls (Accessed 15 December 2005).

Bunting, M. (2004) *Willing Slaves: How the Overwork Culture is Ruling Our Lives*, London, HarperCollins.

Callaghan, G. (1996) *Flexibility, Mobility and the Labour Market*, Aldershot, Ashgate.

Department for Education and Skills (DfES) (2004) *Student Loans and the Question of Debt* [online], http://www.dfes.gov.uk/hegateway/uploads/Debt%20-%20FINAL.pdf (Accessed 10 November 2005).

Department for Work and Pensions (DWP) (2004) *Family Resources Survey 2003–04* [online], available from http://www.dwp.gov.uk/asd/frs/index/publications.asp (Accessed 30 November 2005).

Department of Trade and Industry (DTI) (2006) 'National Minimum Wage' [online], http://www.dti.gov.uk/employment/pay/national-minimum-wage/index.html (Accessed 6 June 2005).

Elias, P. and Purcell, K. (2004) *The Earnings of Graduates in Their Early Careers*, Research paper no.5 from the project 'Researching graduate careers seven years on', Employment Studies Research Unit, University of the West of England and Warwick Institute for Employment Research.

Elias, P., Hogarth, T. and Pierre, G. (2002) *The Wider Benefits of Education and Training: A Comparative Longitudinal Study*, Department for Work and Pensions (DWP), Research Report no.178, Leeds, Centre for Development Studies.

GlaxoSmithKline (GSK) (2005) 'GlaxoSmithKline annual report' [online], http://www.gsk.com/reportsandpublications.htm (Accessed 31 May 2006).

Gordon, D.M., Edwards, R. and Reich, M. (1982) *Segmented Work, Divided Workers: The Historical Transformation of Labour in the United States*, Cambridge, Cambridge University Press.

Her Majesty's (HM) Revenue and Customs (2005) *Net Receipts of Inland Revenue Taxes*, Table 1.2 [online], http://www.hmrc.gov.uk/stats/tax_receipts/menu.htm (Accessed 15 August 2005).

Her Majesty's (HM) Treasury (2003) *EMU and Labour Market Flexibility*, London, HM Treasury.

Her Majesty's (HM) Treasury (2005) 'What does the Government spend money on?' [online], http://www.hm-treasury.gov.uk/economic_data_and_tools/finance_spending_statistics/pes_function/function.cfm (Accessed 16 August 2005).

Learning and Skills Council (LSC) (2005) *Young People Set to Miss Out on £4,000 a Year by Dropping Out* [online], press release, 24 August, http://www.lsc.gov.uk/National/Media/PressReleases/young-people-missout_ema.htm (Accessed 11 November 2005).

McIntosh, S. (2004) 'Further analysis of the returns to academic and vocational qualifications', Research Report no. 35, London, Centre for the Economics of Education, London School of Economics.

Paton, M. (2004) 'Exposing the fat cats', 10 August [online], http://www.fool.co.uk/qualiport/2004/qualiport040810.htm (Accessed 14 December 2005).

Purcell, K. and Elias, P. (2004) *Seven Years On: Graduate Careers in a Changing Labour Market*, Manchester, The Higher Education Careers Services Unit.

Schifferes, S. (2002) 'In business: discrimination in the workplace' [online], http://news.bbc.co.uk/hi/english/static/in_depth/uk/2002/race/in_business.stm (Accessed 15 December 2005).

Small Business Council (2004) *Small Businesses in the Informal Economy: Making the Transition to the Formal Economy*, London, Small Business Council.

Social Trends (2004) no.34, London, The Stationery Office (TSO) for The Office for National Statistics (ONS); also available online at the ONS website (National Statistics Online), http://www.statistics.gov.uk/downloads/theme_social/Social_Trends34/Social_Trends34.pdf (Accessed 14 November 2005).

Social Trends (2005) no.35, Basingstoke and New York, Palgrave Macmillan for The Office for National Statistics (ONS); also available online at the ONS website, http://www.statistics.gov.uk/downloads/theme_social/Social_Trends35/Social_Trends_35.pdf (Accessed 14 November 2005).

Social Trends (2006) no.36, Basingstoke and New York, Palgrave Macmillan for The Office for National Statistics (ONS); also available online at the ONS website, http://www.statistics.gov.uk/downloads/theme_social/Social_Trends36/Social_Trends_36.pdf (Accessed 30 May 2006).

Expenditure and budgeting

Chapter 3

Martin Higginson

Contents

1   Introduction

In today's society there are many opportunities to spend money: goods and services can be bought online, from catalogues, through the TV, and from shopping malls which provide whole shopping experiences. Advertising continually tempts people to spend money – whether it's money they already have, or money they can borrow. Spending provides the way to obtain the essentials of life such as food and accommodation. But the reasons for spending can go far beyond such practical or functional uses. Living in the twenty-first century UK involves being part of a 'consumer society' where spending money has become a leisure activity in its own right. Opinions are often formed about people based on what they buy and the possessions they own. Spending can be a means to signal who we are, and it forms an integral part of the way in which people relate to one other.

You saw in Chapters 1 and 2 that not all spending in the economy is done by households: the government spends money on goods and services, which then directly impact on the quality of everyone's lives – this spending is paid for by taxes, which in turn are another call on household incomes. At household level, we tend to keep spending more. Real average weekly household expenditure in the UK (in 2003/04 prices) increased from £270 in 1980 to £416 in 2003/04, an increase of 54.1 per cent (*Family Spending*, 2005, Table 4.1). Choices about spending levels are crucial because they affect household finances directly. Spending more than the individual or household income will lead to debt, whereas spending less than the income allows savings to be accumulated.

I begin this chapter by exploring some of the economic and social influences which affect the way that households and individuals spend money. This broader discussion provides an important context for Section 4, which introduces the technique of household budgeting. This technique is a way of improving household finances by planning spending in relation to income, and it is an important component of developing financial planning. Budgeting is explained first with reference to a one-person household, before discussing the more complex issues about the management and control of finances that arise in multi-person households (in Section 5), and those with children (in Section 6).

2   Economic influences on expenditure

Let's start by looking at expenditure patterns and by exploring some of the economic influences that affect this expenditure. The pie chart in Figure 3.1, drawn from Office for National Statistics (ONS) data (*Social Trends*, 2004), shows the different categories of spending expressed as a percentage of total household expenditure in the UK. It's like a 'shopping basket' of goods and services on which people typically spend their money. In practice, different households will spend their money in different proportions to this 'typical' pattern of expenditure. From Figure 3.1, it can be seen that, in 2004, housing accounted for the largest proportion of total expenditure (20.9 per cent), followed by motoring (14.6 per cent) and then food (11.1 per cent). The figure for housing includes spending on mortgage payments and Council Tax.

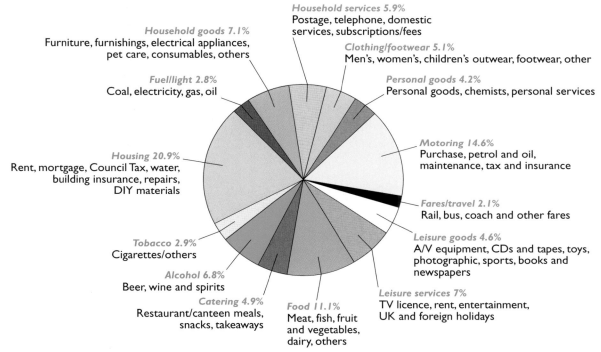

Figure 3.1 *Pattern of household expenditure in the UK, 2004*
Source: *Economic Trends*, 2005, Table W2

Spending patterns are not fixed, and have changed in recent years. For example, spending on housing (including mortgage interest payments and Council Tax) has become more important, increasing from 15.7 per cent in 1987 to 20.9 per cent of total household spending in 2004. Over the same period, spending on leisure services increased from 3 per cent to 7 per cent, while spending on food decreased from 16.7 per cent to 11.1 per cent (*Economic Trends*, 2005).

The changing pattern of spending can in part be explained by economic factors such as how the prices of different goods and services have changed. To illustrate, in the 1990s and the early 2000s, the prices of food and basic clothing increased less quickly than those for other goods. In particular, imports from countries with low production costs, such as

China, have actually reduced the price of some clothing for UK consumers. When the prices of some goods fall, or increase less quickly than those of other goods, the goods become relatively cheaper. Depending on the sort of goods, people may buy more of the goods that have become cheaper, perhaps even increasing their total expenditure on that type of good. Mobile phones are an example of a good where falling prices resulted in more being purchased in 2003 than in 1996, as Figure 3.2 shows. While mobile phones were owned by less than 20 per cent of households in 1996, over 70 per cent of households owned a mobile phone by 2002/03.

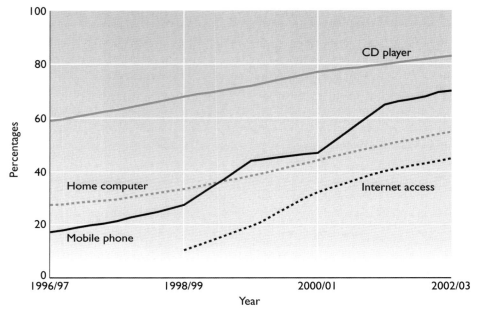

Figure 3.2 *Change in ownership of selected goods, 1996–2003*
Source: *Social Trends*, 2004, no. 34, Figure 13.10

There are some types of goods which people do *not* buy more of when their price falls. For instance, in countries where people generally have enough to eat, people do not tend to buy more food when food prices fall. Rather, the fall in food prices allows them to have more money to spend on higher quality food or other things such as leisure goods. Therefore, price changes can help to explain why the proportion of total household spending has risen for some goods and fallen for others.

Another major factor which explains the increasing proportion of expenditure on items such as leisure goods and services is the rising real disposable income experienced by most households in the UK since the 1980s due to the growth of the UK economy. A household's level of income affects the types of goods and services that it buys, as well as how much it spends in total. With more money available, households can afford to spend money on leisure goods and services which may previously have been seen as unaffordable luxuries, for example, the items in Figure 3.2. With higher income, a smaller proportion of it is needed for necessities, and money can be spent on those types of goods and services which households enjoy consuming. Spending on necessities like food doesn't tend to increase much with a rise in income, while spending on some other goods, such as tobacco, will actually tend to decrease as income increases. This is because people's tastes also change as their income increases so that, for instance, as income rises people may consume more health and leisure goods or services, and fewer things that are harmful to health.

Although spending on some goods falls with increasing income, overall spending increases. Figure 3.3 shows that total household expenditure has tended to respond to movements in disposable income, with both real disposable income and real household expenditure increasing over the period 1980–2003/04. Moreover, when the growth in real disposable income slowed down in the late 1980s and early 1990s, there was also a related slow down in the growth of real household expenditure.

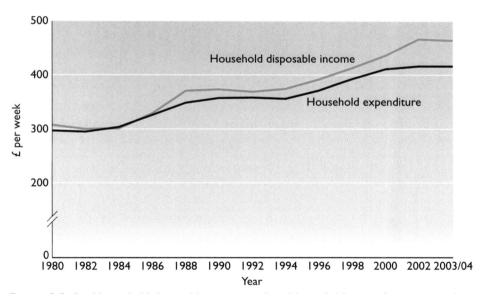

Figure 3.3 *Real household disposable income and real household expenditure per week, 1980–2003/04)*
Source: *Family Spending*, 2005, pp. 56–7, Table 4.1

This link between income and spending is also evident when examining the distribution of expenditure across households with different levels of income. The uneven distribution of income within the UK, described in Chapter 2, results in an uneven distribution of spending. In 2003/04, dividing households in terms of disposable income, the lowest 10 per cent had an average weekly expenditure per person of just £112.80 compared with £903.10 per person in the 10 per cent of households with highest incomes (*Family Spending*, 2005, Table 3.2).

One of the reasons why households spend more as their income increases is that it enables them to enjoy a higher standard of living. To illustrate, a family on a low income which struggles to make ends meet can clearly benefit from additional income, enabling it to afford more, and perhaps better quality, goods and services. Such a household will therefore spend most, if not all, of any extra income it receives. It may seem surprising, but this remains true at all levels of income. As income increases, households generally keep increasing spending (although higher income households will, generally, also be able to save a higher proportion of that extra income). Surely, there is a level of income at which all household needs can be satisfied, so that they do not need to keep spending more? In Section 3, I will consider why this may not be the case.

3   Symbolic consumption, marketing and advertising

3.1 Symbolic consumption

This section aims to make you think more broadly about consumption and spending – perhaps to think differently from how you do now. When reading this section, try to reflect on the spending behaviour of both you and other people. Thinking in this way can help to inform later discussions on planning future spending, through a deeper understanding of the motives behind purchasing decisions.

One of the reasons why people seem to have to keep spending is because there is more to spending and consuming than simply satisfying needs. The concept of **social status** can provide a way to understand this. The sociologist Max Weber (1948 [1924]) saw a person's social status as their position in society based on the level of authority and/or prestige that they hold in the eyes of others.

Social status
A social position within a society; or the social honour or prestige that a particular individual or group is accorded by other members of a society.

Like income, status is unevenly distributed, and while it is common that people with higher incomes have higher levels of status, this is not always the case. For example, in many societies ministers of religion with modest incomes can carry high levels of status; in Hindu societies, status is more likely to be achieved through non-material achievements; and in the UK, the perceived status of, say, teachers and plumbers may not reflect their respective incomes. None the less, in a consumer society like

Max Weber, 1864–1920

the UK's, status *is* often linked to what we can buy. This can create pressure on household and individual finances, and is sometimes used by marketing departments to help sell products. If status is connected to what we buy, to define ourselves in a consumer society we have to keep spending. As Bauman (1999) puts it, in a consumer society, 'The road to self-identity, to a place in society, to life lived in a form recognisable as that of meaningful living, all require daily visits to the market place ... one needs to be a consumer first, before one can think of becoming anything particular.'

You may be familiar with the idea of the **status symbol** as a way of publicly displaying status to others. In traditional societies, status is symbolically displayed in ways such as body marks, clothing, and crowns, jewels and other objects which are often passed down through generations. In a consumer society, status is closely associated with consumption. The goods that are bought may have useful properties, but they also act as status symbols. Consequently, buying a particular type of mobile phone not only enables us to make phone calls on the move,

Status symbol
A status symbol is something that indicates the social status of its owner. Usually a status symbol is a mark of high status.

Symbolic consumption
Consuming products or lifestyles for social meanings attached to those products or lifestyles for others to see.

but the particular type of phone also acts as a status symbol, and buying it is an act of **symbolic consumption**. Looking at consumer behaviour as symbolic consumption can help us understand more about people's spending behaviour. The idea of symbolic consumption suggests that people are concerned about what others think of them, and that the opinions we hold about other people are based partly on what they consume and the material things they own. This makes the possessions that people acquire symbolic of their character and status in society. Symbolic consumption gives a powerful motivation for spending. To explore these ideas further, I will introduce two influential writers, Thorstein Veblen and Pierre Bourdieu. Both had ideas that connected why we spend to the concept of status, and they can help us to reflect on why people spend money in certain ways.

Veblen (1925) saw much spending as a way of displaying an individual's wealth. Rather than being bought simply for their function, some expensive and luxurious products are bought so that others can see how 'well off' their purchasers are. People who say things such as 'Andrew must be loaded because he drives a Ferrari' are expressing Veblen's point: people will infer from Andrew's purchase of an expensive car that he is wealthy. If others often react that way, then purchasing the Ferrari was a successful way for Andrew to acquire the status that is accorded when a person is perceived to be wealthy. According to Veblen, this is what Andrew would want; people want to be seen as wealthy in a society in which being wealthy confers high status. Consumption has taken on a symbolic role: the symbol of wealth is the Ferrari that Andrew drives; it is the price tag that confers status.

Conspicuous consumption
The ostentatious display of wealth in order to gain recognition by others of an increase in one's status.

Veblen called this type of expenditure **conspicuous consumption**. Veblen's own views on this were scathing: he deplored the ways in which the 'leisure class' (or what we might call the 'upper classes') lived a life of waste and ostentatiousness, and how they marked it with their symbols of conspicuous consumption (Abercrombie et al., 2000). Whether you share Veblen's views or not, his point – that the aim of such expenditure is for other people to see it – is one that we can use to develop an understanding of symbolic consumption, and reflect on how people consume goods and services. Veblen's analysis can be extended to modern-day life and to why people buy clothes with 'designer labels' and other such 'obviously' expensive goods. While it may be easier for people who are wealthy, or have a high income level, to indulge in this conspicuous consumption, a possible consequence for those on lower incomes, or with few assets, is the temptation to borrow money and perhaps go into debt to buy more expensive goods and services, in order to obtain perceived higher social status.

A somewhat different view of symbolic consumption is taken by Bourdieu (1977), who has written extensively on how consumption is used as a way of distinguishing people by **social class**. Status here is obtained by being in a higher social class. What defines social class is argued at length among academics, with factors such as income, occupation, education and cultural habits all being considered. Although a complex idea, for our purposes the significant thing about social class is that it divides the population into groups of different social status – people may make some effort to demonstrate to which social class they belong and to distinguish themselves from members of other classes.

For Bourdieu (1977), consumption and our tastes are influenced by experiences in childhood, family and schooling, but most crucially by social class. In turn, what we buy is part of what shapes our position in society. People try to distinguish themselves from people in other, lower, social classes through what they buy. Like Veblen, Bourdieu believes that people consume for symbolic reasons, but for Bourdieu our consumption patterns are a symbol of social class. The higher the social class, the more status its members have and the more they will work to maintain their position of superiority in this hierarchy.

Clearly, income is important in deciding what you can buy, and those in higher social classes can, in general, afford more expensive items. Yet Bourdieu also explains how tastes are important in differentiating people. People demonstrate their membership of higher social classes by having more 'refined' and 'artistic' tastes. Even when consuming what appear to be similar goods, there can be subtle distinctions to show someone's class. For instance, people from different social classes may all buy wine. However, people in higher social classes are likely to be able to buy more expensive wine (perhaps from a specialist wine merchant rather than from a supermarket), and they will also be able to talk more knowledgeably about the grape, the year and the vineyard, possibly because they have even visited the Chateau where it is made. According to Bourdieu, while individuals have some freedom in their purchasing decisions, their social class and tastes restrict the way in which they carry out these decisions. How one spends money then becomes an ongoing struggle to maintain differences between social classes, notably an attempt to distinguish oneself from those in lower social classes.

Social class
An informal ranking of people in a society based on their income, occupation, education, and other factors.

Activity 3.1

Do you think that Veblen's idea of conspicuous consumption explains the spending behaviour of people you know? Does it explain your own behaviour?

Do you think Bourdieu's idea of spending to distinguish oneself from other social classes is more useful than Veblen's idea of conspicuous consumption?

It's always easier to classify other people's consumption as conspicuous than it is to think of your own spending as spending for purely symbolic reasons. We usually think that we make our spending decisions based on the material proprieties of the things we buy: whether we like the shape of a particular sofa or want a high-tech digital camera to take better photos. That's where Bourdieu's (1977) theory is particularly interesting. It is saying that our taste – our liking for a sofa of that particular shape or our wish to produce high-quality photos – is produced by living in a particular social class. Therefore, simply following our tastes when we go shopping has the result of distinguishing ourselves from people in different social classes. We simultaneously buy what we want and engage in symbolic consumption. ■ ■ ■

Thus, the idea of symbolic consumption isn't so much about how we see our *own* behaviour as it is a means of looking at the type of society we live in. In common with other aspects of society, status symbols change over time. For example, consider the fashion brand Burberry, once a symbol of the rich. At the time of writing this chapter, you are as likely to see working-class football fans wearing the Burberry check as people from higher classes. Moreover, it can be the working class that influences the middle and upper classes, as often happens in trends related to music or fashion.

Burberry is a classic example of how symbols of consumption can change over time

3.2 Marketing and advertising

Recognising the importance of symbolic consumption as one explanation of spending patterns does not imply that most things that are bought are actually useless: most products need a function for us to consider buying them. For example, we want a vacuum cleaner to suck up dust, or we want a car to take us from A to B. However, the advert for the car in Figure 3.4 seems to suggest something that is far more than just a machine to transport us. There's symbolism in the advert too – perhaps suggesting that the car 'has spirit' or is 'funky' – as there is also in the advertisement for a brand of vodka.

Figure 3.4 *Citroën and Smirnoff advertisements*

You'll doubtless be able to think of other contemporary examples of advertising campaigns with symbolic messages. Marketing departments have long recognised that products and brands have these symbolic characteristics, and advertising often uses symbolic images to sell products. Naomi Klein (2001), writing about brands and their role in a modern society, describes her view of what marketing departments are thinking about when they use symbolic images:

> They dream ... about their brands' deep inner meanings – the way they capture the spirit of individuality, athleticism, wilderness or community ... Savvy ad agencies have all moved away from the idea of flogging a product made by someone else, and come to think of themselves instead as brand factories, hammering out what is true value: the idea, the lifestyle, the attitude.
>
> (Klein, 2000, pp. 195–6)

It can be hard to escape the feeling that marketers are targeting us relentlessly. There are 'cold' phone callers selling a kitchen; tick boxes asking if your details can be passed on; TV commercials selling anti-ageing creams; stores offering loyalty cards; billboards showing dream holidays; and even internet 'spam' (or junk emails) offering to find your 'dream date'. Marketing departments use the information that they collect about us, individually or as members of the public, to produce advertisements which they hope will make us want to buy their products. One marketing technique is to 'segment' (split) the population into different socio-demographic categories. People are identified by certain common characteristics such as age, gender, income, social class, sexuality and ethnicity. Sophisticated databases identify where different categories of people are likely to live, what TV programmes they are likely to watch, what newspapers they buy, and marketing messages can be placed carefully to market products. This helps to explain why adverts differ between national newspapers and why junk mail in different areas of the same town may be selling different products.

One view about advertising is that it provides information for consumers to help them make informed choices on how to satisfy their needs. The argument is that people do not have enough time to search for information on all the choices available or to discover all the attributes of products, and so marketing and advertising helps people to decide. This view suggests that products are carefully considered by potential buyers, alongside the price and how much money is available, and then an informed decision is made. This view fits in with the idea that there is **consumer sovereignty** in the economy; so that marketing is merely a facilitating influence, helping to provide information to satisfy existing needs. This helps markets to work more efficiently by linking up consumers and producers.

A rather different view is that marketing creates wants that are not previously there, and provides incomplete and biased information. This argument places more emphasis on the power of producers and sellers of goods, and on marketing manipulating emotions to persuade people to spend money, rather than on the power of the consumer.

Consumer sovereignty
An assumption that consumers have the power to dictate the types, quality and quantity of the goods and services provided in a market place.

Activity 3.2

1   How does the idea of symbolic consumption help to explain how marketing influences expenditure?

2   What scope would there be for advertising in a society in which people did not buy things for symbolic reasons? How might advertisements differ from the ones we are used to?

Comment

1   When Klein (2001) describes a brand's deeper meaning, she seems to suggest that the messages conveyed by advertisements are more about 'the lifestyle, the attitude' and what buying the product would say about the consumer, not about the functional attributes of that product.

Marketing departments construct symbolic images to deliver such messages in order to tempt people to buy their products. In many advertisements, we hardly see the product at all.

2   In a society without symbolic consumption, people's interest in buying things would depend on their useful properties, on which they would need information. There would still be a place for informative advertising, telling people about new products, and saying why a particular company's product is better. There would still be reason to be sceptical about adverts, since advertisers would be trying to sell their particular product. However, they would not use techniques that associate the product with status symbols, or with a particular social class. Therefore, advertisements might be more straightforward, but perhaps a little duller because much creative energy in marketing is directed at people as symbolic consumers. ■ ■ ■

4   Budgeting

For most people, there is considerable pressure to spend money on a variety of goods and services. Yet, at the same time, there is a need to save and invest for the future. The process of budgeting can help to reconcile these competing demands on income by planning future income and expenditure flows. It is to this important financial technique that we now turn. A **budget** looks forward to estimate income and expenditure over a future time period. In preparing a budget, we will bring together ideas from Chapter 2 and the earlier sections of this chapter in a practical way.

Budget
A detailed plan of income and expenditure expected over a certain period of time.

Setting a budget aids the management of household finances in three ways:

1   It helps to control spending by comparing actual and planned spending.
2   It checks to see if there is enough spare income to pay current and future bills without having to borrow.
3   It enables planning to meet goals.

Carrying out a budgeting exercise once is useful to help assess whether spending is under control, but budgeting is most effective in managing finances when it is used as part of an ongoing process.

Let's start with an example using an income and expenditure profile. I am going to look at Jenny, a twenty-eight-year-old woman who works as an insurance clerk. Figure 3.5 shows her expenditure and income between 1995 and 2006. It includes a line for Jenny's income, similar to that drawn for Sarah's income in Figure 2.4 in Chapter 2, but Figure 3.5 shows real net income rather than real gross income. I have drawn it that way because it is net income that matters for budgeting purposes. In order to think about planning expenditure, an individual or household needs to know how much income they have available to spend, save and invest, or borrow. Gross income does not provide this information because Income Tax and other deductions are not taken into consideration, whereas net income takes such deductions into account. For the same reason, the income side of the cash flow statement in Chapter 2 showed net income.

Figure 3.5 has an extra line added to it showing Jenny's real expenditure. From this, we can see that her expenditure has been higher than her net income since 1998. From 1998, the gap between the two lines shows the amount that Jenny is spending over her income, and the shaded area from 1998 to 2006 between the two lines gives the total amount that she has spent above her net income. In such a situation, Jenny will have had to borrow to pay for this excess expenditure, unless she had savings to draw upon. Between 1995 and 1997, when her net income was higher than expenditure, Jenny will have accumulated some savings, but these are not enough to prevent her having to borrow in the later period when she spends more than her income.

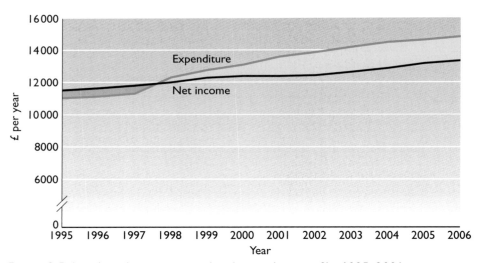

Figure 3.5 *Jenny's real net income and real expenditure profile, 1995–2006*

Assuming Jenny doesn't want to accumulate larger debts, she needs to either increase her income or reduce her expenditure, or both: effectively, she would like to move her income line up and/or her expenditure line down. If she manages to do this sufficiently (and budgeting is one way to achieve this aim), in the future she will be in a position where expenditure no longer exceeds income.

Figure 3.5 examines total net income and total expenditure per year. This is useful because it gives a graphic picture of what is happening to finances and provides an idea of why there may need to be changes in the future. Budgeting can help to plan such changes by looking at the details of income and expenditure. This requires examining income and expenditure flows over a shorter time horizon than a year, usually as often as income comes in (weekly or monthly), and then projecting the flows forward to work on an annual level and beyond.

Similar to the examples of financial planning throughout *Personal Finance*, budgeting will be approached using the four-stage process introduced in Chapter 1. I now want to take you through these stages in the context of setting a budget.

Stage 1: Assess the situation

The start of the budgeting process could be described as the 'reality check'. The cash flow statement introduced in Chapter 2, Section 8 is a good starting point. It provides a snapshot of the income of a household during a particular week or month. I will use a month as the time period here, but the process is the same whatever time period is chosen. In addition, I will add the expenditure side of the cash flow statement to see whether expenditure is less, more than, or equal to income.

A system of carefully filing and keeping all bank and credit card statements helps to collect the information on how money is being spent by recording debit card transactions, direct debits, standing orders, and goods and services bought on credit. However, to obtain a full picture of how money is used, the spending diary that records all cash transactions, as described in the Introduction, is needed too.

Once all such information about expenditure has been collected, it needs to be classified under different headings of expenditure. The level of detail to include and how broad the headings are under which expenditure is classified are personal choices. Nevertheless, it is important to have some different headings if the budget is to be useful when thinking about change. Individual circumstances will influence this decision, as well as the amount of detailed information available to record transactions. For instance, if you go out frequently, you may want to have a more detailed set of headings for specific areas of 'going out' – such as meals out, cinema, the pub, lunch, going to football, etc. Amounts under the different headings can then be recorded on the cash flow statement, alongside the income section described in Chapter 2, Section 8.

Figure 3.6 shows the various parts of budgeting on one sheet. For convenience, it groups all three parts as three columns together: the first shows the cash flow statement for a particular month; the second average monthly expenditure; and the third the budget. We will start by considering Jenny's cash flow statement for June 2006 – the first column. We will examine the other columns later in this section. (The purpose here is to explain the process of how to set a budget, so the details in the columns are kept simple in that the numbers appear to be very neat.)

	Cash flow £ per month	Average month £ per month	Budget £ per month
NET INCOME			
Earnings	1115	1115	1115
TOTAL NET INCOME	1115	1115	1115
Rent	250	250	250
Council Tax	50	50	50
Regular bills (gas, electricity, water, etc.)	30	60	50
Telephone (mobile and landline)	40	40	30
Home insurance (contents and building)	12	12	10
Household goods	15	30	30
Food and non-alcoholic drinks	150	150	120
Alcohol	40	40	40
Tobacco	30	30	0
Clothing and footwear	50	50	40
Medicines, toiletries, hairdressing (personal)	30	30	30
Going out	120	120	80
Holidays/other leisure	20	100	50
Motoring costs (insurance, petrol)	70	130	130
Birthday presents/charity/other gifts			
Christmas presents/gifts	10	45	30
Credit card payments	100	100	150
TOTAL EXPENDITURE	1017	1237	1090
SURPLUS/DEFICIT	98	−122	25

Figure 3.6 *Jenny's budget in June 2006*

The income side of the cash flow statement for Jenny is straightforward as her only income is from her salary. If she had other earnings or we were considering a household with more than one person, then there would be different sources of net income which should all be recorded, as discussed in Chapter 2. Jenny's cash flow statement doesn't seem quite as bad as we might have anticipated from Figure 3.5, which showed expenditure being consistently higher than income for several years. In fact, in June 2006 she has a surplus of £98. We know this because her net income was £1115 and her expenditure was £1017, and so she has a surplus of £98.

Activity 3.3

Can you think why Jenny's cash flow statement might not give an accurate picture of how she spends her money over a whole year?

Comment

The information in the cash flow statement shows only one particular month. June 2006 may not be a typical month. To illustrate, there will be some commitments that only come up every so often such as road tax, quarterly bills, TV licence, and other occasional spending such as going on holiday, buying a new piece of furniture, or buying Christmas presents. This is why people can sometimes underestimate their spending – for budgeting, an 'average' or 'typical' month is needed. ■ ■ ■

A budget has to include *all* expenditure – it's very important that irregular expenditure or occasional items are included. This is normally achieved by recording the amount of any such payment, and the frequency at which it occurs, and recalculating it as an equivalent monthly figure. For example, if electricity charges are £180 for a year, this is recalculated as a monthly figure of £15 (that is £180 per year, divided by 12 months). If Jenny spends £600 on a holiday once a year, then this would equal £50 per month. Similarly, if in the month of recording the cash flow statement, a once-a-year expenditure was undertaken, this would need to be annualised, which would reduce the monthly expenditure figure by spreading that sum across all twelve months. Starting with a cash flow statement and averaging out the more infrequent expenditure should produce a reasonably accurate picture of current income and expenditure per month.

Jenny's average monthly expenditure and net income are shown in the second column in Figure 3.6. This provides a more accurate picture of her finances by looking at monthly, rather than at one specific month's, income and expenditure. With these estimates of monthly spending and income recorded, the 'reality check' is complete, and an assessment can be made about the expenditure and income situation.

Having made the adjustments to gain a more accurate monthly picture, you can see that Jenny's expenditure actually exceeds her income by £122 per month. This is very different from her initial cash flow estimate of a £98 surplus! This completes the essential background

"FROM LIVING BEYOND OUR MEANS, WE'VE GONE TO LIVING BEYOND OUR WILDEST EXPECTATIONS!"

Source: www.CartoonStock.com; ©Elmer Parolini

information needed before going on to the next stage of setting a budget – the plan for the future time period.

It's useful to think about goals before the next stage of setting a budget. As Section 5 of Chapter 1 noted, people's goals vary enormously and have a variety of different time horizons. Yet most short-term goals (such as saving for a holiday in six months' time), medium-term goals (such as saving for a deposit on a flat in eight years' time) or long-term goals (such as saving for retirement) involve making sure that there is sufficient income left over *after* spending on goods and services.

Stage 2: Decide on a financial plan given goals and constraints

Deciding on the financial plan in this context means setting a budget. Both income and expenditure need to be considered to decide on a budget. First, what does the *total* amount of spending need to be in relation to income each month, now and in the future, to work towards the desired goals? Second, should the *pattern* of expenditure be changed?

It's possible to be happy with the total amount of expenditure in relation to income, but to want to alter how that money is being spent, that is, the pattern of spending. To illustrate, if someone has goals of wanting both to do more for charity and to lead a healthier lifestyle, they may decide to give money to their favourite charity while buying less CDs, and to join a gym instead of smoking so many cigarettes. These don't require a change in the *total* amount of expenditure, just a change in the *pattern*. Making decisions on changing the pattern of expenditure involves trade-offs: giving more to charity requires a trade-off in terms of buying fewer CDs. Another way to put this is in terms of opportunity costs: the opportunity cost of giving that money to charity is the CDs that could have been bought. It doesn't sound much of a contest put like that, but a trade-off like this also applies to more hedonistic options such as going out clubbing versus paying to see your favourite football team. Remember that opportunity costs work both ways: the opportunity cost of smoking those cigarettes is not being able to join the gym (as well as the direct health risks), and the opportunity cost of buying the CDs is not being able to give that money to charity.

In Jenny's case, she has set herself the goal of reducing, or eventually eliminating, the gap between her income and her expenditure, and the goals of building up an emergency saving fund and paying off her credit card – all at the same time! There are different approaches she might take to achieve all of this:

1   Do nothing and hope things get better! Things may get better (such as an unexpected Lotto win), but things may also get worse, for instance, the arrival of an unexpected car repair bill. Unexpected bills are a common reason why people go into debt.

2   Increase income. Box 2.4 in Chapter 2 briefly discussed some of the ways to do this such as working overtime or taking a second job.

3   Reduce total spending and change the pattern of expenditure.

I am assuming that Jenny has rejected the first approach, and that the second is not realistic for her at the moment, and so I shall concentrate on the third – reducing total expenditure and changing her pattern of expenditure. Although reducing her total expenditure is all that is necessary to achieve Jenny's goal of lessening the gap between income and expenditure, in practice this will involve changing her pattern of expenditure too. This is because there are some forms of spending which are difficult to reduce, and so others will have to take a more than proportionate cut. Furthermore, it's very hard to carry out a plan to simply reduce total expenditure – where and in what way the cuts are to fall has to be decided.

The first step in deciding where to make such cuts involves thinking about what constitutes essential and non-essential expenditure. While spending on food and housing would be defined as essential, other items are less defined. The discussion in Section 3.1 of how people make social comparisons is relevant here. These comparisons can make the distinction between what is essential and non-essential more difficult.

Figure 3.2 showed that, in the mid to late 1990s, only a minority of UK households owned mobile phones and had access to the internet – yet most people now have access to these technologies. Are these essential items? Many people would argue that to participate fully in contemporary society they are. Although not essential for physical survival, not having these items can make someone feel socially excluded from society. If everyone else is communicating by mobile phone, for example, this creates pressure to own one.

New technological innovations can soon become 'must have' or essential items

Activity 3.4

Looking at the goods and services you spend money on, which would you consider as essential?

How did you decide on whether something was essential or not?

Comment

Although you will have your own answers to this question, your thinking will probably be affected by your income and social class. Bourdieu (1977) would have pointed out that the size of one's income or being in a particular social class may affect the distinction between what is seen as essential and non-essential. ■ ■ ■

Where particular goods or services are seen as essential, expenditure on them can't be cut out completely. In this instance, budgeting is more about reducing the costs of these and other items, for example, by buying fewer of them, or a cheaper version. Part of this process usually involves careful 'shopping around', searching and comparing prices. Some examples of advice on reducing expenditure found on consumer sites on the internet can be seen in Box 3.1. Many of these 'tips' have been shaped by some of the changes in the social and economic environment that you have examined in this and earlier chapters.

Box 3.1   Tips to help make ends meet or release more free income

There are many ways to save money. Here are a few of the more common ideas from personal finance experts:

- Paying some bills by direct debit may save money; for example, utility bills. (But check this carefully as some bills such as household and car insurance may cost more if paid monthly by direct debit.)
- Think about remortgaging. Saving 1 per cent on a £100,000 mortgage saves £83 a month (Chapter 6 looks at re-mortgaging in more detail).
- Shop around when it is time to renew insurance premiums. Premiums are often increased each year, relying on you not bothering to switch to another company. Also check that you are not paying for any 'extras' you didn't ask for or want (Chapter 9 looks at insurance in detail).
- If you are paying high interest on your credit cards, look for 0 per cent deals on balance transfers but check for transfer fees.
- Switch suppliers of gas, electricity, telephone or internet connection. Consider a water meter. There are major savings to be had in these areas.
- Reconsider being a member of a gym, and pay as you go instead – this can save money depending on how often you go.
- Think about whether a branded item is really value for money.
- Cut down on the number of takeaway meals you have – cutting from two to one a week would typically save over £250 a year!
- Call your mobile phone supplier and ask them if there is a better tariff to suit your needs.

- Buying in bulk for items such as contact lenses saves a lot of money.
- Taking packed lunches to work can save lunch costs.
- Buy fresh fruit and vegetables in season. Check whether a local market is cheaper than the supermarket.
- Turn off lights; don't leave stand-by buttons on; turn down the thermostat, etc. to save large amounts on energy bills (and help the environment) each year.
- Make a shopping list and stick to it. Try to use money-off coupons from papers and magazines where possible.
- Think carefully about buying extended warranties – it may be better to simply put aside some money in case of a problem.
- If you shop online, look for price comparison websites to find the best deals.

Activity 3.5

Can you identify any social and economic changes that have influenced the list of tips in Box 3.1?

Comment

It could be argued that many of the tips in Box 3.1 have arisen as a result of some of the social and economic changes examined in Chapters 1 and 2. Some, such as being able to shop around for a cheaper energy or landline telephone company, reflect the liberalisation and increased competition discussed in Chapter 1, with more suppliers available in the marketplace. Others, such as thinking about the cost of gym membership or cutting down on takeaways, reflect the increased importance of leisure spending as real disposable income has increased. Technological change is also important with reference to mobile phones, buying online and comparing prices online. A consumer society and symbolic consumption are relevant when considering the motives behind buying certain branded items. The list of money saving tips in Box 3.1 is particularly interesting because it highlights how social and economic changes can both increase household expenditure through more choice and pressure to buy, yet at the same time can provide ways in which expenditure can be reduced. ■ ■ ■

One reason why people sometimes pay higher prices for certain goods and services is that they think that a higher price equates to higher quality. The price of a product is often used as a mental short cut to assess quality. Such short cuts are called **heuristics**, and they are used to help assess situations when there is limited information available. A link between price and quality may sometimes be accurate, but it may not always be the case; or at least the differences in price may not reflect differences in quality, especially when buying more expensive branded items. Consumers have other, accurate or inaccurate, mental short cuts which lead to certain beliefs about the characteristics of the goods and services that they buy. Marketing departments try to use these market beliefs to help persuade people to buy their products.

Heuristics
Rules of thumb used to guide one in the direction of probable solutions to a problem.

Activity 3.6

Below is a list of some common market heuristics. Think about what each heuristic is suggesting to you to do, and who wants you to believe it.

- Generic products are just brands sold under a different label at a lower price.
- When in doubt, a national brand is always a safe bet.
- Larger stores offer lower prices than smaller stores.
- Small shops give you better service than large stores.
- Stores that have just opened usually charge attractive prices.
- Higher prices indicate higher quality.
- Items tied to 'give aways' are not good value.
- Larger sized containers are cheaper per unit than smaller sizes.
- When buying heavily advertised goods, you are paying for the label not quality.
- If manufacturers invest a lot in advertising they must believe that their product will sell well.
- More recent products are likely to incorporate newer and better technology.
- Best to look for products that have been tested by the market for some time.

(adapted from Solomon et al., 2002, p. 255)

Comment

Some of these heuristics are suggesting that you should buy from large stores; some from small stores. Some are signifying that you should search out bargains; others that it's not worth doing so. Some suggest that buying named brands is a protection; others that they are a waste of money. In each case, there are some particular groups, producers or retailers, who would like you to believe in what is being said so that you spend your money on their products rather than on those of their competitors.   ■ ■ ■

In addition to avoiding the assumption that price is an automatic guide to quality, it is also a mistake to think that good budgeting necessarily means always looking for the lowest price. This may ignore quality, which has many aspects such as functionality, durability and design. A higher price may also be paid for ethical reasons, such as choosing a product that is environmentally friendly or organically grown, or for avoiding products produced using exceptionally low-wage labour in the developing world. These can all be seen as aspects of the quality of the good being purchased.

Having weighed up all of the options, and made the necessary adjustments, the final result is a budget showing planned expenditure and income for the following month(s). In Jenny's case, after making all of her adjustments to the pattern of her expenditure, her budget might look something like the third column in Figure 3.6. By listing the budget together with her starting position, it is easier to see the changes Jenny is planning to make. The new overall difference between income and expenditure is at the bottom of the budget.

Activity 3.7

Compare Jenny's budget (shown in the budget column) with her previous pattern of spending (shown in the average month column) in Figure 3.6. On what things is she spending more and on what less? Do you think this budget will help her to meet her goals?

Comment

The only item of expenditure that has increased is Jenny's payments on her credit card. If Jenny sticks to her budget, she can save £25 a month and increase her credit card repayments to £150 per month. If Jenny's budget was implemented as planned, her income and expenditure profile would look much healthier in financial terms. In Figure 3.7, for example, after 2006 Jenny's income increases and her expenditure falls, and from 2007 her income exceeds expenditure. She is no longer adding to her debt (even though it may take her some time to pay off her existing debt), and she now has some surplus income, shown by the shaded area from 2007. Jenny could use this surplus to pay off some more of her debt and/or use it for saving. Chapter 4 explores debt and Chapter 5 looks at savings and investments in detail.   ■ ■ ■

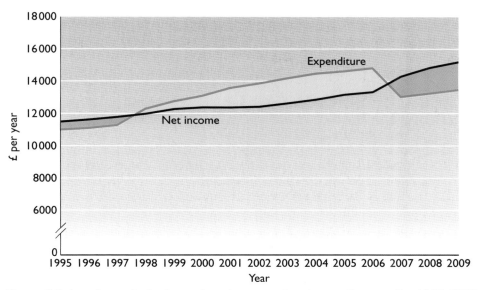

Figure 3.7 *Jenny's post-budgeting real net income and real expenditure profile, 1995–2009*

Stage 3: Act on the financial plan

The best of intentions and plans can be difficult to implement. One method suggested by personal finance experts to help implement a budget is an 'envelope system'. This system makes hypothetical envelopes for each type of expenditure and allocates the amount of money planned for that type of expenditure to its envelope. This doesn't (although it could) mean literally putting cash in envelopes, but thinking in this way helps to understand the system.

Once the different directions of spending and their 'envelopes' have been worked out, money is allocated to each of them and the 'envelopes' filled, by putting that money into different accounts. For example, the bank current account may be allocated an amount each month to pay for food and regular living expenses, such as travel costs, and commitments, such as gas bills. A savings account may be allocated money for infrequent expenditure, so that money is built up to pay for holidays, birthdays or Christmas, while another savings account may be used for saving in case of an unexpected crisis. A fixed amount of cash each week is also needed for those areas usually paid for in cash, such as entertainment. The idea of the envelope system is that you do *not* then switch money between these areas – when the envelopes run out, they run out. This creates a strong discipline to keep to the allocated budget amount.

As budgeting is an ongoing process, a review date is usually fixed. Initially, this review may be in just one month's time, since at the beginning there may be some trial and error in the budgeting process.

The envelope system is often suggested by personal finance experts

After a while it should settle down, and the review dates can be extended to, say, every six months.

Stage 4: Review the outcome of the plan

At the review date, a new cash flow statement needs to be calculated, including entering all the necessary information, to see whether the budget is working. To do this, another spending diary is necessary. The new cash flow statement allows the plans of the budget to be compared to what actually happened. It's probable that more amendments may be needed as it becomes clear how easy or difficult the budget was to implement. A new budget is also required if the goals for which the budget was designed change. A further reason for review would be if income changes and a new budget with more adjustments in expenditure is then required.

External influences, such as price rises and interest rate changes, are also likely to impact on budget plans. For example, a 5 per cent annual inflation rate applied to Jenny's expenditure would increase it from an annual figure of £13,080 (12 × £1090) to £13,734, an increase of £654. Jenny's income may have increased to accommodate this increase, but *incomes may not always change at the same rate as prices* so monitoring and reviewing these changes is important. It's easy to see how such external changes can greatly impact on financial plans, given that after her budgeting exercise Jenny was only planning to save £300 p.a. (£25 × 12 months; see Figure 3.6). This is one reason why financial experts suggest adding a little on to planned expenditure to allow for price increases. For instance, a look at previous gas and electricity bills can show how much energy prices have risen. This precautionary approach may help to avoid some unpleasant surprises!

5 Couples, budgeting and the management of money

Section 4 showed how budgeting can help a one-person household to manage its money. The process is the same when applied to a multi-person household. Table 1.1 in Chapter 1 showed most people do not live alone; they live in a multi-person household, perhaps as part of a couple, with or without children, or as a lone parent. This section examines some of the financial issues that arise when living with others. In particular, it considers how being part of a couple can have implications for budgeting, and looks at some of the budgetary implications of having children.

5.1 Economies of scale

There are ways in which living with others is cheaper than living on your own, and this should help the household budget. Many purchases are collectively consumed in households. To illustrate, the housing and heating costs of a couple living together are likely to be less than twice those of one person living on their own, and that also might be true (to a lesser extent) of their food expenditure. Such savings result from what are called **economies of scale**; that is, the savings in cost per unit that arise because of the overall scale being greater. For a large household, items (for instance, housing, heating and food) generally cost less per person than for a smaller household. Another example would be car ownership: if a couple share a car they each have to pay less overall than if they both owned a car because they save on the **fixed costs** of car purchase, road tax, depreciation, parking permits and so on.

Economies of scale arise for two reasons: one is to do with the way in which some goods and services are consumed; the other is to do with how goods are sold or marketed. First, some goods and services have what is known as a **public good** element. A 'pure' household public good is one that, even though one person consumes it, is still available for anyone else in the household to consume at the same time. Heating a room is much like that – even though it could be heated for one person, the rest of the household can still make use of its warmth. In practice, few things are pure public goods because there may be some disadvantages in sharing, but not enough to negate all the benefits. For instance, sharing a car can have logistical problems when both people need it for different purposes. Second, economies of scale can also apply when shopping. Many things are

Economies of scale
Decreases in the unit cost of production or consumption associated with increasing scale.

Fixed costs
Costs that remain the same regardless of how much is consumed or produced.

Public good
A good or service that can be consumed simultaneously by different people, and from which each person can benefit, and cannot be excluded.

cheaper per unit if bought in larger sizes. Pensioners and people living alone often complain that many of the things they need are expensive because they have to buy them in small amounts. Food is an example of a good where there are often economies of scale in purchasing. A quick look at a supermarket shelf soon shows this point.

Supermarket shelves quickly illustrate economies of scale!

Activity 3.8

Why are there economies of scale in housing? Are they due to the public good element of housing or to economies of scale in purchasing housing?

Comment

Housing is probably the most significant contributor to the economies of scale that larger households enjoy. There is a large public good element in this. It's not a 'pure' public good, as sharing a room wouldn't leave your use of it completely unchanged. This is more important for some rooms than others and may depend on relationships within the household. While unrelated adult sharers generally want their own bedroom, this is not usually the case for married or cohabiting couples, and children of the same sex are often expected to share. Therefore, the number of bedrooms needed may go up with the number of people in a household, but the number of kitchens usually doesn't. There may also be economies of scale in the purchasing involved in housing costs. A large house may not cost twice the amount of one half its size. ■ ■ ■

We can obtain some guidance about the size of these household economies of scale by looking at household equivalence scales. These are used to calculate the effects of living in households of different sizes. Box 3.2 explains one such scale, known as the 'McClements equivalence scale'. It is the one most frequently used by the UK Government, both in its official statistics and in calculating the relative levels of various benefits for different size households.

Box 3.2   Household equivalence scales

The income that a household needs to attain a given standard of living will depend on its size and composition. For example, a couple with dependent children will need a higher income than a couple with no children to attain the same material living standards. To adjust a household's income for size and composition, official income statistics use the McClements (1977) equivalence scale, in which an adult couple with no dependent children is taken as the benchmark with an equivalence scale of 1 (i.e. head 0.61 + partner/spouse 0.39). The equivalence scales for other types of household can be calculated by adding together the implied contributions of each household member from the table below.

McClements equivalence scale

Head	0.61
Partner/spouse	0.39
Other second adult	0.46
Third adult	0.42
Subsequent adults	0.36
Each child aged 0–1	0.09
Each child aged 2–4	0.18
Each child aged 5–7	0.21
Each child aged 8–10	0.23
Each child aged 11–12	0.25
Each child aged 13–15	0.27
Each child aged 16–18	0.36

For instance, in a household consisting of a couple with one child aged three, the head of the household would contribute 0.61, the spouse 0.39, and the child 0.18, giving a total equivalence scale of 1.18. In other words, this household would need an income 18 per cent higher than that of a childless couple to attain the same standard of living. To calculate an equivalised household income, a household's unequivalised income needs to be divided by its total equivalence scale. For example, if the above household had an income of £20,000, its equivalised income would be $\frac{£20,000}{1.18}$ = £16,949. So, other things being equal, children will reduce a household's standard of living.

(adapted from IFS, 2005)

You can use an equivalence scale to work out how far income is likely to go in a household of a particular size and composition. It shows how much extra income a large household would need to maintain the same standard of living as a couple, and how much less a one-person household would need to do so. It demonstrates that large households do need more income to achieve the same standard of living, but not proportionately to the number of people. One-person households need less, but more than half as much, income as a couple to attain the same standard of living.

Let's consider John and James, who work together in the same job and both earn £30,000 per year. John lives on his own, while James is married to Anna, who doesn't have any income. Because James and Anna are a married couple, their household equivalence scale is 1. This means that their equivalised income is £30,000 divided by 1, which is £30,000. John, living on his own, has a household equivalence scale of 0.61, which means that his equivalised income is $\frac{£30,000}{0.61}$ which is £49,180. In other words, John, on the same income as James, can live alone with a standard of living that James and Anna would need £49,180 to achieve. In this example, there is only one income for the couple. But if Anna were earning, her income would be added in too.

Activity 3.9

How much income would Anna need to earn if James and Anna were to live at the same standard of living as John (assuming that John spends all his income)?

Comment

Anna would need to earn £19,180 to make her and James' joint income up to £49,180, which we calculated above as the amount needed for a couple to live at the same standard as a one-person household on an income of £30,000. If Anna were to earn £30,000, like John and James, then you can see that James and Anna would enjoy a higher standard of living than John on his own, with their joint income being £60,000, because of the economies of scale that a couple enjoy. We'll revisit equivalence scales in Chapter 8. ■ ■ ■

In practice, as you saw in Chapter 2, most couples of working age have two incomes, and large households tend to have larger incomes than smaller households. None the less, the finances of multi-person households have to be managed carefully.

5.2 Budgeting and managing money

Couples that live together face the important financial decision of how to manage their money. The use of the words '*their* money' immediately raises an important question that can influence this decision. That is, *whose* money is it when you are thinking of the household finances? Is it jointly shared and perceived to be equally accessible to both partners? Or does each person have their own individual money and the couple comes to an agreement about how to pay bills and living expenses? The answer to this question depends in part on the system of money management that a couple adopts. Four examples of how household finances are organised can be seen in Box 3.3.

Box 3.3   Systems of managing household finances

The 'whole wage system' is where one partner is given overall day-to-day management of the household finances. In the female example, the woman manages money for the household with the man handing over his wages to her. In the male example, the male breadwinner retains control of his wages, and any money the woman earns is handed over to him. These patterns are more common in poorer households in which the man is the sole earner, or the female partner earns relatively little compared with the man.

A system of 'housekeeping allowance' is where the person who earns all or most of the income provides an allowance for spending for household purposes and keeps the remainder. This is more commonly found among middle-income households where earnings are relatively unequal.

> The 'pooling system' is where both partners share any income, usually in a joint account. This is the most common form of household financial arrangement in the UK. Both partners manage the finances.
>
> A system of 'independent management' is where the partners keep their incomes separate, and make arrangements about how to split the household expenditure. This relies on both partners having an income and is most frequently found when one or both partners have been in previous marriages or previous long-term relationships. Younger couples, before they have children, also tend to manage money more independently.

The choice a couple makes about how they manage money is influenced by a variety of factors. The attitude towards who the money belongs to is an important aspect, but there are other factors. These include who is deemed to have the most skill in managing money; previous experience of other relationships; attitudes towards gender roles; parent's money management systems; attitudes towards a relationship; and who earns more.

Activity 3.10

If you are part of a cohabiting couple, how do you organise your finances, and why do you manage them in the way you do? Does your system of management fit into any of the systems described in Box 3.3?

Comment

If you do not live in a couple, try to answer this question for a couple you know: perhaps your parents or some close friends. ■ ■ ■

Jan Pahl (2000) argues that there is a difference between the management of money and the control of it. While the management of money is a task that has to be carried out, and can be a burden, control over spending is a form of power and influence in the household. She found that, in many cases, women have less freedom over how money is spent in multi-person households; a woman is less likely to feel that the money she manages is hers to spend on herself than a man does. Burgoyne (2004) found that whatever system of money was adopted, and whoever managed it, the person who earned more of it seemed to retain more control.

The whole wage system is most commonly found in working-class and in low-income households. The daily management of money and budgeting in such situations is often the difficult task of trying to carefully balance income and expenditure. Having to search for bargains and make difficult decisions, between many demands on scarce income, can be a stressful experience. However, some women also find this responsibility beneficial because they can make sure bills are paid on time and gain a level of satisfaction from managing money in the household (DWP, 1999).

While the housekeeping allowance system may provide more freedom for the recipient of the allowance to make purchasing decisions, Burgoyne (2004) argues that the person with the main income decides how much allowance to give, thus retaining a degree of control over how it is spent. The envelope system, discussed in Section 4, is an extended form of housekeeping allowance. In this case, different envelopes may be managed by each partner – with all the responsibility that this entails.

The pooling income system may be thought of as being the fairest arrangement because it gives freedom to both partners to spend money. In such a system, the budget becomes more difficult for either partner to manage since each partner has access to all income. The envelope system helps to overcome this difficulty through allocating different bank or building society accounts for different purposes – perhaps having agreed individual accounts for personal spending. Interestingly though, both Pahl (2000) and Burgoyne (2004) found that even with this arrangement, women tend to feel less free in spending than their male partner: where the male income was higher, it was as if the source of the money exerted power over spending decisions. The source of money – that is, who has brought it into the household – has a psychological label of 'power' attached to it.

The independent management system, managing money completely independently, would seem to allow more control over how money is spent by each partner. There may, though, come a time when this situation changes. To illustrate, the decision to have children often results in one partner (usually the woman) reducing their income by reducing the hours they work in order to help care for the baby/babies. In this case, a system that seemed equitable when both partners were earning similar amounts can result subsequently in great inequalities in control over spending.

The ability to manage and budget money successfully in a way that both partners feel is equitable is not easy. Disagreements over money are a common reason for arguments between partners. Nevertheless, planning a budget and agreeing a system of money management can help to avoid tensions between partners.

The changes in the labour market described in Section 4 of Chapter 2, which have led to women having more economic power, are also likely to lead to them having more financial power within households in the future. Yet when children are present in a household, additional financial pressures arise, and inequalities can result. Having children usually has implications for both the income and the expenditure side of the budget, and this requires careful money management and budgeting.

6　Children and budgeting

Even before we are born, money is spent on our behalf as parents and relatives buy cribs, buggies, toys and what seems like an endless list of items that babies are seen to need. The arrival of a baby into a household will inevitably alter the pattern, and often the total amount, of its expenditure.

Let's return to Sarah and Peter, who you met in Chapter 2, Section 6. Figure 2.6 shows Sarah's and Peter's income changing over time. I now want to add an expenditure line to demonstrate how having children may influence a household budget. First, we will look at their joint household before having children. Figure 3.8 shows their combined income and spending for the period 2004–07.

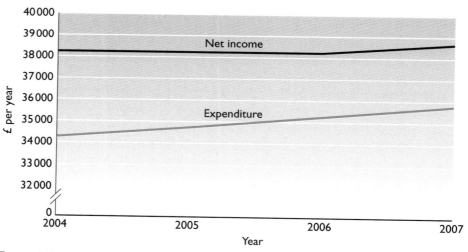

Figure 3.8 *Sarah's and Peter's real net income and real expenditure profile, 2004–07*

In Sarah's and Peter's case, they seem to have their finances in reasonable shape – having two incomes and benefiting from the financial advantages of economies of scale, their income exceeds expenditure across all the years (the income line is higher than the expenditure line), and they are accumulating savings. Although they had a surplus income over expenditure, budgeting was still a useful part of their financial planning process – to plan their pattern of expenditure and think about whether such a surplus was sufficient to meet their various future goals.

We saw in Chapter 2 that Sarah and Peter had their first child in 2008. The result of this was that Sarah gave up work (although either partner could have done so). These events impact on the future projections of both the income and expenditure lines in Figure 3.8. In the short term, at least, income is liable to fall due to maternity and paternity leave and, as Sarah gave up work for a while, there will be a longer-term impact on income. Such changes need to be budgeted for. As can be seen in Figure 3.9, the impact of Sarah giving up work would have the effect of causing the income line to fall after 2008.

Sarah's and Peter's expenditure will also be affected by starting a family. There are three possible scenarios. In the first scenario, if Sarah and Peter don't adjust their expenditure on themselves downwards, but simply add new expenditure on the baby, then the expenditure line will tilt upwards, closing the gap with or even rising above their income line and changing their surplus income into a deficit. This is indicated by the 'Expenditure 1' line in Figure 3.9. The second scenario is that Sarah and Peter may instead budget so that their pattern of expenditure reduces spending on themselves by roughly the same amount as the increased spending on the baby, so that total expenditure remains similar to the situation before the baby was born, as shown by the 'Expenditure 2' line

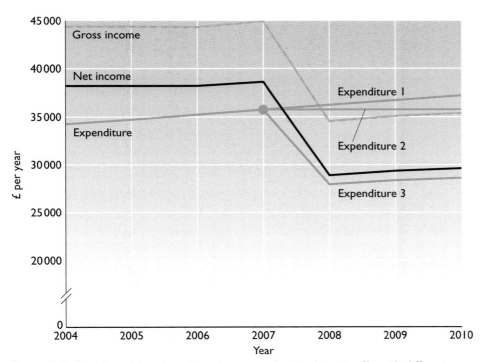

Figure 3.9 *Sarah's and Peter's real net income and expenditure profile with different scenarios, 2004–10*

in Figure 3.9. However, with the reduction in income, this would still lead to expenditure exceeding income. The third scenario shows how, perhaps through very careful budgeting, Sarah and Peter make large cuts in spending on themselves and still manage to keep expenditure just below income, as shown by the 'Expenditure 3' line in Figure 3.9.

Budgeting in situations such as starting a family very much works on the premise of the three purposes of setting a budget described at the start of Section 4: controlling spending; making sure there is enough income available for bills; and planning for the future. One way of estimating how having children impacts on the standard of living of parents is to use the equivalence scale shown in Box 3.2.

Activity 3.11

From the equivalence scale in Box 3.2, work out by what percentage a couple would need to increase their income to maintain their pre-children standard of living if they have:

1   one baby aged 1 year
2   two children aged 1 and 3 years old
3   three children aged 7, 13 and 16 years old.

(NB: Assume that the couple had no spare income to draw on before they had children.)

Comment

1   With just the one baby, the couple's income would have to increase by 9 per cent (the equivalence scale addition for a baby being 0.09).

2   With two children aged 1 and 3 their income would need to increase by 27 per cent (that is 0.09 + 0.18 = 0.27).

3   With three children aged 7, 13 and 16, it would have to increase by 84 per cent! (0.21 + 0.27 + 0.36 = 0.84).

We can see that having children has a major impact on household finances, and emphasises the need to budget carefully in order to plan for changes in expenditure and income. ■ ■ ■

If a parent or parents can increase their income, they may be able to maintain their standard of living at the same level. Yet in practice, as we have seen, having children is more likely to reduce a couple's income. For example, Sarah gave up work, so household income fell. This placed even more pressure on their budget, and more adjustments were needed. Conversely, if Sarah had stayed at work, it's likely that the costs of providing for their child would have been higher. Either way, having children will usually require adjustments to a household's budget in the light of the costs that children place on a household. Children not only need feeding and clothing and other goods and services, they also need looking after, and providing for care is an expensive aspect of having a child (which equivalence scales do not include, as we shall see in Chapter 8). Fortunately, parents in the UK do get some extra income from the government to help with these costs, as discussed in Chapter 2, and to be returned to in Chapter 8. The above discussion on standards of living when having children is based on the *financial* impact of having children. However, many couples would argue that their quality of life has been improved by having children, and that sacrificing expenditure on themselves is more than compensated for.

It is clear, whatever the benefits of having children, that financial planning is beneficial both for the parent(s) and for their children's future. The budgeting process is a useful part of this planning process, and it can help when thinking through how to change both total expenditure and the pattern of expenditure, although there are many pressures to spend more on children.

Expenditure on and by children is shaped by some of the social and economic changes we've seen in Chapters 1 and 2 of *Personal Finance*. One such change is the growth in the number of working mothers in paid employment which has led to increased expenditure on children, both on their care and through parents ensuring that children share in the benefits of having a mother in employment. In 2004, the average age for a mother to have her first child was twenty-seven, and nearly thirty for married women (*Birth Statistics*, 2005, Table 1.7). Twenty years earlier, the average age was twenty-five (*Birth Statistics*, 1999, Table 1.6). With the age at which mothers have their first child rising, the money available to spend on children has also increased – women have earned more before they have children, and as we saw in Chapter 2, many are now able to continue their careers after they have children. Increased separation and divorce is also argued to contribute to spending on children.

Symbolic consumption is also relevant in relation to children: both when parents use the things they buy their children to create their own parental identities and status through their children, and when children themselves use consumption as a way to develop their identities. Belk (1988) sees symbolic consumption as helping children through stages of uncertainty in their lives, such as adolescence, by enabling them to gain prestige or peer approval. This can be seen, for example, in relation to having the 'right' trainers or wearing certain clothes. This can create pressure on children and their parents to buy more expensive, branded items.

Trainers are a classic example of more expensive branded goods that children desire to own, compared with unbranded cheaper alternatives

The role played by advertising adds additional pressure on young children and in turn on parents who often supply the income needed to purchase such items:

> Children's vulnerabilities are played on as advertisers sell images of perfection and increase the pressure to have the latest 'in vogue' fashion and gadgets. Research shows that nearly three-quarters of seven-year-old girls want to be slimmer and the pressure to 'look good' is a constant. As one girl told us, 'I liked these adverts because [they] said your hair could look like Beyoncé's.
>
> (NCC, 2005)

The status that comes with owning fashionable brands can also bring discontentment, particularly among 'brand-aware' children from low-income families who do not have the economic means to meet this demand (NCC, 2005).

7 Conclusion

I have covered a lot of material about expenditure and budgeting in this chapter. In Section 1, I started by looking at how spending has risen in recent years, and how the pattern of that expenditure has changed, in particular with a shift towards leisure expenditure. I then went on to discuss, in Sections 2 and 3, how expenditure is influenced by a wide range of economic and social factors, including symbolic consumption, and marketing and advertising. These are all important components of the changing social and economic context, one of the themes of *Personal Finance*.

The discussion of such economic and social influences was particularly important because it helps to underpin thinking about budgeting by encouraging a greater reflection on what influences expenditure. Section 4 showed how budgeting is a crucial component of financial planning (another *Personal Finance* theme), because budgeting helps to plan and adjust income and expenditure in order to work towards desired goals. This reminds us that budgeting is an ongoing process, and it is important to revisit that process as the life-course unfolds.

The chapter has also helped to develop the other theme of this book: that involving the interrelationship between individuals and households. Most households are made up of more than one person. As we saw in Sections 5 and 6, when people live together there may be financial advantages through economies of scale, but these may not be equally shared, and couples need to think about how best to manage their money. Having children is likely to change the pattern of expenditure and the total expenditure of a household, as well as affecting income.

The budgeting process will lead to different outcomes in terms of the balance between income and expenditure. There will be many, like Jenny after her budgeting process, for whom a surplus will enable savings and investments to be undertaken, and these issues are looked at in detail in Chapter 5. Yet households and individuals also borrow money – because income is exceeded by expenditure or for other reasons – and Chapter 4 explores this aspect of personal finance further.

References

Abercrombie, N., Warde, A. and Deem, R. (2000) *Contemporary British Society*, Malden, MA, Polity Press.

Bauman, Z. (1999) *Work, Consumerism and the New Poor*, Buckingham, Open University Press.

Belk, R.W. (1988) 'Possessions and the extended self', *Journal of Consumer Research*, vol. 15, pp. 139–68.

Birth Statistics (1999) Series FM1, no. 27, London, The Stationery Office (TSO); also available online at the ONS website, http://www.statistics. gov.uk/downloads/theme_population/FM1_27_1998/FM1_27.pdf (Accessed 1 February 2006).

Birth Statistics (2005) Series FM1, no. 33, London, Office for National Statistics (ONS); also available online at the ONS website, http://www. statistics.gov.uk/downloads/theme_population/FM1_33/FM1_33.pdf (Accessed 1 February 2006).

Bourdieu, P. (1977) *Outline of Theory and Practice*, Cambridge, Cambridge University Press.

Burgoyne, C. (2004) 'Hearts and purse strings: money in heterosexual marriage', *Feminism and Psychology*, vol. 14, no. 1, pp. 165–72.

Department for Work and Pensions (DWP) (1999) 'Relying on the state, relying on each other', Research Report No. 103, Leeds, Corporate Document Services.

Economic Trends (2005) no.620, Basingstoke and New York, Palgrave Macmillan for The Office for National Statistics (ONS); also available online at the ONS website, http://www.statistics.gov.uk/downloads/theme_economy/ET620.pdf (Accessed 31 January 2006).

Family Spending: A Report on the 2003–04 Expenditure and Food Survey (2005) Basingstoke and New York, Palgrave Macmillan for The Office for National Statistics (ONS); also available online at the ONS website, http://www.statistics.gov.uk/downloads/theme_social/Family_Spending_2003-04/FamilySpending2003-04.pdf (Accessed 25 November 2005).

Institute of Fiscal Studies (IFS) (2005) 'Interactive models: where do you fit in?' [online], http://www.ifs.org.uk/wheredoyoufitin/about.php (Accessed 25 November 2005).

Klein, N. (2000) *No Logo: No Space, No Choice, No Jobs, Taking Aim at the Brand Bullies*, London, Flamingo.

McClements, L. (1977) 'Equivalence scales for children', *Journal of Public Economics*, vol. 8, pp. 191–210.

National Consumer Council (NCC) (2005) *The Shopping Generation*, London, National Consumer Council; also available online at http://www.ncc.org.uk/protectingconsumers/shopping_generation.pdf (Accessed 25 November 2005).

Pahl, J. (2000) 'Couples and their money: patterns of accounting and accountability in the domestic economy', *Accounting, Auditing, and Accountability Journal*, vol. 13, no. 4, pp. 502–17.

Social Trends (2004) no. 34, London, The Stationery Office (TSO) for The Office for National Statistics (ONS); also available online at the ONS website, http://www.statistics.gov.uk/downloads/theme_social/Social_Trends34/Social_Trends34.pdf (Accessed 14 November 2005).

Solomon, M.R., Barmossy, G. and Askegaard, S. (2002) *Consumer Behaviour: A European Perspective* (2nd edn), Harlow and New York, Financial Times/Prentice-Hall.

Veblen, T. (1925) *The Theory of the Leisure Class: An Economic Study of Institutions*, London, Allen and Unwin.

Weber, M. (1948 [1924]) 'Class, status and party', in Gerth, H. and Mills, C.W. (trans.) *Essays from Max Weber*, London, Routledge & Kegan Paul.

Debt

Martin Upton

Chapter 4

Contents

1 Introduction

Britons going bust: total soars by 46% in a year

- Experts blame easy credit and 'want now' consumers
- Government accused of allowing £1 trillion debts

(*The Guardian*, 5 November 2005)

Record number go bankrupt as debt rises

(*Times Online*, 4 February 2005)

Home repossession orders soar by 66 per cent as debt mounts

(*Daily Telegraph*, 27 October 2005)

High earners struggle with debt

(*The Guardian*, 19 May 2005)

Increasingly, debt has become a part of everyday life in the UK and, as a result, discussion about levels of personal debt made headline news throughout the mid 2000s. As you saw in Chapter 1, the amount of personal debt carried by UK citizens in 2005 topped the seemingly staggering figure of £1.1 trillion (Bank of England, 2005). Everyone who has a mortgage, a personal loan, or owes money on a credit card contributes a part of this total sum. Debt is regularly featured in the news media, with stories about how much some people are borrowing, how some extraordinarily high rates of interest are being charged, or with questions about whether debt is becoming an intolerable burden for some households. This chapter is going to explore some of these issues in detail. Section 2 looks at evidence on the level of debt in the UK, before going on to examine some of the changing social and economic context. Section 3 explores the costs of having debt, and Section 4 considers the relationship between debt and household finances. Finally, Section 5 investigates the borrowing process, and suggests that gathering information and making informed decisions about taking on debt is an important part of financial capability.

2 Exploration of debt

2.1 Debt: concepts and evidence

Let's start by examining exactly what is meant by the idea of 'debt'. You'll recall that in Chapter 2, Section 2 we came across assets: things that people *own* at a point in time. By contrast, a debt is a **liability**. Liabilities are effectively the opposite of assets: they are amounts, or stocks, of money that people *owe* at a particular point in time. Typically, this would include **mortgages**; personal loans; outstanding amounts on hire-purchase agreements; credit card debts; and bank **overdrafts**. If, at the point of time that you read this chapter, you owe money in any of these ways, then you have a liability for that amount. Liabilities can also include money owed on items such as utility bills and Council Tax bills (a situation often referred to as being 'in arrears'), although these are not included in the Bank of England's calculation of the £1.1 trillion of personal debt.

As you progress through *Personal Finance*, you'll see that having an understanding of both assets and liabilities is an essential part of financial capability. At the end of Chapter 6, when you will have examined the main different types of assets and liabilities, you can begin to pull them together in an important personal finance tool called a **financial balance sheet**. This tool is a way of looking at both the assets and liabilities held at a particular point in time. By comparing assets owned with liabilities owed, you will be able to look at concepts such as **net worth** (also referred to as **net wealth**), or the value of all assets *minus* the value of all liabilities.

In this chapter, we'll be concentrating on looking at debt in more detail. Let's start by briefly considering the terms which are often used to talk about debt: 'borrowing', 'debt' and 'credit'. The term 'borrowing' is frequently used to describe the process by which debt is taken out, and is also the amount that is taken out in any one time period, such as 'I borrowed £10,000 this year'. 'Debt' is, strictly speaking, the total amount of money owed at a particular point in time – if you borrowed £10,000 this year and £10,000 last year, then you could say that you now have £20,000 of debt (although in reality the figure would have changed due to interest and repayments). Confusingly, 'borrowing', in popular usage, can also be used to express the total amount outstanding, as in 'I have

Liability
An amount of money owed at a particular point in time.

Mortgage
A loan secured on property or land.

Overdraft
A facility provided by banks and some building societies which allows customers to go into debt on their current account.

Financial balance sheet
A financial tool that records household or individual assets and liabilities at a particular point in time.

Net worth/net wealth
The value of all assets minus all liabilities.

£20,000 of *outstanding borrowing*. Sometimes, the distinction is that 'debt' is used to imply a less voluntary situation, whereas the term 'borrowing' is often used when the debt has been undertaken voluntarily, such as when taking out a mortgage. What is crucial here is that the amount – whether one refers to it as 'outstanding borrowing' or simply 'debt' – is still a liability in terms of the personal financial balance sheet. We'll be developing that further in Chapter 6. To keep things simple, we will primarily use the term 'debt' in this chapter, with 'borrowing' describing the process by which debt is taken out.

The third term that you'll see or hear in the media is **credit**, defined as an arrangement to receive cash, goods or services now and to pay for them in the future. It has been argued that there is a rather subtle distinction between debt and credit, which has been described as follows: 'Debt is the involuntary inability to make payments which the payee expects to be paid immediately, as opposed to credit use, which can be characterised as agreed postponement of payment' (Furnham and Argyle, 1998, p. 113). So debt can have the sense of being more involuntary than credit – and debt is traditionally associated with debt problems, which we shall be looking at later in this chapter. It is perhaps not surprising that the part of the UK financial services industry concerned with lending money is known as the 'credit industry' rather than the 'debt industry'. However, the crucial point – just as with the distinction between debt and borrowing – is that an amount owed at a particular point in time, no matter how it has arisen, is a liability.

Chapter 1 began to explore the UK's £1.1 trillion of personal debt in 2005. We saw that over four-fifths of this debt was accounted for by mortgages. Debts such as these are known as **secured debt**, meaning that the amount owed is secured against an asset – in this case a house – which can be sold by the lender if repayments are not made. Other types of debt are known as **unsecured debt**, and in 2005 these represented some £186 billion, or 17 per cent of the total (Bank of England, 2005). Unsecured debt includes money owed on credit cards; motor and retail finance; overdrafts; mail order catalogues; and other types of personal loan. Liabilities are also frequently categorised by whether they are short-term (often less than a year) or long-term (more than a year).

Levels of debt have been changing over time. Both secured and unsecured debt grew substantially from 1999 to 2004. This can be seen in Figure 4.1. Between these dates, total household debt moved from being 1.1 times bigger than total after-tax household income to being 1.4 times bigger (DTI, 2005; Del-Rio and Young, 2005). This means that over a period of time when household income was growing (as we saw in Chapter 2, Section 3), levels of debt were growing even more rapidly. One important factor, especially with regards to mortgage debt, has been the relatively low rates of interest in the UK since the middle of the

Credit
An arrangement to receive cash, goods or services now and to pay for them in the future.

Secured debt
Debt secured against an asset such as a home. If the debtor fails to make adequate repayments, the lender has a right to obtain money by selling the asset.

Unsecured debt
Debt not backed by any asset.

Bank of XYZ
July 2006 statement

Summary of account

Account Holder
Mr Howie Twiner: 4810 4866 0000

Date
20th Jul 2006

Payment due date
20th Aug 2006*

Current limit
£3000.00

Credit available
£2585.00

Your new balance
£415.00

Minimum payment
£20.75

Reference	Sent	Purchases since last Statement	Amount
000000DS00	22/6	Payment Thank you	−1285.00
22222XX222	3/6	The Noodle Bar	35.00
5555DD5555	10/6	Acme Fashion	85.00
3331AA3331	14/6	Clifftop Chalets	295.00

Previous balance	1285.00	Current amount due	£415.00
Transactions	415.00		
Cash advances	00.00		
Payments	1285.00	**Minimum payment**	£20.75
New Balance	415.00		

Finance summary	Purchases	Please call ▓▓▓▓ ▓▓▓ ▓▓▓▓ immediately if you're unable to meet with the above terms. Our opening hours are between 8am and 4pm, Monday to Friday and between 9am and 1.00pm on Saturdays
Purchase Annual Rate	27.9%	
Cash Annual Rate	27.9%	

20th Aug 2006* Allow 7 days for payments through the post, or 4 working days for bank payments

Have you written your account number and Post Code on the reverse of your cheque?

Credit card balances are a form of unsecured debt

1990s. Interest rates are explained in more detail in Section 3. Another factor is the level of 'economic confidence': when people feel more optimistic about the future, they are more likely to consider taking out a debt than if they are worried about the economy and problems such as potential unemployment.

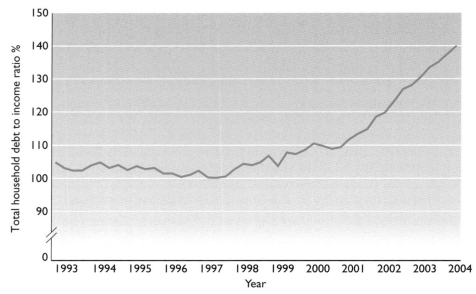

Figure 4.1 *Total household debt to income ratio, 1999–2004 (secured and unsecured debt)*
Source: DTI, 2005, p. 5, Figure 1

One trend in the early part of the twenty-first century is for people to increase the level of secured debt by increasing their mortgage debt. This phenomenon has come about particularly in response to rising UK house prices. These rising prices have tended to increase the **equity** which people have in their homes. People have therefore sought access to this additional equity and used these funds to increase spending in other areas (Del-Rio and Young, 2005). This process is known as **equity withdrawal**. Housing and mortgages (a major form of asset with its corresponding liability) are such important topics in their own right that most of Chapter 6 is devoted to them. Equity withdrawal will also reappear in Chapter 7.

Within the rising level of overall debt, the proportion which is unsecured almost doubled from 1994 to 2004, to stand at 20 per cent (Del-Rio and Young, 2005). To put into perspective what this means at an individual level, you might recall from Chapter 1, Section 2.1 that in 2005 the average level of *unsecured* debt for each adult in the UK was £4071. There has also been a gradual shift in the uses to which such unsecured debts are put, with more people taking on debt to finance expenditure on things like holidays, clothing or special occasions (Del-Rio and Young, 2005). All these changes have helped to shape the consumer society you saw earlier in *Personal Finance*.

At first glance, some of these figures might suggest that UK debt levels are too high. Yet thinking through whether debt levels are a

Equity
Equity in a property is the excess of the market value of the property over the outstanding mortgage debt secured against it.

Equity withdrawal
The process whereby mortgage levels are increased to release funds for additional spending.

problem requires consideration of a number of more complex issues. The first of these issues is the level of debt taking into account all assets and liabilities. A Bank of England report indicated that at the end of 2004 the net worth of *all* households in the UK (that is, the value of total assets minus total secured and unsecured debt) was about £5 trillion, which was substantially up from just over £2 trillion ten years earlier; the majority of this was made up of wealth held in the form of housing, which by 2004 stood at £3.2 trillion (Tudela and Young, 2005). The remainder consisted of other financial assets, such as money held in savings accounts and shareholdings. Therefore, at the level of the UK as a whole, the value of total household assets is substantially *greater* than the total amount of household liabilities, a fact which might be interpreted as meaning increasing levels of debt are affordable (Tudela and Young, 2005).

This might help to explain the findings of a government publication which showed that the proportion of people who saw debt as a 'heavy burden' stayed constant at around 10 per cent between 1995 and 2004 despite rising debt levels (DTI, 2004). Whether debt is a heavy burden on UK household finances is a second important issue in considering whether debt levels are too high. Other studies have concluded that the proportion of people's income spent on loan repayments was broadly constant between 2000 and 2004 (Oxera, 2004), and that UK household debt as a percentage of household income was broadly the same as in the USA, Japan and Australia, only a little higher than in Germany, and lower than in the Netherlands and Denmark (Debelle, 2004).

The third issue in considering whether debt levels are too high is how debt is distributed amongst different individuals and households, and whether debt is causing problems for particular households. And it is certainly the case that while liabilities are more than matched by assets across the UK *as a whole*, debt is a major problem for some individuals and households. There are different ways of defining when individuals and households are facing debt problems, and there is no universally agreed definition. 'Over-indebtedness', 'problem debt' and 'financial difficulty' can all be used as interchangeable terms for the same debt problems (DTI, 2005). 'Over-indebtedness' is a term used to describe debt that has become a heavy burden for the borrower, and Citizens Advice defines 'problem debt' as 'when an individual is unable to pay their current credit card repayments and other commitments without reducing other expenditure below normal minimum levels' (Citizens Advice, 2003, p. 48). The definition of debt problems as having debt considered by the individual to be a heavy burden is especially interesting because it suggests that two individuals with the same financial circumstances might have different views as to whether their debt is a heavy burden or not. So a statistical measure often used in personal finance to measure 'financial difficulty' is whether debt repayments (excluding secured loans like mortgages) are 20 per cent or more of net income – a higher payment figure might signify problems.

Using these definitions, it is clear that a minority of the UK population is 'experiencing difficulty due to problem debt: 4% of the population above the age of 18 are in arrears for more than 3 months on either consumer credit or utility bills, and 5% of borrowers consider their repayments to be a "heavy burden"' (DTI, 2005, p. 1). The prevalence of problem debt varies by type of household. For example, those on low incomes, those with children, and those in their twenties and thirties are more likely to have debt problems (DTI, 2005). Table 4.1 demonstrates how level of income affects the percentage of households with children being in arrears on consumer credit or household bills. Table 4.1 shows that households earning less than £15,000 are around three times as likely to have arrears as those earning more than £35,000 (DTI, 2004).

Table 4.1 Arrears on consumer credit and household bills by level of income (% of families with children in the UK, 2002)

Gross household income	In arrears now (%)	Consumer credit (%)	Household bills (%)
Under £7499	26	14	20
£7500–£14 999	34	14	26
£15 000–£24 999	21	11	14
£25 000–£34 999	18	15	8
Over £35 000	11	5	6

Source: DTI, 2004, p. 15

Debt problems also relate to family type. Families with children are more likely to be in arrears than households without children and, of such families, lone parents are much more likely to be in arrears and to have two or more debt commitments (DTI, 2004). In addition, home ownership plays a role and, in a study of debt among low-income families in the UK, Bridges and Disney (2004) found that tenants are much more likely to be in debt than homeowners.

Moreover, there is a link between low-income households and financial exclusion, including having less access to mainstream banking and loan facilities. This, in turn, means that some low-income households turn to alternative sources of credit. Bridges and Disney (2004) also found that the use of credit for catalogue and mail-order purchases was very common among low-income families.

Although only a minority of UK households have debt problems, the number would appear to be growing. Evidence from Citizens Advice shows that new debt enquiries in the UK increased from 862,019 in 1997/98 to 1,066,509 in 2001/02. Another change noted by Citizens Advice is an association between debt problems and the number of credit cards held (Citizens Advice, 2003). By the end of 2004, there were more credit and charge cards than people in the UK: 74.3 million credit and charge cards compared with around 59 million people (Credit Action, 2005).

Activity 4.1

What kind of pressures do you think substantial debt might place upon individuals and households?

Comment

In a paper called 'Debt and distress: evaluating the psychological costs of credit', academics from Leicester University in the UK found an association between debt and psychological well-being. Their main finding was that unsecured debt, measured by outstanding (non-mortgage) credit, had a greater negative influence on psychological well-being than secured (mortgage) debt (Brown et al., 2005). Citizens Advice found that a quarter of its debt clients were seeking treatment for stress, depression and anxiety. Of those receiving medical treatment for depression, just under half felt that their symptoms were caused by their debt problems (Citizens Advice, 2003). ■■■

Despite the fact that data on debt across the whole of the UK show that household assets are much greater than liabilities, a significant minority of households has debt problems. These households are concentrated in low-income groups, especially lone-parent families, many of whom face great financial difficulties (Brown et al., 2005; Citizens Advice, 2003; Kempson et al., 2004). Nevertheless, even those who own their own home but still have a substantial mortgage may have some cause to be concerned about debt. Any significant rise in mortgage interest rates and/or a crash in the housing market may cause severe financial hardship. As you saw from our examination of the interdependence of the different sectors of the economy in Chapter 1, the repercussions of a large number of households suffering financial hardship would, in turn, have significant impact at the level of the whole economy.

2.2 Liberalisation in the financial services industry

We've already touched upon the changing social and economic context by looking at the growth of debt in relation to income and the way that debt impacts upon different types of household. Yet there are other aspects of the social and economic context relevant to understanding debt. One of the most important is the liberalisation of the UK financial services industry. This process has brought about great change within financial services, dating back to legislation passed in the 1980s. This included the Financial Services Act 1986, the Building Societies Act 1986, and the Banking Act 1987. Together with policy changes by lenders, these acts prompted the diversification by financial institutions into various new activities; relaxed rules on the use by lenders of borrowing from other financial institutions in the world's financial markets to finance their personal lending, and encouraged greater price competition among lenders.

These developments led to a very different environment from that prevailing in the 1970s. Then, credit and store cards were only starting to emerge in the UK. Most mortgage lending was carried out by building societies while the banks largely limited their personal lending activities to providing overdrafts and personal loans; boundaries were clearly drawn. Other features of financial life before the 1980s were starkly in contrast with life in the mid 2000s. Lenders were less proactive in encouraging debt, and marketing was limited. Borrowers expected to have a long-standing – if not lifetime – relationship with financial institutions: one bank for banking and loans, one building society for a mortgage. When seeking a mortgage from a building society, borrowers were often expected to have a savings account with the same lender. Even after having their mortgage applications approved, borrowers sometimes had to queue for funds until these were available for advancing. By the mid 2000s, it was common for households to have multiple relationships with different lenders.

Accompanying this more competitive environment has been a greater emphasis on marketing. Some newer entrants to the UK credit card market introduced more aggressive marketing techniques, such as issuing credit card cheques (as we saw in Chapter 1, Section 2.1), and offering interest-free periods to woo consumers (but often with 'catches'), and higher credit limits, including some limits increased with no reference to the borrower. As Chapter 3, Section 3 pointed out, marketing is used by companies to encourage people to buy goods and services; it's now common for banks and other lending institutions to advertise 'sales' for their debt products in much the same way as traditional high-street stores selling jeans and trainers, for example, might have January sales.

Consequently, it can be argued that the liberalisation of the financial services industry in the UK is linked to the consumer society: the increased availability of debt products helps to provide the money that fuels immediate consumption. One partial explanation for people's willingness to borrow is that there has been a shift from deferred gratification, where one might save before purchasing a good, towards

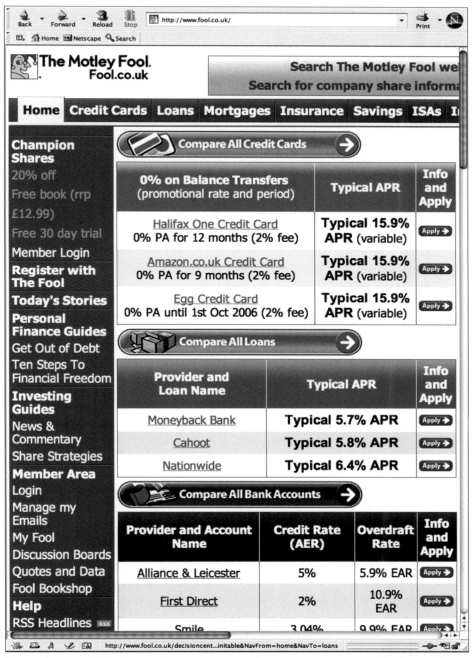

Financial services liberalisation has encouraged price competition amongst lenders and shopping around by borrowers

There are now 'sales' for debt products just as there are for high street goods

immediate reward, obtained through using credit (Lury, 2004). It's possible to see the strength of this argument in practice when you consider the number of adverts encouraging you to 'buy now and pay later'.

This discussion can be carried a step further: it can be claimed that the financial services industry is not simply meeting the demand for debt, but it is part of a process which encourages debt. There is some evidence to support this argument. For instance, a study in the USA found that increases in credit card limits, 90 per cent of which are initiated by the issuers rather than card holders, generated an immediate and significant rise in debt (Gross and Souleles, 2002). Another report in the UK suggests that in the build-up to Christmas each year, lenders send out at least 100 million unsolicited, but pre-approved, credit card application forms. The idea is that any new cards taken out achieve what is called 'top of the wallet' status; in other words, they are the most used cards, and the most lucrative for lenders (Credit Action, 2005).

There are also claims that the liberalisation of financial services has not made the debt market as competitive as it would appear. The Competition Commission found, in a report into store cards, that: 'there is an adverse effect on competition in connection with the supply of consumer credit through store cards and associated insurance in the UK'; this report also found that the charges on store cards were 'on average some 10 to 20 per cent higher across the store card market as a whole than they would have been had they reflected providers' costs, including the cost of capital' (Competition Commission, 2005). In essence, this is arguing that there is a lack of competition in the provision of such cards, and that consequently the charges for them are higher than they need be. The report suggests that the estimated cost to cardholders in terms of the excess prices paid for credit and insurance was in the region of £80 to £100 million a year.

'You heard me, buster. Take out a loan!'

As we saw in Chapter 1, liberalisation also tends to be accompanied by increased regulation. The FSA's role in regulating mortgage lending will be examined when we consider mortgages in Chapter 6. The Office of Fair Trading (OFT) and local authority Trading Standards Departments enforce the Consumer Credit Act 1974. This Act regulates consumer credit and consumer hire agreements for amounts up to £25,000, and lays down rules covering issues such as: the form and content of agreements; what can and cannot be stated in advertisements for debt; the procedures to be adopted in the event of default, termination, or early settlement, and extortionate credit bargains. The Act has been the mainstay of regulation in this area of financial services.

However, the Act has come under increasing strain in recent years, and it has been argued that it is unable to cope with the more liberalised debt market. For example, the Parliamentary Treasury Select Committee in 2003, in a report into the operation of credit and store cards (UK Parliament, 2003), was critical of what they saw as some poor lending and marketing practices, a lack of transparency and some 'excessive' interest rate charges. This has led to some changes, such as the industry's introduction of an 'Honesty Box' in which lenders provide a range of basic information about a credit deal, and the use of existing statutory powers to improve the means by which early repayment charges are calculated. The government has also introduced new consumer credit legislation to update the Act which, in 2006, had cleared Parliament and was awaiting implementation. This new Consumer Credit Act 2006 will, among other things, require annual statements for some types of loan, require more information to be given to customers not keeping up with their payments, and increase the number of credit deals which are regulated.

2.3 Structure of the financial services industry

The UK financial services industry is dominated by the banks. This has become much more the case since the conversion of most of the large building societies to banks in the 1980s and 1990s. These and other types of lending institutions are described in Box 4.1. At the end of 2004, banks accounted for 63 per cent of personal lending, building societies accounted for 15 per cent and other specialist lenders 21 per cent. Retailers and other types of lender accounted for the remaining 1 per cent (Bank of England, 2005).

Box 4.1   The UK lending industry

- **Banks** are mostly public limited companies (plcs) which are owned by their shareholders. These include the major 'high-street' names, such as Barclays, Lloyds TSB, HSBC and the Royal Bank of Scotland group (including NatWest), but also a number of other banks, such as Halifax Bank of Scotland, Abbey, and the Northern Rock, some of which were building societies until the 1990s.

- **Building societies** are 'mutual' organisations. This means that they are owned by their retail savers and borrowers (that is, personal customers). When they were originally founded in earlier centuries, building societies were organisations formed by groups of people who saved together to buy land on which to build their homes. Subsequently, 'permanent' building societies emerged with whom people could save even if they did not need to acquire a home themselves. The Nationwide Building Society is the largest remaining society in the UK, although there are still sixty-two others, such as the Britannia, the Portman and the Skipton Building Societies.

- **Finance companies** are in many cases subsidiaries of banks and building societies. These specialise in personal loans, and motor and retail finance (e.g. Car Select from Lloyds TSB).

- **Direct lenders** are also often subsidiaries of banks, building societies and insurance companies. The chief distinction between these and other lenders is that they do not have a branch network; they deal with customers via the telephone, internet and the postal system, such as Direct Line.

- *Credit unions* are cooperative organisations, often small in size and run on a localised basis. There are two main types: community-based, whose members tend to come from low-income groups; and work-based, whose members are employed with an affiliated organisation. One of the largest is The Open University's credit union.

- *The Student Loans Company (SLC)* is owned by the UK Government, and lends to students in higher education to enable them to meet their expenses. With the cost of higher education increasing in recent years, the SLC has become a major lender.

- *The alternative credit market* consists of 'sub-prime lenders' aimed primarily at people on low incomes. Such lenders include some loans companies, door-to-door money lenders, rental purchase shops, 'sell and buy back' outlets, and pawnbrokers. In addition, this market includes unlicensed lenders who provide loans in an emergency at extremely high rates of interest.

- *Budgeting loans* are available for people on Income Support or Jobseeker's Allowance, or getting Pension Credit. These are interest-free loans which have to be paid back, and in 2006 they had a borrowing limit of £1000.

The UK's lending industry has been affected by the diversification into financial services of many retailing companies, particularly the supermarkets. These lenders are supported by, or have joint ventures with, established banks, and the retailing name is used as an effective means of marketing to the public. For example, the financial services activities of Tesco and Sainsbury's were, in 2006, joint activities with First Active (which is part of the Royal Bank of Scotland) and Halifax Bank of Scotland (HBOS), respectively. The basic business of all lenders is really the same. It involves borrowing funds from the public and institutions, and lending them (at a profit in most cases) to the public, companies, local authorities and even governments.

Activity 4.2

Which of the categories of lender in Box 4.1 have you borrowed from? Why was this? If you haven't borrowed any money, which kinds of institutions might you borrow from in the future?

Thinking through the reasons why you build and maintain relationships with different categories of lender is important. Do you shop around for the best deal or do you accept the first offer? Do you deal with building societies because of their mutual status, or do you turn to the alternative credit markets? Sections 3 and 5 of this chapter will provide information about and examples of the kind of issues someone might work through in order to come to an informed decision about categories of lender and types of loan products. It's important to remember that not everyone has such a choice: low-income households may have to use money lenders or mail-order companies because of a lack of access to mainstream lenders. ■ ■ ■

One key difference between the different types of lenders lies in their differential need to make profits. For example, a major objective of incorporated companies like banks and finance companies is to maximise profits. In recent years, the banks have been very successful in this objective and have made substantial profits. It was against this backdrop that there were some calls for banks to lower their charges and interest rates on debt products, especially on credit cards where the interest rates were argued to be particularly high – a 2003 report from the Parliamentary Treasury Select Committee was one of these voices (UK Parliament, 2003). Building societies have no shareholders since their customers in effect own them, and so they do not have to make dividend payments. With the financial leeway this gives them, these mutual organisations *may* charge lower rates of interest to borrowers. For credit unions, the maximum interest rate that can be charged is set by law, and the interest rate charged by the Student Loans Company is linked to the rate of inflation by law. Therefore, the interest rate of these organisations' lending is likely to be lower than that offered by the commercial sector.

3   Debt costs

3.1   Some basics of debt and interest

When someone acquires a debt, the money that they will have to repay to the lender will consist of three different elements. Let's briefly introduce each of these in turn.

First, there is the amount originally lent – this is normally referred to as the **principal sum** (or sometimes the capital sum). For instance, if £10,000 is borrowed for five years to buy a car, then the £10,000 will have to be repaid. There are two usual ways in which this principal sum

Principal sum (or capital sum)
The original amount of debt taken out.

can be repaid: either in one amount at the end of the **term** of the loan (in this case, five years), or in stages over the life of the loan. The former is often referred to as an 'interest-only loan' and the latter a 'repayment loan'. If the principal sum is to be paid off in full at the end of the loan period, the borrower will need to have the money available – for example, through the proceeds from an endowment mortgage or through building up other savings to pay off the loan.

Second, there is the important additional cost of having debt: the **interest** that has to be paid on it. In effect, interest is an additional charge on the repayment of debt. The **interest rate** is the exact price of this charge. It is normally expressed as a percentage per year – for example 7 per cent per annum, or more commonly abbreviated to '7 per cent p.a.'. The charging or paying of interest is generally rejected by shariah law, as it used to be by some Christians in earlier centuries. (We'll look at an Islamic system of funding house purchases in Chapter 6.) In modern economies, the concept of interest comes about because lenders require payment in return for the access to the money they have given up, in return for the risk associated with not getting their money back, and because they require an amount to cover the expected inflation rate over the coming year.

Third, there may be charges associated with taking out, having or repaying debt. We'll look at these in more detail in Section 3.4.

Term
The period of time over which a debt is to be repaid.

Interest
The charge a borrower pays for the use of someone else's money.

Interest rate
The exact price that a borrower pays for debt, normally expressed as an annual percentage.

3.2 The official interest rate

In the UK, the official interest rate is set monthly by the Bank of England, as explained in Box 4.2.

Box 4.2   High noon in Threadneedle Street

Prior to 1997, 'official' interest rates in the UK were determined by the UK Government, usually after consultation with the Bank of England. Arrangements changed in May 1997 when the incoming Labour Government passed responsibility for monetary policy and the setting of interest rates to the Bank of England to make them independent of political influence. This matches the arrangement in the USA and in the 'euro zone', where the Federal Reserve Bank and the European Central Bank respectively set official rates. The rate set by the Monetary Policy Committee (MPC) is the rate at which the Bank of England will lend to the financial institutions. This, in turn, determines the level of bank 'base rates' – the minimum level at which the banks will normally lend money. Consequently, the 'official' rate effectively sets the general level of interest rates for the economy as a whole.

Each month, the Bank of England's MPC meets for two days to consider policy in the light of economic conditions – particularly the prospects for inflation. The MPC's decision is announced each month at 12 noon on the Thursday after the first Monday in the month. The objective, in 2006, was for the MPC to set interest rates at a level consistent with inflation of 2 per cent p.a. For example, if the MPC believes inflation will go above 2 per cent p.a., they may increase interest rates in order to discourage people taking on debt – because if people spend less, it may reduce the upward pressure on prices. Conversely, if the MPC believed inflation would be much below 2 per cent p.a., they might lower interest rates (also known as 'easing monetary policy') – people may then borrow and spend more.

Cyclical
A recurring pattern of a variable over time showing peaks and low points at regular intervals.

As you can see from Figure 4.2, official rates of interest tend to be **cyclical**, rising to peaks and then falling to troughs. Since 1989, the trend in the UK has been for nominal interest rates to peak at successively lower levels. Nominal interest rates peaked at 15 per cent in 1989, 7.5 per cent in 1998 and 6 per cent in 2000. They then reached a low point of 3.5 per cent in 2003. As 2006 began, UK interest rates stood at 4.5 per cent.

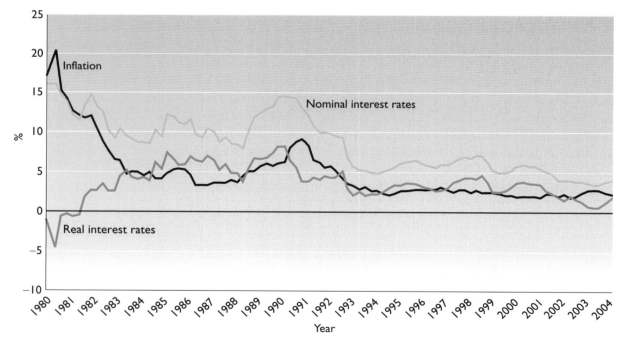

Figure 4.2 *Nominal and real interest rates and inflation in the UK, 1980–2004*
Source: Bank of England, 2005, p. 11, Chart 3

Real interest rates are interest rates which have been adjusted to take account of inflation. Looking at Figure 4.2, when inflation is higher than the nominal interest rate, this means that real interest rates are negative (as they were in 1980/81). Real interest rates are at zero when the rate of inflation and the nominal interest rates are the same; and are positive when the nominal interest rate exceeds inflation. Real interest rates have also been low in the 1990s and early 2000s, falling from 7 per cent in 1990 to just over 2 per cent by 2004 (Bell, 2005). Most mainstream lenders link interest rates, including mortgage rates, to the official rate of interest, and so the cost of debt, including mortgage debt, declined over this period. This is another reason why debt levels may have risen. Some economists have suggested that we are living in an era of low real interest rates, and will be for some time to come, but others suggest that higher real interest rates could return again in the future. These alternative future scenarios, of low or high interest rates, would have very different impacts on people holding significant amounts of personal debt.

The Governor of the Bank of England in 2006, Mervyn King

3.3 More on interest

Let's look at interest payments in more detail. We can return to the car loan I mentioned in Section 3.1. If £10,000 is borrowed and no repayments of this principal sum are made during the year, and the interest rate is 7 per cent p.a. with interest being paid once a year at the end of the year, the interest charge for that year is £700. Thus, provided that the principal sum owed to the lender remains at £10,000 and interest rates are 7 per cent p.a., the borrower will have to pay £700 each year to the lender.

Activity 4.3

How much would you pay in interest per annum if you make no repayments on a principal sum of £50,000 and the rate of interest is as follows?

1 5 per cent p.a.

2 35 per cent p.a.

3 7.5 per cent p.a.

4 6.7 per cent p.a.

Comment

The answer to Activity 4.3 is given at the end of the chapter. ■ ■ ■

As you completed the calculations in Activity 4.3, you may have started to think of some factors that could complicate the calculation of the interest charge. For example, what would be the interest charge if some of the principal sum is repaid during the course of the year? In many cases, the answer is that the interest rate calculation will be based on the average balance of the principal sum during the year. For instance, if £10,000 is owed at the start of the year and £100 is repaid halfway through each month, then the outstanding balance at the end of the year would be £8800. The average balance of principal outstanding during the year would be the average (mean) of the balance at the start and at the end of the year, or £9400 ($\frac{£10000 + £8800}{2}$) . Based on this average balance, the interest for the year at 7 per cent p.a. would be £658 (£9400 × $\frac{7}{100}$) – rather less than the £700 if no repayment of the principal sum had been made.

The precise practice for computing the interest charge varies among different lenders – and interest can be calculated by different lenders at different time intervals. One of the pieces of financial small print it is always vital to read is the basis on which interest is charged – that is, how often and by reference to what terms. For instance, if someone was repaying some of the principal sum of their loan regularly, the interest charged would be lower if the interest charge was calculated on a daily basis, rather than a monthly, or an annual, basis (an annual basis would be the least favourable if repayments of the principal sum were being made).

Another question may be what happens if the borrower does not repay the interest due to the lender? Again, this will depend on the details of the contract with the lender and their attitude to borrowers who fall into arrears. Normally, the lender will add the interest charge left unpaid to the principal sum. This means that the following period's interest charge is going to be higher since the borrower will be paying interest not only on the original principal sum but also on the unpaid interest. This is known as **compounding**, and can quickly enlarge debts. Box 4.3 and Figure 4.3 provide an example of compounding, illustrating what happens if someone borrows £1000 at an interest rate of 35 per cent and makes no repayments over ten years. Over this period of time, the debt would rise from £1000 to £20,107.

Compounding
The process by which interest repayments are added to the original amount borrowed to give a higher total figure which, in turn, attracts interest rate charges.

Box 4.3 An example of compound interest

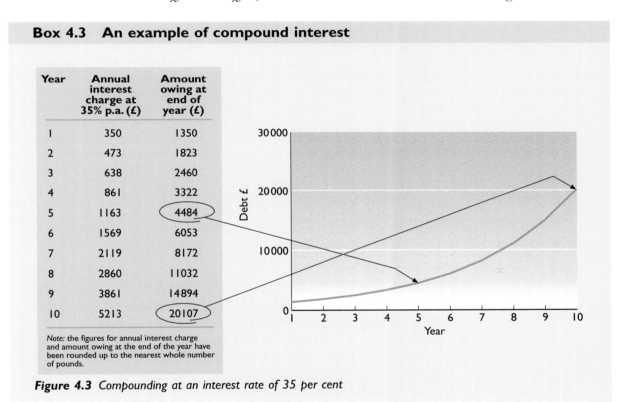

Year	Annual interest charge at 35% p.a. (£)	Amount owing at end of year (£)
1	350	1350
2	473	1823
3	638	2460
4	861	3322
5	1163	4484
6	1569	6053
7	2119	8172
8	2860	11032
9	3861	14894
10	5213	20107

Note: the figures for annual interest charge and amount owing at the end of the year have been rounded up to the nearest whole number of pounds.

Figure 4.3 Compounding at an interest rate of 35 per cent

The dangers of compounding were demonstrated vividly in a famous case which came to court in 2004. This is reported fully in Box 4.4. A debt of £5750 grew to the staggering sum of £384,000 in fifteen years. In the event, the debt was (unusually) cancelled for being 'extortionate'. Yet it showed the risks of compounding very clearly!

Box 4.4 Landmark ruling as judge erases couple's debt

A judge today wiped out a couple's debt of £384,000 which had spiralled out of control from an original loan of £5,750 due to 'extortionate' interest rates. Tony and Michelle Meadows, from Southport, Merseyside, faced losing their home after they were taken to court by London North Securities for failing to keep up with repayments on their loan.

The couple, who have two children, took out the loan in 1989. Mr Meadows, 45, a car windscreen salesman, claimed he had taken out the loan, designed for people with poor credit ratings, to install central heating and convert a bathroom into a third bedroom. The small print of the loan agreement revealed that the couple would be charged a 'compounded' interest rate if they ever fell into arrears.

Essentially this meant that the money lenders were charging 34.9 per cent interest on the arrears as well as on the repayments, which soon resulted in the debt growing to an enormous amount.

Judge Howarth said: 'Where the rate concerned is as high as 34.9 per cent it seems to me that the combination of factors is so potentially exorbitant that it is grossly so and does grossly contravene the ordinary principles of fair dealing.' He added: 'This is one of the few credit bargains which is extortionate.'

When the couple failed to keep up with repayments, their debt soared and London North Securities attempted to take possession of the couple's £200,000 family home to pay off the loan.

Speaking outside court, Mr Meadows said 'It wasn't a wanton spending spree we went on back then, it was just something we had to do at the time. I would advise people thinking of taking a loan to read the small print very carefully.'

The court heard the couple ended up with a loan for £5,750 to pay for £2,000 home improvements, around £3,000 to pay off their mortgage and £750 for an insurance policy they did not want ...

[Subsequently the Court of Appeal] dismissed a challenge by the lender, London North Securities, to a County Court judgment that wiped out the debt run up by the Meadows. They said the loan agreement was unenforceable under the Consumer Credit Act after the original loan company had wrapped insurance payments into the debt and then added interest and penalty payments to the total.

(adapted from *The Guardian*, 2004 and 2005)

Interest rates can also be set in a number of different ways. These are:

- *A variable rate* which can move upwards or downwards during the life of the loan. In the UK, these usually move in tandem with movements in the official rate of interest (see Box 4.2). Some products (called 'trackers') are specifically linked to official Bank of England rates.

- *A fixed rate* where the rate is determined at the start of the loan and remains unaltered throughout the fixed rate term. The rate will be based on what the lender has to pay for fixed rate funds of the same term.

- *A capped rate* where the rate cannot rise above a defined maximum (the 'cap'), but below this 'cap' it can move in tandem with movements of official interest rates. A variation to a capped rate loan is a 'collared' rate loan where rates can move in line with official rates but cannot either go above a defined maximum (the 'cap') or below a defined minimum (the 'floor'). Such products usually require the payment of a fee to the lender at the start of the loan.

Most commonly, personal loans are set at a fixed rate, credit card debt and overdrafts at a variable rate, while mortgage lending (covered in Chapter 6) is split between the three interest rate forms defined above. In 2004, new mortgage lending in the UK was divided in the following ways: 64 per cent variable rate; 34 per cent fixed rate; and 3 per cent on a capped or other rate basis. Therefore, the majority of mortgage holders, along with most of those with credit card and overdrafts, are at risk to increases in the official rate of interest made by the Bank of England. As mortgages account for a large proportion of personal debt, it is easy to see why the UK economy can be easily affected by even relatively small changes in interest rates.

Activity 4.4

Under what circumstances do you think it might be attractive to borrow at the following types of interest rate?

1   Fixed rate of interest.
2   Variable rate of interest.

Comment

Assuming that borrowers have a choice and want to pay as little interest as possible, choosing a variable rate may be preferred if interest rates are expected to fall, and fixed rates may be preferred if rates are expected to rise. However, to assess which would be cheaper requires a forecast of how rates will move during the life of the loan, and making such forecasts is difficult because it is difficult to predict future rates of inflation and interest rates. In addition, the choice may reflect the borrower's household budget. For example, households on a tight budget may choose a fixed rate because this would provide certainty of monthly expenditure. ■ ■ ■

3.4 Annual Percentage Rate (APR)

You have seen that borrowers have to repay both the principal sum and interest to the lender, and that the interest charge may be fixed, variable or capped. On top of this, there are often extra costs. Some of these costs arise from fees which may have to be paid on obtaining a loan and, under certain circumstances, on repaying the loan before the end of the term. Such extra costs include:

1   *Arrangement fees paid to the lender:* These are usually flat rate, one-off fees and are generally charged when the borrower takes out a fixed rate or capped rate loan, or when remortgaging.

2   *Intermediary fees:* These may be paid when a borrower deals with a broker rather than directly with a lender.

3   *Early repayment (or 'prepayment') fees:* These may have to be paid to a lender if a loan is repaid early. The argument used by lenders is that earlier repayment can incur additional costs. In the case of personal loans, early repayment charges mean the lender gets a share of the interest which would have been paid had a borrower kept the loan for the full term.

4   *Tied insurance:* Taking out insurance (for instance, payment protection insurance, life insurance, home insurance) may be required with a loan. In other cases, insurance may be optional, although this is not always made clear to borrowers, who might end up paying for inappropriate policies. The commissions earned on such sales add to the profits made on lending. Insurance is covered in more detail in Chapter 9.

Annual Percentage Rate (APR)
APR or Annual Percentage Rate is a summary figure for comparing debt costs which brings together interest rates and other charges.

Given all these different potential charges, and the different methods of calculating interest, it's important to have a good means of comparing the total cost of debt on different debt products. Fortunately, in the UK there is a way of ensuring an accurate 'like for like' comparison, and of assessing which is most appropriate. This is known as the **Annual Percentage Rate (APR)** of interest. This accommodates interest and the compulsory charges discussed above. The APR also takes into account *when* the interest and charges have to be paid. The method for calculating the APR is laid down by the Consumer Credit Act 1974. Generally, a low APR means lower costs for the borrower.

The APR is only a guide, and not a *perfect* measure. It does not include any costs which might occur that are not a compulsory part of the loan (for example, premiums on non-compulsory insurance). In 2003, the Parliamentary Treasury Select Committee report into credit and store cards found that there were, in practice, two different precise methods used to calculate the APR, and 'up to 10 different ways in which charges are calculated, meaning that users of cards with the same APR can be charged different amounts' (UK Parliament, 2003). The Department of Trade and Industry responded by publishing regulations that tightened up the assumptions that could be used in the calculation of the APR. These difficulties were one of the drivers behind the Consumer Credit Act referred to Section 2.1.

3.5 Interest rates and individuals

You saw in Box 4.2 that the Bank of England determines the official interest rate. Yet this is not the interest rate that will be charged to individuals taking out different types of debt. Lenders will tend to take into account a number of different factors when setting the rates for a particular individual. I mentioned in Section 3.1 that one of the reasons for charging interest was the need for lenders to have a return for taking the risk associated with not getting their money back. Customarily, the basic principle here would be that the greater the estimated risk of loss, the greater the interest charged. This means that 'higher risk' borrowers may be charged more interest than those who are deemed 'lower risk'. In a similar vein, interest charges will vary according to the security offered to the lenders by the borrowers. This takes us back to the distinction between secured and unsecured debt introduced in Section 2.1 – secured debts will, other things being equal, usually have a lower interest rate than unsecured debts. Another factor which may affect interest rates is the size of the loan. Sometimes, larger loans may attract lower interest rates than smaller loans. The extent of competition between lenders will also be a factor: typically, the greater the competition between lenders who wish to lend money, the lower the interest rate you would expect them to be able to charge.

One question which arises from this is whether such factors can explain the different interest rates charged, especially the higher rates often charged to people on much lower income. A Citizens Advice survey, for instance, found that APRs charged to clients with debts owed to money lenders and home-collected credit providers ranged from 25 per cent to a staggering 360 per cent, while interest rates charged on mainstream credit card debts ranged from 9.9 per cent to 25.4 per cent and on bank loans from 8 per cent to 32.9 per cent (Citizens Advice, 2003). Box 4.5 describes some of the experiences of those on low incomes.

Box 4.5   Credit for those on low incomes

A Citizens Advice Bureau in Hampshire reported that their clients, a couple with two children, had taken out a £500 loan to repay their rent arrears which were the subject of possession proceedings. The total cost of the loan was £800 in total, with a 60 per cent rate of interest.

A West of Scotland Citizens Advice Bureau reported a client couple who have over £16,000 in debts. The couple had two recent loans from doorstep providers, both granted within two months of each other. The first loan was for £500, with a £275 interest charge. The second loan was for £100 with a £55 interest charge. These loans were being used to help meet the income shortfall on existing credit agreements.

(Citizens Advice, 2003, pp. 27, 28)

4   Debt and household finance

In this section, we shall return to some ideas that you met earlier in *Personal Finance*, in particular, the model of income and expenditure flows changing over time. This will enable us to investigate how debt fits into the overall picture of household finances.

4.1   Income and expenditure, and debt

An important reason why people take on debt is because of a continued excess level of expenditure over net income: a situation which could be caused by a number of factors. Let's use the example scenario of the Syme family: a household consisting of a lone parent and two children. We can use the Syme household to look at how flows of expenditure and income relate to debt. In this case, shown in Figure 4.4, the main income earner in the household loses her full-time job in year 2, and so household income falls below expenditure. This is a realistic scenario: according to Citizens Advice, job loss is one of the three main reasons for problems with debt, along with living long term on low income and overcommitment to high levels of spending (Citizens Advice, 2003). In the case of the Symes, from year 3 onwards net income, made up of benefits and earnings from part-time work, totals £9000 per year. Expenditure remains constant at £14,000 in year 3, and then the household manages to cut expenditure down to £12,000 in year 4. However, the shortfall between expenditure and income must be financed. This can be done by either using up any savings, or taking on debt, or a mixture of the two. For simplicity, in this example we'll assume that the Symes have no savings and that they take out debt to finance the

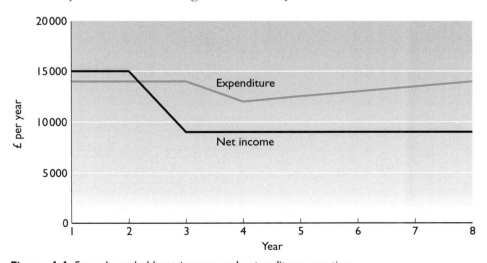

Figure 4.4 *Syme household net income and expenditure over time*

expenditure over and above net income. This debt leads to expenditure increasing from year 5 onwards as interest and other charges are added to existing household expenditure. This, in turn, would require more debt. Such a situation is not sustainable in the long term and, eventually, the Symes would either have to make other cuts in expenditure or find a way to increase income.

The Syme scenario highlights how certain life events, such as job loss, relationship breakdown or illness might lead to households having to take on debt. Other more predictable life events, such as full-time study, are easier to build into financial plans. A household, for instance, with one member who intends to go to university, might plan to finance current levels of expenditure through taking out debts and then use the benefit of the graduate earnings premium discussed in Chapter 2 to pay these debts off after graduation.

One reason why individuals and households take on debt is to finance expenditure which is above income. Another reason is to spread the cost of expensive purchases, such as a car or house, over a number of years. In these cases, a household takes out a relatively large debt which is repaid over time. This cannot be taken to imply that taking out a debt to pay for such items means that the debt can be considered part of income – it might sometimes appear that credit can be used like income, to pay for items, but of course, unlike income, it forms a liability which is then owed. Debt problems often arise when a household already has debt, but then faces unexpected life events like those mentioned above.

4.2 Liabilities and expenditure

As you saw in Section 2.1, debts are liabilities: a stock of money owed at a certain point in time. Such liabilities include long-term debt, such as a mortgage, as well as short-term debts such as an overdraft. You will see more about recording these liabilities in the financial balance sheet in Chapter 6. For now, I want to explain the interrelationship between such liabilities and expenditure. This is illustrated in Figure 4.5.

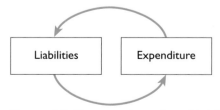

Figure 4.5 *The interrelationship of liabilities and expenditure*

Figure 4.5 shows that liabilities and expenditure are inextricably linked. For example, taking on a liability will generate a future flow of expenditure in the form of debt repayments (both of the principal and, crucially, of the interest). It's important to realise that having liabilities will give rise to higher future expenditure.

Similarly, higher levels of expenditure can give rise to liabilities. If, for instance, a household's expenditure exceeds its income (and has no savings to draw on), then in order to fund that expenditure, a liability will arise. For example, people might run up a credit card bill, or have to increase their overdraft. Conversely, repayments of debt would gradually reduce the stock of liability over time if the repayments are of sufficient size to cover all the interest and to repay some of the capital.

Remembering this relationship is important as we work towards the financial balance sheet. To illustrate, someone may want to borrow £10,000 to buy a car. This stock of debt will be a liability in their financial balance sheet; it will also give rise to monthly repayments which will be part of that person's expenditure in the budgeting process that you saw in Chapter 3, Section 4.

Activity 4.5

Can you think of any situations where taking out a debt to fund a purchase can also lead to the acquisition of an asset?

Comment

The most common answer to this question would be a home, where the house's market value would be an asset in the financial balance sheet and the amount of mortgage outstanding will be a liability. There are other possible examples – ranging from jewellery or collectibles to financial assets such as stocks and shares. You could refer back to Chapter 2, Section 2 to remind yourself of what the different types of assets are. ■ ■ ■

5　The borrowing process

In the example in Section 4, the Syme family fell into debt due to some unexpected circumstances. This section uses an example of someone deciding to take out a debt in order to work through the issues involved in borrowing money. It also relates these issues to the financial planning model introduced in Chapter 1 (see Figure 1.8).

5.1 How to finance a purchase

Let's look at the example of Philip, who wants to purchase a music system costing £1000. (We'll assume that Philip cannot simply fund it out of his monthly budget.) In order to finance the purchase, options would include:

1 using existing savings
2 building up savings first, and purchasing the item later
3 using a mixture of savings and debt
4 taking out a debt of £1000.

Philip wants a new music system

Which option is chosen will obviously depend on a number of factors including, crucially, Philip's initial financial position. Let's start by running through some generic issues related to each of these options.

The first option involves using existing assets held in the form of savings. If Philip has built up savings, he could draw upon these to fund the music system purchase. In coming to a decision on whether to use savings, he may think about opportunity cost – the savings used to buy the music system will not then be available for him to purchase something else. He will also be giving up the future income, in the form of interest earned, on the savings that will be spent on the item. He might also compare debt costs with the loss of income on savings. Generally, you'd expect the cost of debt, in terms of the interest that will be paid, to be rather higher than income from savings for two reasons. First, savings products and debt products are provided by the same institutions – such as banks and building societies – and these institutions make their profits from the difference between them. It is likely, therefore, that in normal circumstances the interest rate for debt will be higher than the rate earned on savings. Second, interest on savings will be taxed as income unless there is a means of sheltering the earnings – for example, by saving in tax-exempt products. If savings are taxed, the likelihood is that the rate of interest received after tax will be lower than the interest paid for borrowed money. (Savings are covered in more detail in Chapter 5.) Thus, other things being equal, it would usually be the case that using existing savings will be cheaper than taking out debt to fund a purchase.

The second option is to build up savings before purchase. Again, this will depend on having disposable income above expenditure, which would allow savings to be built up. It also depends upon Philip being prepared to defer the enjoyment associated from having a music system for the period of time it takes to build up the savings. For the same reasons as the first option, this second option would most likely be cheaper than using debt to fund the purchase.

The third and fourth options both involve taking on debt. For the reasons given above, it's likely that using a mixture of savings and debt would be cheaper than funding the purchase solely through debt. For the sake of clarity, in the rest of this section we'll assume that Philip chooses to borrow the full amount.

Activity 4.6

Think back to the framework associated with the financial planning model (see Chapter 1, Figure 1.8). If, in our example of buying the music system, Philip was using the 'Stage 1: Assess the situation' part of the model, what issues would he need to consider?

Comment

Under the financial planning model, Philip would need to consider the relative importance of buying the music system within the wider context of his existing goals. He would need to think about the constraints on his resources, and calculate whether repayments can be afforded within his household budget. In thinking through affordability, individuals should also consider the possibility that their circumstances may change. For instance, if household income were to fall or be interrupted during the term of the loan, could repayments be afforded? ■ ■ ■

5.2 Which debt product?

Philip may or may not have been thinking through all of the issues discussed above, but we have assumed that he is going ahead and wants to fund the purchase by taking out debt. Philip will then need finance, and the debt product which is used will depend upon a number of factors, including price, flexibility and the length of time over which repayments are made. Box 4.6 describes the different debt products.

Box 4.6   Debt products

- *Overdrafts:* These provide a flexible means of accessing debt on a bank current account, up to a limit approved by the lender. Unapproved overdrafts normally attract penalty fees and higher interest charges than approved overdrafts.

- *Credit cards (including store cards):* These will have a credit limit set by the lender and normally require a minimum amount to be repaid each month – typically between 2 per cent and 5 per cent of the balance of debt. Prior to the time when the payment is due, there may be a short period of interest-free credit. Credit cards will vary widely in the interest rate charged on the balance that is not paid off, and some may have an annual fee attached, although many do not. Store cards are a form of credit card which may only be used for buying from specified outlets, and the interest rate charged on store cards tends to be much higher than that of credit cards.

- *Charge cards:* These can be used like credit cards to make purchases and obtain up to around two months' free credit between purchase and paying off the outstanding amount. The difference from a credit card is that, with a charge card, a borrower is required to pay off the entire balance each month. The two-month free credit period arises from the fact that the charge card bill will be sent out monthly, with up to around a further month to settle the bill. A fee may be payable for the card. A famous brand of charge card is the American Express charge card.

- *Personal loans:* These are loans, typically of terms between one and ten years, which may be either unsecured or secured against a property (such as a house) or other assets. Unsecured personal loans are not contractually linked to any assets the borrower buys. These are available from credit unions, banks, building societies, direct lenders and finance companies.

■ ***Hire purchase (HP):*** This is a form of secured debt where hire payments (interest and part repayment of the principal) are made over a period, normally of up to ten years in order to purchase specific goods. The legal ownership of the product only passes to the borrower when the final instalment has been paid.

■ ***Mortgages:*** These are loans to purchase property or land, and are secured against these assets. Debt terms for mortgages are normally up to twenty-five years. There are many different types of mortgages and, as mentioned in Section 2.1, it's possible to fund spending through equity withdrawal. Chapter 6 looks at mortgages in detail.

■ ***Alternative credit:*** These are the areas of sub-prime lending described in Box 4.1, and include buying on instalments through mail-order catalogues, doorstep lending and lending on the high street. Commonly, interest rates are high and there are heavy penalties for late payment. In fact, one report found that a fifty-week loan for £400 from one of the weekly-collect credit companies would cost £700. The same report found that a £400 loan from an unlicensed lender could cost up to £2000 in repayments spread over six or more months (Kempson, 2001).

In terms of price, as Section 3.4 noted, the APR can be used to compare the costs of different debt products. One first possible step for Philip might be to gather information on different APRs. Sources of information include adverts and offers for loans in newspapers, on television, radio and the internet, the finance sections of newspapers, or financial advisers.

Connected to price is whether the debt product is secured or unsecured. One trend in recent years, encouraged by advertising, has been for individuals to consolidate a number of unsecured debts in one loan, usually secured against a property, and thus withdrawing 'equity' from that property. The attraction of doing this is that the mortgage rate – which tends to be the lowest of the rates charged on the different forms of debt – may now be applied to all debts and the term of debts may be extended, reducing the size of monthly repayments.

However, there are risks in adopting this course of action because swapping existing loans for a consolidated loan increases the risk of losing one's home. Additionally, if consolidating debts in this way involves extending the term of indebtedness, there is the possibility of a mismatch between the life of the debts and the life of the assets acquired. Therefore, for example, if the music system was expected to need replacing in five years but the debt was repaid over ten, Philip might still be paying for a music system which was no longer in use. None the less, consolidating debts is popular: a survey of borrowers conducted on behalf of the Bank of England in 2004 (May et al., 2004, pp. 420–1) found that 25 per cent of respondents who took on an additional mortgage did so to fund the consolidation of debts.

The price of the debt product is clearly important when making a decision on which product to choose. Indeed, an accurate price is essential for household budgeting and planning ahead, but it's not the only factor. A second issue is flexibility. For instance, Philip might find that debt through hire purchase (HP) is cheaper than debt through an unsecured personal loan but, because HP tends to be tied to a particular deal, there may be less flexibility in shopping around for a particular commodity or brand.

Credit cards offer a flexible way to borrow, but interest rates can be high. You saw, in Section 2.1, that possessing and using credit cards is very popular in the UK. One feature of the credit card market is the use of discounts to attract new customers. These may be in the form of 'low start' loans, where the initial rate charged is lower than the standard rate, but with the cost rising to the standard rate after the introductory period. One extreme example of this is where credit cards are offered at an interest rate of zero (0 per cent) for an introductory period, including for sums of existing debt transferred to the card. These rates are designed to encourage customers to move from one lender to another or, in fact, to take on debt which might not otherwise have been contemplated. If a debt product has an initial discount, borrowers need to calculate whether they can afford the rate which will apply once the discount period ends.

Credit cards can offer a flexible way to borrow

A third issue when choosing a debt product, and which contains both elements of price and flexibility, is deciding over what term to borrow. Table 4.2 uses an example of borrowing £1000 on a repayment loan at 6.7 per cent APR to illustrate the difference this makes. In this example, taken from a high-street building society, total repayments vary from £1035.48 to £1173.60. Because it is a repayment loan, the interest charged is calculated on the average balance of the principal outstanding, as discussed in Section 3.1. Although the monthly charge (and hence the expenditure in the household budget) is higher per month for a shorter loan, the total cost of repayment is less.

Table 4.2 Examples of borrowing £1000 at 6.7 per cent APR

Repayment period	Monthly payment (£)	Total amount paid (£)
1 year (12 months)	86.29	1035.48
3 years (36 months)	30.65	1103.40
5 years (60 months)	19.56	1173.60

Consequently, price, flexibility and length of term are all important factors in choosing a debt product. This is all significant information needed in the 'Stage 2: Decide on a financial plan' part of any financial planning process about the taking out of debt. However, the notion of choice itself is influenced by the social and economic circumstances of individuals such as Philip. As we saw in Section 2.1, low-income groups have only limited access to mainstream finance: in fact, this is one of the characteristics of financial exclusion. People who do not own their own home, for instance, will not have the same access to secured lending as homeowners. This narrows their ability to access the kind of low interest debt which is associated with secured lending. Such individuals might, of course, choose not to borrow to fund a music system purchase, but any borrowing they do undertake would most likely involve more expensive forms of debt than homeowners can access.

Activity 4.7

The data below show some real interest rates for different products in a high-street bank in December 2005. Given that the rate for the personal loan is substantially the lowest, why might someone use any product *other* than a personal loan to buy the music system?

Debt product	Typical APR (%)
Overdraft	14.9
Personal loan	6.9
Credit card	13.9
Charge card	25.0

Comment

When choosing a debt product, many of the aspects you've seen in Box 4.6, and in Section 5 generally, will be important, such as flexibility, convenience, the desired term of repayment, and the price (the interest rate). Another factor that may influence someone's decision is how these different financial products are marketed. Therefore, many factors other than the price will play a part in selecting the specific debt product, and that is why the personal loan, which is the cheapest, may not always be the product chosen. ■■■

A crucial factor in being able to access debt products is the credit standing of the borrower. People with poor 'credit scores', even if they have relatively high incomes, will have limited access to cheaper forms of debt. Most lenders 'credit score' loan applicants before releasing money. Although the exact practices vary from lender to lender, the credit score analysis can be broken down into four main areas:

1 *Factors which might automatically prevent approval:* For example, if the individual has a County Court Judgement (CCJ) – or a decree in Scotland – against them for previously defaulting on debts.

2 *Affordability testing:* This looks at the income and prevailing expenditure commitments of applicants, with an emphasis on existing debts.

3 *Characteristics of applicants:* For example, how long someone has lived at their current address (and at previous addresses), and how long they have maintained their current banking arrangements will be scored. Frequent changes of address and banking arrangements attract unfavourable credit scoring.

4 *Security:* This relates to the importance of security in deciding the level of risk and the interest rate.

The range of outcomes from this process is more than just a 'yes' or a 'no'. It also determines the maximum the lender is prepared to advance and the interest rate charged. Moreover, it can involve the lender making use of the credit reference agencies (CRAs) that provide databases on the credit histories of individuals. Those seeking to borrow have the right both to ask if a CRA was employed by the lender and which CRA was used. For a small fee (£2 per file in 2006), anyone can ask to see their statutory credit report from the major CRAs (Experian, Equifax and Call Credit).

Let's return to the financial planning model and financial capability. The financial planning model can be applied to the process by which individuals like Philip decide upon a generic type of debt product and then shop around for the best deal on a specific product. They then act

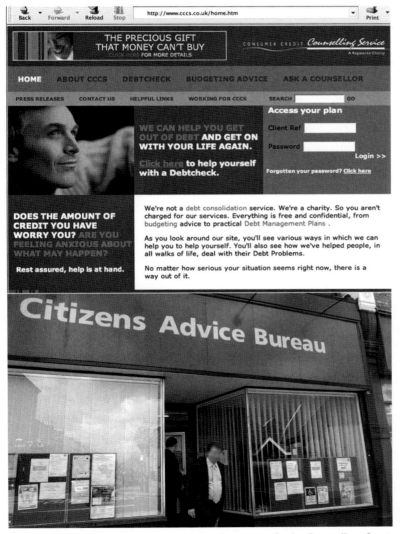

Debt advice could be obtained from the Consumer Credit Counselling Service or from a Citizens Advice Bureau

upon that decision (in Stage 3) and, in turn, review the decision (Stage 4). As part of the review process, it's important to be able to tackle problems with debt if they arise. To where do people with debt problems turn if they get into difficulty? The nearest Citizens Advice Bureau (the local branch of Citizens Advice, whose research has been drawn on throughout this chapter) is one organisation which helps people with such problems. Other organisations include the National Debtline and the Consumer Credit Counselling Service. It can also be important to contact a lender and tell them about problems with repayment. Box 4.7 gives an example of the kind of tips for dealing with debt that are available from many organisations without charge – in this case from the OFT (2005).

Box 4.7 Money and credit: tips on debt

- Get free advice.
- Don't panic or ignore the problem: unopened bills won't go away.
- You can't ignore your debts. Better to pay a small amount than nothing at all – those you owe money to may be prepared to accept low repayments.
- If struggling with store or credit cards, stop using them.
- Work out a realistic budget that covers all your income and spending. Check whether there are any benefits or tax credits you are entitled to that you are not getting.
- Decide which debts take priority – like mortgage or rent – and which cost you most through penalties or higher interest rates.
- Only agree to pay off debts at a rate that you can keep up – don't offer more than you can afford.
- Contact those who you owe money to as soon as possible. Let them know that you are having problems. Many companies will be helpful if you talk to them.
- If organisations won't accept your repayment offers, seek advice.
- If you get a threatening letter, get advice from your local Citizens Advice Bureau or trading standards service.
- If a debt collector calls at your home, you don't have to let them in. If you want time to get advice arrange a later appointment. If a debt collector or lender harasses you contact your local Citizens Advice Bureau or trading standards service.

- Check if a loan will be secured on your home. If it is and you do not keep up repayments you could lose your home. If you do not understand the terms of a loan get advice.
- If you're thinking of taking out a new loan to pay off debt, make sure you find out the total cost of the loan, not just the monthly repayments.
- Think very carefully before borrowing more to pay off your debts. Get impartial advice and don't rush into signing anything you don't understand.
- If you are thinking of using a fee-charging debt management company, then make sure you understand exactly what you are signing up to – check what fees you will be paying to a debt management company and how long it will take you to pay off your debts.
- Keep copies of all letters you send and receive about your debts.

(OFT, 2005)

6 Conclusion

This chapter has explored personal debt within the UK. In Section 2, we examined overall levels of debt, before going on to explain how debt affects different households in different ways. Specifically, low-income households and families with children are more likely to get into difficulties, mostly linked to unsecured debt. Section 3 also explored the different costs associated with debt and highlighted the role of APR in making cost comparisons. The position of debt as a liability in the financial balance sheet and the interrelationship between such liabilities and expenditure was explained in Section 4. Section 5 investigated the issues related to funding a purchase through debt, and again highlighted the role of an individual's social and economic circumstances in shaping available choices.

Thinking through and understanding the issues covered in this chapter, such as an awareness of the social and economic context, and knowledge of the mechanics of debt, helps to build financial capability. Chapter 5 will add to this knowledge and understanding by focusing on savings and investments.

Answer to Activity

Answer to Activity 4.3

1 £50,000 × $\frac{5}{100}$ = £2500

2 £50,000 × $\frac{35}{100}$ = £17,500

3 £50,000 × $\frac{7.5}{100}$ = £3750

4 £50,000 × $\frac{6.7}{100}$ = £3350 ■■■

References

Bank of England (2005) 'Table A5.8 Quarterly total lending to individuals: growth rates'; 'Table A5.9 Quarterly total lending to individuals: net lending' [online], http://www.bankofengland.co.uk/statistics/ms/2005/may/taba5.8.xls and http://www.bankofengland.co.uk/statistics/ms/2005/may/taba5.9.xls (Accessed 18 August 2005).

Bell, M. (2005) 'A matter of no small interests: real short-term interest rates and inflation since the 1990s', speech by Marion Bell, member, Monetary Policy Committee (MPC) to the Institute of Directors and Milton Keynes Chambers of Commerce at Cranfield University, 2 March.

Bridges, S. and Disney, R. (2004) 'Use of credit arrears on debt among low income families in the United Kingdom', *Fiscal Studies*, vol. 25, no. 1, pp. 1–25.

Brown, S., Taylor, K. and Price, S.W. (2005) 'Debt and distress: evaluating the psychological cost of credit', *Journal of Economic Psychology*, vol. 26, pp. 642–3.

Citizens Advice (2003) *In Too Deep: CAB Clients' Experience of Debt*, Citizens Advice and Citizens Advice Scotland [online], http://www.citizensadvice.org.uk/in-too-deep.pdf (Accessed 20 December 2005).

Competition Commission (2005) *Store Cards – No Competitive Pressure on APRs and Insurance Charges*, News Release, 14 September [online], http://www.competition-commission.org.uk/press_rel/2005/sep/pdf/57-05.pdf (Accessed 21 December 2005).

Credit Action (2005) *Debt Facts and Figures – Compiled 1st November 2005* [online], http://www.creditaction.org.uk/debtstats.htm (Accessed 7 November 2005).

Debelle, G. (2004) 'Household debt and the macroeconomy', *BIS Quarterly Review*, March, pp. 51–64.

Del-Rio, A. and Young, G. (2005) 'The determinants of unsecured borrowing: evidence from the British Household Panel Survey', Bank of England Working Paper Number 263, London, Bank of England.

Department of Trade and Industry (DTI) (2004) *Tackling Over-indebtedness: Action Plan 2004* [online], http://www.dti.gov.uk/ccp/topics1/pdf1/overdebt0704.pdf (Accessed 20 December 2005).

Department of Trade and Industry (DTI) (2005) *Over-Indebtedness in Britain: A DTI Report on the MORI Financial Services Survey 2004* [online], http://www.dti.gov.uk/ccp/topics1/pdf1/debtdtionmori.pdf (Accessed 20 December 2005).

Furnham, A. and Argle, M. (1998) *The Psychology of Money*, London, Routledge.

Gross, D.B. and Souleles, N.S. (2002) 'Do liquidity constraints and interest rates matter for consumer behavior? Evidence from credit card data', *The Quarterly Journal of Economics*, vol. 117, pp. 149–85.

Kempson, E. (2001) Select Committee on Social Security, *Minutes of Evidence*, Memorandum submitted by Elaine Kempson, Bristol, Personal Finance Research Centre, University of Bristol (SF 41).

Kempson, E., McKay, S. and Willitts, M. (2004) 'Characteristics of families in debt and the nature of indebtedness', Research Report No. 211, London, Department for Work and Pensions.

Lury, C. (2004) 'Everyday life and the economy', in Bennett, T. and Watson, D. (eds) *Understanding Everyday Life*, Oxford, Blackwell.

May, O., Tudela, M. and Young, G. (2004) 'British household indebtedness and financial stress: a household-level picture', *Bank of England Quarterly Bulletin*, Winter, pp. 414–28.

Office of Fair Trading (OFT) (2005) *Money and Credit – Tips on Debt* [online], http://www.oft.gov.uk/consumer/money/tips.htm (Accessed 19 December 2005).

Oxera (2004) *Are UK Households Over-indebted?*, Oxford, Oxford Economic Research Associates.

The Guardian (2004) 'Landmark ruling as judge erases couple's debt', 28 October [online], http://money.guardian.co.uk/creditanddebt/debt/story/0,1456,1338330,00.html (Accessed 21 December 2005).

The Guardian (2005) 'Court cancels debt that grew from £6,000 to £380,000', 28 July [online], http://money.guardian.co.uk/creditanddebt/story/0,1456,1537662,00.html (Accessed 21 December 2005).

Tudela, M. and Young, G. (2005) 'The determinants of household debt and balance sheets in the United Kingdom', Bank of England Working Paper no. 266, London, Bank of England.

UK Parliament (2003) *Report Published on Transparency of Credit Card Charges*, Treasury Committee Press Notices, 17 December [online], http://www.parliament.uk/parliamentary_committees/treasury_committee/tc171203_04.cfm (Accessed 20 December 2005).

Savings and investments

Chapter 5

Janette Rutterford

Contents

1 Introduction

In Charles Dickens's *David Copperfield*, Mr Micawber infamously mused that an annual income of £20, coupled with an expenditure of £19, 19 shillings and sixpence (leaving sixpence over to save) was happiness itself. Whereas the result of spending £20 and sixpence (and having to borrow the difference) would be misery. Linking happiness or misery to having surplus income or surplus expenditure may be somewhat simplistic, but for many people having spare income, and thus an ability to save, can indeed help make life easier and more rewarding. This chapter, along with Chapter 7 which specifically focuses on saving for retirement purposes, explores the situation where households do have surplus income and can hence save money. We'll look at the importance of savings, why households save, and the different ways in which they can save.

I will begin the chapter by defining some terms you are going to come across. First, I want to draw a distinction between the definitions of saving and savings. **Saving** refers to a *flow* of money in a particular time period – such as putting money into a building society account. By contrast, **savings** (note the plural) is the current value of the total accumulated sum of previous saving. Savings is therefore the value of the *stock* of such savings that a household has at a particular point in time. Saving is connected to savings because saving in any given time period will add to the accumulated stock of savings. Consequently, if I already have £100 in a building society account, that £100 is my savings, but if I put in an additional £25 a month into the account, I am saving £25 a month – after another two months, my savings will have increased to £150 (plus any interest earned).

In Sections 2 and 3, I use the terms 'saving' and 'savings' in the same way as the UK Government's official definitions, to encompass putting money into both 'savings products', such as deposit accounts, and 'investment products', such as shares and government bonds. However, you will notice that this chapter is called 'Savings *and* investments'. This is because in personal finance a distinction is often made between the two. Sometimes, the distinction isn't too clear, but we shall explore the difference between them in Sections 4 and 5. I will then look at how the different savings and investment products can be analysed in Section 6. Section 7 considers ethical investments, and Section 8 applies the financial planning model to decisions about savings and investments.

A key thing about saving is that it *defers* (or puts off) consumption today for consumption at some time in the future. This future may be next month (such as a night out), next year (perhaps for a holiday), or many years ahead (in the case of a young person saving for retirement). Saving can even be for after death, such as when people save in order to bequest or leave money for their children. This contrasts with the taking out of debt which, as you saw in Chapter 4, Section 5, was described as *bringing forward* consumption by buying now and paying later.

Chapter 4, Section 4.2 showed the interrelationship between liabilities and expenditure. There is a similar link to point out here between assets (such as savings) and income. The receipt of income immediately adds to assets, for instance, when income is paid into a bank account. Such assets may only be temporary because the money is then used in the typical outgoings of a household paying bills and living expenses, but any surplus income that isn't used adds to the households' assets over the longer term. In turn, assets like savings usually produce an income such as interest on a savings account. This interrelationship is summarised in Figure 5.1.

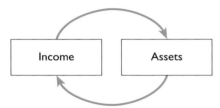

Figure 5.1 *The interrelationship between assets and income*

One other important point to note is that households often simultaneously have debts *and* savings – they are not mutually exclusive. For example, many households have a mortgage and a savings account. They can also be saving (for example, contributing to a pension fund) and taking out more debt (for instance, adding more to a credit card bill).

2   Savings in the UK

So how much savings do UK households have? Data based on the *Family Resources Survey 2003–04* (DWP, 2005) provide evidence to explore this question. Remember, by referring to savings we mean the *stock* of such savings that UK households have. Table 5.1 shows the percentage of households that have different levels of savings (excluding savings through pension schemes). As you might expect, households have different levels of savings, with 27 per cent having no savings at all, while 15 per cent have savings of more than £20,000.

The Office for National Statistics says significant caution needs to be exercised when drawing firm conclusions from data on savings such as that presented in Table 5.1.

Table 5.1 Percentage of households with different amounts of savings, 2003/04

Savings	All households (%)
No savings	27
Less than £1500	19
£1500 but less than £3000	8
£3000 but less than £8000	16
£8000 but less than £10 000	4
£10 000 but less than £16 000	7
£16 000 but less than £20 000	3
£20 000 or more	15

Note: Figures do not add to 100, due to rounding.

Source: DWP, 2005, Table 5.9

Activity 5.1

Why do you think the ONS might suggest such caution?

Comment

The reason for the caution is linked to how data on savings are collected. Much official government data are based on surveys where households are asked questions via a questionnaire. An estimated one in ten households simply does not know the value of its savings, while others may deliberately understate the value of any assets they have. Disclosing financial data can be seen as sensitive, and so collecting such data accurately can be problematic. ■ ■ ■

The data are interesting, but do not tell us very much about why some households save and others don't. The *Family Resources Survey* (DWP, 2005) breaks down savings by some of the social and economic variables that have already been discussed in this book, such as income, household composition, age and ethnicity of households, and these can help explain the differences in household saving. The findings can be summarised as follows:

■ In general, low-income households have lower levels of savings, and higher-income households have higher levels of savings.

- Households where the named head or spouse of a household is unemployed or disabled are much more likely to have no savings at all.

- Pensioner couples, single male pensioner households, and couples without children tend to have higher savings, while single adults with children households have the lowest savings.

- Levels of savings among Asian and Black ethnic groups are on average lower than White households.

Some of the above points remind us that saving will not be as easy for everyone. It is easier to build up savings as household income increases. For those on lower incomes, savings have to be built up through the kind of careful budgeting that you saw in Chapter 3, Section 4.

Table 5.2 below and overleaf provides a breakdown of the types of savings, investments and accounts that households have in the UK. As you can see, almost nine out of ten households have a current account, and over half have other (savings) accounts with a bank or building society. Over one-fifth of households have stocks and shares, and over one-fifth of households have Premium Bonds. We shall be looking at all of these products in more detail in this chapter in Sections 4 and 5. It's noteworthy that 6 per cent (about 1 in 16) of households don't have *any* kind of bank account, let alone any savings.

Table 5.2 UK households with types of savings, 2004

Type of account	%
Current account	89
Post Office account	6
Basic bank account	3
Tax-Exempt Special Savings Account (TESSA)	7
Individual Savings Account (ISA)	33
Other bank/building society accounts	54
Stocks and shares/member of a share club	22
Personal Equity Plans (PEPs)	8
Unit trusts	5
Gilts	1
Premium Bonds	23
National Savings Bonds	4
Guaranteed Equity Bonds	–

Table 5.2 (Continued)

Type of account	%
Company share scheme/profit sharing	4
Save As You Earn	1
Any type of account	94
No accounts	6
Direct Payment Account	93

Source: DWP, 2005, Table 5.3

2.1 The UK's saving ratio

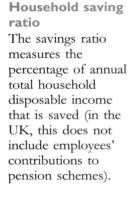

Household saving ratio

The savings ratio measures the percentage of annual total household disposable income that is saved (in the UK, this does not include employees' contributions to pension schemes).

Another type of data to look at, apart from that of savings, is data about saving. This is usually done by examining what is called the **household saving ratio**. This is the percentage of annual household disposable income that is saved rather than spent. Figure 5.2 shows the household saving ratio for the UK. It shows that the household saving ratio has ranged from a peak in 1980 (at 12.4 per cent) to a low in 1988 (of 4.9 per cent); then another peak in 1992 (of 11.6 per cent) and back to a low of 4.9 per cent in 1999. It therefore shows how the household saving ratio tends to be quite cyclical.

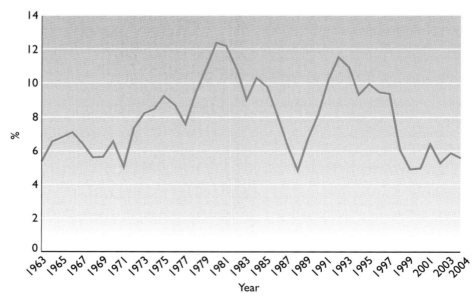

Figure 5.2 *UK household saving ratio, 1963–2004*
Source: adapted from Halifax Financial Services, 2005, p. 2

How can we explain these changes? One factor has been the state of the UK economy. When the economy has been growing quickly and so personal incomes have been rising, the household saving ratio has been lower. This can be explained by the fact that when things are going well, confidence is high and people tend to spend more. This was the picture in the late 1980s and in the early 2000s. When the economy has experienced very low growth or even **recession**, such as in the early 1980s and again during 1989–92, and incomes were not rising as fast or falling, the household saving ratio was higher. This is because when people are more concerned about their future, they tend to cut back on spending and save more.

Other factors also help to explain the changes in the UK household saving ratio. When inflation was high, for example, in the mid and late 1970s, households needed to save more to stop the real value of their savings falling – consequently the household saving ratio increased. The household saving ratio averaged 8.5 per cent during the period of relatively higher inflation between 1969 and 1991 (inflation averaged 10 per cent), but it averaged 6.2 per cent during the periods of relatively low inflation in the 1960s, and 5.6 per cent since 1998 when inflation has again been low. More recent data suggest the state of the housing market may also be important. Figure 5.3 shows changes in the household saving ratio and changes in house prices in the UK between 1984 and 2004.

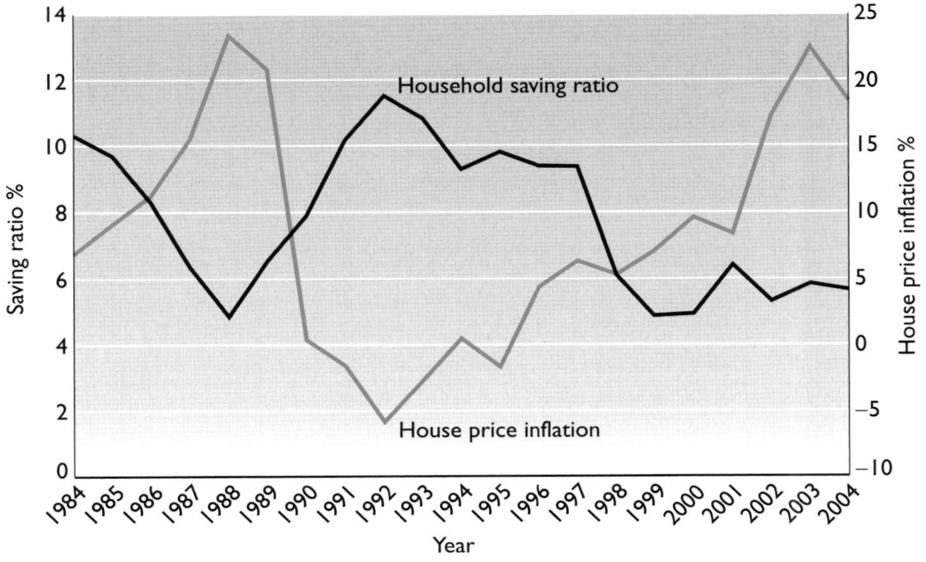

Recession
A reduction in the level of economic activity measured by two consecutive quarters of negative economic growth.

Figure 5.3 *House prices and the household saving ratio, 1984–2004*
Source: Halifax Financial Services, 2005, p. 2

Activity 5.2

1   Look at Figure 5.3 and describe any pattern between house prices and the household saving ratio.

2   Can you think of any reasons to explain this pattern?

Comment

1   There appears to be an **inverse relationship** between house prices and the household saving ratio. That is, when house price increases were higher (for example in the late 1980s and early 2000s), the household saving ratio was lower, and when house prices were lower (for instance, in the early 1990s), the household saving ratio was higher.

2   This may be because people often feel that they do not have to save as much when their wealth is increasing due to the increased value of their house. Conversely, in the early 1990s there was an increase in saving as house prices fell and households repaid some of their borrowings. Chapter 6 discusses housing in detail and explores some of the reasons for such changes in house prices, and how this is linked to net wealth and the financial balance sheet. ■ ■ ■

The UK has a relatively low household saving ratio compared with other countries, as shown in Figure 5.4.

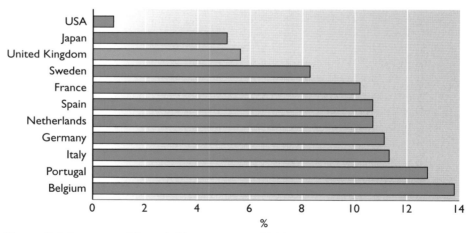

Figure 5.4 *International household saving ratios, 2004*
Source: Halifax Financial Services, 2005, p. 3

The data in Figure 5.4 show the household saving ratio varying significantly between countries. The data are **cross sectional** – a snapshot of a moment in time. As a result, we cannot draw too many conclusions, but the data are still interesting – the UK household saving ratio is far higher than that of the USA, it is slightly above Japan's, but far lower than that of many other European Union (EU) countries. This may reflect different cultural approaches to the importance of saving. At the end of 2005, there was some evidence (see Box 5.1) that UK households were increasing the amount they were saving, perhaps due to worries about the levels of debt discussed in Chapter 4. Such an increase in saving would increase the UK's household saving ratio.

Cross sectional
Data relating to different variables at the same time period.

Box 5.1 Savings hit record high as concerns mount over debt

Press Association
Wednesday December 14, 2005

Consumers are increasing the amount they save each month as they finally show signs of tightening their belts, research revealed today.

People saved an average of 7.2% of their income during the three months to the end of November, the highest proportion since National Savings and Investments first started the survey in September 2004.

They are now setting aside an average of £174.43 a month – another record figure and up from just £158.26 over the summer and £163.40 during the same period last year.

Going forward people hope to save even more, planning to set aside an average of 14.8% of their income, also the highest figure since the survey first began. Overall 55% of people said they were now paying money into a savings account on a regular basis.

The group said the rise in people's level of saving had coincided with a fall in spending on the high street, suggesting people were finally beginning to heed warnings about taking on too much debt.

(*Guardian Unlimited*, 14 December 2005)

2.2 Why is the level of savings important?

Household savings are important for the individuals within those households. In Table 5.1, you saw that 27 per cent of UK households reported that they have no savings at all. An unexpected event that results in financial costs could easily lead such households into debt – or compel them to make cuts on their other expenditure. Having savings also allows people to take advantage of opportunities – such as being able to pay for education or start a business. I will look at the importance of savings for households in more detail in Section 3.

Savings are also important for the broader economy. As you saw in Chapter 1, Section 3, there is interdependence between the household sector and other sectors of the economy. The level of household savings has important effects for the corporate sector, and is another example of that interdependence. For example, by the act of saving (to increase the accumulated level of savings), households are not buying the goods and services that firms sell. However, by saving, households are placing money in financial institutions, and this provides an important source of funds for firms to expand and to invest themselves.

In addition, governments have an interest in household savings. One reason for this is that governments often spend more than the receipts they have from taxation. Thus, they have to borrow the difference, including directly from the public. Governments have encouraged people to save in government savings schemes (and, effectively, loan the government money), such as through National Savings & Investments Certificates and Premium Bonds. Figure 5.5 shows some of the different messages that have been used to promote national savings at different times. In the first part of the twentieth century, advertising for Post Office accounts often encouraged workers to save for 'adversity and ill-health' or to grow 'big oaks from little acorns'. During the Second World War, saving was strongly encouraged to provide funds for the war effort. By 1969 an advert encouraged people to save at a time when there was concern that inflation would erode the real value of savings. The final advert is for National Savings & Investments from 2006 – on television, such adverts also featured Sir Alan Sugar.

So, saving can be important for households, firms and governments. Here, I will concentrate on households, and consider first the crucial question of: 'Why do households save?'

Figure 5.5 *Advertisements for government savings schemes over the years: early twentieth century (top left); Second World War (top right); 1960s (bottom left); 2006 (bottom right)*

3 Why do households save?

In Section 1, I explained how saving defers consumption from the present to sometime in the future. Therefore, when thinking about the reasons for households to save, we are really thinking about why households are deferring consumption rather than consuming now.

3.1 Reasons for saving

One important reason for saving is known as the 'precautionary motive' to save – perhaps more commonly known as 'saving for a rainy day'. This involves building up savings to provide for unexpected events and bills. If a household doesn't have *any* savings, and an unexpected event with financial consequences occurs (such as a car being damaged or someone becoming too ill to work and losing their income), then there are only three alternatives:

1 Receiving a pay out from any insurance taken out against such an unexpected event (which is looked at in detail in Chapter 9).
2 Borrowing money (from family, friends, or financial institutions) to pay the unexpected bills.
3 Defaulting on any commitments, for example, not making payments on a car loan or mortgage, with the consequent risk of repossession and negative impact on future credit ratings.

Having savings is an important means of preparing for unexpected life events – the savings act as a buffer to protect a household against these other possibilities.

Savings are an important buffer against unexpected bills

A second reason for saving is to do so for a specific purpose. The advantage of saving for a purpose is that a household can budget more easily, putting so much aside each month (or week), based on a calculation of how much they need for a particular goal. One of the most significant purposes for saving is for retirement, but saving can also be for many other reasons, for instance, saving for a child's university education, sending money abroad to family, or paying the costs of a nursing home for a parent.

A third reason for saving may be to accumulate wealth for which, as yet, there is no defined purpose. The savings may later be spent on a variety of things, for example, a second home, cosmetic surgery, a series of holidays after retirement, or leaving an inheritance to children.

These three reasons all underline an important overall aim of having savings – to give a sense of independence and autonomy to do things. For instance, having sufficient savings may enable someone to leave a job or take a break for a few months, or buy things or do things that they wish, or take advantage of opportunities that arise.

3.2 Saving and the life-course

Economists have argued that households' overall levels of savings are linked to the life-course. This can be explained with the income and expenditure diagram shown in Figure 5.6. A theory called the 'life cycle hypothesis' (Modigliani and Brumberg, 1954) predicts that people start their adult life with expenditure exceeding disposable income. For the majority of adult life, people then accumulate savings until retirement (or near retirement), and then use their accumulated savings to provide income. A key motivation for saving is thus saving for retirement.

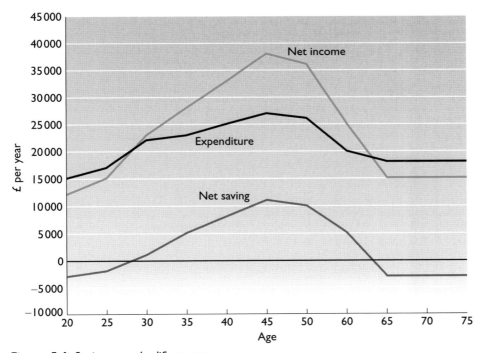

Figure 5.6 *Saving over the life-course*

The line labelled 'Net saving' in Figure 5.6 shows the difference between the two other lines labelled 'Net income' and 'Expenditure'. It starts as negative (where expenditure exceeds net income), then is positive during mid-life when households save, and is negative again in retirement. Such a pattern does not mean that households cannot save and borrow at the same time; indeed, many households will be doing both. For example, taking out a mortgage or borrowing on a credit card while also saving money in a savings account. The important point is that this line shows the **net saving**, after taking into account any borrowing and any repayments of debt. (You saw in the budgeting exercise in Section 4 of Chapter 3 that paying back debts is included in expenditure.) Figure 5.6 clearly does not apply to every household, but it is a useful, visual way of showing how income and expenditure, and net saving, typically change over a life-course.

The various motives for saving can also be linked to the life-course, but in a different way. These are summarised in Table 5.3, which highlights some typical saving motives at different ages for different household types. Often, the marketing departments of financial institutions selling different types of savings and investment products will target different households, depending on what stage of the life-course they are at or on what type of household they are.

Net saving
Household net income minus household expenditure.

Table 5.3 Life-course stage and saving motives

Life-course stage	Examples of saving motives
Young, single	Car, house
Young couple, no children	House
Couple with dependent children	Saving for children's future, retirement
Single with dependent children	Saving for children's future, retirement
Older couple with nearly independent children	Saving for children's future, retirement
Older, single, no children	Retirement
Older couple with independent children	Retirement
Couple, retired	Use savings for income, bequests
Single, retired	Use savings for income, bequests

There is also evidence that motives for household saving differ between countries. Some research carried out on Dutch households (Alessie et al.,

1997) investigated motives for saving over time. Figure 5.7 shows four possible motivations:

1   Saving for a house.

2   Saving for unforeseen circumstances (our 'rainy day').

3   Saving for a child.

4   Saving for old age.

The vertical axis of Figure 5.7 shows the frequency, or proportion out of 1, of households mentioning each possible motive (so that a value of 0.20 is the same as saying that 20 per cent of respondents stated a particular motive). The data covers respondents from age 17 to 78.

The 'rainy day' line is the highest line for the majority of age points in the graph. This means that saving for a rainy day is the most frequently mentioned motive for people of most ages interviewed in the research. Figure 5.7 also shows that housing is most important for Dutch people in their twenties, whereas saving for a child is important at around age forty, and then again in old age, perhaps when the issue of bequests looms large.

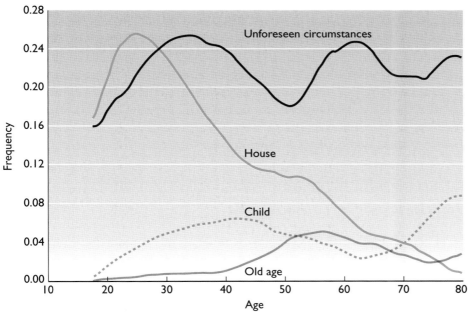

Figure 5.7 *Motives for saving in relation to age for Dutch households*
Source: Alessie et al., 1997, p. 30

It's noticeable that the Dutch do not see saving for old age as their number one concern, at any age. This may be because government policy on welfare provision can also influence saving. With the Dutch state pension scheme being relatively generous, people approaching retirement may not feel that they have to set aside additional personal savings to supplement the pension they expect to receive from the state.

Other research, such as that by Horioka and Watanabe (1997), showed that Japanese households saved mainly for retirement and for the 'rainy day' motive. Webley et al. (2000) compared the saving motives of households in Italy and the UK. The research concluded that for Italians the most important motives were to save for their children's education and for medical care. For UK savers, saving towards future purchases was more important – perhaps reflecting the importance of the UK's 'consumer society'.

The above discussion highlights how motives for saving can differ in different countries, and how they are also linked to the life-course. None the less, whatever the motive to save, life events at any age can have an impact on saving plans – sometimes leading to starting, or undertaking more, saving, but at other times to less saving or ceasing to save altogether. Table 5.4 highlights the effect of certain life events on saving behaviour.

Table 5.4 Effect of selected life events on saving behaviour of people of working age in Great Britain, 1991–2000[1]

	Percentage of non-savers starting to save after the event	Percentage of savers ceasing to save after the event
Divorce/separation	15	46
Marriage	25	29
Having a first child	23	41
Having a second or subsequent child	14	38
Becoming unemployed	8	71
Moving into employment from unemployment	29	38
Moving house	20	40
Becoming a carer for at least 20 hours per week	18	33

[1] Data have been pooled for the period 1991 to 2000.

Source: *Social Trends*, 2005, no. 35, p. 82, Table 5.27

It is highly likely that you either have experienced, or will in your lifetime experience, one of the events in Table 5.4, and so it is important to think about some of their consequences. The data show unemployment as having the greatest impact on stopping saving, with 71 per cent of savers who experienced unemployment ceasing to save. Moving back to employment has the biggest impact in causing non-savers to start to save, with 29 per cent starting to save. Unemployment and employment have a large direct impact on an individual's or household's income and, hence, their ability to save. The figures for divorce/separation, marriage, and having children are also interesting. For example, you saw in Chapter 3, Section 5 that people joining together to form a household brings economies of scale, thus giving more scope for saving in a household budget. So the high figure for non-savers starting to save after marriage isn't too surprising. Similarly, divorce or separation may lose such economies of scale, making saving harder. So, again, it is perhaps not surprising to see that 46 per cent of savers cease to do so after divorce or separation.

3.3 Saving within the household

One of the themes of this book is to explore the interrelationship of individuals and households. In Chapter 3, Section 5 you saw that the way in which money is managed by couples may influence control over expenditure. This is also true of saving, as having access to income in the household is fundamental to being able to save. Having individual savings, as well as joint savings, can provide more financial security for people in relationships. This can be linked back to the idea that independence is an important overall aim for having savings. This is particularly important in terms of saving for retirement, but also when relationships break down. With over one-third of marriages ending in divorce (and higher rates of separation among non-married couples), preparing for such an eventuality may be sensible. As the numbers of women in paid employment have increased, women can increasingly save from their own income and make their own saving choices.

There are also practical considerations in deciding who should save in a household. As you shall see in the next section, the UK Government gives tax incentives to save, and it may be advantageous to spread these across all members of the household when building up savings, for example, by putting the savings in the name of a non-earning spouse or partner. Similarly, splitting savings and particular investments that are likely to generate capital gains in the long run, can reduce the future liability to Capital Gains Tax.

4 Making sense of different savings products

The remainder of this chapter is going to explore the different saving choices available when a household has surplus income. As mentioned in Section 1, in this section and in Section 5, I distinguish between savings products that earn interest where the nominal value of the capital stays the same, and investment products that can make capital gains but also capital losses. I will return to this distinction in more detail in Section 5.

Starting with savings products, there are thousands of different products available, and such choice may seem daunting. Yet it is possible to make sense of the choice with reference to available interest rates (considered in both nominal and real terms), and the taxation of that interest. An understanding of these, as well as a clear idea about the reason for wanting to save, should provide enough background information to make a more informed decision about a product.

4.1 Interest rates

Annual Equivalent Rate (AER)
AER or Annual Equivalent Rate is the rate of interest on savings products calculated to take into account different payment patterns.

The financial services industry is now required to show interest rates on all savings products so that they can be easily compared. You saw in Chapter 4, Section 3 how interest rates on debt products are expressed as the Annual Percentage Rate (APR). For savings products, the comparable rate is called the **Annual Equivalent Rate (AER)**. The AER and the APR are similar in principle, and allow a comparison of financial products with different payment patterns. The AER is the annual interest rate that savers receive, taking into account when interest is actually paid (for instance, annually, quarterly or monthly).

Activity 5.3

Suppose that a savings account offers an interest rate of 5 per cent, with interest payable either weekly, monthly or quarterly. Which account will have the highest AER?

Comment

The more frequent the payment, the more *compounding* of interest there will be. Therefore, 5 per cent interest paid weekly will have a higher AER than 5 per cent paid monthly, which in turn will have a higher AER than 5 per cent paid quarterly. ∎ ∎ ∎

Chapter 4, Section 3 also introduced the idea of real interest rates. Thinking in real terms can help to understand what is happening to the value of savings over time. For example, if savings can earn 5 per cent interest, the significance of this is very different if inflation is at either 1 per cent or 6 per cent. In the latter case, the real interest rate is actually negative, that is, your savings could buy less in a year's time, even after the receipt of interest. Theoretically, this could cause some people to decide to consume more now and save less. Conversely, as you saw in Section 2.1, when inflation has been high in the UK, it can make people want to save more to make sure the real value of their savings is not reduced.

One way to avoid the risk of having the value of savings eroded by unexpected inflation is to invest in inflation-proofed savings products. These are offered by National Savings & Investments in the form of their Index-linked Savings Certificates. In 2006, these offered holders a real annual interest rate of 1.05 to 1.10 per cent, with inflation protection, that is, interest of 1.05 to 1.10 per cent over and above the rate of inflation. The downside is that this is a relatively low real rate of interest. However, there have been times, for example the early 1980s (as we saw in Figure 4.2 in Chapter 4), when inflation and nominal interest rates were both high but real interest rates were low so that this kind of inflation protection was an attractive proposition.

With many accounts, the rate of interest varies when the Bank of England changes base rates (see Chapter 4, Box 4.2). With 'variable rate' deposit accounts with a high-street bank, building society, or internet bank, the interest rate changes over time in response to changes in base rates.

Some savings products, often called 'term bonds', lock the saver in for a fixed period of, say, two, three or five years, at a fixed interest rate. Some products pay regular interest during the period; others roll up the interest into the final repayment, as do National Savings Certificates. These products may allow money to be kept in for longer than the fixed term, but not necessarily at the same interest rate. Depending on the product, interest can be paid monthly, quarterly, six monthly or yearly. Fixed term savings products paying regular (usually monthly) interest are sometimes called 'pensioner' bonds because they are designed for people (typically pensioners) who rely on the income from their savings as a large part of their total household income.

The attraction of fixed term interest rates is that the rate is guaranteed for the whole period, and not subject to the fluctuations of the base rate. The rate may also be higher than a straightforward savings account because the financial institution is sure of the saver's money for the whole term. The disadvantage is that there may be no provision for early access to the money, or there may be penalties on early withdrawal, such as the sacrifice of 90 days' worth of interest. These penalties tend to make such products less attractive for 'rainy day' saving. In addition, if interest rates or inflation rates increase, such fixed rates would appear less attractive.

Savings products are available from many banks and building societies

A different savings product from the fixed term account is the notice account. Here, the bank or building society requires a certain number of days 'notice' if the saver wants to withdraw their money (for example, 30, 60, 90 or even 180 days' notice). If the saver wants the money immediately, they can have it, but at a price. The price is usually the deduction of the equivalent number of days' worth of interest, whatever the notice period is, and regardless of how long the money has been deposited for. Conversely, the traditional attraction of the notice account is a higher interest rate than on the straightforward instant access account. This is because, like the fixed term product, the saver is lending the financial institution their money for a longer period of time.

4.2 Before and after tax

Governments have encouraged household saving for many years. Besides advertising campaigns, governments encourage saving through providing tax advantages when people save, either through a lower tax rate on interest (for example, in 2006 in the UK, for basic rate Income Tax payers, Income Tax on income from savings was 20 per cent, compared to the basic rate of Income Tax of 22 per cent) or through certain specific savings products that are exempt from tax.

The interest on savings accounts can either be paid gross (before tax) or net of tax (after tax has been deducted). Most building societies and banks pay interest on accounts net of tax (that is, after deduction of the

20 per cent savings rate Income Tax). In the UK, if someone's income is low enough to attract no tax charge or the lower 10 per cent tax charge, they can claim a refund of the tax deducted by the bank or building society or, in the case of non-tax payers, arrange to be paid interest without deduction of tax. Non-tax payers in the UK have to complete HM Revenue & Customs form R85 in order for the financial institution to be able to pay interest gross. If, on the other hand, someone is a higher rate tax payer, they will have to pay additional Income Tax on the interest on their savings – the difference between the higher Income Tax rate and the basic savings rate: in 2006 in the UK, this was 40 per cent less 20 per cent.

As mentioned above, another way in which governments encourage saving is to allow particular savings products to be exempt from tax completely. In the UK, the most popular is the **Individual Savings Account (ISA)**. In 1999, these accounts replaced TESSAs (Tax-Exempt Special Savings Accounts) and PEPs (Personal Equity Plans). Until at least 5 April 2010, up to £7000 per annum (p.a.) can be put into an ISA, including £3000 in a cash savings account called a 'Cash ISA'. The balance of £4000 (or the full £7000) can go into investments, which I will discuss in Section 5. The tax advantage of Cash ISAs is that no income tax at all is payable on the interest, and no tax is payable when any money is withdrawn. This means that, if an interest rate of 5 per cent p.a. is offered on a Cash ISA, the saver receives the full 5 per cent. In contrast, another bank or building society account may offer 5 per cent gross, but if 20 per cent is deducted on behalf of a basic rate tax payer, the net interest paid will only be 80 per cent of 5 per cent, that is, 4 per cent net.

As a result, Cash ISAs have been popular with the general public. From Table 5.2, you can see that one-third of households held an ISA in 2004. Many of these households save the full £3000 in a Cash ISA each tax year. As well as having tax advantages, Cash ISAs are attractive because money from many can be withdrawn at short notice; there is also no need to fill out a tax return for an ISA. The interest paid on Cash ISAs is typically higher than the 'net' interest offered on conventional savings products. The only savers for whom ISAs do not necessarily improve the net return are savers who do not pay income tax. For tax payers, the higher the tax rate they pay, the more attractive Cash ISAs will be.

4.3 Savings and the internet

In the mid 2000s, there were major developments in 'e-banking' or online banking. Online savings accounts can usually only be accessed online. When the savings are needed, with many accounts the saver transfers

Individual Savings Account (ISA)
An ISA allows up to £7000 savings per tax year, with no tax on the capital gain or interest received (dividend and share-based income is taxed at 10 per cent). In each tax year you can either save in one Maxi ISA, which can include both cash (up to £3000) and shares, or you can have two Mini ISAs – one for up to £3000 cash, and one for up to £4000 shares. You cannot invest in both a Mini ISA and a Maxi ISA in the same tax year, and you can only open one Maxi ISA in each tax year.

money from their online savings account into their current account electronically, and can then access the money from the current account. Some online accounts have a cash card, so money can be withdrawn via cash machines. Interest rates are usually higher for such 'e-savings' accounts because savers themselves manage the account, thus reducing the costs to the bank or building society in terms of issuing a passbook or requiring branch availability to make transactions. This does mean that the saver has to have access to the internet, and some institutions, although not all, require a current account to be held with them as well as the online savings account.

To help think about some of the ideas covered in this section, I want you to look at an example of some different savings products. For this example, I am going to use some typical high-street bank and building society savings products that were on offer in 2006 (see Table 5.5).

Table 5.5 Examples of different savings accounts

Name of account	Interest tier	AER (gross p.a.) %	Net p.a. %
Internet Savings An instant savings online savings account	£1+	4.75	3.80
Instant Access An instant access account with passbook or cash card	£1–£4999 £5000–£19 999 £20 000–£49 999 Over £50 000	1.30 1.50 1.90 2.20	1.04 1.20 1.52 1.76
Notice Account A 60-day notice account with passbook	£1–£19 999 £20 000–£49 999 Over £50 000	2.80 2.90 3.00	2.24 2.32 2.40
1 Year Fixed Rate Bond (interest paid annually)	£1–£250 000	4.50	3.60
Instant Access ISA A tax-free instant access account with passbook	£1+	4.60	n.a.

Activity 5.4

Look at the examples of different types of savings account in Table 5.5.

1   What are the key factors that explain why some accounts offer higher rates than others?

2   Why would anyone want to take out an 'Instant Access' account?

Comment

The time period for which savings are tied up affects interest rates. For instance, the 1 Year Fixed Rate Bond and the Notice Account have higher net rates than the Instant Access account. The ISA (maximum £3000 cash savings a year at 4.60 per cent) is not subject to tax. The amount saved also influences the rates offered for both the Instant Access and Notice accounts: the higher the savings deposited, the higher the rate. The Internet Savings account can offer higher rates due to the lower costs of managing the account. None the less, some people will still choose the most basic Instant Access account, mainly because it provides plenty of flexibility, with instant access by using a cash card so that money can be accessed night or day – the downside is the lower interest rate. ■ ■ ■

In this section, I have explained why interest rates offered on savings products vary, but we have not yet considered the question of risk. In Chapter 4, it was the credit risk of the individual borrowing money that mattered. Here, it is the risk to the saver that is important. One risk is that savers will not receive their money back plus the promised interest. What would happen if a bank or building society were to collapse? In the UK, the Financial Services Compensation Scheme provides protection; this scheme offers compensation of 100 per cent of the first £2000 of savings, and 90 per cent of the next £33,000 of savings, to a maximum compensation payment of £31,700 (in 2006). Another risk is that inflation can erode the value of the savings if the interest rate is less than the rate of inflation (i.e. there is a negative *real* interest rate).

5   Making sense of investment products

I now want to examine investment products. In personal finance, the terms 'savings' and 'investments' have different meanings. As explained earlier, savings accounts refer to any form of deposit account that pays interest on top of the amount deposited. The amount deposited is not at risk unless the institution defaults. Investments also allow interest or dividends to be paid but, crucially, the investment itself can fall or rise in value. Financial investments are those products with the phrase in the small print: 'the value of your investment can go down as well as up'.

Remember that investments can fall in value

Financial investments, which for simplicity I shall call 'investments', include shares and bonds. The amount invested, called the 'principal' or 'capital', is usually at risk, as well as the rate of return on the investment. This means that for investments it is not income alone that is relevant (as the rate of interest is on savings products) but the *total* return, which may be made up partly of income and partly of the change in the value of the capital. Consequently, if the price of the investment has gone up, a capital gain will be made, or if the price goes down, a capital loss is made.

Newspapers often print cases of investors who have lost money on investment schemes. With increased regulation of **financial intermediaries** and other financial firms, including the actual providers of savings and investment products and their company salespeople, and the requirement to explain fully the characteristics of the financial products they sell, mis-selling of financial products should in theory be unlikely, but it still happens. Not everyone reads the small print or understands all of the choices, and all of the products' details, but the saying 'the safest way to double your money is to fold it in half' is perhaps a reminder that promises of high returns usually carry higher risks. This can be linked to a risk–return spectrum. Products with low risks tend to have lower returns, and those with higher risks have *potentially* higher returns (see Figure 5.8).

Financial intermediaries
Persons and institutions who arrange investments (and other products) on behalf of others, such as financial advisers and brokers.

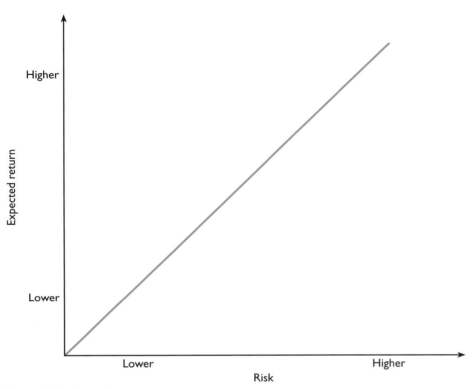

Figure 5.8 *The risk–return spectrum*

Box 5.2 offers a cautionary tale by describing how investors lost money through investing in what were called 'high income bonds'. With these particular products, people were offered very attractive guaranteed interest rates. In fact, the interest was guaranteed, but *not* the capital.

Box 5.2   The risk of investing

Some top fund management companies fear the UK savings industry could be brought into disrepute as controversial high-income bond funds launched at the height of the **bull market** reach maturity with devastating losses.

Senior executives at UBS and Skandia have broken their silence, warning that an 'ugly story' surrounding the selling of high-income bonds could haunt the savings industry as it struggles to deal with the Equitable Life and split capital trust scandals.

The warnings come as the Financial Services Authority, the UK's City watchdog, steps up its campaign to stamp out mis-selling. It is understood to have launched formal investigations into some leading fund managers and product distributors that could lead to fines and public 'naming and shaming'.

Some 250,000 investors bought high-income bond funds, pouring in

Bull market
A market in which prices are rising. A 'bull' is a person who expects that the stock market or the price of a particular share will rise and so buys in the hope of making a profit on selling at a higher price.

£5bn of their savings. Several high-income funds are controversial because they guarantee a certain level of income – but not the capital. With markets plunging dramatically, it means that some investors may not get back any of their original capital.

(*Financial Times*, Financial Times Report – FT Fund Management, p. 1, 3 February 2003)

I will now look at the two main types of financial investment: shares and bonds.

5.1 Shares

Shares (or equities)
A part ownership in a company.

Dividends
The part of a company's post-tax profits distributed to shareholders, usually expressed as an amount per share.

Shares are also sometimes called 'equities'. They are a form of investment that entitles the holder to a share or part ownership in a company. Depending on the type of share, this may entitle the shareholder to vote on how the company is run. Shares also usually entitle their owners to the receipt of **dividends**, paid by the company out of the profit that it makes. The receipt of these dividends is, for the shareholder, the income element of the return from their investment in the shares.

The price at which a particular share can be bought and sold will vary from minute to minute; for example, on the day of writing this chapter, I looked up the price of British Petroleum (BP) shares and saw how they had changed during one day (see Figure 5.9).

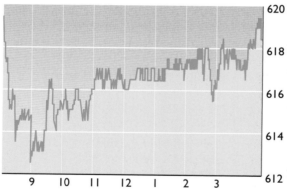

Figure 5.9 *BP share price, 11 November 2005*
Source: FT.com, 2005

In Figure 5.9, the price of the share is expressed in pence, and shown on the right-hand axis. You can see that it ranged from a low of 613 pence at 9 a.m. to over 619 pence at the beginning and end of the day (the bottom axis indicates the time of day).

Shares are bought through a **broker.** A broker can be found in high-street banks, on the internet, or in a stockbroking firm. For online broking, there is typically a flat-rate charge for any transaction, say £12 for one-off trades, or £10 per trade for frequent traders, so it is not usually worth buying or selling shares in very small amounts. Conventional stockbrokers may also charge a percentage commission on the value of the transaction as well as a minimum commission. Stamp Duty of 0.5 per cent is paid when shares are bought, with a minimum £5 charge in 2006 for paper-based transactions (paperless trading, including all internet trading, has no minimum). Stamp Duty is not paid when shares are sold. As an example, Box 5.3 shows what the total bill of buying some British Telecom (BT) shares priced at 217p might be.

Broker
A person who buys and sells securities on behalf of others in return for brokerage or commission.

Box 5.3 The cost of buying £500 worth of BT shares		
230 shares of BT at 217p each		£499.10
Other charges:		
Broker's commission	£12.00	
Stamp Duty: 0.5% of £499.10 (minimum £5)	£ 5.00	
Total other charges		£17.00
Total cost		**£516.10**

Buying shares in a single company, or even holding shares in, say, three companies, is generally considered to be a risky form of investment. This is because owning shares means owning part of a company, and companies are subject to all sorts of risks, both broader economic risks, such as a recession or an increase in the cost of oil, and specific risks to the company, such as the loss of a major contract or increased competition. The share price can go up or down depending on whether the news is good or bad. You saw in Figure 5.9 how the value of BP shares changed in one day; Figures 5.10(a)–(c) show how the share price changed for three major companies – BT, BP and HSBC – over a decade. The share price in pence is on the right-hand axis.

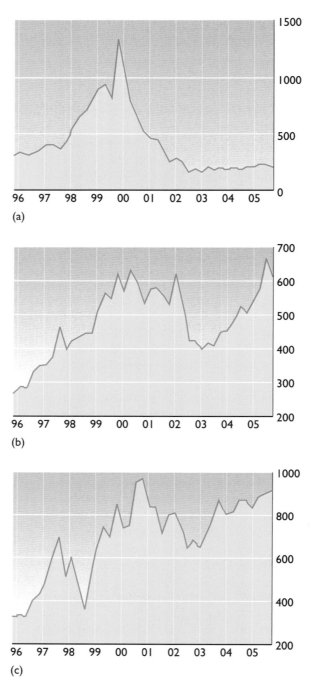

Figure 5.10 *Share prices for (a) BT, (b) BP, and (c) HSBC for the decade 1996–2006*
Source: FT.com, 2005

Activity 5.5

Based on Figures 5.10(a)–(c), if you had decided to buy shares in 1996, which shares would it have been best to buy to make a capital gain?

Comment

The answer isn't straightforward! Both HSBC and BP have made gains over the decade, the former having the greatest increase from just over 300 pence to over 900 pence, while BT's share price decreased over the time period. However, if someone had sold their BT shares in 1999, they would have received around 1300 pence having bought them for around 300 pence in 1996, an excellent return in just three years. Yet what if someone had bought their BT shares in 1999? They would have bought the shares for 1300 pence and in 2005 they would be worth less than 250 pence – quite a loss. In all three companies' cases, it is evident that timing is vital to whether gains or losses are made. ■ ■ ■

Share prices can be seen in most newspapers that report daily on share prices as well as on other information (see Figure 5.11).

You may want to look up the current share prices of the companies listed in Figure 5.11 and see how each price has changed from November 2005 and, if you had invested money in November 2005, whether you would have made a gain or a loss.

Besides the risk of share prices falling and making a capital loss, there are other risks attached to investing in shares. For instance, not all profits are paid out as dividends. Companies tend to keep money back to re-invest in the business; the proposed level of dividends is at the discretion of the directors. In good years, directors may recommend payment of large dividends, but in bad years they may decide not to pay a dividend at all; conversely, they may decide to smooth the level of dividends from year to year. Companies must first pay the interest on their bank loans and on other forms of debt finance before paying out profits to shareholders as dividends.

In Table 5.2, you saw that 22 per cent of households held shares in the UK in 2005. In addition to owning shares directly, shares are also held through individuals having investment funds, such as **unit trusts**, pension funds or investment-linked life assurance. If someone has a pension fund, it is probable that shares are being bought on their behalf. As the percentage of shares held by individual investors on the London Stock Exchange has fallen, so unit trusts and pension funds have taken up the slack. We'll look at this in more detail in Section 6.2.

The better that stock markets perform, the more comfortable may be the retirement for people with such funds. This is why the part of the

Unit trusts
Collective funds that allow private investors to pool their money in a single fund.

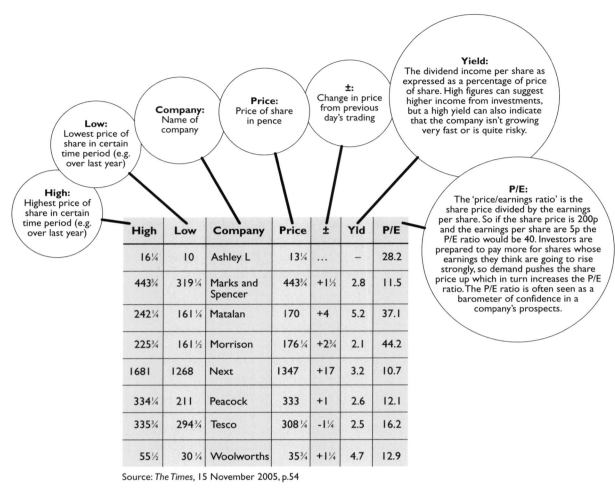

High: Highest price of share in certain time period (e.g. over last year)

Low: Lowest price of share in certain time period (e.g. over last year)

Company: Name of company

Price: Price of share in pence

±: Change in price from previous day's trading

Yield: The dividend income per share as expressed as a percentage of price of share. High figures can suggest higher income from investments, but a high yield can also indicate that the company isn't growing very fast or is quite risky.

P/E: The 'price/earnings ratio' is the share price divided by the earnings per share. So if the share price is 200p and the earnings per share are 5p the P/E ratio would be 40. Investors are prepared to pay more for shares whose earnings they think are going to rise strongly, so demand pushes the share price up which in turn increases the P/E ratio. The P/E ratio is often seen as a barometer of confidence in a company's prospects.

High	Low	Company	Price	±	Yld	P/E
16¼	10	Ashley L	13¼	...	–	28.2
443¾	319¼	Marks and Spencer	443¾	+1½	2.8	11.5
242¼	161¼	Matalan	170	+4	5.2	37.1
225¾	161½	Morrison	176¼	+2¾	2.1	44.2
1681	1268	Next	1347	+17	3.2	10.7
334¼	211	Peacock	333	+1	2.6	12.1
335¾	294¾	Tesco	308¼	-1¼	2.5	16.2
55½	30¼	Woolworths	35¾	+1¼	4.7	12.9

Source: *The Times*, 15 November 2005, p.54

Figure 5.11 *Share prices of selected UK high-street retailers, 15 November 2005*

television and radio news dealing with the 'markets', and the business pages of the newspapers, are relevant to many households, even if they do not own shares directly. In the UK, the Financial Times Stock Exchange (FTSE) 100 Index is often quoted. This is an index that tracks the prices of the shares of the top 100 listed companies on the London Stock Exchange.

5.2 Bonds

Bond

A certificate of debt that is issued by a government or corporation in order to raise money.

The other main kind of investment product is a **bond**, which can be issued by companies or governments. A bond generally represents a promise to pay a regular rate of interest over a fixed period, from one to fifty years, plus the promise to repay the principal at the maturity date. The interest rate is normally fixed, for instance, at 5 per cent or 10 per cent

The FTSE 100 Index is often quoted in the media

each year. The principal is the nominal amount on which the interest is calculated and is divided into small amounts for sale, usually £100 or less. Therefore, for example, an investor could buy £100 nominal of a 'Five-year 5 per cent bond'. This will pay 5 per cent a year for five years on £100 nominal – that is, £5 a year. The interest may be paid quarterly, semi-annually or annually, depending on the type of bond bought. At the end of the five-year period, an investor would receive £100 in repayment of principal.

Bonds tend to be less risky than shares because they have a promised interest rate and because company bonds rank in front of company shares in the event of a liquidation of a company. However, although less risky than shares, bonds are riskier than savings accounts. This is because with savings products typically the amount of capital you receive back is fixed – if you deposit £100, you get £100 back. With a bond, the amount paid back on maturity is also fixed, but if the bond is sold before maturity, then more or less than the promised nominal amount may be paid.

To illustrate, suppose a variable rate savings account initially pays 5 per cent, and £100 is saved. If market interest rates go up to 6 per cent, the interest rate on the savings account will go up too. With the bond, on the other hand, the promised interest rate is fixed at 5 per cent and so will always pay £5 on £100 nominal. What changes is the *price* that investors will therefore pay for that bond. In order to receive the market interest rate of 6 per cent on the bond paying a fixed 5 per cent, the price of the bond will have to fall to £83.34 (because £83.34 × 6% = £5). If the bond was held for the full five years, it would mature at £100 nominal, but over the life of a bond, the price will fall below £100 or rise above £100 as interest rates change. This volatility in the price makes bonds riskier than savings. The longer the time left until maturity, the more scope there is to be susceptible to this risk. If money needs to be taken out before the five years are up, all or part of a bond holding would need to be sold and a capital gain or loss made, affecting the overall return. Thus, bonds are riskier than variable rate savings but less risky than shares, which have even more volatile price movements. For shares, there is also no equivalent to the promised maturity date of bonds, when investors know they will get their money back.

An additional risk of bonds is if the issuer of a bond defaults. UK Government bonds, known as **gilts**, are seen as safer than bank and building society accounts, in the sense that the government is even less likely than a bank or building society to default.

Gilts

Gilts raise money for the UK Government by offering a secure investment, usually over a fixed period with a fixed rate of interest. Gilts can be bought and sold on the London Stock Exchange. At the end of the term, the holder is repaid the original purchase price.

United Kingdom Debt Management Office	*This Notice is for information only and does not constitute an offer of securities* AUCTION OF £3,000,000,000 OF **4¼% TREASURY GILT 2011** ON A BID PRICE BASIS ON THURSDAY, 26 JANUARY 2006

The United Kingdom Debt Management Office ("DMO") announces the issue of £3,000,000,000 of 4¼% Treasury Gilt 2011, for auction on Thursday, 26 January 2006 and settlement on Friday, 27 January 2006.

The Gilt will be repaid at par on 7 March 2011. Interest will be payable on 7 March and 7 September.

The price payable will include an amount equal to the accrued interest from 9 November 2005, the first issue date of the Gilt, to 27 January 2006, the settlement date of this auction, at the rate of £0.927486 per £100 nominal of the Gilt. This further issue of the Gilt will rank for the interest payment of £1.385359 per £100 nominal of the Gilt due on 7 March 2006.

The Gilt may be stripped and holdings of the Gilt reconstituted. The minimum stripping unit will be £1,000,000 until the payment of the non-standard first coupon on 7 March 2006.

Application has been made to the UK Listing Authority for the Gilt to be admitted to the Official List on 27 January 2006. Application has also been made to the London Stock Exchange for the Gilt to be admitted to trading on the London Stock Exchange's Gilt-Edged and Fixed Interest Market.

Members of the public applying for gilts at auctions must be members of the DMO's Approved Group of Investors, details of which can be found at www.dmo.gov.uk/gilts/press/ml150803.pdf.

The full prospectus for this issue of the Gilt was published on 17 January 2006 and can be obtained from the DMO or the Registrar, Computershare Investor Services PLC, at the addresses below or viewed on the DMO's website at www.dmo.gov.uk/gilts/public/prospectus/prosp170106b.pdf.

UK Debt Management Office Eastcheap Court 11 Philpot Lane London EC3M 8UD Telephone: 020 7862 6500	Computershare Investor Services PLC PO Box 2411 The Pavilions Bristol BS3 9WX Telephone: 0870 703 0143

17 January 2006

The *United Kingdom* **Debt Management Office** is an Executive Agency of HM Treasury

The UK Government announces a new issue of gilts

Table 5.2 shows that only 1 per cent of UK households directly owned gilts in 2004, despite the fact that there is a wide variety of government bonds available that can be bought through the Debt

Management Office (which is accessible online) or a stockbroker. Households prefer to buy National Savings & Investments products (e.g. 4 per cent of households have various types of savings bonds from National Savings & Investments, according to Table 5.2), including fixed term bonds with two-, three- or five-year maturities. The difference between these and gilts is that gilts can be sold at any time – for a gain or at a loss – whereas fixed term bonds impose penalties for early redemption. The greater flexibility of gilts is paid for by the risk that the price may go down as well as up.

One problem with bonds is that not everyone means the same thing when they talk of a 'bond'. The kinds of bonds I have described above are company or government bonds that have a fixed interest rate and fixed repayment date. Recently, though, the term 'bond' has sometimes been taken in vain. Financial intermediaries have sold bonds that were in effect shares by another name, as Box 5.4 shows. Similarly, long-term savings products may not only be bank accounts promising interest, but also linked to company bonds or shares. There is no regulation in the UK on terminology, and consequently *it is important to read the small print of any product*.

Box 5.4   A rose by any other name would smell as sweet

Many investment products are called bonds, but not in the sense of company or government bonds with a fixed interest rate and repayment date. For example, an 'insurance bond' or a 'high-income bond' is what the industry calls a 'wrapper'. This is a structure into which a bank, an insurance company, or other financial services company puts real bonds and shares to offer a particular risk–return trade-off. For instance, in the (relatively) small print at the bottom of an advert for a so-called 'high-interest bond', the make-up of the bond was given as 35 per cent shares and 35 per cent high-yield bonds, as well as 30 per cent investment grade bonds. So the risk of this bond is much greater than its name implied.

Therefore, in reality, the term 'bond' can be applied to products that are very different, and not just company and government bonds. It is also applied to various National Savings & Investments savings products such as Premium Bonds, Income Bonds, Pensioners Guaranteed Income Bonds and Capital Bonds. There are also Guaranteed Equity Bonds, some of which are savings products, others of which are much more risky investment products, for example, Guaranteed Income Bonds with a defined three- or five-year life and a guaranteed income of 10 per cent a year over the 'bond's' life. With words like 'guaranteed income' and 'bond', how could such products be risky? In fact, the bonds in question were not bonds, but structures or wrappers investing in equities. Although the income was guaranteed, the capital was most definitely not. Reading the small print is definitely worth the effort.

An important product that does not fit within the bonds category that I have described, but that is mentioned in Box 5.4, is the Premium Bond. **Premium Bonds**, owned by 23 per cent of households in the UK in 2004 (see Table 5.2), are a lottery-based form of savings account backed by the UK Government, where instead of everyone receiving annual interest of 2.95 per cent (in June 2006), a lottery is held every month and the equivalent of 2.95 per cent p.a. on all the Premium Bonds is paid out in tax-free prizes. Box 5.5 takes a brief look at National Savings & Investments, and shows examples of some of the savings and investment products they offer.

Premium Bonds

A Premium Bond is a bond issued by the UK Government's National Savings & Investments scheme. The government pays interest on the bond, but instead of the interest being paid into individual accounts, it is paid into a prize fund, from which a monthly lottery distributes tax-free prizes.

Box 5.5   National Savings & Investment Products

'The safest home for your money'

At National Savings & Investments we offer a range of savings and investments to suit different people's needs. Because National Savings & Investments is backed by HM Treasury, you can rest assured that any money you invest with us is 100 per cent secure. Our range [includes]:

- *Premium Bonds:* Two £1 million jackpots and still over a million other prizes a month
- *Cash mini ISA:* The easy way to save tax-free
- *Fixed Interest Savings Certificates:* Guaranteed returns, tax-free
- *Index-linked Savings Certificates:* Inflation-beating savings, tax-free
- *Children's Bonus Bonds:* Tax-free investment for your children's future

- **Income Bonds:** Regular monthly income at attractive variable rates
- **Pensioner Guaranteed Income Bonds:** Guaranteed monthly income, exclusive to investors over 60
- **Fixed Rate Savings Bonds:** Guaranteed returns with a choice of growth or income
- **Capital Bonds:** Fixed interest rates that rise over 5 years
- **Guaranteed Equity Bonds:** Stock market growth potential with no risk to your capital
- **Investment Account:** Straightforward one-month notice account with passbook
- **Easy Access Savings Account:** Tiered interest rates, cash card and telephone service.
         (adapted from National Savings & Investments, 2006)

There is one last point I want to make in this section. My definition of the difference between savings and investment is not a universal one. In particular, some products that are *advertised* as being 'long-term savings products' may well involve shares or other forms of investment, and so their value can go down as well as up.

6   Analysing products

Sections 4 and 5 described a range of savings and investment products that a household may choose to have. This section aims to build on this knowledge by exploring some of the key factors that may influence whether and how to save or invest.

6.1 Risk and return

We know that bonds and shares are riskier than savings products since the prices of bonds and shares can go down as well as up, and you can make a capital loss as well as a gain. If they are riskier, why do people buy them? The answer is that historically bonds and shares earn, on average and over time, higher returns than savings products. Earning 9 per cent a year over ten years on an initial investment of £1000, instead of 4 per cent a year, means a final savings pot of £2367 instead of only £1480, an improvement of 60 per cent. Over twenty-five years, the equivalent figures would make a savings pot of £8623 compared with £2666!

The trade-off between risk and return discussed in Section 5 is a *crucial* element in thinking about different products.

Where would you place the following products on the risk–return spectrum in Figure 5.12?

- Corporate bonds
- Individual shares
- Unit trusts
- Savings account
- Current account
- Government gilts.

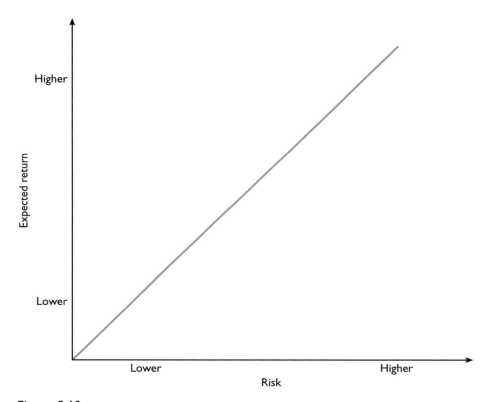

Figure 5.12

The answer to Activity 5.6 is given at the end of the chapter.

The choice of a product will in part be determined by someone's attitude towards risk. This is influenced by how much risk someone can afford and also the purpose of the saving, for example, is it short term or long term? If someone is risk averse (a term you first came across in Chapter 1, Section 5.2), they would in effect need a greater potential return in order to take the same risk as someone who is more willing to take risks.

For example, someone may be happy with a 4 per cent return on savings, require a 5 per cent return on gilts, and may hope to achieve an 8 per cent return on corporate bonds and 10 per cent on equities. If a savings account promises 4 per cent, then unless interest rates change, 4 per cent will be paid. If a gilt offers 5 per cent, then 5 per cent will be received if the gilt is held to maturity. If a corporate bond promises 8 per cent, it will return 8 per cent if held to maturity and if the company does not default. A share that currently has a 3 per cent dividend yield would return 10 per cent if the dividend is maintained at 3 per cent and if a capital gain equivalent to 7 per cent a year is made when the share is sold, which is influenced by the performance of that company.

While evidence suggests that there is no guarantee that what has happened in the past will happen in the future, historical performance of products is still informative. Table 5.6 shows the average annual returns on UK equities, gilts and cash deposits for the period 1963 to 2005. Note that throughout Section 6, when I talk about 'cash deposits' I am referring to bank or building society savings accounts. They are similar to cash in that they are liquid assets, and 'cash deposits' is the term that you will come across in this kind of product analysis in advanced personal finance literature. Before looking at the table, it is worth pointing out that the table is looking at a **portfolio** of equities – in this case the performance of the FTSE All Share Index, which includes around 1000 companies' shares listed on the London Stock Exchange.

Portfolio
A set of financial assets held by an individual (or a bank or other financial institution).

Table 5.6 Average annual returns on UK equities, gilts and cash deposits (1963–2005)

% per year	Nominal return (%)	Real return (%)
UK equities	13.0	6.6
Gilts	9.2	2.8
Cash deposits	8.8	2.4

Source: UBS Global Asset Management, 2005

Table 5.6 shows that, over the forty-three-year period of 1963–2005, a diversified portfolio of equities outperformed gilts, which in turn outperformed cash deposits on a yearly returns basis. The nominal returns in Table 5.6 look high compared with what the returns on offer in the mid 2000s were, because there was an average annual inflation rate of 6.4 per cent between 1963 and 2005. The real returns, after allowing for that inflation rate, were lower. Compounded over a number of years, the differences in annual average returns between equities, bonds and cash can make a huge difference in money terms.

If investing in shares makes higher returns, why don't people put all of their money in UK equities rather than in gilts or cash? There may be ethical reasons (as you will see in Section 7) but, furthermore, such returns are only an *average* on a portfolio of shares achieved over the period shown in Table 5.6. The actual return on a portfolio of shares in any one year has ranged from a staggering −51.7 per cent (the loss of more than half of the capital) in 1975 to a rebound the following year of a 150.9 per cent gain.

Figure 5.13 shows movements in the FTSE All Share Index from 1989 to 2005. While there were movements up and down between 1989 and 2000, the general trend was up. However, UK equities returned a loss of 13.3 per cent in 2001, followed by an even worse loss of 22.7 per cent in 2002 – a total loss of 34 per cent over two years. For the three years up to and including 2003, the loss was closer to 50 per cent.

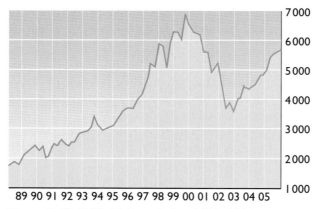

Figure 5.13 *FTSE All Share Index, 1989–2005*
Source: FT.com, 2005

A person's attitude to volatility in returns will determine how much someone invests in equities, in bonds, and in cash (or savings products). If someone is highly risk averse, they are more likely to stick to savings products and bonds. If someone is less risk averse, they will be happy to buy at least some shares for their overall investment portfolio.

Risk also relates to the length of time of any investment. Normally, the longer someone intends to invest without needing to sell, the more risk can be afforded. Table 5.7 uses past data to show how likely it is that the shares will beat cash deposits or gilts as an investment over different time periods or horizons – from two years to eighteen years – without withdrawing any money, that is, allowing for compounding of interest. The probability (from 0 per cent to 100 per cent) is based on the number of periods in which equities outperformed either cash or gilts expressed as a percentage of the total number of periods between 1899 and 2004. Therefore, for example, if we consider all possible two-year time periods between 1899 and 2004, there were 104 of them. For these two-year time periods, equities outperformed cash deposits 69 times out of the total of 104, giving a probability of 69 divided by 104, then multiplied by 100, to give 66 per cent. These numbers are shown in bold in Table 5.7.

Table 5.7 The effect of time on equity outperformance, 1899–2004

Time period (years)	2	3	4	5	10	18
Number of times equities outperformed cash deposits	69	72	75	76	89	87
Number of times equities underperformed cash deposits	35	31	27	25	7	1
Total number of time periods	104	103	102	101	96	88
Probability equities will outperform cash deposits (%)	**66**	**70**	**74**	**75**	**93**	**99**

Time period (years)	2	3	4	5	10	18
Number of times equities outperformed gilts	72	78	80	77	80	80
Number of times equities underperformed gilts	32	25	22	24	16	8
Total number of time periods	104	103	102	101	96	88
Probability equities will outperform gilts (%)	**69**	**76**	**78**	**76**	**83**	**91**

Source: adapted from *Daily Telegraph*, 26 February 2005, Money Section, p. B3

So past evidence suggests that the longer the time period, the more likely it is that equities will outperform bonds and cash – assuming that past returns are good predictors of the future. Studying the past seems to say that, with as short a time horizon as two years, there is a two-in-three chance of doing better if you held all equities rather than all bonds or all cash deposits. With a ten-year time horizon, there is more than a nine-in-ten chance of doing better with equities than with cash deposits. Put another way, the risk of underperformance with an equity portfolio over ten years is less than 10 per cent.

History would seem to suggest that someone is unlikely to lose when investing in equities compared with buying bonds or putting their money in a savings account. Nevertheless, the past would not have been a good forecast of the future if someone had been investing £1000 for five years in 2000. As you saw from Figure 5.13, 2000 was at the start of

Bear market
A market in which prices are falling. A 'bear' is a person who expects that the market or the price of a particular share will fall and so sells – perhaps in order to buy the shares at a lower price later on.

a **bear market**. In fact, £1000 would have only been worth £956 at the end of the five years if invested in UK equities, even allowing for all dividends received over the five years, compared with £1255 invested in gilts over the same five-year period, and £1280 if money had been placed in a three months' notice cash savings account for the same five-year period. An important issue is that the probabilities in Table 5.7 are calculated over a very long time period and may not take into account more recent changes. Consequently, the past is not necessarily a good indicator of a particular future.

The introduction of the tax-efficient savings and investment vehicle called the Child Trust Fund (CTF) was very clearly aimed at the longer term. Since April 2005, all UK children born on or after 1 September 2002 receive £250 at birth from the government, with a further £250 payable to children in low-income households, with a further £250 (or £500 if a low-income household) at age 7, and possibly another tranche at secondary school age.

The introduction of the Child Trust Fund was designed to encourage long-term saving

In order to encourage a nest egg, parents, family and friends can also contribute up to £1200 a year to the fund. The fund can be invested in a variety of ways, for example, in a savings account or an investment fund. Interest earned on savings and investments held in the fund are tax-free, and dividends are taxed at 10 per cent. From the age of 16, children will be able to manage their accounts and, from 18, use the money as they so wish. One option introduced by the government is the 'Stakeholder Child Trust Fund'. This has certain rules about how the money is invested which providers must comply with. In 2006, UK government statistics showed that of 2.3 million CTF vouchers issued, less than two-thirds had been taken up by households – if a parent does not invest the money within twelve months, the government invests the money in a Stakeholder CTF.

6.2 Risk reduction strategies

Lengthening the time over which an investment is held can usually reduce risk, but even if not investing over the long term, **diversification** can reduce risk. That is, instead of making a single investment in one company's shares, someone may hold a portfolio of different UK shares, some of which will go up and some of which will go down, but they are less likely to all go up or all go down at the same time. We can take this principle further. Instead of holding just UK shares, a portfolio could hold, say, US, Japanese and European shares, or a mix of shares, bonds and cash.

Diversification
An investment strategy that aims to reduce market risk by combining a variety of investments, such as stocks and bonds, that are unlikely to all move in the same direction at the same time.

Buying unit trusts can lead to a more diversified portfolio. These are investment funds that invest in shares and/or bonds. They are bought in units, and the value of units is an investor's share of the underlying portfolio. Unit trusts can either be bought directly from a fund manager, through a stockbroker or bank, or via a fund supermarket on the internet. There are many different types of fund, ranging from balanced funds that invest in cash, bonds and equities, taking the asset allocation decision out of the private investor's hands, to others specialising in a country, such as the USA, or a sector, such as technology. Some funds look for capital growth, others emphasise income. These kinds of investment offer diversified investment for amounts from as low as perhaps £30 to £50 a year. However, they are not cheap in terms of transaction costs. The typical fee on a unit trust is a 5 per cent 'entrance fee' plus a further 1.5 per cent p.a.

Different unit trusts will do well or badly according to what assets they hold and how good the fund managers are. It is very difficult, reading a newspaper, to identify which managers are good and which are bad. An alternative is to buy what are known as 'tracker' unit trusts, which mirror an index, such as the FTSE All Share Index, and give you the performance of the index plus dividends, no more and no less. These funds are passively managed, in contrast to actively managed funds where the managers buy and sell to try to get their market timing right, and so,

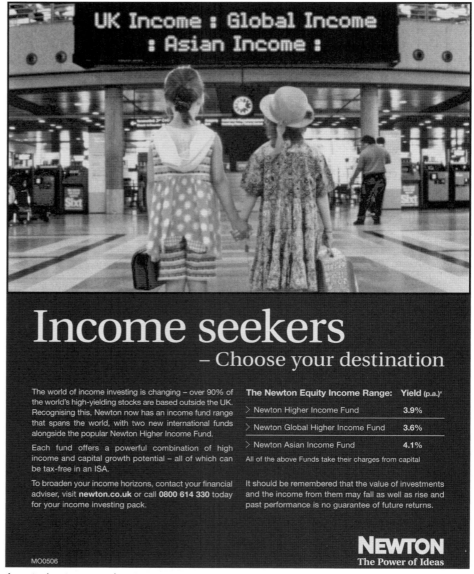

A typical unit trust advertisement

as a result, trackers usually have lower fees. Remember, as explained in Section 4.2, that up to £7000 p.a. can be invested in equities tax-free (apart from 10 per cent tax on dividends) in an ISA.

Allocating money to a range of different assets instead of just one type of asset can be described as not putting all your eggs in one basket, with your attitude to risk being the key to the split.

The reduction in risk through diversification need not necessarily sacrifice returns. This is because not all investments rise and fall together.

Don't put all your eggs in one basket

For example, bond prices can rise when shares are doing badly. Interest rates on cash deposits can go up when share prices go down. This cash/bond/equity split is called the **asset allocation decision** because each one of cash deposits, bonds and equities is called an 'asset class'. An important factor when making decisions about the asset allocation is someone's age.

Asset allocation decision
The choice of how to divide a savings and investments portfolio across cash deposits, bonds and equities.

Activity 5.7

Why do you think that age is an important factor in determining approaches to investment risk?

Comment

As you have seen, investing solely in equities is more suited to long-term investment. If someone is retiring in five years, then investing solely in equities may be very risky. Looking back to Figure 5.13, imagine what would have happened to the value of their investments if they were only holding shares and they retired in 2002/03 – they would have seen the value of their fund severely hit. If, on the other hand, someone is twenty-five, with thirty years or more to save, they can afford to invest more in equities. If not saving directly, but through a company pension fund, the pension fund managers will look at the age distribution of the members of the scheme when deciding on the asset allocation. ■■■

So the asset allocation decision that may be appropriate when someone is relatively young may not be appropriate when close to retirement. This suggests that the pre-retirement years shouldn't be entered into with too much risk. Indeed, the asset allocation should be regularly revised and reviewed over the life-course. This is a clear example of the *Personal Finance* theme of change over the life-course. Box 5.6 discusses 'lifestyling' products as a way of achieving this asset re-allocation.

> ### Box 5.6 Lifestyling
>
> This kind of investment strategy takes age into account. It will automatically point an investor towards equities if they are under 30, and the cash/bond/equity mix will gradually be changed as someone gets older to put them into lower risk investments as they approach retirement. Imagine if someone had 100 per cent equities as they approached 65. If the market did well, they might retire in splendour; if the market did badly, they might retire with little. In order to reduce this risk, an investor gradually sells equities and buys bonds over time, so that by the time the investor retires their savings and investments are fully in cash and bonds and no longer bear stock market risk.

Market timing
A technique of buying and selling stocks in conjunction with the ups and downs of the market.

Pound cost averaging
The investment technique of allocating a fixed sum for the purchase of particular investments on a monthly (or other periodic) basis. When prices fall, the fixed amount will buy more shares/units, and when prices rise, fewer shares/units are bought.

Planning a budget for making savings and investments can be difficult, but, for example, contributing to a pension scheme (see Chapter 7) or a unit-trust regular savings plan helps in making regular investments. These products also have the advantage of spreading the risk of buying or selling at the wrong time. **Market timing** – that is, buying when markets are low and selling when markets are high – is very difficult. You have already seen in relation to individual company shares, the FTSE and other market indices, and with bond prices, how timing can be all-important in avoiding capital losses.

In the recent past, this would have meant buying shares in the early 1990s and selling them before the crash of 2000. However, there is little evidence that individuals or fund managers are particularly good at market timing. Individuals (or 'retail investors' as they are called) tend to be influenced by advertising. When markets have already gone up, advertisers are able to advertise good recent returns and so people often buy after the market has risen.

A way to reduce mistakes of market timing is to invest on a regular basis, such as monthly, quarterly or yearly. This is called **pound cost averaging**, and reduces the risk of buying at the high and selling at the low. It also reduces the chance of getting market timing right – buying at the low and selling at the high. If someone invested, say, £50 a month in a unit trust that invested in shares, then if the market fell they would buy more units and if the market rose they would buy less units, since they would be spending an equal amount each month on units that varied in price over time. It is also worth adopting a similar approach for selling. If someone wants to sell, it makes sense to sell holdings in regular amounts, since it is difficult to tell when the market has reached a peak. Using this technique may be preferable in order to receive a reasonable average return rather than to hold on, possibly miss the height of the boom, and have to sell when prices have already fallen.

In this section, we have looked at the risks and returns associated with different savings and investment products, and we have seen how the time horizon may affect the choice of savings or investment products. We have also seen how regular saving and diversification of investments into different asset classes can help to reduce risk.

7   Ethical investments

Another factor that some people wish to take into account is the knowledge that their money is invested ethically or in a socially responsible way. **Ethical investment** refers to investments that avoid companies that are engaged in what some people consider to be unacceptable activities. To be sure that an investment fits with an individual's ethical views, some investigations have to be made into the detail of a particular product since even products advertised as being ethical vary in exactly how 'ethical' is defined. Box 5.7 outlines some of the different factors that may constitute ethical investment.

Ethical investment
Investments made in companies that are deemed to be socially responsible. Ethical investments tend to exclude companies involved in tobacco, gambling and the arms industry.

Box 5.7   What is ethical or socially responsible investment?

Ethical investment has been described as putting your money where your morals are, or investing according to your beliefs. Ethical investments tend to use negative criteria to avoid investing in companies involved in areas such as:

- environmentally damaging practices
- trading with oppressive regimes and countries with poor human rights records
- pornography and offensive advertising
- gambling
- tobacco and alcohol production
- unnecessary exploitation of animals
- unsafe products and services
- genetic engineering, abortion and embryonic research
- armaments.

Socially responsible investments, as well as adhering to [the above] agreed negative criteria, actively seek out firms that make a positive contribution to society, for example:

- products and services that are of long-term benefit to the community
- conservation of energy and natural resources
- environmental improvements and pollution control
- good relations with customers and suppliers
- high employee welfare standards
- organic farming and foods
- strong community involvement
- a good equal opportunities record
- respect for the sanctity and dignity of human life
- openness about their activities.

(adapted from The Ethical Partnership Ltd, 2006)

Is there a trade-off between investing ethically and making good returns? Figure 5.14 compares ethical unit trusts with all unit trusts in the UK from 1994 to 2004.

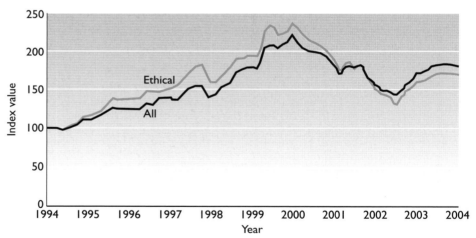

Figure 5.14 *Comparison of ethical unit trusts with all UK unit trusts, 1994–2004*
Source: smile.co.uk, 2006

Look at Figure 5.14 and describe the performance of all ethical UK unit trusts compared with that of all UK unit trusts.

When interpreting such a graph, it is important to look at the unit of measurement. In this case it is an index number. Between 1994 and 2002, ethical unit trusts outperformed all unit trusts, but between 2002 and 2004 this trend was reversed. The index value of both lines peaked at over 200 at the turn of the century, which means they had doubled in value compared to the base figure in November 1994. The last date of May 2004 shows ethical unit trusts having slightly lower returns than all unit trusts over the whole ten-year period. ■ ■ ■

Religious background can also influence decisions on how to save or invest. For example, shariah law stipulates that investments that are halal (permissible) must exclude companies with income from alcohol, pork-related products, conventional financial services (that charge and pay interest), insurance, gambling, tobacco, weapons and similar activities. Buying other shares and receiving dividends are acceptable, but speculation is not allowed.

Some savers also take a different ethical stance by choosing, on principle, to save or invest with a mutual institution such as a building society. As you saw in Chapter 4, Box 4.1, these are organisations that are owned by their members. Such members have certain rights to vote on the running of the organisation. Each member has one vote, and this does not depend on the amount of money they have invested, thus making (so its proponents argue) a more democratically run organisation. Moreover, some people feel strongly that a system based on share ownership reinforces inequalities in society, as those with higher incomes gain at the expense of those on lower incomes. Building societies are perhaps the best-known form of a mutual, and approximately 15 million adults have building society savings accounts (BSA, 2006). In fact, it has also been argued that mutuals can offer better savings rates compared to shareholder-owned organisations, a point argued below by the Building Societies Association (BSA):

> Building societies are different from banks, which are companies (normally listed on the stock market) and are therefore owned by, and run for, their shareholders. Societies have no external shareholders requiring dividends, and are not companies. This

normally enables them to run on lower costs and offer cheaper mortgages and better rates of interest on savings than their competitors.

(BSA, 2006)

Friendly Societies
Mutual organisations that provide savings and life insurance plans to their members. They benefit from special tax treatment but investors can only put in small amounts, currently £25 per month.

Friendly Societies also offer tax-efficient investing. These societies are mutuals and non-profit making, and have the advantage of allowing a limited amount of largely tax-free investing. In 2006, up to £25 a month (or an annual one-off sum of up to £270) can be invested in these products free of tax.

There are also situations that are less to do with 'ethics' and more to do with the difficulty for some groups of accessing conventional saving schemes, and of having different cultural backgrounds and experiences. For example, there are informal 'clubs' where people undertake collective saving in order to fund purchases by individuals. South Asians refer to these as 'communities' or 'bond committees', while Black Caribbeans tend to refer to them as 'pardner' systems. There are also the more formalised credit union systems that were mentioned in Box 4.1 in Chapter 4.

8   Planning savings and investments

The financial planning model we have used in *Personal Finance* can also help when planning savings and investments. First of all, the reasons for saving need to be examined as part of the 'Stage 1: Assess' part of the process. This is important information needed for the 'Stage 2: Decide' part of the process and specifically deciding how much has to be saved and for how long. The goals an individual or household have will influence this process.

Activity 5.9

Take a minute to reflect on whether any of your goals require you to save or invest. If so, are they short-, medium- or long-term goals?

Comment

Obviously people's goals vary enormously. You may want to save for a holiday later in the year (which would be a short-term goal) or you may want to save towards a 'once-in-a-lifetime' cruise holiday in, say, twelve years' time (which would be a long-term goal). It is important to reflect regularly on such goals and their time frames because this will impact on your financial planning process. ■ ■ ■

The 'Stage 1: Assess the situation' part of the financial planning model would require a household to examine its financial situation and assess carefully if it can save and, if it can, how much to save and how regularly. This may require adjustments to the household's budget. It may be that someone feels they really do not have enough spare income to save. In the case of many households, having a low income may prevent savings, but for others making relatively simple cuts in expenditure can lead to surplus income, as you saw in Chapter 3, Section 3. Personal finance experts often use the expression 'pay yourself first', meaning that saving should be allocated before other outgoings are budgeted for.

We have already seen in Section 3 how many people are both savers and borrowers at the same time. This may be for sensible reasons. Suppose Sarah and Peter, who you met in Chapters 2 and 3, have bought a house and are paying interest on a mortgage, and yet are also putting money aside each month to pay for their children's education and their retirement. Why not use the savings to pay off the mortgage early? One reason might be to do with cost: it may be expensive to pay back a mortgage, partly or in full, because of early payment penalties – this may be particularly true if it is a repayment mortgage backed by investment in a life assurance policy (we'll look at the repayment of mortgages in more detail in Chapter 6, Section 5). A second reason might be to retain flexibility: paying off a mortgage early may mean a reduction in the emergency fund of savings available for a rainy day. A third reason is that saving can be a disciplined way of making sure that you will be able to work towards a particular goal, for example, of having enough money to pay university fees, or to retire in comfort. This is particularly the case with regular saving or investing, such as a commitment to pay £50 per month into a savings account, or £100 per month into a Maxi ISA. These would be good examples of the principle of 'pay yourself first'. If savings are used to pay off a debt like a mortgage, it might be more tempting to stop saving. On the other hand, as you saw in Chapter 4, the interest paid on debt products is likely to be higher than the interest received on savings products. Consequently, it may make sense to pay off debt and reduce savings, especially if the habit of disciplined saving can be maintained afterwards.

When wanting to buy things like a car, a holiday, or an in-house entertainment system, the trade-off between consuming now (perhaps through acquiring debt) or saving to buy later may be a difficult choice. Part of this choice is about finance, but part is also about attitudes towards debt and consumption more generally. We started to look at this in Chapter 4, Section 5, and used the example of the choices of how to finance a music system purchase. Now that we have looked at the details of saving and savings products, we can carry that one stage further and look at a numerical example. One way of doing this is shown in Box 5.8.

Box 5.8 Borrowing or saving for Kelly's motorbike

Let's suppose that Kelly wants a new motorbike that costs £2400. She hasn't any savings or debt, and she thinks she can budget to save £100 a month. She would like to buy the bike straight away and her credit card limit of £3000 would cover the £2400 needed. Her credit card has an APR of 12.9 per cent, and she can pay back £100 a month, or she could save £100 a month with a Cash ISA at 4.75 per cent AER. We'll assume that the price of the bike stays the same over the two years.

By using her credit card Kelly can buy her bike straight away, but with payments of £100 a month it will take her 28 months to pay the debt off. Alternatively, she can postpone purchasing the bike until she has saved. By saving £100 in her ISA with an initial deposit of £100, it will take her 22 months to save £2400. It is cheaper to pay for the bike when she has saved the money, but she has to give up the use she could make of it now. This is a classic example of the kind of trade-off discussed in Chapter 1, Section 5.

There is another way to look at the same process of comparison. Kelly could budget for the bike over a fixed period of two years. If she saved £100 a month in the Cash ISA, at the end of two years she would have £2626.85 (with over £200 left over after paying for the bike). If she wanted to have the bike now and pay for it on the credit card, and she wanted to pay off the card over two years, she would have to pay £113.19 a month, so that the total paid would be £2716.67 (with over £300 paid in interest).

Returning to thinking about just saving or investing, the next stage in the financial planning process (Stage 2: Decide) is to choose what type of savings or investment product is most appropriate. You've seen that the decision depends on attitude to risk, the investment time horizon, and ethical considerations.

Activity 5.10

Examine the three case studies below and think about what the options for saving and investing may be in each. You may want to look at Tables 5.3, 5.4, 5.5 and 5.7 to help think about this.

1   Shirin and Ade want to save at least £10,000 towards a deposit for a house in two years' time. They do not want to take any risks with their money and they are sure they will not need to access the money during that time.

2   Paul wants to put some money aside in case of an emergency, but wants easy access and to be able to withdraw money when he wants, night or day, and he can probably save about £50 a month.

3   Sue has just had her first baby and is thinking about how to use the Child Trust Fund (CTF).

Comment

1   Shirin's and Ade's motive for saving is for the specific purpose of their deposit, and they can budget to save the money. They can save up to £3000 a year in a Cash ISA (using the example of the interest rates in Table 5.5, at an AER of 4.6 per cent). Given they don't want to risk any of their savings, they would probably not want to invest in equities, so they may want to have a Cash ISA each to maximise their returns. Another option may be to open a high-interest internet savings account (the example one in Table 5.5 has a net interest rate of 3.80 per cent).

2   Paul's options are a little more limited because he wants complete flexibility in access to his savings, which are primarily for a 'rainy day'. In such a case, he needs an account with no withdrawal penalty, such as the 'Instant Access' account seen in Table 5.5. This is likely to suit him best because, while it has lower interest rates compared with other products, the cash card enables him to access his money. There is a trade-off between flexibility and return. If Paul did not want or need such immediate access, an internet savings account, a notice account or a Cash ISA would give better returns.

3   For Sue, the time horizon most appropriate for a CTF is eighteen years. Using the numbers in Table 5.7, and assuming the past is a good indicator of the future, equities are 99 per cent likely to outperform cash deposits, and 91 per cent likely to outperform gilts, so Sue may well think about investing the money in equities. Nevertheless, she may be more risk averse and/or want to have a more diversified portfolio of different asset classes. She might well consider a Stakeholder CTF.

In all three cases, ethical concerns may shape exactly what product is chosen. ■ ■ ■

Once the decision has been made about what products to use, the 'Stage 3: Act' step in our financial planning model involves making and then managing savings and investments. At this stage, 'shopping around' may mean finding the most attractive products in terms of the rates offered on specific different, comparable products across the various banks, building societies and other organisations that offer them.

For example, the FSA provide 'comparative tables' on their website that enable consumers to shop around for an account type and find the highest interest rates available. Many newspapers also offer 'best buy' tables for savings accounts in their financial pages.

It is possible for an individual or household to manage their own savings and investments, but another choice is to delegate the management to others. Savings products may be relatively easy to manage; investments, on the other hand, are not. The latter may need regular watching, for instance, to check if there is a problem with the companies chosen if individual shares have been invested in. The costs of managing investments are relatively high if investments are relatively small sums. Using an investment fund, such as a unit trust, avoids these problems by passing the work to the fund's investment manager.

The final stage in the financial planning model is 'Stage 4: Review the situation'. I have already commented in Section 6.2 on how market timing and lifestyling are important. You also saw in Section 3.2, particularly Table 5.4, how certain events, such as divorce, having children and being made unemployed, may necessitate adjustments to any savings plans.

9 Conclusion

This chapter started by examining the importance of savings and investments to both households and the broader economy in Sections 2 and 3. We then examined, in Sections 4 and 5, the kinds of products available in the marketplace, and the factors that influence the decision on which product(s) to use.

In Section 6, the concepts of risk and return were described as central to savings and investment decisions, with an individual's attitude to risk shaping their savings decisions. An individual's savings and investment decisions relate to their goals, and the length of time for that goal to be achieved can influence how much risk is taken. Section 6 also suggested a number of ways of analysing the different products on offer, and what kind of 'portfolio' may be best. In Section 7, we introduced the idea of 'ethical investments'.

For many people, the main form of savings is the savings account. Other households have shares, and many more households have an indirect interest in shares through their pension fund. But it's also important to remember that for many households, savings and investments are not possible due to limited income.

In Section 8, we also considered how, for many households, savings and debts are experienced simultaneously. Indeed, many UK households have one very large asset with an associated liability – their home – to which we turn next in Chapter 6.

Answer to Activity

Activity 5.6

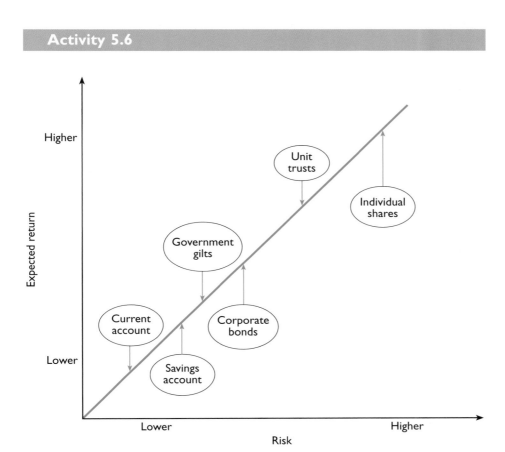

Figure 5.15

References

Alessie, R., Lusardi, A. and Aldershof, T. (1997) 'Income and wealth over the life cycle: evidence from the panel data', *Review of Income and Wealth*, vol. 43, pp. 1–32.

Building Societies Association (BSA) (2006) 'Home page' [online], http://www.bsa.org.uk (Accessed 23 March 2006).

Department for Work and Pensions (DWP) (2005) *Family Resources Survey: United Kingdom 2003–04* [online], http://www.dwp.gov.uk/asd/frs/2003_04/pdfonly/frs_2003_04_report.pdf (Accessed 6 March 2006).

FT.com (2005) 'Market data: equities: UK companies' [online], http://mwprices.ft.com/custom/ft-com/html-marketsDataTools.asp?c=uk (Accessed 11 November).

Guardian Unlimited (2005) 'Savings hit record high as concerns mount over debt' [online], http://money.guardian.co.uk/news_/story/0,1456,1667152,00.html (Accessed 10 January 2006).

Halifax Financial Services (2005) 'Savings ratios over the decades' [online], press release, 4 June 2005, http://www.hbosplc.com/economy/includes/04-06-05SavingRatio.doc (Accessed 15 November 2005).

Horioka, C.Y. and Watanabe, W. (1997) 'Why do people save? A micro-analysis of motives for household saving in Japan', Papers 412, Osaka, Institute of Social and Economic Research.

Modigliani, F. and Brumberg, R. (1954) 'Utility analysis and the consumption function: an interpretation of cross-section data' in Kurihara, K.K. (ed.) *Post-Keynesian Economics*, New Brunswick, NJ, Rutgers University Press.

National Savings & Investments (2006) 'The safest home for your money' [online], http://www.nsandi.com/ (Accessed 23 February 2006).

Nationwide (2005) 'Savings rates' [online], http://www.nationwide.co.uk/savings/rates.htm (Accessed 11 November 2005).

Smile.co.uk (2006) 'Ethical investing: what is it? (performance)' [online], http://www.smile.co.uk/servlet/Satellite?cid=1039596326377&pagename=Smile%2FPage%2FsmView&c=Page (Accessed 23 March 2006).

Social Trends (2005) no. 35, Basingstoke and New York, Palgrave Macmillan for The Office for National Statistics (ONS); also available online at the ONS website, http://www.statistics.gov.uk/downloads/theme_social/Social_Trends35/Social_Trends_35.pdf (Accessed 14 November 2005).

The Ethical Partnership Ltd. (2006) 'What is ethical investment' [online], http://www.the-ethical-partnership.co.uk/about (Accessed 23 March 2006).

UBS Global Asset Management (2005) *Pension Fund Indicators 2005: A Long-term Perspective on Pension Fund Investments* [online], USB Global Asset Management, http://www.ubs.com/1/ShowMedia/globalam/emea/uk/institutional/publications?contentId=78721&name=pfi2005.pdf (Accessed 11 May 2006).

Webley, P., Burlando, R.M. and Viner, A. (2000) 'Individual differences, savings motives and saving behaviour: a cross national study' in Hölzl, E. (ed.) *Fairness and Cooperation: IAREP/SABE Conference Proceedings*, pp. 497–501, Vienna, WUV.

Housing and the financial balance sheet

Ian Fribbance and Martin Upton

Contents

1 Introduction

'Home sweet home.'

'Home is where the heart is.'

'A man's home is his castle.'

Three of the best-known phrases in the English language relate to homes, and that isn't surprising when we consider how central our homes are to our lives – they are a key place where individuals and households live. Not everyone's home will be sweet, it won't necessarily be where the heart resides, and it is unlikely to be a castle literally! However, everyone needs somewhere to live, and options about where to live and how to pay for the home we reside in are among our biggest financial decisions. Therefore, housing is an important and often emotive subject. In Section 2, we look at the major economic and social forces which affect everyone's housing options, and then consider the choice of renting or buying property in Section 3. After we have looked at renting (in Section 4) and buying (in Section 5) in detail, we can examine financial balance sheets in detail in Section 7: it makes sense to do this after we have thought about housing because property often forms a major part of such balance sheets.

How and where individuals and households live will vary tremendously according to factors such as income levels; goals, tastes and preferences; other types of expenditure; life events such as the formation, growth and dissolution of households; and money management skills. Some people will rent a home for long periods or throughout their lives. Others will find that, perhaps after an initial period of renting, they are able to buy a series of properties that increase in size or desirability. Some people might want and be able to buy a second or holiday home, or buy property for investment purposes.

In order to start considering some of these issues, we need to define some of the main types of housing tenure, or means of occupying a home. The most common type is **owner-occupation**. This is when people own, or are buying, the home they live in. As very few people have the resources to purchase a home outright, most people purchase property by obtaining a mortgage on it. In common with many financial products, the market for mortgages is highly competitive and we explore that market, its impact on taking out a mortgage, and buying more generally in Section 5.

Owner-occupation
To own outright, or to be in the process of buying, the property you are living in.

Homes come in all shapes and sizes

Another form of housing tenure is **renting**. Most renting is where the whole home is rented by an individual or household. Sometimes renters will share with other people, such as in a flat-share or where a lodger rents a room in a privately owned property. Historically, the main component of the housing rental sector was renting from a private landlord. There are also various types of renting from what is called the 'social sector': renting from a local authority (or 'council housing') and

Renting
A form of housing tenure where the person who lives in the house is a tenant, paying rent to the landlord, who owns the property.

Registered Social Landlords (RSLs) Providers of rented social housing who are registered with, and regulated by, the relevant national body in the four nations of the United Kingdom (such as the Housing Corporation in England). Most RSLs are housing associations, but others include trusts and cooperatives.

renting from **Registered Social Landlords (RSLs)** including housing associations (HAs) or housing cooperatives. There are also 'shared equity' schemes whereby people can part-rent from an RSL and part-buy the rest of the property. Section 4 covers the rented sector in detail.

2 The social and economic background to housing issues in the UK

2.1 Changes in housing tenure

Most people in the UK own their own home or are purchasing a property through a mortgage. Many others plan to buy a home or hope to do so in the future. Home ownership is very much a part of British popular culture: witness British TV schedules which reveal what seems to be a national obsession with programmes about buying, selling, auctioning, improving, buying-to-let and redesigning property, as well as shows encouraging us to relocate to the seaside, the sunshine or even another continent.

Housing and homes are popular subjects in magazines too

The latest property price trends and changes in mortgage interest rates are also given great prominence in UK news and media outlets. This attention, which is particularly noticeable at the time of the Bank of England's Monetary Policy Committee's (MPC's) monthly meeting (see Box 4.2 in Chapter 4), reflects the importance of home ownership and mortgages to individual households and the broader economy. Yet is this apparent fascination with home buying in the UK the same elsewhere? Let's first look at Figure 6.1, which shows the comparative position for owner-occupation in the then fifteen countries of the European Union (EU) at the start of the 2000s.

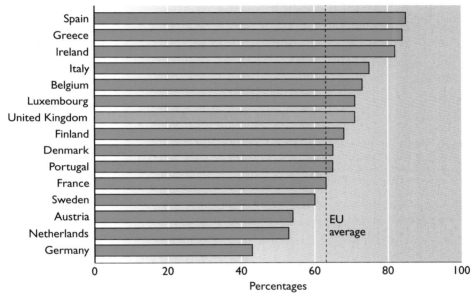

Figure 6.1 *Owner-occupied dwellings: EU comparison, 2000*
Source: *Social Trends*, 2004, no. 34, p. 154, Figure 10.8

Owner-occupation levels in the UK are, in fact, only a little above the EU average, albeit somewhat above that in the other two largest economies, France and Germany, where renting property is more common than in the UK. One difference that Figure 6.1 may hide is that owner-occupation in the UK at younger ages is greater than that of other countries – for those where the age of the household head is between 25 and 29 years, the owner-occupation level is 59 per cent. This is the highest in the EU and well above the 48 per cent in Spain, 31 per cent in Italy, 21 per cent in France and 11 per cent in Germany (Chiuri and Jappelli, 2000, p. 27).

Over time, the composition of housing in the UK has varied considerably between types of tenure. Data on such composition are sometimes difficult to compare directly because housing figures have been compiled in various ways and by different bodies across the four UK nations. For purposes of consistency, we use English data in Figure 6.2 to examine changes in tenure across the last century.

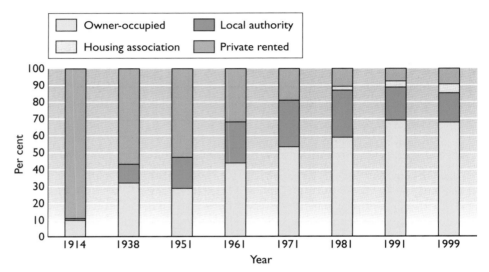

Figure 6.2 *Housing tenure in England, 1914–99*
Source: House of Commons Library, 1999, p. 12

Examine Figure 6.2. How did the pattern of housing tenure change in England between 1914 and 1999?

Figure 6.2 tells a dramatic story. From 1914 to 1999, owner-occupation in England rose from just 10 per cent to around 70 per cent of homes, while privately rented housing fell from 89 per cent to just over 10 per cent. By contrast, the proportion of local authority housing initially rose but has been falling sharply since the 1980s. The share of HAs has been growing since their first appearance in Figure 6.2 in 1981. ■ ■ ■

Now we can look a little more closely at the trends in more recent years in the whole of the UK (see Table 6.1).

Table 6.1 UK dwelling stock by tenure, 1983–2003

	1983 (%)	1993 (%)	2003 (%)
Owner-occupier	59.2	66.2	70.4
Rented privately	10.7	9.9	9.8
Rented from local authorities	27.8	20.6	12.6
Rented from RSLs	2.3	3.4	7.2

Source: adapted from ODPM, 2005a, Table 101

The picture over the last few decades is interesting. The decline in private rental has slowed significantly. This is partly due to changes in legislation designed to make it easier for landlords to rent property, which we shall consider in Section 4. It is local authority housing that has continued to fall much more sharply, while there has been an increase in rental from RSLs. It is worth noting that this change has been even more marked in some parts of the UK such as Scotland. As late as 1983, a majority of Scotland's dwelling stock was local authority rented, but by 2003 it was little more than 16 per cent – a significant change (ODPM, 2005b). In Northern Ireland, the proportion of local authority stock fell from 36 per cent in 1983 to 16 per cent in 2003, and in Wales the equivalent figures were 24 per cent and 14 per cent (ODPM, 2004, 2005c).

While there has been a general shift to owner-occupation across the UK, there are variations within the UK and between different types of household. Box 6.1 summarises information from the Office for National Statistics (ONS, 2005a) about these variations.

The information contained in Box 6.1 also indirectly suggests that income levels are important to housing tenure. For example, we know from Chapter 2 that lone-parent households have lower levels of disposable income. We now also know that an additional characteristic of such low-income households is that they are much more likely to rent, particularly from local authorities and RSLs.

Box 6.1   Housing tenure, regions and households

Figure 6.3 *Dwelling stock: by region and tenure, 2003*
Source: ONS, 2005a

In 2003/04, 70 per cent of houses (18 million) in Great Britain were owner-occupied. ...

Tenure varies markedly according to the type of household. Lone parents with dependent children are much more likely to rent property than own it. In 2003/04 only one in three (36 per cent) of these households in the United Kingdom were owner-occupiers, 50 per cent rented from the social sector [local authorities and RSLs] and 15 per cent rented privately. In contrast, four in five households comprising a couple with dependent children were owner-occupiers, most of whom were buying with a mortgage. Outright home ownership is highest among those over pensionable age. Almost three fifths (56 per cent) of one person households over pensionable age owned their home outright, compared with around a third of households overall.

Tenure also varies regionally. In 2003/04 owner-occupation was highest in the South East, East Midlands and East (75 per cent) and lowest in London (58 per cent) and Scotland (67 per cent). The South West region and Wales had the highest percentage of homes owned outright (34 per cent) and the South East outside of London had the highest proportion

owned with a mortgage (44 per cent). London had by far
the highest proportion rented from the private sector
(17 per cent).

(adapted from ONS, 2005a)

The rapid growth in home ownership in the UK is the consequence of a
mixture of economic, political and social developments. As we saw in
Chapter 4, the growth of real income in the second half of the twentieth
century enlarged the scope for households to finance the mortgages
required to buy their own property. Growing affluence also provided
mortgage lenders with more comfort about the creditworthiness of the
individuals they were lending to. High rental costs also encouraged more
people to purchase property.

Another major factor, which runs through many chapters of *Personal
Finance*, is liberalisation. Section 2.2 of Chapter 4 examined the
liberalisation of the financial services industry. This process substantially
widened the availability of a variety of mortgage types, and increased
competition between mortgage lenders. The resulting increase in the
supply of finance, combined with the availability of comparatively cheaper
deals to potential homeowners, further fuelled the move to home
ownership.

Another related element of liberalisation was the sale of local
authority housing to tenants. In 1980, the Conservative Government
introduced legislation allowing local authority tenants to buy their rented
properties, often at a discount. Since then, over 2 million properties have
been sold under this **right-to-buy** legislation and related policies, and
this was the largest single factor boosting owner-occupation in the 1980s
and 1990s (Joseph Rowntree Foundation, 1998). The legislation was
controversial since, in the longer term, it reduced the stock of local
authority property available for rental for those on lower incomes who
could not afford to purchase property. Some argued that it led to
increased homelessness. The sales also achieved a form of risk
transference, with the new owners, rather than the local authorities, being
responsible for the upkeep of their properties and bearing the risk of
changes in property prices. The political impetus towards a 'home-owning
democracy' remains strong: in April 2005, the Labour Government
announced their intention to increase the proportion of property
ownership to 75 per cent.

Wider social factors may also be at work. In Chapter 3, we looked at
some theories of conspicuous consumption, and property may be another
example of this. The common use of phrases such as 'getting on to the
property ladder' may imply a progressive or inevitable upward movement

Right-to-buy
The entitlement of
the tenant of a rented
public sector property
to buy that property
from the owner.

of households to more expensive or desirable purchased properties – perhaps emphasising an aspirational mindset, and hence reinforcing the increased move towards owner-occupation. However, remember that this is a social phenomenon: there is nothing 'inevitable' about the fact that most people live in owner-occupied homes.

The popular term the 'housing ladder' encapsulates the aspiration of home ownership

It is also important to note that high levels of owner-occupation affect the economy. This is another example of the interdependence we saw in Chapter 1. For example, owner-occupation may make the UK economy somewhat more volatile than other comparable economies with lower home-ownership levels. This is because changes in property prices will significantly affect the wealth of many households, and changes in mortgage rates will affect their expenditure, and both of these will impact on how much is then spent in the high street.

2.2 Property prices

For most people who buy a home, it is their biggest asset, and this is why the media closely follows the movements in property prices. Prices are tracked by the government and also by indices published by the Nationwide Building Society, the Halifax Bank of Scotland plc, and others. For owner-occupiers, one aspect of the experience for the greater part of the last half-century has been very positive: the trend has been for house prices to grow, usually at a rate in excess of price inflation, thereby raising their 'real' value. Though there have been periods when prices fell, the overall trend since the 1950s has been upward.

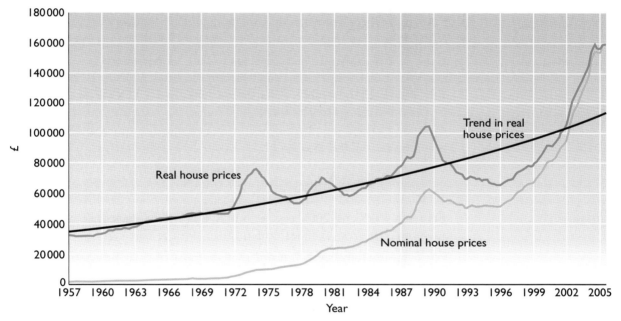

Figure 6.4 *UK nominal and real house prices, 1957–2005*
Source: Nationwide Building Society, 2005

Figure 6.4 shows the movement in property prices since 1957. It illustrates both the move in 'nominal' (or actual) prices, and also in 'real' prices – that is, house prices adjusted to price levels in 2005. It shows that even after allowing for inflation, the value of properties has risen almost fivefold from 1957 to 2005. You can see that 1989–95 is the only period when house prices actually fell in nominal as well as real terms (from an average £62,782 in 1989 to £50,930 at the end of 1995). There are two other periods when house prices fell in real terms (i.e. failed to keep up with inflation) – from 1974 to 1977 and from 1980 to 1982. In these periods, house prices were rising (as you can see on the line labelled 'Nominal house prices') but not by as much as inflation, which was then very high. The period 1989–95 therefore stands out most strongly as the exceptional time for housing in the UK. The overall picture is very clear: house prices have risen dramatically in the last five decades. You should also be able to see a substantial rise in both nominal and real house prices from 1995 to 2005.

Activity 6.2

According to data from the Nationwide Building Society, in April 2005 the average UK house price was £156,128, and average gross earnings in April 2005 were £27,010. Ten years earlier in April 1995, the average house price was £52,063 and average gross earnings were £17,432.

1   Using this Nationwide Building Society data, calculate the ratio of average house prices to average earnings in both 2005 and 1995. (To do this, divide the house prices by the earnings figure.) What has happened to this ratio between 1995 and 2005?

2   Can you suggest any implications of this change for those wanting to buy a home for the first time?

Comment

1   Between 1995 and 2005 the ratio of average house prices to average earnings rose from 3 times to 5.8 times average earnings.

2   For first-time buyers this meant that the cost of their first purchase was much more onerous – not surprisingly, this contributed to a drop in first-time buyer activity in 2004 and 2005. ■ ■ ■

Demography
The study of population and its composition and changes.

What has brought about this upward pressure on property prices? The answer is to do with the forces of demand and supply. There has been an increase in demand for homes. This is partly due to **demography**. There has been population growth since the 1950s – due to increased longevity and the impact of net immigration into the UK – which has more than offset a falling birth rate. More importantly, the average size of households has been shrinking – so for any given population size, more homes are needed. For example, in 1971 the average household size in Great Britain was 2.91. By 2003, that had fallen to 2.32 people per household (ONS, 2003). This is the consequence of changes in the nature of the family such as more people staying single for longer and an increase in the number of divorces, up from 27,200 in 1961 to 166,700 in 2003 (ONS, 2005b). A mixture of growing affluence, rising house prices and the comparatively weak performance of other long-term investments like stocks and shares since the mid 1990s has also generated additional demand for property from existing homeowners, such as the purchase of holiday homes, houses bought-to-let and homes bought for investment purposes.

Another boost to demand has been the low level of interest rates since the early 1990s. As we saw in Figure 4.2 in Chapter 4, low inflation has enabled interest rates to be maintained at much lower levels than those experienced between the early 1980s and the early 1990s. Lower interest rates make mortgages cheaper and therefore more affordable. Employment levels have also remained high, and with real incomes rising there has been further capacity for people to afford larger mortgages. As people can obtain larger mortgages, so competition between buyers forces up the price of property. The UK housing market since 1995 has demonstrated a general economic principle that when interest rates go down, asset prices rise.

There have also been issues of limited supply. In many areas of the UK, the construction of new property has not kept pace with demand. It has been estimated that on average 155,000 new households are formed each year in the UK, but during 2002/03 the number of private sector completions of new houses amounted to only 125,000 (Gray and Gray, 2004). One explanation is that some local authorities are reluctant, or have insufficient appropriate sites available, to release land for residential development. Demand for homes is often highest in areas where supply is most limited – such as suburban or rural areas protected by 'green belt' or other legislation. This supply shortage helps to put further upward pressure on house prices.

In 2005, after ten years of property price growth, there was increasing controversy about the future direction of house prices. Some commentators were suggesting that property price rises would have a 'soft landing' and simply level off. Others were sounding warnings that property prices might fall in real terms, perhaps back to the 'trend' line shown in Figure 6.4, or even possibly in nominal prices, i.e. that they might 'crash' as they did in the early 1990s. Box 6.2 gives an example of such predictions from the magazine *The Economist*.

Box 6.2 'The worldwide rise in house prices is the biggest bubble in history: prepare for the economic pain when it pops'

In come the waves: the global housing boom

Britain's housing market has ... cooled rapidly. The Nationwide index ... rose by 5.5 per cent in the year to May, down from 20 per cent growth in July 2004. But ... other surveys offer a gloomier picture. The Royal Institution of Chartered Surveyors (RICS) reports that prices have fallen for ten consecutive months, with a net balance of 49 per cent of surveyors reporting falling prices in May, the weakest number since 1992 during Britain's previous house-price bust. The volume of sales has slumped by one-third compared with a year ago as both sellers and buyers have lost confidence in house valuations ...

The rapid house-price inflation of recent years is clearly unsustainable, yet most economists in most countries (even in Britain and Australia, where prices are already falling) still cling to the hope that house prices will flatten rather than collapse. It is true that, unlike share prices, house prices tend to be somewhat 'sticky' downwards. People have to live somewhere and owners are loath to accept a capital loss. As long as they can afford their mortgage payments, they will stay put until conditions improve. The snag is that eventually some owners have to sell – because of relocation or job loss – and they will be forced to accept lower prices.

... If house prices stop rising or start to fall, owner-occupiers will largely stay put, but over-exposed investors are more likely to sell, especially if rents do not cover their interest payments. House prices will not collapse overnight like stock-markets – a slow puncture is more likely. But over the next five years, several countries are likely to experience price falls of 20 per cent or more.

(adapted from *The Economist*, 18 June 2005, pp. 66–8)

Activity 6.3

You've just looked at some of the factors that affect house prices in Box 6.2. House prices don't always rise, and they fell in the UK between 1989 and 1995. Under what circumstances do you think house prices might fall again in the future?

Comment

House prices tend to fall when the demand for homes reduces or the supply of homes increases. High interest rates would dampen demand by making mortgages more expensive. Higher unemployment would reduce the ability among the unemployed to finance existing mortgage payments. Moreover, those in financial difficulties might be forced to sell their properties, increasing supply. Another possibility is that if house prices are very high, above the 'trend', some people, such as potential first-time buyers, will withdraw from the market, causing prices to drop.

In the longer term, a significant increase in the supply of housing or a reversal of the demographic trend to have more households would also help to dampen house prices. ■ ■ ■

This balance between the demand and supply for housing varies substantially across the UK, at both regional and local level. For instance, many commentators have noted a 'North–South' divide in property prices. Figure 6.5 gives an overview on regional variations in property prices and price rises. As you can see, prices in London rose by 211 per cent over the ten years to 2004, compared with a 135 per cent rise in Scotland over the same period, leaving the average property price ranging from £272,886 in London down to £110,188 in Northern Ireland.

The picture is somewhat more complicated, with many large and localised variations within each of the regions. In addition to generally high prices throughout London and the South and East of England, prices have also risen substantially throughout the UK in various local places such as revitalised urban areas, some suburban commuter areas, and places where second or holiday homes are popular. These are often referred to as 'property hot spots'.

The rapid house price inflation from 1995 to 2006 has had some important social consequences. Rising property prices have meant that many more people's assets have become potentially subject to **Inheritance Tax** upon their death, as higher property prices have pushed their net wealth above the Inheritance Tax threshold. Another effect has been the impact on young potential first-time buyers, who have been priced out of the market in some parts of the country. Some are forced to carry on living at their parental home, and UK media reports 'discovered' the phenomenon of the stay-at-home 'Kippers': the 'kids in parents' pockets eroding retirement savings' after a survey by The Prudential (BBC, 2003). A related issue has been the pricing out of lower paid public sector workers from the housing market in places such as London, threatening the provision of public services and forcing

Inheritance Tax
Tax on the value of a deceased person's net assets (also known as the person's 'estate') above a tax-free threshold. Tax may also be levied on any gifts made during the seven years before death, and on a few lifetime gifts.

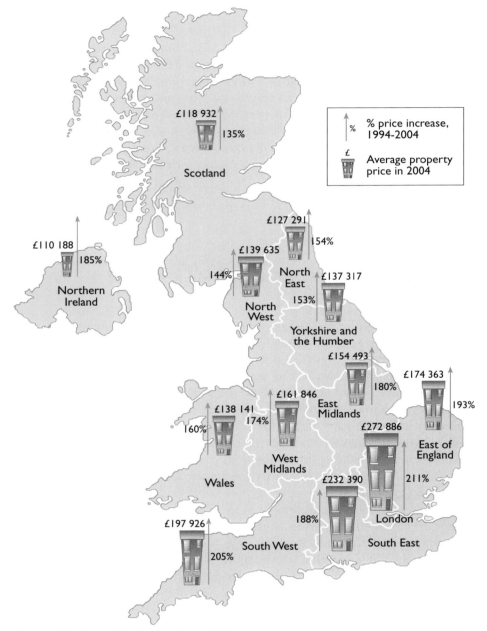

Figure 6.5 *Regional property prices, 2004, and percentage price increase, 1994–2004*
Source: adapted from ODPM, 2005d, Table 505

government initiatives to provide homes for such 'key workers'. More generally, there has been a shift from seeing home ownership as giving people somewhere to live to seeing it as a long-term investment in its own right.

How would you explain the unevenness in property prices across different parts of the UK?

The different levels of demand for property are strongly connected to changes in economic activity and the labour market. The growth of the service sector and the decline of the manufacturing sector in the UK, described in Chapter 2, have resulted in a shift in labour market demand geographically to the South and East. This has led to a consequent shift in the demand for housing. ■ ■ ■

3   The financial implications of buying or renting

This section examines the financial implications of buying or renting a main home. In making choices about whether to rent or buy, most people have personal goals and preferences. Some may prefer to rent in order to avoid costly, time-consuming responsibilities like property maintenance and buildings insurance, which instead fall on the landlord. Conversely, people may want to buy so that they have somewhere to maintain, style and decorate as they wish, and in order to avoid any restrictions on what can be done, as might apply in rented property.

There are substantial financial considerations in any decision between renting and buying. The first means of evaluation might be a comparison of monthly outgoings. This is complicated because any such calculations have to allow for future unknowns such as maintenance expenditure and inflation rates. Inflation is very important in this comparison because it will reduce the real value of a mortgage debt, whereas rents would generally increase. Therefore, it is difficult to do a simple comparison of the costs. Box 6.3 summarises some 2005 research by the Abbey Bank. The research suggested that, considered over a twenty-five-year period and making the assumption of 4.6 per cent inflation per annum (p.a.), monthly outgoings are significantly less when buying.

Box 6.3 Abbey's 2005 survey into the costs of buying and renting

Abbey's annual survey into the difference in cost between buying and renting shows that homebuyers still have the upper hand – but the gap is at its narrowest yet. On average, a homebuyer will pay £37,650 (11 per cent) less over 25 years than renters. Last year [2004], the equivalent saving was £49,977 (or 16 per cent), so the difference has reduced.

The Abbey report shows that:

- The average cost of renting a property in the UK over 25 years is £364,499 compared with £326,849 for buying a property. The average saving [is] £37,650.
- The most expensive areas to rent or buy are London and the South East. However, buying a property in Greater London rather than renting could still save someone an average of £25,100 (or 4 per cent) over 25 years.
- The cheapest area to rent is North West England although people could still save £42,212 (or 14 per cent) ... if they choose to buy a property instead.
- The cheapest area to buy is the west of Scotland, where the average saving to be made by homeowners over 25 years is 32 per cent, or £112,616.
- Even in the North [of England], where the gap is the narrowest, a homeowner could still spend on average £11,692 less than a tenant over the long term.

(Figures are calculated by assuming a 4.6 per cent inflation rate over 25 years. Buying costs are based on a 90 per cent repayment mortgage at a fixed rate of 5.5 per cent over 25 years and include average maintenance costs at 4 per cent per annum inflation rate.)

(adapted from Abbey, 2005)

The Abbey research (2005) did attract some criticism. For example, in regions like London, where property prices are much higher in relation to incomes than elsewhere in the UK, it may be simply impossible for many people to buy a property. Also, it could be argued that Abbey's assumption about future inflation may be too high – and higher inflation figures tend to favour buying. Another factor complicates such comparisons: it's cheaper (and quicker) to move when renting because selling a property can be a lengthy process involving legal costs, probably estate agency costs, and the costs of creating a 'Home Information Pack' (when these come into force in England and Wales in 2007). Buying another property also has substantial costs attached such as **Stamp Duty Land Tax**. Consequently, when people need or want to move often – perhaps for employment reasons or as a young adult – the financial attraction of renting correspondingly increases.

Stamp Duty Land Tax
A tax payable by the purchaser when a property is bought and its price is over a certain threshold, the amount payable being calculated as a percentage of the total purchase price.

For people who need to move home often, renting can be an attractive option

The most important of all financial considerations is the long-run effect of either renting or purchasing. A major argument for buying a home is that purchasing creates a non-financial asset for the individual or household. The mortgage on the property will be a corresponding liability. Once the mortgage is paid off, the owner/s will be left with an asset that has no corresponding liability. A house is an unusual asset in so far as there are some opportunities to generate an income from it (for instance, renting out a room), but also plenty of ways in which it can cost money, such as when maintaining it. This latter characteristic is usually associated with liabilities. None the less, acquisition of such an asset can increase future financial options, for example, moving to another property, downsizing, using it to create an income, or building up an inheritance.

On the other hand, renting can improve financial flexibility. Large sums of money are tied up when a property is being purchased with a mortgage, such as in a deposit on the purchase. There are opportunity costs involved in having that money tied up in property because it could alternatively be invested in the range of investments (for instance, shares or bonds) seen in Chapter 5. These investments are also likely to be more liquid than the value tied up in a property. Furthermore, renters are not subject to the risk of a sharp fall in the housing market or increases in interest rates.

The relative importance of these two points will depend on the future direction of property prices. The more they rise, the more powerful the argument about the acquisition of an asset becomes. Looking back to Figure 6.4, we can see that property prices have increased over most timeframes. Looking at any possible twenty-five-year period (a standard mortgage term) in Figure 6.4, all of them would have produced an increase in the real value of the property. Even someone buying a home in 1973 and selling it in 1998 – the worst twenty-five-year period – would have made a small real terms gain. Home ownership in the UK also enjoys a tax advantage – your 'primary residence' (the home you live in) is usually exempt from **Capital Gains Tax** when it increases in value, unlike almost all other assets. This is another means by which UK governments have encouraged home ownership. Many people have achieved large increases in the equity in their home, and hence of their net wealth, because of these increased property prices.

However, we can also see from Figure 6.4 that, between 1989 and 1995, property prices fell in most regions of the UK. As a result, some people who bought homes in the late 1980s or early 1990s found themselves suffering from **negative equity**. This is a situation where the amount of debt on a mortgage exceeds the value of the property on which it is secured. This tends to occur in periods when nominal property prices fall. We consider this again in Section 5.4.

House prices rose rapidly from the mid 1990s, but as you saw in Box 6.2, in 2005 *The Economist* was predicting future house price falls. When property prices do fall, or are flat or rising slowly, other investments can make a better return – although in practice this has not often been the case. Nevertheless, the decision between buying and renting is worth reviewing, even after a home has been purchased. Remember that – as we saw in Chapter 1, Section 5.3 – an important step in the financial planning process is 'Stage 4: Review'. For example, if prices look set to fall, it may produce a financial gain to sell and then rent to obtain greater returns on the capital elsewhere. For many households, especially families, this may be difficult in practice. Such plans might only entail a temporary retreat from the property market: if prices did actually fall, it would then be possible to buy a better property than before.

Capital Gains Tax
A tax on capital 'gains'. If an asset has increased in value when it is sold or given away, the 'gain' (profit) above a certain threshold (£8800 in 2006/07) may be taxable.

Negative equity
Where the market value of a property is exceeded by the outstanding mortgage debt secured against it.

People can sell their properties for different reasons

One last important point to remember is that many people do not have a choice between renting and buying. As we saw in Chapter 4 in relation to financial exclusion and debt, financial choice is heavily constrained by household income. In terms of housing, this means that low-income households may have to rent even though they would prefer to buy – especially since the sustained rise in property prices since the mid 1990s in the UK.

4   Renting a property

Let's look in more detail at the mechanics of the rental sector. As we saw in Section 2, the total amount of local authority stock has declined substantially since the 1980s. This has happened largely through 'right-to-buy' legislation but also through stock transfers from local authorities to RSLs, often accompanied by government money to improve the quality of the housing. The type, range and quality of housing still owned by local authorities is very diverse, ranging from flats to substantial houses. Whether someone qualifies for local authority accommodation depends on their income and circumstances, and on the amount of housing stock available to that local authority.

HAs and other RSLs are non-profit-making organisations which provide accommodation for people who need a home but cannot afford to buy or rent privately. They differ from local authorities in that they are formed and run by a voluntary committee, which is usually connected in some way with the area in which the HA operates or it has some particular expertise in housing. RSLs can be charities, industrial and provident societies and not-for-profit companies. There are also a number of housing cooperatives which are jointly owned and run by their tenants. RSLs are regulated, supported and funded by different bodies in the four nations of the UK such as the Housing Corporation (in England) and Communities Scotland. HAs also often offer 'shared equity' schemes. This is where homes can be part-bought and part-rented – a response to the rise in property prices making it harder for some people to buy their own home.

Housing Associations provide homes for people who can't afford to buy outright

Private rentals take many different forms, both in terms of type of accommodation and the legal basis on which the tenant lives in the property. The rights and responsibilities of a tenant and landlord of a property are generally determined by a tenancy agreement between the two parties. This contract usually states the amount of rent payable; the upfront 'deposit' required; the minimum length of occupancy; the notice required from either side for the tenant to leave; the division of responsibilities between the landlord and tenant in terms of the upkeep (perhaps with inventory attached); and various other matters.

One type of private rental is as a 'lodger', where the landlord, who is normally the owner and main occupant of the flat or house, rents out a room to someone. This type of arrangement is excluded from the legal protection given to other types of tenant, and so a lodger has no security of tenure. The landlord needs only to give reasonable notice for the tenant to leave, usually the same period of time as how often the rent is paid. Rent levels are set by agreement between landlord and lodger with no reference to any other authority. Despite the apparent lack of protection offered to a lodger, it is an arrangement which will suit some people at certain times in life, for instance, young people moving to a new area. It often suits homeowners too, as they can receive up to £4250 (in 2006/07) of tax-free income each year under the 'Rent a Room Scheme' in the UK.

Another type of rental is that of a private 'bedsit' – usually a room with its own 'front door' inside a larger building, perhaps with a kitchen and bathroom that may be shared between two or more such bedsits in a building. These and other 'Houses in Multiple Occupation' (any shared house on three or more stories and let to three or more people forming two or more households) will have individual agreements with each tenant and are covered by special laws such as those covering fire regulations and facilities.

Private rentals also include the renting of whole flats or houses – ranging from a studio apartment to a large house. Flats and houses can either be rented as a flat- or house-share where people (who may or may not have known each other before) live together and share all the facilities, and usually share responsibility for the payment of bills and Council Tax on the property. When sharing, the tenants will usually prefer to be responsible for their own rent and no one else's, whereas landlords may wish to have all the tenants sharing responsibility for all the rent. Flats and houses can also be rented by a single person or by a multi-person household. This means not having to share the facilities with others, but the costs may be more expensive per person.

Most tenancy agreements covering rentals of flats and houses now take the legal form of an 'Assured Shorthold Tenancy', known as a 'Short Assured Tenancy' in Scotland. This type of tenancy assures the right of the tenant to live in the property for a specified period (the Shorthold), such as six months, which is often automatically renewed for another six months on a rolling basis, but guarantees that the landlord may take back possession at the end of that period if they wish. All new tenancies granted are automatically Assured Shorthold Tenancies unless specified otherwise. The introduction of this type of tenancy agreement has arrested the long-term decline of private rented accommodation as a tenure type, as we saw in Table 6.1 and Figure 6.2, because it is more favourable to landlords than its predecessor. An older alternative is for an 'Assured Tenancy'. This gives security of tenure to a tenant as the landlord can only regain possession of the property via a possession order gained in court. Consequently, these agreements are being offered less by landlords, though they are still common with local authority rentals. (This broad description applies to most parts of the UK, although there are some minor differences, especially in Scotland).

5 Buying property

We can now move on to examine the different issues involved in buying property. Note that there are variations across the different parts of the UK; for example, Scotland has a different legal system, and the system of property purchase differs.

5.1 Affordability

Thinking back to the four stages of the financial planning process outlined in Chapter 1, Section 5.3, the first of these is to 'Assess'. In taking out a mortgage, one issue which a household or individual would have to assess is the question of its 'affordability'. Conventionally, this means taking on a mortgage debt no larger than three times the main earner's gross income, plus one times the second earner's gross income. Another conventional 'income multiple' is to use two and a half times a couple's joint pre-tax income. These days many lenders will offer mortgages based on higher income multiples, depending on the borrower's status.

Lenders use such income multiples, together with a 'credit scoring' process similar to that described in Section 5.2 of Chapter 4, to decide what size of mortgage they are prepared to lend. Usually, they will not advance more than 95 per cent of their valuation of the property, with the rest to be met from the borrower's own resources. For example, if the lender valued a property at £140,000, the maximum they would lend would be £133,000. Some lenders may be prepared to offer an advance of up to 100 per cent of the property value (termed 100 per cent **loan-to-value – LTV**). Other lenders, however, have a lower LTV maximum, especially when lending to those with a lower credit score. Certain lenders will be prepared to add some of the other associated costs (such as upfront fees), discussed in Section 5.3 below, to the mortgage advance, particularly if the amount lent in total does not exceed the value of the property. Some lenders specialise in lending to those with a poor credit history, and also in lending more than a property's current value.

Loan-to-value (LTV)
A measure of a loan (or mortgage) as a proportion of the lender's valuation of the property on which the loan (or mortgage) is secured.

5.2 Interest rates and mortgage products

Two choices about mortgages are linked with the question of affordability: the way interest is going to be charged on the mortgage, and the way the mortgage is going to be repaid.

How mortgage interest is charged

Partly because of the liberalisation in financial services, there are a large number of different mortgages on offer. In the second stage of the financial planning process, the 'Decide' stage, it is necessary to consider what mortgage product is most suitable. There are a number of issues which must be considered. The first of these is whether a fixed or variable rate mortgage should be chosen and whether a short- or long-term 'interest rate deal' is preferred. In the UK, variable rates are still the most common but there are a growing number of mortgage products offered at fixed rates. In 2004, the split in new mortgage lending in the UK was 64 per cent variable rate, 34 per cent fixed rate and 3 per cent on a capped or other rate basis.

There are many varieties of mortgage on offer, and Box 6.4 illustrates the main types.

Box 6.4 The main types of mortgage

Fixed rate mortgages: The interest rate is 'fixed' for a period of up to five years (although there are a limited number of ten- and twenty-five year products available). This gives the advantage to borrowers of knowing what their mortgage expenditure will be for several years ahead. The borrower is protected from an interest rate rise, but is locked into an uncompetitive rate if they fall. Fixed rate mortgages often have early redemption penalties. These are fees payable for repaying the mortgage early and are discussed further in Section 5.4.

Capped rate mortgages: The interest rate is variable, but cannot exceed a maximum level and so the borrower's maximum monthly mortgage payment is known in advance. These products are also likely to have early redemption penalties.

Variable rate mortgage: The rate of interest varies with movements in the official rate set by the Bank of England. Some 'tracker' mortgages may guarantee to be only a certain amount above the Bank of England official rates.

Discounted rate mortgages: Another type of variable rate mortgage which offers a discounted rate for an initial period. Borrowers need to calculate whether they can afford the rate which will apply once the discount period ends. Another incentive from lenders is to offer a 'cashback' payment to the borrower. These packages can be attractive for those borrowers who have particularly tight budgets in the first few years of purchasing a house. Discounted and cashback mortgage products are likely to have early redemption penalties.

Flexible mortgages: A type of variable rate mortgage which provides a number of repayment options, including a facility to overpay, underpay, re-borrow amounts previously repaid or take a 'payment holiday' if needed.

Offset mortgages: A type of variable rate mortgage which sets off cash surpluses in current or savings accounts against mortgage debt before monthly mortgage interest is worked out.

Top-up loan: A further mortgage on top of the main loan often used as a way to withdraw equity following an increase in house prices.

Equity release: A mortgage taken out against a property that was previously 100 per cent owned in order to release wealth locked up in the house for other purposes. The lender recoups the equity when the home is eventually sold.

Shared ownership mortgages: The borrower part-owns their own property while the rest is owned by another party – typically an HA.

Mortgage lending is also influenced by cultural difference. An important example of this is the development of Islamic home finance. Such products are compatible with shariah law, and avoid the payment of interest. Media reports suggest that this market is growing among the UK's Muslim population (Levine, 2005), with six banks offering Islamic home finance by mid 2006. The basic principles are that the lending institution and individual share ownership of the property and that the individual then makes rent payments which, over a number of years, end with complete ownership transferring to the individual. Box 6.5 illustrates an example of shariah lending.

Box 6.5 Example of Islamic home finance with Lloyds TSB

Islamic Home Finance is based on the ... Islamic finance principles of Ijara [lease agreement] and Diminishing Musharaka [equity participation]. You make two contracts with the bank: In this scheme, the bank and you jointly own the property although the title deeds will be in the bank's name. You will then buy back the bank's share over a number of years. During that period the bank will charge you rent for living in the property on the percentage of shares it has. With each payment your share of the property increases while the bank's percentage decreases. At the end of the term the bank will transfer the title deeds of the property into your name.

Figure 6.6 shows how the process works.

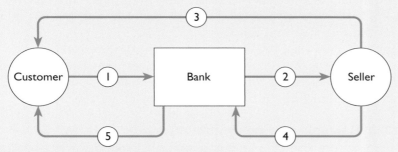

Figure 6.6 *The Islamic system of home finance*

Step 1 – You make an initial payment to the bank of at least 10 per cent of the property value. You sign two contracts, the Diminishing Musharaka contract and the Ijara contract. You promise to purchase the remaining 90 per cent of the property over an agreed period and you agree to pay rent to the bank.

Step 2 – The bank contributes up to 90 per cent of the property value and buys the property on your behalf.

Step 3 – The property is then transferred to you from the seller.

Step 4 – The property deeds are transferred to the bank.

Step 5 – When you have purchased the property completely, the property deeds are transferred to you.

(adapted from Lloyds TSB, 2005)

How a mortgage is repaid

The second major choice to be made about a mortgage is to decide how it is to be repaid. The options are a 'repayment' mortgage and an 'interest-only' mortgage (or perhaps a combination of the two).

Repayment mortgage
A mortgage where the periodic repayments made to the lender are the sum of the interest due and an amount of the original capital (or 'principal') sum borrowed.

With a **repayment mortgage**, the capital or principal sum (the original amount of debt), is paid off in stages throughout the life of the loan. Table 6.2 shows the pattern of payments on a repayment mortgage. The typical structure is a reducing balance loan where payments are made which, apart from any change in interest rate, would be a set amount each month throughout the mortgage term. The effect of this is that the amount of the principal sum repaid accelerates over the term of the mortgage – initially the majority of annual mortgage costs is made up of interest payments, and then towards the end of the mortgage term these costs are mainly repayments of the principal sum. One consequence is that a borrower who wishes to repay early might be surprised at how much of the principal sum remains.

Table 6.2 shows a £100,000 repayment mortgage payable over twenty-five years, at 7 per cent APR with interest calculated monthly. Results will vary slightly if different periods are used – for instance, a daily calculation of interest. Only selected years are shown.

Table 6.2 Example of a repayment mortgage

Year	Interest	Capital	Total for year
1	£6736.41	£1581.05	£8317.46
5	£6245.02	£2072.44	£8317.46
10	£5410.76	£2906.70	£8317.46
15	£4240.66	£4076.80	£8317.46
20	£2599.54	£5717.92	£8317.46
25	£297.79	£8019.67	£8317.46

Interest-only mortgage
A mortgage where the periodic repayments made by the borrower to the lender are solely the interest due and where the capital or principal sum borrowed is paid off in full at the end (or 'maturity') of the mortgage.

Conversely, with an **interest-only mortgage**, the principal sum outstanding is unchanged through the life of the loan and the only payments made to the lender until the end of the loan period are interest. At the end of the period, the borrower must have the means to repay the lender the principal sum. Failure to do this will result in the property, because it is secured against the debt, being repossessed. With interest-only mortgages, repayment of the principal is typically achieved by putting money throughout the life of the mortgage into a savings or investment scheme such as an ISA or unit trusts. To determine how much to save each month, the investment is projected to grow at an assumed rate in order to produce a lump sum large enough to repay the principal sum in full on the maturity of the mortgage.

Activity 6.5

What is the main financial risk with an interest-only mortgage?

Comment

The biggest risk with an interest-only mortgage is that the savings or investment scheme chosen does not produce enough money to pay off the mortgage. It's important to remember that the investment projections mentioned above may not materialise in reality because they usually do not have a guaranteed return. As you saw in Chapter 5, if investments are based on stock market gains, there are significant risks attached. Section 5.4 of this chapter explains that the fact that such projections can be wrong has led to financial difficulties for a number of households. ■■■

Comparing mortgage products

When comparing the interest charges on different mortgage products, there are some key points that need to be considered. As discussed in Section 3.4 of Chapter 4, in order to obtain an accurate comparison of the interest charges on different debt products, it is useful to look at the APR quoted. This calculates the cost of the mortgage over its life, taking account of discounts and additional costs (which are not included in the quoted interest rate of the mortgage) and the timing of interest payments and charges. The APR does not include charges for early repayment or options such as insurance or payments into an investment product for an interest-only mortgage. In addition, the APR will not take into account the cost of any **mortgage indemnity guarantee (MIG)** which may be levied on a higher risk borrower, for example, where there is a high LTV. Provided the products are comparable, a low APR indicates a mortgage is cheaper than one with a higher APR.

To help the process of making decisions in such a complex mortgage market, the Financial Services Authority (FSA) has stipulated that each mortgage seller must provide a **Key Facts Illustration (KFI)**. This document is produced as part of the mortgage application process and includes details of the features, terms and conditions of the mortgage product, enabling a comparison of different products on the same basis. Among the details included in the KFI are information on the overall cost of the mortgage, the amount of regular repayments, the APR and whether there are any early redemption penalties. For those on a variable rate mortgage, the KFI also illustrates by how much monthly mortgage repayments would increase if there were a 1 per cent increase in the rate of interest. The introduction of the KFI can be seen as an example of

Mortgage indemnity guarantee (MIG)
An insurance policy which insures the lender for any losses on lending above a defined minimum loan-to-value sum. This is charged to the borrower.

Key Facts Illustration (KFI)
Details the features, terms and conditions of a mortgage on a standard basis, enabling comparisons to be made between different lenders' products.

regulators responding to the complexity which accompanies increased competition, in this case by insisting that lenders provide information which enables mortgage customers to compare products more easily (see Box 6.6).

Box 6.6 FSA regulation of mortgages

How will I benefit from regulation?

On 31 October 2004 the FSA took over the regulation of most mortgage sales. The new regime means that:

- you will get clear information about mortgages and mortgage services in a standard keyfacts format. This makes it easier for you to compare mortgages and services from different lenders
- price information (including the APR) in any mortgage advertising and marketing material must be clear
- when you receive advice from a firm they must make sure that they recommend a suitable mortgage based on your needs and circumstances
- charges must not be excessive
- there are new standards offering greater protection should you get into arrears with your mortgage.

What is keyfacts?

To help make things easier for you firms will give you documents with this sign:

Make sure you read and understand them.

(FSA, 2005)

5.3 Other costs and the purchasing process

After choosing a mortgage and deciding upon how it is to be repaid, the house actually needs to be purchased – this is equivalent to the 'Stage 3: Act' part of the financial planning process. Let's first look at the other costs usually associated with buying property:

■ Legal costs for local searches. These are required to ensure that there are no problems with the property rights, and for the completion of documentation.

■ The cost of surveys undertaken on the property. Lenders normally require a valuation survey to be undertaken to ensure that the property is worth at least the mortgage amount. (Note that after the introduction of 'Home Information Packs' in England and Wales in 2007, the cost of surveys – but not a mortgage valuation – *may* shift to the seller at some subsequent date.)

■ Possibly fees payable to the lender (these often apply to fixed rate or capped rate mortgages).

■ Possibly fees payable to a financial services intermediary (or broker) who organises the mortgage. There may be commission paid to the broker by the lender of the mortgage product and ultimately borne by the borrower through charges for the mortgage.

■ Stamp Duty Land Tax on the purchase price. In 2006/07 this was 0 per cent on property purchases up to £125,000; 1 per cent on property purchases above £125,000; 3 per cent on purchases above £250,000; and 4 per cent on purchases above £500,000. These rates apply to the total purchase price. (Note that in some 'Disadvantaged Areas' properties under £150,000 are free of Stamp Duty Land Tax.)

■ The costs of moving into the accommodation, including removal costs and connection fees payable to utilities companies (for example, telephone line connection).

Activity 6.6

Your offer of £150,000 on a property has been accepted. The following costs apply: legal fees, £500; valuation survey, £250; structural survey, £750; arrangement fee to the mortgage broker, £250; Stamp Duty Land Tax paid at 1 per cent; removal costs, £1000.

1   How much does it cost in total to buy your property?

2   What are the extra non-purchase costs as a percentage of the property purchase price?

Comment

1   Stamp Duty (£150,000 × 1 per cent) = £1500

The other costs are £500 + £250 + £750 + £250 + £1000 = £2750

The total cost of buying the property is therefore £154,250

2   The extra costs are $\frac{4250}{150,000} \times 100 = 2.83$ per cent of the cost of the property ■ ■ ■

The largest cost when buying a property will be the price of the property itself, which a buyer can try to negotiate down from the seller's 'asking price'. Once a price has been agreed, both parties approach their solicitors (or other conveyancer) to seek completion of the transaction. Is the agreed price binding? In Scotland, the buyer submits their offer to the seller by an agreed date and the seller selects the best offer. Usually, at this point, the price agreed is binding so the mortgage needs to be arranged before the offer is made. In England, Wales and Northern Ireland, until the legal contracts are 'exchanged' between the two parties, both the buyer and seller are able to seek to change the price originally agreed. Sellers may accept a new, higher offer up to the point when contracts are exchanged – an unpopular process known as 'gazumping' – but if the market is weak, there is the risk of 'gazundering' where the buyer cuts the level of their offer at the last minute.

The exchange date is particularly important if there is a long 'chain' of sales involved. Usually buyers and sellers in a chain of housing transactions coordinate to try and ensure that no one remains committed to buying a property without having secured a commitment to have their existing property bought. The longer the chain, the greater the risk of problems that will prevent completion of the individual transactions. When the documentation is agreed and exchanged, the buyer pays a deposit to the seller and a 'completion date' is agreed, when ownership passes legally from the seller to the buyer and the money is paid. This is also usually moving day. Box 6.7 looks at the different ways in which property can be owned.

A property chain can be a major cause of stress when buying a home

Box 6.7 Freehold and leasehold

Properties in England, Wales and Northern Ireland are generally owned on either a freehold or leasehold basis. (The system in Scotland is different and leasehold for domestic properties is extremely rare. In Scotland, freehold is referred to as 'feuhold'.) With freehold properties, the owner has use of a property for an indeterminate time up to the point at which it is sold to another party. With leasehold properties, ownership is for a limited time, typically of ninety-nine years. Many flats are leasehold properties; most houses are freehold.

Leaseholders may have to pay 'ground rent' – a nominal sum due to the owner of the freehold on the property – and 'service charges' to cover maintenance of common parts of the whole property within which the leasehold property is situated. As the period of the unexpired lease shortens, the property may become less attractive to buyers, so extending the lease or determining whether there are any rights to buy the freehold may need investigating. Full details of recent changes to the rights of leaseholders arising from the Commonhold and Leasehold Reform Act 2002 can be found on the website of the Office of the Deputy Prime Minister (ODPM).

One decision that needs to be made if two people are going to buy together (whether as partners or not) is how the property will be owned legally. For instance, if they own it as **joint tenants**, each jointly owns the entire property, so upon the death of one party their interest in the property would pass automatically to the survivor. Therefore, couples will usually buy a property as joint tenants. By contrast, **tenants-in-common** each have a distinct share in the property. In Scotland, the equivalent terms are joint owners and owners-in-common. However, in Scotland, joint owners will have to have a 'survivorship destination' clause in the deeds to determine what happens to the property if one of the joint owners dies.

Joint tenants
Two or more people who own a property together. The joint tenants do not own distinct shares in the property.

Tenants-in-common
Two or more people who own a property together. Each has a distinct share.

Bridging loan
A temporary loan to extend further funds during the selling of one property, when the seller has already acquired another.

Selling property

Having entered the property market, moving home will usually involve both buying *and* selling a property. In these circumstances, it is necessary to ensure that the processes of exchanging on the sale and the purchase coincide to avoid owning two properties, while desperately trying to sell one of them. There are **bridging loans** for such a situation. When you are a seller, you will want to achieve as high a price as possible and the TV shows mentioned in Section 2.1 give endless tips about making homes attractive to buyers. One practical consideration, unless selling at auction, is to decide how to sell and how many estate agents to engage in the process. Typically, selling commission is between 1 per cent and 2 per cent of the sale price. If using one agent only (a 'sole agent'), it may be easier to negotiate the estate agent's commission than if several are used. Selling without agents, using the media and the internet, is an alternative. Sellers will have to pay for the production of 'Home Information Packs' when these are introduced in England and Wales in 2007. Legal costs will be higher when both buying and selling since there is more documentation to be completed.

5.4 The risks

Once a home has been purchased, some people might believe that all they have to do is sit back and watch their property rise in value. However, taking on a mortgage exposes households to financial risks.

These risks include the possibility that, due to sickness, unemployment, increases in interest rates or other unexpected events, mortgage repayments cannot be met. The risks will be higher as the size of the mortgage debt increases in relation to income. The lender will often allow a degree of leeway involving a small number of missed payments, provided they are advised of what the borrower believes to be a temporary problem. None the less, if payments are missed for a sustained period, the lender is likely to take action, including possibly repossessing the property. A mortgage is a secured loan and if the repayments are not met, the security (that is, the property) will be taken by the lender.

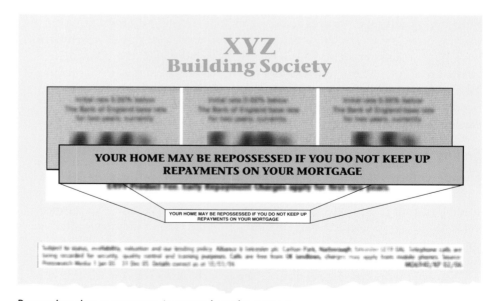

Remember that a mortgage is secured on the property

One possibility is to take out Mortgage Payment Protection Insurance (MPPI), also known as accident, sickness and unemployment insurance (ASU) (this is also discussed in Chapter 9, Section 7.2). This usually covers against accident, sickness and unemployment. Typically, a period of up to two years' cover on mortgage repayments is insurable, but because of exclusions, this type of insurance is not suitable for everyone. The UK Government may pay mortgage interest payments after nine months' unemployment for mortgages taken out after 1 October 1995 (or after eight weeks for mortgages taken out before then), but only where certain conditions are met.

Another risk, mentioned in Activity 6.5, is that the savings or investment vehicle used to pay off the principal sum in interest-only mortgages doesn't produce enough money. Investment policies sold in the late 1980s and 1990s were based upon assumptions about future investment performance that turned out to be too high. Low inflation and interest rates since the early 1990s, and the weakness of global stock markets after 1998, mean that some borrowers are at risk of finding that the principal sum of their mortgage cannot be paid off by the proceeds from their investment product. This is particularly true if borrowers did not regularly review how much they were setting aside.

So this highlights the importance of the 'Stage 4: Review' part of the financial planning process: in this case, reviewing the progress of the investment regularly and making adjustments if the investment is unlikely to repay the loan in full. Sellers of the investment products should advise borrowers about this risk when the borrowers take out such a mortgage, and should follow up with regular re-projections of how the product is performing (see Box 6.8). If the risk looks as though it will materialise, the borrower has the following options:

- Increase monthly payments on the investment product to increase the projected earnings by the maturity of the investment.
- Increase savings by paying extra into a different investment product that then supplements the original.
- Move to a repayment mortgage for some or all of the outstanding debt.
- Find additional resources when the mortgage reaches the end of its term. This could include borrowing again to meet the outstanding debt.
- Switch from the original product into another, although this is likely to incur penalties.
- Sell another asset or perhaps use a lump sum paid from a pension scheme.

Investment products can produce a return that exceeds the principal sum. While more recent policies have seen projected shortfalls, older policies have often produced returns in excess of the principal sum of the mortgage since these benefited from the higher investment yields seen in the 1980s and the early 1990s, and from tax reliefs which have now been abolished.

Box 6.8   When a 'red letter day' is bad news

Under Association of British Insurers guidelines, life companies providing endowment policies linked to mortgages must provide customers with an update, generally every two years, to state whether the policies are on track to meet the sum intended at the outset. If the product is projected to meet or exceed the target, the borrower gets a green letter. Slightly below target, indicating a risk of underperformance, generates an amber letter. A red letter results when there is a high risk that the target sum will not be met. In making these assessments, the investment companies must use FSA-required projections of annual returns of 4 per cent p.a., 6 per cent p.a. and 8 per cent p.a.

In *some* cases, endowments were 'mis-sold' in the past. This might be the case if, for example, the person who sold the policy did not explain that the endowment would not necessarily pay off the mortgage in full and that this depended on investment performance. In such cases, there is an official complaints procedure to be followed. If the complaint is upheld, it *may* be the case that some compensation is payable, according to a formula laid down by the FSA.

Another risk is that of negative equity. You saw in Section 2.2 how house prices fell between 1989 and 1995, and could do so again in the future. Many of those who bought houses in the late 1980s found themselves in a situation of negative equity, where the size of the mortgage debt exceeded the market value of their property. Moving into negative equity is not critical if the borrower is still able to meet their mortgage repayments and doesn't have to move home. However, if moving is necessary and house prices have fallen, there is the risk that the sale proceeds will be less than the amount owed on the mortgage. Either the shortfall has to be made up from other resources (for instance, savings or a loan) or it has to be added to the size of any new mortgage on a new property – provided the lender agrees to this.

Activity 6.7

Read the following description of the Max 130 mortgage from Mortgage Express, the lending arm of Bradford & Bingley. What issues should be considered if you are taking out such a mortgage?

Max 130 mortgage

A mortgage that allows borrowing up to 130% of property value – designed for people who haven't got a deposit, need some extra cash, or [are] looking to debt consolidate. This mortgage is only available through a Financial Adviser for re-mortgagers, first-time buyers and home movers.

(Mortgage Express, 2005)

Comment

For some people, this kind of mortgage will enable them to buy a property that they otherwise could not buy. However, it should be remembered that anyone taking on a debt for a sum greater than a property's value is immediately in negative equity. This means that if they want to move home in the future, they will have to finance the difference between the total debt and the property's value. The above quotation also mentions debt consolidation. You saw in Chapter 4, Section 5.2 that this is where a number of smaller, short-term debts are replaced by larger, long-term debt. ▪▪▪

A further risk of having a mortgage is that the mortgage ends up costing more than it needs to. It is possible, even if the best available mortgage was arranged at the time of purchase, that either circumstances have changed or other mortgage deals have become available – such as if a fixed rate product is taken out and interest rates subsequently fall. Increased competition in the mortgage market has increased the popularity of 'remortgaging'. This involves repaying an existing mortgage and taking out a new mortgage at a lower rate now available from either an existing or new lender. Such remortgaging may arise from a regular review of household finances such as that described in Stage 4 of the financial planning process. Possible events which might trigger a review include changes in household income, changes in interest rates, or the end of a period of time when someone is locked into a particular mortgage contract.

Remortgaging might seem simple, but there are costs. In addition to legal costs, there may be 'early redemption' or 'prepayment' fees. Generally these fees last for the first few years of the mortgage, or the period of any special deals, but sometimes they extend beyond a special deal (called a 'penalty overhang'). The terms of early redemption fees will be included in the KFI. When repaying a longer-term, fixed rate mortgage early, the prepayment fees may be substantial – a fee of six months' interest is not uncommon. This does not necessarily mean that remortgaging might not save money, particularly if interest rates have fallen a long way since the initial mortgage was arranged; it simply means that households need to make careful comparisons. Any savings made from remortgaging will help with the budgeting process we saw in Chapter 3. Activity 6.8 offers an example.

Activity 6.8

An interest-only mortgage of £100,000 ends in three years. Currently the Barnett household is on a fixed rate deal at 8 per cent p.a. If they repay now, the lender will charge an upfront six-month interest penalty. They have savings earning 4 per cent p.a. net of interest which could cover this cost, and another lender has offered them a three-year mortgage at 6 per cent p.a. and will cover all the other costs of remortgaging. Should the Barnetts pay the penalty and remortgage?

Comment

The six-month penalty costs the Barnetts 4 per cent (i.e. 8 per cent for half a year), which is £4000 (4 per cent of £100,000). If they had kept the £4000 invested at 4 per cent for the three years, leaving the interest in the account, this would have totalled £4499 at the end of the three years. This is because the interest would be compounded. You learned about compounding in Chapter 4.

The calculation is:

$(£4000 \times 1.04 \times 1.04 \times 1.04) = £4499$.

The annual savings with the new lender are 8 per cent minus 6 per cent = 2 per cent. For each year, the household would save £2000 (£100,000 × 2 per cent), totalling savings of £6000 over three years.

So even if the Barnetts do not invest the annual sum saved, the minimum benefit from remortgaging is £6000 minus £4499 = £1501, implying the financially capable household should remortgage. ■■■

6 Property as an investment and 'buy-to-let'

Investment in property is now considered a serious alternative to the kinds of investments discussed in Chapter 5. This isn't surprising: the liberalisation of financial services has made obtaining mortgages much easier, and the sharp rise in property prices that we saw in Section 2.2 has encouraged the view that capital gains on property can be easily achieved. The popular media, including the TV shows I mentioned in Section 2.1, also seems to encourage the idea that we can all become property developers!

Don't overlook the investment in your own home. It's easier to raise finance on the 'primary residence' than on second homes; there is only one set of interest costs to worry about and, as mentioned earlier, there is normally no liability for Capital Gains Tax on any profit made. The objective with your home (apart from having somewhere to live) would be to increase its capital value and thus the equity in it. There are several ways in which that can happen over and above any general rise in property prices. For example, homes can be bought in an 'up and coming' area where property prices will rise more than the average; they could be bought at below the 'true' market value; or someone can add value to a property by finding, for instance, a rundown home suitable for refurbishment and, when completed, sell at a profit over and above the total cost of the purchase, interest and refurbishment. As mentioned in Section 4, another way to make money from a home is to rent out a spare room, effectively using the home as an income-producing asset. Some people may carry these ideas substantially further and rent out several rooms, or regularly buy, develop and then sell individual properties. Doing either would move into the realms of trading, and Income Tax 'Rent a Room', and Capital Gains Tax exemptions would be lost.

Another development – particularly from the mid 1990s on – has been the growth of the 'buy-to-let' sector. This has become more common both as a result of the introduction of the Assured Shorthold Tenancy (described in Section 4) and the development of specialist buy-to-let mortgages in the competitive mortgage marketplace. The main change was that the buy-to-let mortgages allowed expected rental income to be taken into account when assessing the borrower's ability to take out a mortgage on a property intended for rental. Buy-to-let can be an alternative to, or complement, other investments or pension plans. Properties are bought to be rented out, perhaps with the hope of additional return from an increase in the capital value of the property. In the mid 1990s, buy-to-let returns of 12 or 13 per cent per annum could sometimes be achieved. However, when the stock market performed badly in the late 1990s, and money consequently flowed from there into the buy-to-let market, the supply of rental property increased and returns fell. This was another major reason why the decline in private rented homes was halted, as we saw in Section 2. The introduction of Real Estate Investment Trusts (REITs) from January 2007, which will enable individuals to invest in the property market without the risk of direct ownership, may give a further boost to the idea of investment in property.

Activity 6.9

What are the risks of buy-to-let? Your answers to Activity 6.3 will suggest some issues, although you will need to think of others.

Comment

Some of the risks include: property prices falling; the landlord being unable to find tenants for the rental property for a period of time; higher than anticipated costs on the property (for instance, on maintenance or renovation). These reinforce the need for careful calculation and advice. ■ ■ ■

7 Revisiting assets and liabilities

7.1 Financial balance sheets

Given the material covered so far in *Personal Finance*, we are now ready to explore the financial balance sheet more fully. Chapter 4 briefly outlined the purpose of a financial balance sheet: to estimate the value of assets and liabilities at a particular point in time, for either an individual or a household. Liabilities were introduced and explained in Chapter 4, and the most common assets in Chapters 2 and 5. This chapter has so far focused on housing, which for many people will provide both their biggest asset (their home, if they own one) and their biggest liability (their mortgage). The financial balance sheet allows an individual or household to have a snapshot of their overall financial position at a particular point in time. Such information, taken together with cash flow and budgeting statements, is crucial for financial planning.

Figure 6.7 in Activity 6.10 lists the main items recorded in a financial balance sheet, most of which should be familiar from earlier discussions in this and other chapters. Assets are split between liquid and other assets, while liabilities are split between short-term and other liabilities. The difference between total liabilities and total assets provides an estimate of the net worth (or wealth) of an individual or a household – rather like a summary of their overall financial position at a particular point in time.

You may have noticed that I said that net worth is *estimated* rather than *recorded*. This is because it can be difficult to obtain an accurate valuation of certain assets without actually selling them. For example, the value of houses can be estimated, but their actual value will depend on a price obtained in the marketplace. You may also notice that contributions to pension schemes are not included in the assets column. This is because, generally, pensions cannot be sold and turned into cash, making it hard to get a precise estimate of their worth. (Pensions are considered separately in Chapter 7.) Despite these reservations, the estimate of net worth provided by the financial balance sheet is useful in giving an overview of an individual's or household's financial position.

Activity 6.10

Use Figure 6.7 overleaf to complete your financial balance sheet. You can do this individually, or for your household, as you feel appropriate. ■■■

The financial balance sheet can also be used to calculate the **current asset ratio**. This compares total liquid assets with total short-term liabilities and is useful in assessing how finances can be managed in the short term. It is calculated in the following way:

$$\text{Current asset ratio} = \frac{\text{Total liquid assets}}{\text{Total short-term liabilities}}$$

Personal finance experts say that the current assets ratio should always exceed 1. If it is below 1, then that tells us that short-term liabilities (such as bills and credit card debts) could not be met if circumstances made it necessary to do so. This can indicate that potentially serious financial difficulties could lie ahead. The risks are **insolvency** and potentially even **bankruptcy**. Personal finance experts often argue that a good target to aim for – when well into adult life – would be a current asset ratio of 4, though a less conservative target might be only 3.

Current asset ratio
Total liquid assets divided by total short-term liabilities.

Insolvency
When someone is unable to pay the debts they owe.

Bankruptcy
A process that happens when an individual cannot pay their debts, and all their property is distributed to the people to whom they owe money.

Assets	Liabilities
LIQUID ASSETS	**SHORT-TERM LIABILITIES**
Cash	Bills you owe
Current account balance	Credit card and store card debts
Savings account(s) balances	Loan balances repayable within one year
Debts owed to you and repayable within one year	Overdrafts
	Other money owed and repayable within one year
TOTAL LIQUID ASSETS _____	**TOTAL SHORT-TERM LIABILITIES** _____
OTHER ASSETS	**OTHER LIABILITIES**
Home	Mortgage balance
Other land and buildings (e.g. second home, buy-to-let property)	Other mortgages or long-term loans
Investment funds (e.g. unit trusts, investment trusts)	Loan balances repayable in more than one year
Shares	Amount outstanding on hire purchase agreements
Gilts and corporate bonds	Other liabilities
Collectables (e.g. antiques and paintings)	
Debts owed to you and not repayable within one year	
Other financial assets _____	_____
TOTAL OTHER ASSETS _____	**TOTAL OTHER LIABILITIES** _____
TOTAL ASSETS _____	**TOTAL LIABILITIES** _____
MINUS _____	
TOTAL LIABILITIES _____	
= NET WORTH (OR NET WEALTH) [ ]	

Figure 6.7 Financial balance sheet

Activity 6.11

Use the figures you produced on your personal balance sheet in Activity 6.10 to calculate your current asset ratio. How might this be used in financial planning?

Comment

One possible use of your current asset ratio would be to assess the progress of particular financial plans. Someone with the goal of getting out of short-term debt, for example, could calculate their current asset ratio every three months and track it as it (hopefully) moves to a figure above 1. ■ ■ ■

7.2 Assets and liabilities: their relationship with income and expenditure

We now want to draw together the discussions in Chapters 4 and 5 which started to look at the relationship between liabilities and expenditure and assets and income. This is summarised in Figure 6.8, which describes the interrelationship between the *stocks* of assets and liabilities and the *flows* of income and expenditure. Assets are on one side of the scales and liabilities on the other. In reality, these scales would be in constant motion, as money continually flows into and out of individuals' and households' pockets, and the value of assets and liabilities is continuously changing. For the sake of simplicity, let's assume the scales have stopped at a particular point in time. This allows an exploration of both how assets relate to income and how liabilities relate to expenditure.

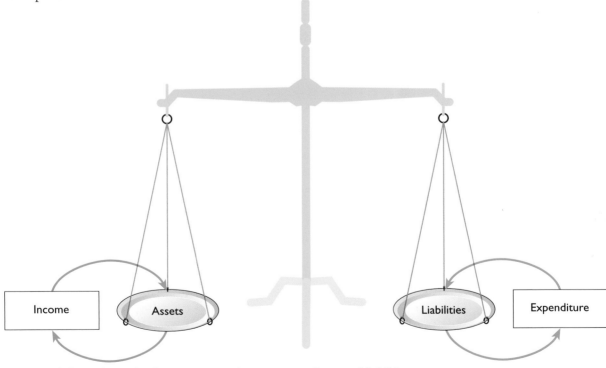

Figure 6.8 *Interrelationship between assets, income, expenditure and liabilities*

The receipt of income adds to the asset side of the balance sheet (at least in the short term) as money flows, such as pay from employment, go into a current account, or can be used to purchase shares, bonds or other forms of saving and investments. In turn, many assets produce flows of income, such as interest payments or share dividends. Non-financial assets (for instance, a piece of art) generally do not produce an income flow, and would have to be sold to generate money. Yet even these assets could theoretically produce an income, for example, lending a work of art to an exhibition for a fee.

Similarly, expenditure is related to liabilities in the sense that having debts generates future flows of expenditure. Expenditure either reduces assets – perhaps by depleting the current account or by causing other assets to be sold – or increases liabilities, perhaps by taking out debt to pay for it. Expenditure which is higher than income generates liabilities because individuals or households will have to take on debts, for example, by using credit cards or overdrafts, to fund the gap between expenditure and income.

To return to the subject of housing, it can be interesting to reconsider how homes fit into the balance sheet. Homes are typically regarded as the biggest asset of an individual or household. Yet an interesting point put forward by Robert T. Kiyosaki in his famous book *Rich Dad, Poor Dad* (Kiyosaki, 2000) is that one of the key mistakes contributing to making people 'poor' rather than 'rich' is buying a home that is bigger than strictly needed. Rather than buying assets that produce *income* (like shares or investments), the large mortgage actually causes *expenditure* to escalate. It's a salient point which provides an interesting counterweight to the British dedication to house buying.

8 Conclusion

In this chapter, you have seen that there are many important financial decisions that have to be taken about homes and housing – probably several times over a life-course, and often in response to changes in household circumstances or other changes over time. In Section 2, you saw how the social and economic context is crucial in affecting decisions about where we live – from government legislation to property price trends. You also saw how changes in household composition and demographics have played a big role in the housing market.

In terms of the financial planning process, we have added several important components. The practicalities of the process of renting and buying were discussed in Sections 4 and 5. It was shown how the financial planning process can offer a useful framework, particularly in the buying process, by assessing affordability, deciding upon repayment options and reviewing decisions. You also saw in Section 7 that homes, when purchased through a mortgage, form a major component of both sides of a financial balance sheet. Such balance sheets provide a snapshot of individual or household net worth and are an important tool in personal financial planning. This tool adds to the cash flow statement and budgeting process explained in Chapters 2 and 3, and together these offer a crucial toolkit in financial planning and money management. The size and composition of the financial balance sheet is also very important as you become older – it will affect how you approach later life, retirement planning and issues of inheritance, subjects we turn to in Chapter 7.

References

Abbey (2005) 'Gap between the cost of renting and buying narrows', press release, 21 June [online], http://www.aboutabbey.com/csgs/ Satellite?c=GSNoticia&cid=282596140586695&idBack=1127562008772& pagename=AboutAbbey/GSNoticia/PAAI_newCompletCentre& printable=si (Accessed 12 May 2006).

BBC (2003) 'The Kippers who won't leave home' [online], http://news. bbc.co.uk/1/hi/business/your_money/3276039.stm (Accessed 29 March 2006).

Chiuri, M.C. and Jappelli, T. (2000) 'Financial market imperfections and home ownership: a comparative study', Centre For Studies In Economics and Finance, Working Paper no. 44, December.

Financial Services Authority (FSA) (2005) 'FSA regulation of mortgages' [online], http://www.fsa.gov.uk/consumer/07_MORTGAGES/ about_keyfacts.html (Accessed 9 December 2005).

Gray, P.P. and Gray, D.P. (2004) 'Housing foundations remain rock solid', *The Times*, Business Section, p. 53, 23 November.

House of Commons Library (1999) 'A century of change: trends in UK statistics since 1900' [online], Research Paper 99/111, http://www. parliament.uk/commons/lib/research/rp99/rp99-111.pdf (Accessed 26 January 2006).

Joseph Rowntree Foundation (1998) 'Reviewing the right to buy', December [online], http://www.jrf.org.uk/knowledge/findings/housing/ hrd28.asp (Accessed 11 January 2006).

Kiyosaki, R.T. (2000) *Rich Dad, Poor Dad: What the Rich Teach their Kids about Money – That the Poor and Middle Class Do Not!*, New York, Warner Business Books.

Levine, T. (2005) 'Banks meet the demands of UK's 1.8m Muslims', *The Guardian*, Jobs and Money Section, 2 April, p. 10.

Lloyds TSB (2005) 'How does Islamic home finance fit with my faith?' [online], http://www.lloydstsb.com/mortgages/islamic_home_finance_faqs.asp (Accessed 27 January 2006).

Mortgage Express (2005) 'Max 130 mortgage' [online], http://www.mortgage-express.co.uk/pdf/max130%20mortgage.pdf (Accessed 6 December 2005).

Nationwide Building Society (2005) House price data available at http://www.nationwide.co.uk/hpi/downloads/UK_house_prices_adjusted_for_inflation.xls (Accessed 9 July 2005).

Office for National Statistics (ONS) (2003) 'Table 3.1 Trends in household size: 1971 to 2003' [online], *General Household Survey 2003*, http://www.statistics.gov.uk/statbase/Expodata/Spreadsheets/D8705.xls (Accessed 11 January 2006).

Office for National Statistics (ONS) (2005a) 'Housing tenure: 70% of GB dwellings are owner-occupied' [online], http://www.statistics.gov.uk/cci/nugget.asp?id=1105 (Accessed 9 August 2005).

Office for National Statistics (ONS) (2005b) 'Divorces: fourth successive annual increase in UK' [online], http://www.statistics.gov.uk/cci/nugget.asp?id=170 (Accessed 11 January 2006).

Office of the Deputy Prime Minister (ODPM) (2004) Housing Statistics, Live Tables on Stock, 'Table 108 Dwelling stock: by tenure, Northern Ireland (historical series)' [online], http://www.odpm.gov.uk/pub/14/Table108Excel36Kb_id1156014.xls (Accessed 9 September 2005).

Office of the Deputy Prime Minister (ODPM) (2005a) Housing Statistics, Live Tables on Stock, 'Table 101 Dwelling stock: by tenure, United Kingdom (historical series)' [online], http://www.odpm.gov.uk/pub/7/Table101Excel38Kb_id1156007.xls (Accessed 11 January 2006).

Office of the Deputy Prime Minister (ODPM) (2005b) Housing Statistics, Live Tables on Stock, 'Table 107 Dwelling stock: by tenure, Scotland (historical series)' [online], http://www.odpm.gov.uk/pub/13/Table107Excel38Kb_id1156013.xls (Accessed 9 September 2005).

Office of the Deputy Prime Minister (ODPM) (2005c) Housing Statistics, Live Tables on Stock, 'Table 106 Dwelling stock: by tenure, Wales (historical series)' [online], http://www.odpm.gov.uk/pub/12/Table106Excel39Kb_id1156012.xls (Accessed 9 September 2005).

Office of the Deputy Prime Minister (ODPM) (2005d) Housing Statistics, Live Tables on Housing Market and House Prices, 'Table 505 Housing market: simple average house prices, by new/other dwellings, type of buyer and standard statistical regions, from 1969' [online], http://www.odpm.gov.uk/pub/114/Table505Excel102Kb_id1156114.xls (Accessed 27 January 2006).

Social Trends (2004) no. 34, London, The Stationery Office (TSO) for The Office for National Statistics (ONS); also available online at the ONS website (National Statistics Online), http://www.statistics.gov.uk/downloads/theme_social/Social_Trends34/Social_Trends34.pdf (Accessed 14 November 2005).

Pensions

Chapter 7

Jonquil Lowe

Contents

I   Introduction

Crisis looms for private pensions

(Scotland on Sunday, 12 June 2005)

One in four 'heading for poverty in retirement'

(Daily Telegraph, 28 April 2005)

Closure of final salary schemes set to expand

(Financial Times, 4 June 2005)

Retirement age will rise to 68

(The Guardian, 25 May 2006)

These were familiar headlines in the mid 2000s. Pundits were full of doom, predicting a future of impoverished pensioners and overburdened tax payers. Why was this, and were the commentators right to be so gloomy? By the end of this chapter, you will have an insight into the background to the claims, the implications for retirement planning generally, and what households and individuals can do to improve their chances of financial security in later life.

The key to financial security is having enough income to finance a desired level of spending. Chapter 2 showed how earnings from work are the most important source of income for most people during their working-age years. Yet they expect to retire one day, and earnings then either stop or markedly fall. Other sources of income will be needed to support the chosen standard of living in **retirement**. We shall explore the options open to society and to individuals to ensure that these alternative

Retirement
The period of life after (the main source of) paid employment ends.

sources are available, and how the outcomes vary for different types of household and individual, in particular, the different experiences of men and women. Section 3 introduces the different types of schemes available to individuals, whilst Section 4 focuses on the significance of an ageing population. Sections 5 and 6 focus on some of the choices and decisions that individuals and households need to consider.

A future of overburdened tax payers?

2   Pensions and pensioners

2.1   Pensions policy

The question of providing financial support in old age is important to every society. The UK Government, in common with that of many other countries, has provided some sort of payment to people in old age, known as a **pension**, for around 100 years. However, decisions about what is an 'adequate' pension, who qualifies for such a pension, and who has the responsibility to provide pensions have always been, and continue to be, a matter of debate among politicians, policy makers and wider society.

At the centre of this debate is deciding upon the share of economic output which goes to those receiving pensions. Each year different productive elements of an economy combine to produce a level of output (called **Gross Domestic Product** or **GDP**) which is shared by society. If one section of society, such as those receiving pensions, is to have a larger share of economic output, other sections of society, such as workers or

Pension
A regular payment that forms part of financial support in old age.

Gross Domestic Product (GDP)
The value of all goods and services produced by an economy over a set period of time, usually a particular year.

corporations, must have less. Therefore, if pensions were to increase, for example, this would mean less economic output would be available for other uses, such as pay, profits or other forms of government expenditure.

Another important issue is the mix between private and public pension provision. In 1979, about 70 per cent of a UK single **pensioner**'s gross weekly income came from the state; by 2003/04 this percentage had fallen to around 60 per cent (DWP, 2005). What is more, one government report cited the aim of reducing the proportion of UK pensioner incomes coming from the government to 40 per cent by 2050 in order to 'maintain public expenditure at prudent levels' (Department of Social Security, 1998, pp. 31–2). In fact, UK governments from 1979 to the 2000s took steps to reduce future state spending on retirement pensions, including changing state pensions so that they increase in line with prices rather than earnings, making several reductions in the pensions accumulating through the state additional pension scheme (explained in Section 3.1), and increasing the age at which women become entitled to the state pension from 60 to 65.

As these changes take effect, so state spending on retirement pensions in the UK is forecast to fall from 5 per cent of GDP in 2004 to 4.4 per cent in 2051 – despite a rising number of pensioners (House of Lords, 2004a, paragraph 10.11). Another report showed public spending on pensions declining as a percentage of economic output from 5.5 per cent in 2000 to 4.9 per cent in 2020 and 4.4 per cent in 2050 (Pensions Commission, 2004). The effect of this on the future level of government spending per pensioner will depend on how big the economy grows (as measured by GDP), but the likely impact is even greater when taking into account the fact that the number of pensioners is rising.

It is not just the UK Government which has been seeking to minimise its liability for paying pensions. Employers have also been implementing changes. The main shift has been from 'defined benefit' to less generous 'defined contribution' occupational pension schemes. We'll look at these schemes in detail in Section 3. An indication of the rate of change is given by the National Association of Pension Funds Survey 2004. This survey reported that, in 2003, 26 per cent of the more generous private sector defined benefit pension schemes closed to new members, and that, in 2004, another 10 per cent closed (NAPF, 2004).

Such changes represent a shift in the risk associated with providing financial security in old age from the collective, in the form of the state or employer, to the individual. So the area of pension provision, perhaps more than any other area of personal finance discussed in *Personal Finance*, highlights the need for increasing levels of financial self-reliance.

This clearly has implications for financial planning, many of which are discussed in the following sections. None the less, as you read through this chapter it is important to remember the role of political decisions in

Pensioner
A person who has started to draw a pension whether or not they continue to do some paid work.

shaping the current and future social and economic environment. At present, the emphasis is on individuals increasingly bearing the risk of providing adequate pensions. Yet if in the future citizens choose to elect a government with different policies – for instance, one which increases taxes to fund higher pensions – then this emphasis may change. In other words, the interdependence between individuals and their social and economic environment works both ways: the environment shapes individual choices and decisions, and at present encourages people to provide for their own pensions, but individuals acting collectively through the political process can also shape and change their social and economic environment.

Political action over the level of the state pension is an example of how the social and economic context can be shaped by collective action

2.2 Pensioner income inequality

Standards of living are not uniform for pensioners. Indeed, as Figure 7.1 shows, there is significant inequality in income among UK pensioners. In Figure 7.1, data has been divided into five groups (called 'quintiles') according to the income of each group. (Quintiles are similar to the percentiles explained in Chapter 2, except that here we are dividing the populations into five equal parts). These figures rank the poorest fifth (bottom quintile) of pensioners from the left up to the richest fifth (top quintile) on the far right. In UK Government statistics, a single pensioner is a single person over **state pension age** and a pensioner couple is a household where the man is over state pension age.

State pension age
The age at which a person becomes eligible to draw a state pension. In the UK, this is 65 for men and, until 2010, 60 for women but then rises to 65 for women born after 5 March 1955. In 2006, the government proposed raising the state pension age in stages to age 68 by 2044.

Figure 7.1 shows that the poorest fifth of single pensioners had an income of only around £100 a week, which is just one-quarter of the amount (over £400 a week) that the richest fifth receives. The poorest pensioner couples have less than £200 a week, which is only one-fifth of the £900 plus that the richest fifth have. What is more, the differences between the poorest and richest pensioners have grown since 1979 (DWP, 2005).

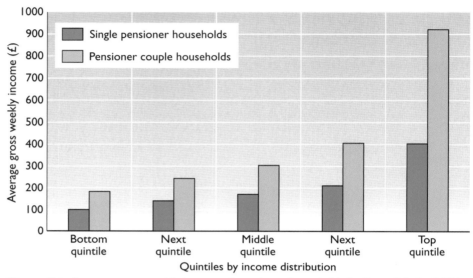

Figure 7.1 *Average gross weekly income of pensioner households in Great Britain, 2004*
Source: data from DWP, 2005, p. 51, Table 19

State pension
Pension provided by the government to everyone in the UK who qualifies.

Occupational pension
Pension from a scheme provided by an employer for workers and their dependants.

Personal pension
Pension from a retirement savings scheme taken out by an individual to provide for themselves and their dependants.

Let's now look at where pensioner income comes from by examining data on income sources. Figure 7.2 uses data from 2004 to show the sources of income for the poorest fifth of single pensioners and the richest fifth (the data relates to Great Britain only). You can see from Figure 7.2 that the poorest single pensioners are relying heavily on **state pensions** and benefits, whereas the richest single pensioners also have other sources of income: **occupational pensions**, **personal pensions**, investments and earnings. Although less reliant on them, richer pensioners also have bigger state pensions than poorer pensioners. (This is because older pensioners, who also tend to be poorer pensioners, generally have lower state additional pension, which will be explained in Section 3.) The story is similar for pensioner couples.

Clearly, one of the most important distinguishing factors between rich and poor pensioners is the amount of income which comes from occupational pension schemes. However, given the findings of the National Association of Pension Funds Survey 2004, mentioned in Section 2.1, it is unlikely that better-off pensioners will continue to receive similar returns from occupational schemes in the future. It is possible that richer pensioners will receive more income from other sources such as investment income in the future, but the amount coming from occupational schemes is likely to fall as employers seek to minimise their future financial liability by moving away from the more generous defined benefit schemes.

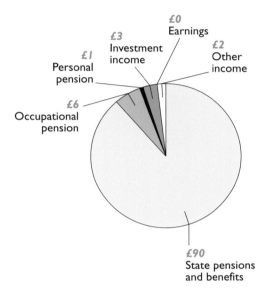

(a) Poorest fifth of single pensioners

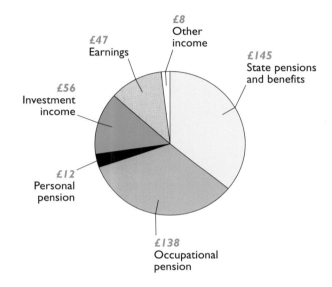

(b) Richest fifth of single pensioners

Figure 7.2 *Sources of gross weekly income, 2004*
Source: data from DWP, 2005, p. 51, Table 19

I now want you to think a little more about income distribution among different groups of pensioners. What does the information in Table 7.1 tell you about differences in income distribution among pensioners according to their age, gender and whether they are single or part of a couple?

Table 7.1 Average gross weekly income of different pensioners, 2004

Type of pensioner	Gross weekly income	Percentage of income from:	
		State pensions and benefits (%)	Other sources of income (%)
Pensioner couple where man is under age 75	£456	38	62
Pensioner couple where man is aged 75 or over	£344	53	47
Single male pensioner under age 75	£265	48	52
Single male pensioner aged 75 or over	£225	56	44
Single female pensioner under age 75	£214	58	42
Single female pensioner aged 75 or over	£184	71	29

Source: data from DWP, 2005, pp. 17 and 23, Tables 2 and 5

Comment

Table 7.1 shows that older pensioner households, whether couples or single people, have less income on average than younger pensioners. It also shows that single women pensioners have lower incomes than their male counterparts, whatever their age. Older, single women pensioners have the lowest incomes of all. It also confirms that the poorest pensioners tend to be more reliant on state benefits than better-off pensioners. For example, the older, single female pensioners receive 71 per cent of their income from state pensions and benefits compared with just 38 per cent for the younger pensioner couples. ■ ■ ■

2.3 Age and gender

As Activity 7.1 showed, lower pensioner incomes are particularly noticeable among the older and female pensioner population. In 2002, there were just under 11 million people in the UK who were over state pension age. Of these, nearly 7 million were women. Thus, overall, there were approximately two female pensioners for every male. Moreover, women make up an even greater proportion of the oldest pensioners with, for instance, three women to every man over the age of 85 (ONS, 2004a).

Older pensioners tend to be poorer than younger pensioners because modern occupational pension schemes became widespread only from the late 1950s onwards (Pension Law Review Committee, 1993, pp. 64–8). This means that many of today's older pensioners did not have the opportunity to build up good occupational pensions during a large part of their working life. Older pensioners are also less likely than younger pensioners to be supplementing their income with earnings from paid work. Overall, just one pensioner in eleven works, but the proportion in the first five years of retirement is higher: one in eight for men, and one in four for women (DWP, 2003, p. 14, Table 2.2; DWP, 2004a, p. 6, Table 1).

Some of the reasons for greater pensioner poverty among women lie in the social and cultural background of the last century. Stereotypically, this was the model of women looking after the home and family, rather than having their own career, while the husband earned income and hence built up the household's retirement savings. In addition, wives often had little control over the family income and few opportunities to accumulate any savings of their own. The state pension scheme was built around this stereotype of family life, allowing husbands to claim extra pension for their wives, and originally giving married women the right to 'opt out' of building up their own state pension.

Reliance on their partners means that women generally see a big drop in income if the relationship breaks down or the man dies. Take, as a fictional example, Phil and Mary Simms. In 2005, they were living fairly comfortably in retirement on their state pensions and Phil's occupational pension, which together came to around £14,000 a year after tax (£269 a week). Unfortunately, Phil then died. Mary qualified for only a small widow's pension from Phil's occupational scheme. Her state pension was boosted and she was also able to claim Pension Credit (a state benefit which we shall briefly look at in Section 3.1). Even so, her income dropped to just £6500 a year (£125 a week). Figure 7.3 shows the impact of Phil's death on the household income. While Phil was alive, the couple lived within their means and were even able to save a little. Mary on her own cannot manage on her income. Despite cutting back her spending as much as possible, she risks running into debt problems.

Although more women are now in paid employment, as we saw in Chapter 2, their caring roles mean that they often have less opportunity than men to build up adequate pensions of their own. It is still far more common for women than men to work part time or to take career breaks

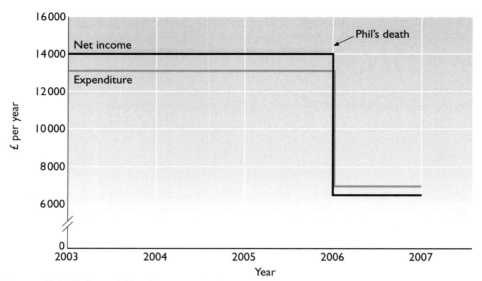

Figure 7.3 *Phil's and Mary's income and expenditure*

in order to bring up children or care for elderly relatives. As you will see in Chapter 8, this affects women's labour market prospects not only during the caring years, but also beyond. It also has a major impact on the pension they can expect in retirement because:

- during breaks from paid employment, people generally build up low or no retirement savings
- part-time work tends to be low paid, so any pension entitlement linked to it or financed out of it is also low
- part-time jobs often used to be with employers who chose not to offer pension arrangements at all or excluded part-timers. (Since October 2001, all but the smallest employers must offer some type of pension through the workplace, and since October 2002 part-timers may no longer be excluded.)

The issue of women's lower pensions is further compounded because women tend to live longer than men – in the UK, women's life expectancy at birth is 81, but for men it is 76. This means that it costs more to provide a pension for the average woman than for the average man of the same age, because her pension will have to be paid out for longer. In turn, this means that if a woman is to have the same pension as a man of the same age, she needs to save more.

3 Types of pensions in the UK

In this section, we are going to look in more detail at the main types of pension that I introduced in Section 2.2.

3.1 State pensions

Limited state retirement pensions were first paid in the UK in 1908. These were improved in 1946 when the National Insurance Act brought in flat-rate universal state pensions. Since the Second World War, the levels of pensions and the mechanisms for paying pensions have been a matter of continual public debate. While various developments in state pensions have taken place, the main thrust of policy, especially since 1980, has been a shift to limit public expenditure on pensions.

The level of the flat-rate universal state pension has been debated since it came into being in the UK in the late 1940s

There are two main parts to the state pension. The first is the basic state pension which is paid at a **flat rate** (£84.25 a week in 2006/07 for a single person), which in 2006 was equivalent to approximately 15 per cent of national average earnings for full-time employees. This is normally increased each year in line with price inflation. This compares to the early 1980s when it was worth 20 per cent of average earnings

Flat rate
Describes an amount of pension where the value is not linked to a person's earnings.

Working life
An official definition meaning the tax years from age 16 to state pension age. For a person whose state pension age is 65, working life is 49 years.

Registered civil partner
A same-sex partner treated in the same way for tax, benefit and most legal purposes as a husband or wife. Two people of the same sex can form a civil partnership by signing a registration document.

State additional pension
A state pension available mainly to employees. The amount received varies from one person to another depending largely on their average earnings while the pension was building up.

(Smith, 2001, p. 1). Everyone who has a nearly full record of National Insurance contributions and credits over their **working life** receives this flat rate basic state pension. People with a reduced record receive less. There are special rules to prevent or lessen any reduction in the basic pension for people who are out of paid work caring for children or dependent adults. In 2006, the government proposed that the number of years of National Insurance contributions needed to qualify for the flat rate basic state pension will be reduced to 30 years for both men and women.

Husbands (and from 2010, wives and **registered civil partners**) can claim extra pension (up to £50.50 a week in 2006/07) for their spouse unless the spouse qualifies for more than that based on their own National Insurance record. (This means that the maximum basic state pension for a married couple, or civil partners, will normally be £134.75 a week in 2006/07.)

The second part of the state pension is the **state additional pension**, which is an earnings-related pension restricted mainly to employees. The amount a person receives depends on their earnings averaged over their working life since 1978 (when the scheme started). In general, the higher their average earnings, the higher the pension. However, employees earning less than a set threshold (£12,500 in 2006/07), carers and some people with disabilities receive extra pension by being treated as if they have earnings equal to the threshold.

In theory, the state additional pension can be substantial, more than doubling the total state pension a person can receive. In practice, many higher earners are 'contracted out' of the state additional pension. 'Contracting out' means ceasing to build up state additional pension and building up pension in an occupational scheme or personal pension instead.

In 2006/07, the UK Government's assessment of the minimum weekly income required by pensioners was £114.05 for a single person, and £174.05 for a couple (whether married or not). Consequently, for a single pensioner, the basic state pension is, in 2006/07, *only three-quarters of the minimum means-tested income* that a pensioner is deemed to need. This contrasts with the situation twenty years ago, when the basic state pension was about *the same* as the minimum level of income that was deemed enough for a single householder to live on. Therefore, anyone relying solely on the basic state pension is now also eligible to claim a means-tested top up.

In 2006, there was a range of means-tested benefits, in particular, 'Pension Credit', as well as some non means-tested benefits – for example, for people who need help with personal care and to help with winter fuel costs. Pension Credit has two elements:

1 ***Guarantee Credit:*** To raise pensioners' incomes to the minimum level they are deemed to need to live on (£114.05 for a single person and £174.05 for a couple in 2006/07).

2 ***Savings Credit:*** Anyone who has retirement income above the level of the full basic state pension (£84.25 for a single person and £134.75 for a couple in 2006/07) qualifies for Savings Credit at a rate of 60p for each £1 of such income up to a maximum credit (£17.88 per week for a single person and £23.58 for a couple in 2006/07). If income exceeds the guaranteed minimum income described above, the maximum Savings Credit is reduced at a rate of 40p for each £1 of excess income.

A problem with such means-tested retirement benefits can be that they actually discourage saving for retirement. Activity 7.2 will show you why this can be the case.

Activity 7.2

For the moment, let's suppose that Pension Credit is made up of just 'Guarantee Credit' and no 'Savings Credit'. In 2006/07, a single person is guaranteed an income of £114.05 a week. How much Guarantee Credit would they get if they had an income before Pension Credit of:

1 £84.25 per week basic state pension?

2 £84.25 per week basic state pension and £10 per week from a personal pension?

Comment

The answer to Activity 7.2 is given at the end of the chapter. ■■■

I hope you can see from Activity 7.2 that, in a system where £1 of state benefit is lost for every £1 of extra income (as was the case until October 2003), there is no incentive for a person to make their own savings for retirement unless they can save enough to bring their income above, or perhaps well above, the guaranteed minimum income level.

The Savings Credit was introduced to tackle this problem. In part 2 of Activity 7.2, the person has £10 of savings over and above the level of the basic pension. This would qualify them for a Savings Credit of £6 (60p × 10) as well as the Guarantee Credit of £19.80. Therefore, their total income including Pension Credit would be: £84.25 + £10 + £19.80 + £6 = £120.05. So the £10 pension from their savings has produced an increase of £6 in the income they would otherwise have got.

That's certainly much better for them than the previous system, but is it an incentive to save? Looked at another way, keeping £6 out of £10 is similar to paying a tax rate of 40 per cent.

3.2 Occupational pensions

Occupational pension schemes are set up by employers for their employees. They typically provide a package of benefits:

- a retirement pension for the employee payable from the scheme's normal pension age (often 65) or later
- a tax-free lump sum for the employee at retirement
- a pension payable if the employee has to retire early due to ill health
- pensions for a widow, widower, registered civil partner and dependent children if the employee dies either before or after retirement. Some schemes also pay such a pension to an unmarried partner
- lump sum life insurance if the employee dies before retirement.

Occupational pensions generally work on one of two bases: **defined benefit** or **defined contribution**. (Defined contribution is also sometimes called **money purchase**.) Some schemes combine the two bases; for example, working out a pension on both bases and paying whichever amount is the highest.

In a defined benefit scheme, the yearly pension and lump sum payment is worked out according to a formula. The most common type is a final salary scheme where the yearly pension formula is:

Yearly pension = accrual rate × number of years in scheme × final salary

The accrual rate is a fraction, typically $\frac{1}{60}$ th or $\frac{1}{80}$ th. Final salary means pay just before retirement if the member stays in the scheme until retirement or pay at the time of leaving if they leave before then. For example, a person earning £36,000 a year and retiring after thirty years in a $\frac{1}{60}$ th scheme would receive a pension of: $\frac{1}{60}$ th × 30 × £36,000 = £18,000 a year.

Defined benefit
Describes a pension scheme where the pension is worked out according to a formula, usually linked to pay and length of time in the scheme.

Defined contribution/ Money purchase
Describes a pension scheme where the pension depends on the amount paid in, how the invested money grows, and the amount of pension that can be purchased from an insurance company at retirement.

Activity 7.3

Work out how much pension each person receives from their final salary scheme:

1   John retired after 20 years in a $\frac{1}{80}$ th scheme. His pay at retirement was £34,000.

2   If Paula stays in her $\frac{1}{60}$ th scheme until retirement, she will have been a member for 15 years. Assume her pay then will be the same as today: £51,000.

3   Lewis is 27 now and has just joined his scheme. He expects to be a
     member of his $\frac{1}{80}$th scheme until age 65. Assume his pay then will be
     the same as today: £25,000.

Why do you think using pay today in the pension formula might give a
reasonable guide to pension at retirement?

The answer to Activity 7.3 is given at the end of the chapter. ■ ■ ■

Another type of defined benefit scheme is a 'career average salary
scheme', where an average of the employee's pay during the whole time
they belonged to the scheme is used in the pension formula instead of
final pay. Usually pay from earlier years is increased to take account of
inflation before the average is worked out. (The state additional pension
works on the same basis.)

     It is defined benefit occupational pension schemes like the ones
described above which have been closing to new members or changing in
some way, as I mentioned in Section 2.1. One of the main changes has
been a shift from defined benefit to defined contribution schemes. Under
defined contribution schemes, a pension depends upon the amount paid
in, investment returns, charges and **annuity** rates (annuities are covered
in Section 6.1). All defined contribution schemes work in essentially the
same way and are described in Section 3.3.

     The pension from a defined benefit scheme is usually increased each
year in line with price inflation, at least up to a set amount such as 2.5
per cent a year. The pension from an occupational defined contribution
scheme used to be covered by similar rules but, since April 2005, the
retiring employee can usually choose whether or not the pension will be
increased each year.

3.3 Personal pensions

Personal pensions and defined contribution occupational schemes are
both examples of defined contribution schemes, and all work in
essentially the same way. Under such schemes, the pension depends on:

■ the amount paid in, which is invested in a pension fund

■ how much the invested pension fund increases in value

■ how much is taken out of the pension fund in charges

■ how much pension the fund can buy at retirement (most commonly
   the fund is used to buy an annuity).

Annuity
A type of investment
where the investor
pays a lump sum and
in return receives an
income paid either for
a set period or, as in
the case of most
pensions, for the rest
of their life. Once the
investment is made,
they cannot change
their mind or get
their lump sum back.

Anyone can have a personal pension and anyone can pay into a personal pension for someone else. For example, with a couple, the main earner may pay into a plan for a partner who has a caring role in the household. You will see in Chapter 8 why this may be an important point to consider.

Personal pensions (unlike occupational defined contribution schemes) do not necessarily offer a package of benefits. It is up to the individual to choose whether to buy extra benefits. For instance, life cover, a pension for a partner, or increases to the pension once it starts to be paid.

The shift away from defined benefit to defined contribution occupational schemes and personal pensions has involved a shift in risk. This is because, while under defined benefit schemes the employer has to guarantee to pay a certain pension each year, and thus the pensioner knows what the pension will be, with defined contribution schemes and personal pensions, the amount of pension depends upon investment returns and other factors.

To understand these risks, imagine someone who is currently many years from retirement and who has to organise their own pension scheme to provide themselves with retirement income. How much should they invest in the scheme? They can't be certain of the correct amount because the eventual cost of the pension will depend upon the following factors:

■ *Investment returns:* As discussed in Chapter 5, when investing for the long term – and pension savings are very long term – stock market investments, like shares and bonds, are likely to be most suitable. It's impossible to know in advance how well these investments will perform. If the person planning for retirement assumes they will perform well, they don't need to invest too much. Yet if their assumption is wrong and the investments turn out badly, they will have too little in the fund to provide the pension they wanted.

■ *Inflation:* Chapter 2 described how rising prices reduce the buying power of money. To protect against this, the person planning for retirement would need to invest extra money to compensate for the effect of inflation both over the years when the savings are building up and once the pension starts, but they will have to estimate what rate of inflation to guard against. If their estimate is too low, in real terms they will have a smaller pension than planned.

■ *Longevity:* When it starts, the pension will provide a regular income, usually paid monthly, until the person dies. The longer they live, the more months of pension that have to be paid out, and the greater the total cost of the pension. In deciding how much to save, the person planning for retirement needs to make an assumption about how long they will live. If their assumption is wrong, either the money will run out before they die or they will have saved more than they needed to.

There are three main risks for personal pensions and defined contribution schemes

Therefore, defined contribution schemes, including personal pensions, lead to individuals shouldering the risks up to the time when the pension starts. This means that different people saving the same amount can receive very different pensions, and a person's pension can be markedly different depending on when they retire. On reaching retirement, individuals can protect themselves from further longevity risk by buying an annuity which will provide an income for the whole of their remaining life, however long they live.

Activity 7.4

As you've seen, some employers in the UK have been closing final salary schemes and offering workers career average salary schemes instead.

1   Why do you think the employers are making this switch?

2   Which workers might gain and which might lose from such a switch?

1   For many employers, average salary pensions are cheaper to provide than final salary schemes because, even after adjusting for inflation, a worker's average pay over many years is often lower than their pay just before retirement. Thus, companies can save money by closing final salary schemes.

2   Workers whose pay tends to peak in mid-career may gain from such a switch. Workers whose pay tends to peak towards the end of their career would lose. ■■■

3.4 Funded and pay-as-you-go schemes

With most occupational schemes and all personal pensions, money is paid in to the scheme to create a pension fund – a pool of investments. These are called **funded schemes**. Employers pay into occupational schemes and can require employees to contribute too. With other types of scheme, there is no obligation for any employer to pay in and individuals usually fund the whole scheme. In most large, occupational defined benefit schemes, experts are appointed to manage the investments, and pensions are paid directly from the fund as they fall due. With defined contribution arrangements, an insurance company normally looks after the investments, and the pensions are typically paid by taking money out of the fund to buy annuities.

Funded scheme
Pension scheme where an investment fund is built up from which to pay pensions and other benefits as they fall due.

By contrast, state pensions are **pay-as-you-go (PAYG)** schemes. There is no pension fund. Instead, the pensions paid out today are financed from National Insurance and other tax revenues collected today. Sometimes this is referred to as a 'contract between the generations', with today's tax payers paying for today's pensions on the understanding that when they retire, their pensions will be paid for by the tax payers of the future.

Pay-as-you-go (PAYG) scheme
Pension scheme where pensions and other benefits paid out today are paid for out of tax revenues collected today.

Most public sector occupational schemes (covering, for example, civil servants, teachers and National Health Service (NHS) workers) are also financed on a PAYG basis, with employees' contributions and general tax revenues used to pay the pensions of most retired public service workers. In contrast, the schemes for local authority employees and university lecturers in 'old' universities are funded schemes. Table 7.2 provides a summary of the main types of pension provision in the UK.

Table 7.2 Summary of main types of pension provision in the UK

Pension scheme	Organised by	Basis on which pensions are provided	How pensions are financed	Who pays?
State scheme: basic pension	State	Defined benefit	Pay as you go	Taxpayers
State scheme: additional pension	State	Defined benefit	Pay as you go	Taxpayers
Occupational scheme: final salary	Most public sector employers	Defined benefit	Pay as you go	Taxpayers, usually employee too
	Private sector and some public sector schemes	Defined benefit	Funded scheme	Employer, usually employee too
Occupational scheme: defined contribution	Private sector employers	Defined contribution	Funded scheme	Employer, usually employee too
Personal pension	Individual	Defined contribution	Funded scheme	Individual (employer occasionally)

4   Pensions and an ageing population

So far, you have looked at income inequality among pensioners, examined the different types of pension, and explored some of the debates around pension policy. Let's now look at one of the most important aspects of these policy debates: an ageing population.

4.1 How the population is ageing

In 2003, in the UK, 18 per cent of women and 14 per cent of men were aged 65 or over. These proportions have changed little over the last 30 years, but they are set to grow rapidly over the next 30. There are two key reasons for this:

1   ***People are living longer (i.e. longevity is increasing):*** Table 7.3 shows, for example, that a man reaching age 65 in 2031 is predicted to live nearly 7 years longer than a man who reached 65 in 1981.

2   ***Changing birth rates:*** There was a big increase in the birth rate after the end of the Second World War in 1945 (often referred to as the 'post-war baby boom'). These children have grown up and will be retiring around the period 2010–2030. In addition, nowadays people are having fewer children.

Table 7.3 UK life expectancy at age 65

Someone reaching age 65 in the year ...	... could expect on average to live for this many more years	
	Men	Women
1981	14.0	18.0
1991	15.8	19.2
2001	18.3	21.3
2011	19.6	22.5
2021	20.3	23.2
2031	20.9	23.7
2041	21.4	24.1
2051	21.7	24.4

Table 7.3 shows 'cohort' expectations of life, which are based on how long people have lived in the past, but are adjusted for known or expected changes that improve or reduce life expectancy.

Source: data from GAD, 2005

4.2 The support ratio

The ageing of the population lies behind the press headlines that were reproduced in the Introduction to this chapter, which stated that the UK faces a 'pensions crisis'. There is much to be celebrated in the fact that most UK citizens are living longer. Nevertheless, this also gives rise to some financial concerns. The biggest of these is based around changes in the relationship between the number of people over state pension age and the number of people of working age. There are two ways of measuring this relationship. One is the 'dependency ratio'. This ratio refers to the number of old people (typically measured as people over state pension age) in the economy divided by the number of people of working age. The second measure, which I shall use in this chapter, looks at the same thing from the other way around. This is the **support ratio**. If we define the number of people of working age as 'W' and the number of people over state pension age as 'P', then the support ratio is $\frac{W}{P}$. For example, if there are three workers to one pensioner, this could be expressed as a support ratio of $\frac{3}{1} = 3$. (The dependency ratio would be $\frac{1}{3}$ or 33.3 per cent.) If the number of workers fell to two per pensioner, then the support ratio would fall to $\frac{2}{1} = 2$. (And the new dependency ratio would be $\frac{1}{2}$ or 50 per cent.)

As the population ages, the UK support ratio is expected to fall from around four workers to support each pensioner in 2000 to around two workers per pensioner by the middle of the century (United Nations, 2001, p. 458). Falling support ratios are a worldwide phenomenon, as you can see from Table 7.4. In fact, many other countries, especially in Europe, will see a much larger decline than the UK.

Support ratio
The number of people of working age divided by the number of people over state pension age.

Table 7.4 Support ratio in selected regions and countries, 2000 and 2050 (predicted)

Region or country	Support ratio in the year	
	2000	**2050 (predicted)**
World as a whole	9.1	4.1
More developed regions:	4.7	2.2
Australia	5.5	2.7
Europe:	4.6	1.9
Germany	4.1	1.8
Netherlands	5.0	2.2
Spain	4.0	1.4
UK	4.1	2.1
Japan	4.0	1.4
North America	5.4	2.8
Less developed regions:	12.2	4.6
China	10.0	2.7
India	12.4	4.4

Note: in this table, the support ratio has been defined as the number of people aged 15 to 64 divided by the number aged 65 and over.

Source: data from United Nations, 2001, pp. 48, 50, 52, 78, 96, 122, 178, 244, 270, 286, 346, 420, 458

There is a case for exercising caution in using the support ratio as the best basis for determining society's capacity to cope with an ageing population. The main reasons for this are:

1 Not everyone of working age is in productive work, because of, for instance, unemployment, illness or disability, caring roles, early retirement or full-time education.

2 Not everyone of retirement age has stopped productive work.

3 People over retirement age are not the only dependants requiring support. In particular, children might also be included.

4 The ratio as defined assumes that workers are uniformly productive, but a part-time worker will generally produce less than a full-time one and, over time, average **productivity** per worker may change. So the ratio might over- or understate the amount of economic support available.

5 The ratio assumes dependants are uniformly needy but, over time, the average cost of dependency might change. For example, if an increasing proportion of pensioners lives alone, the resources that each person requires may tend to rise.

Productivity
The amount of output (of goods and services) per unit of inputs used to produce it. If productivity increases, there will be more output from the same inputs.

Some of these issues may be overcome by using a support ratio which measures the proportion of people actually working divided by the number of non-workers, including children. On that basis, the UK Government estimates that the support ratio in 2003 was about 0.9 and it would fall to 0.8 by 2031 (House of Lords, 2004b, p. 10). This is an 11 per cent fall in the ratio over thirty years, which is much less than the 48 per cent fall over 50 years suggested by the crude support ratios in Table 7.4.

A more difficult challenge, however, is how support ratios take account of changing levels of productivity in the economy. Such ratios depend on estimates of how many people are defined as workers, but it is possible that due to technological and other changes an economy's output might improve even when the number of workers is in decline. In other words, a smaller number of workers have the potential to produce increasing levels of output, meaning the UK's GDP could rise substantially even with a relatively small workforce. This would allow everyone – workers and pensioners – to share in higher living standards despite the falling crude support ratio.

In its evidence to a House of Lords Select Committee, the Bank of England estimated long-term growth in the productivity of the UK labour force at an average of 1.75 per cent a year which, over the fifty years to 2051, would have an effect equivalent to doubling the number of workers in the economy (House of Lords, 2004a, paragraph 3.4). If that estimate turns out to be correct, there may be little change or even

Arguments over who shares the 'economic cake' may overlook the fact that increased productivity can make the cake bigger

an improvement in the *effective* support ratio. The House of Lords Select Committee concluded that:

> Population ageing does not pose a threat to the continued prosperity and growth of the United Kingdom economy; in this sense, therefore, there is no looming 'crisis' of population ageing in the United Kingdom.

> This does not mean that the future growth of the economy is in any sense guaranteed; that depends on how we manage our economic resources. A failure, for example, to sustain historic rates of technological progress and productivity growth might drastically reduce future growth rates below those projected here. We conclude, nevertheless, that such risks exist independently of any demographic pressures on the economy.
>
> (House of Lords, 2004a, p. 15, paragraphs 3.7 and 3.8)

None the less, the concern over an ageing population and its possible impact on pensions prompted the UK Government to set up a Pensions Commission in late 2002, also known as the 'Turner Commission'. The Commission's purpose was to review the adequacy of pension savings in the UK and to make policy recommendations. It produced two reports: the first, *Pensions: Challenges and Choices* (Pensions Commission, 2004), set out an analysis of pension provision in the UK and looked at historical trends; the second, *A New Pension Settlement for the Twenty-First Century* (Pensions Commission, 2005), outlined recommendations for policy change.

Lord Turner chaired the Pensions Commission

The Pensions Commission recommended two main elements of reform:

- The creation of a low-cost, national funded pension savings scheme into which individuals will be automatically enrolled, but with the right to opt-out, with a modest level of compulsory matching employer contributions, and delivering the opportunity to save for a pension at a low Annual Management Charge [an administration charge].

- Reforms to make the state system less means-tested and closer to universal than it would be if current arrangements were continued indefinitely. In order to achieve this while maintaining the standard of living of the poorest pensioners it will need to be more generous on average. In the long term this implies some mix of both an increase in taxes devoted to pensions expenditure, and an increase in State Pension Ages.

(Pensions Commission, 2005, p. 6)

These proposals helped to highlight the ongoing debate about how the UK's economic output should be distributed among different groups. This debate was touched upon in Section 2.1, and the second Pensions Commission report added to it by arguing that to deliver the proposed changes, the amount of public expenditure spent on pensions as a percentage of the whole of the economy's output (or GDP) must increase, and/or the age at which citizens receive the state pension must increase. The Commission suggested raising the state pension age in proportion to the increase in life expectancy, while at the same time increasing public expenditure on state pensions by around 1.5 per cent of GDP – reversing the trend we saw in Section 2.1. In May 2006, the UK Government published a White Paper setting out its proposals for the future of state pensions. It proposed raising the state pension age to 66 from 2024, to 67 from 2034 and 68 from 2044. It also proposed that the flat-rate basic state pension will be increased in line with average earnings rather than inflation, probably from 2012.

Activity 7.5

How would raising the state pension age impact on different parts of the population?

Comment

There are several ways of thinking about this. First, some groups have a shorter life expectancy than the average for the whole population. Even allowing for some increase in their life expectancy, raising the normal retirement age may mean that they never reach retirement or that they have only a few years in retirement. Vulnerable groups include those living in poverty, manual workers (who on average die three years younger than non-manual workers), and smokers, who die seven years younger on average than non-smokers (House of Lords, 2004a, paragraph 4.18). Second, given that older people suffer from poorer health than younger citizens, any increase in the state pension age implies that many retired people would enjoy fewer retirement years in good health. ■ ■ ■

This section raises many interesting political questions and choices. For example, how should support ratios be used in pension planning? Should increasing productivity mean that today's workers and corporations receive smaller increases in pay and profits so that today's pensioners can share in economic growth? In addition, should today's workers and corporations forgo some of the increases in pay and profits which result from higher productivity, in order to fund saving for their own retirement? Or should government expenditure on pensions be controlled in order to keep taxation low?

These are tough questions which are likely to mean redistributing income among different elements in society, and possibly substituting future for present consumption. Given this, it is not surprising that pensions policy will continue to be a topic of hot political and policy debate.

4.3 Policies to promote private saving for retirement

One reason why it is difficult to persuade people to substitute future for present consumption is that people generally display what economists call **time preference**, which means they prefer to consume goods and services now rather than waiting to consume them at some time in the future. This happens for several reasons. First, there are many competing demands for a household's money – for example, paying off student loans, buying a home, raising children – and saving for a future pension may seem relatively unimportant compared with current needs. Second, the future is uncertain. Prices could rise, which means money set aside might buy less in future than expected. Third, and worse still, a pension provider may fail so that savings are lost; an individual might even die and miss out on the potential future consumption altogether. We came across time preference in Chapter 4, when we looked at how people sometimes borrow to pay for present consumption.

Consequently, because time preference can deter saving towards pensions, governments have tried to boost the amount that people save by increasing the return they effectively get. Typically this is done by offering tax incentives, as outlined in Box 7.1.

Time preference
The tendency of people to prefer 'present goods and services' (those available for consumption now) to 'future goods and services' (those expected to be available for consumption at a future date).

Box 7.1 UK incentives to encourage saving for a pension

In 2006, the following incentives were available to encourage saving for retirement through occupational schemes and personal pensions:

- Full tax relief on the amount an individual paid in. With personal pensions, a bonus equal to the tax relief at the basic rate (see Chapter 2, Section 7) was given even if the individual was a non tax payer or paid tax at a lower rate.
- Payments into an occupational scheme by an employer were treated as a tax-free fringe benefit of the employee.
- All the capital growth and some of the income building up in the invested pension fund were tax-free (but dividends from shares and similar income were taxed).
- At retirement, a quarter of the savings could be taken as a tax-free lump sum (the rest had to be drawn out gradually as a pension which was taxable).

A further problem with saving for retirement is that people often don't like to think about getting old. They shut out thoughts of retirement and fail to plan ahead. Governments and pension providers can use information to try to make people more aware of their eventual retirement needs. For example, in 2003, the UK Government started a program of sending state pension forecasts to all UK adults showing the amount of state pension they are likely to get when they reach retirement. (A state pension forecast can also be requested from The Pension Service, which is part of the Department of Work and Pensions.) Similarly, pension schemes are required to provide regular information to members about their pensions, in an easy-to-understand format.

Another reason why it is difficult to persuade people to give up consumption now in favour of saving for retirement is a lack of trust. Over the years, there have been several scandals involving pensions, such as the mis-selling of pensions (see Box 7.2), the near collapse of Equitable Life, and the closing down of some occupational defined benefit schemes with too little in the pension fund to pay the promised pensions. These knocked public confidence. As a result, some people are unwilling to save for retirement because they do not trust pension providers. Government, regulators and the pensions industry can try to restore confidence through measures such as tough regulation to prevent abuse, and compensation schemes to pay out if things do go wrong. In the UK, a Pensions Regulator oversees occupational schemes, the Financial Services Authority regulates personal pensions, and various compensation arrangements have been set up.

Box 7.2   Pension mis-selling

From the late 1980s to the mid 1990s, hundreds of thousands of customers were wrongly advised to take out a personal pension and lost out on the benefits of an occupational scheme ... In 1994 the regulators set up a review of pension business from 1988–1994 to help customers get any redress due ... The pensions review is now largely complete and over 1.1 million customers have had offers of redress. So far, offers of redress exceed £10 billion.

(FSA, 2004, p. 30)

If individuals cannot be persuaded to save voluntarily, governments could make saving for retirement compulsory. In the UK, state pensions (and their contracted-out alternatives) are compulsory for those people covered by them. Many other countries also have compulsory state schemes but only a few – for example, Switzerland, Australia, Sweden and the

Private pension
Used collectively to
refer to occupational
pensions and personal
pensions as opposed
to state pensions.

Netherlands – have so far made **private pension** saving compulsory (Pensions Commission, 2004, p. 95). The 2006 White Paper proposed a system of 'personal pension savings accounts' in which employees will automatically be enrolled (unless there is an existing occupational scheme). Companies, employees and government would all contribute to the scheme.

5 Planning ahead for retirement

To consider how an individual or household can plan ahead for their retirement years, we return to the financial planning model you've seen throughout *Personal Finance*, which is reproduced in Figure 7.4. We can use this model to develop a financial plan for achieving a financially secure retirement. This would be a common approach to planning for retirement, but it's not the only possibility – Box 7.4 has a different approach to retirement planning.

5.1 Assess the situation

Central to the situation is the goal of a comfortable retirement. The need is to have enough income throughout retirement to finance a certain standard of living. The amount required will be determined largely by expectations of spending in retirement.

This raises a question: whose spending needs? Should the financial plan look at the individual or the household? The danger of basing the plan on the household is that many households change over time as, for example, couples split up, family members and friends decide to share a home or leave, or people die. Traditionally, married couples have adopted the household approach, and the resulting financial plans have often proved inadequate in the face of death or divorce. This is a key reason why women account for such a high proportion of the poorest pensioners today. The advantage of a retirement plan based on the individual is that each member of the household has their own pension arrangements which they retain even if the make-up of their household changes.

Spending in retirement can be estimated from the individual's or household's current level and pattern of spending. Yet there are some good reasons to think that spending in retirement may be different from spending while working, and that spending needs in early retirement may differ from those later on. I've listed a few reasons in Box 7.3, and you can probably think of others.

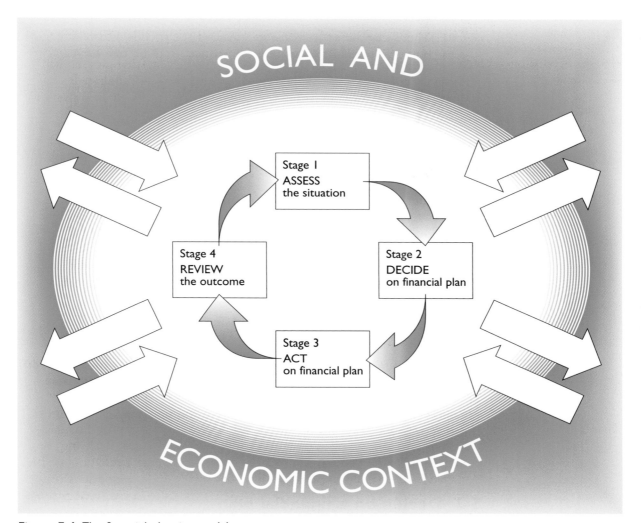

Figure 7.4 *The financial planning model*

Box 7.3 Some reasons why spending in retirement might differ from pre-retirement spending

- By retirement, most homeowners will have finished paying off any mortgage, so the amount that these pensioners spend on housing may fall.
- Pensioners often spend more time at home, so bills for gas and electricity could rise.
- There will be savings on work-related costs such as pension contributions and commuting.

- There may be an increase in travel to see friends and relatives, but pensioners often qualify for reduced-rate or free travel, especially on public transport.
- Pensioners may spend more on holidays, especially in early retirement, but may save money by going away at off-peak times.
- In later retirement particularly, pensioners may have to spend significantly more on health-related items such as help with personal care.

Activity 7.6

Think about your own current spending. How do you think your own spending might change when you reach retirement (or if you are already retired, over the next ten years)?

Comment

Your spending may change for reasons of both necessity and choice, as you saw in Box 7.3. One thing to remember is that these are only estimates – no one can be sure of the spending they will need to undertake in retirement, because personal circumstances at the time may differ from those anticipated beforehand. ■■■

5.2 Decide on a financial plan

I have already introduced you to the main financial tools that are used to build up retirement income: state pensions, occupational pensions and personal pensions. The key differences between them are summarised in Table 7.5. Any other types of saving and investing, as discussed in Chapter 5 – for example, unit trusts – can also be used but, as Box 7.1 showed, there are some incentives to saving through occupational schemes and personal pensions.

Most UK adults will already have some pension arrangements in place, not least because some are compulsory: most employees and self-employed people have to pay National Insurance contributions and so build up a basic state pension; most employees must also build up state additional pension or a contracted-out occupational or personal pension instead. People may also have opted voluntarily to build up additional retirement savings.

Table 7.5 Key differences between the main ways to save for retirement

	State scheme	Occupational defined benefit scheme	Occupational defined contribution scheme	Personal pension
Who can join?	Most people aged 16 and over automatically belong	Employees of the employer providing the scheme	Employees of the employer providing the scheme	Anyone regardless of age or employment status
Employer (if individual has one) pays part or all of the cost of the pension	Yes (through National Insurance)	Yes	Yes	Not usually
At any date the scheme commits to a given level of pension at retirement	Yes	Yes	No	No
Pension automatically keeps pace with inflation while it is building up	Yes	Yes	No	No
Pension keeps pace with inflation once it starts to be paid out	Yes	At least partially	Not unless chosen as an option	Not unless chosen as an option
Scheme includes pensions for dependants if individual dies either before or after retirement	Yes	Usually	Usually	Not unless chosen as an option

The first step in the financial plan is to check what arrangements are already in place, and how much pension these arrangements are expected to produce by the chosen retirement age. This is done by gathering forecasts and statements for the various arrangements. The expected pensions can then be deducted from the target retirement income to see if the existing arrangements are likely to produce enough income.

If there is a shortfall, extra pension savings may be required if the retirement income target is to be met. There may be a tension between the amount a person needs to save and the amount they can afford to save given their current budget. In that case, either the retirement target will have to be revised or adjustments made to current income and spending via the budgeting process described in Chapter 3.

To see how the process of planning works in practice, let's use the fictional example of Dibyesh. He is 36, thinks he should start saving for retirement, and so follows the initial steps of the financial planning model:

- ■ ***Stage 1: Assess the situation:*** The first step is to decide how much retirement income he might need. Dibyesh currently spends about £480 a week and, thinking about how his spending needs might change in retirement (this is the exercise you did in Activity 7.6), he reckons he would then need about £240 a week in today's money. Allowing some adjustment for tax, that would mean a before-tax retirement income of, say, £265 a week or about £13,700 a year.

- ■ ***Stage 2: Decide on a financial plan:*** Dibyesh recently asked for a forecast of his state pension, which showed he was likely to get £110 a week (£5700 a year) in state pension from age 65. Currently, he has no other retirement savings. He needs a plan to produce another £8000 a year of pension. He is self-employed, so there is no occupational scheme to join. Therefore Dibyesh looks at a personal pension. The pension provider helps him to work out that to produce a pension of £8000 a year by age 65, Dibyesh needs to start saving about £220 a month, assuming he increases this each year if his earnings rise. Dibyesh already saves about £100 a month, but this is earmarked for other things. To save enough for retirement, Dibyesh decides he will have to cut back his current spending.

Figure 7.5 summarises how deciding to save for retirement alters Dibyesh's income and spending. Part (a) shows Dibyesh's income and expenditure without any savings for retirement. Part (b) shows his income and spending when he does pay into a pension. Up to age 65, Dibyesh's income is the same whether or not he saves for retirement. Without retirement savings, Dibyesh's income drops very sharply once he reaches age 65 and his budget is so stretched that his spending actually exceeds his retirement income. If he saves for retirement, his spending between the ages of 36 and 65 is reduced, but at age 65 the drop in Dibyesh's income is much smaller and his retirement income is enough to cover an enhanced level of spending. Dibyesh decides that giving up some spending today is a worthwhile trade for a better standard of living when he retires.

5.3 Act on the financial plan

Having decided on the financial plan, the next stage in the model is to act on the financial plan. For most people, because it is compulsory, little action is needed regarding the state pension while it is building up. To join an occupational pension scheme or to find out about increasing the

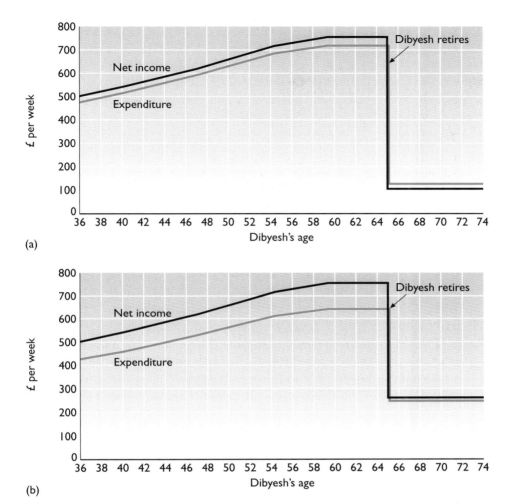

Figure 7.5 *Dibyesh's expected weekly income and expenditure: (a) without saving for retirement; (b) with saving for retirement*

benefits from it, an employee would talk to their personnel department at work.

Personal pensions are more complex. The individual needs to make choices, for instance, about the provider to choose and how to invest their pension fund. They might decide to get help from a financial adviser.

5.4 Review the outcome of the plan regularly

There are many uncertainties in retirement planning because of the long timescale, the risks involved and the potential for all sorts of life changes (such as work breaks to raise a family, redundancy, or long-term illness). It is also likely that the social and economic environment might change. For example, if the UK Government implemented its White Paper proposals to increase the state pension age, then Dibyesh's financial planning for retirement would clearly have to change. For example, if he was 36 in 2006, the proposals would mean he could not draw his state pension until he was 67. Therefore, this is one of the most important areas of financial planning that needs to be reviewed carefully – for example, he would need to monitor closely the implementation of the government's proposals.

Most pension schemes and plans issue statements yearly. This enables people to check regularly how their pensions are building up, and to take steps in good time if their retirement planning is no longer on track for the income they expect to need in later life.

In the example above, because the return from a personal pension varies as the value of investments goes up and down, Dibyesh checks each year to see if he is on track for a retirement income of £265 a week, and adjusts the amount he is saving as necessary.

Box 7.4   Different approaches to retirement planning

The main goal of the financial planning model described in this section is to ensure financial independence in later life. However, this is not the only way to plan for financial well-being. You've seen in earlier chapters how financial plans are always affected by cultural values. The following is an extract from a research report called *Ethnic Minorities and their Pension Decisions*. It shows how planning for later life is another area of finance affected by different values:

> Commitment to and reliance on family and community appeared to have a powerful influence on the outlook of all groups of respondents. The older white respondents accepted that they might need to provide material or financial support for their own parents but had no intention of in turn becoming reliant on their children in old age. Nor did they appear to have any responsibilities to their extended families. ... the younger white respondents had no real expectations of either supporting their parents in old age or being reliant themselves on their own children. ... young Pakistani and Bangladeshi respondents had financial commitments (*Izzat*) not only to their extended families but also to the community. ... both older and younger Pakistani and Bangladeshi respondents attached considerable importance to the perpetuation of traditional Moslim values, particularly with regard to respect for and duty towards parents. ... open

disapproval was sometimes expressed towards the 'western' style of raising children – a view founded on the belief that many white Britons uncaringly put their elderly parents into residential care rather than look after them themselves. ... most of these respondents said with certainty that in their old age they expected to receive social care from their younger family members, and they linked this either to Islam or to 'traditional' ways of doing things.

(Nesbitt and Neary, 2001, pp. 39, 40, 41)

6   Financial planning approaching retirement

This section examines some of the financial decisions and choices facing people approaching and during retirement. We'll be looking at issues of care separately in Chapters 8 and 9.

6.1   Buying an annuity

This is an issue for those with a defined contribution scheme (whether an occupational scheme or a personal pension). At the point of retirement, such a pension fund needs to be converted into pension. The usual way of doing this is to buy an annuity. An annuity is an investment where the investor swaps a lump sum for an income. In the case of a pension, the annuity is usually a type where the income is paid out for the rest of the person's life, however long they live.

Annuities offer a choice of different types of income. The option selected affects the cost of the annuity (see Box 7.5). The most basic option is a level annuity, which provides the same income year in, year out. It is the cheapest type of annuity – that means, as you will see from Box 7.5, that it pays out the largest income each year. In other words, you get a relatively high income in return for the amount you invest. The drawback is that, as time passes, inflation reduces the buying power of the income.

Box 7.5   The cost of an annuity

The cost of an annuity is expressed as the 'annuity rate'. This states how many pounds a year of income the investor receives for each £10,000 of lump sum they invest. The lower the annuity rate, the more costly an annuity. For example, an annuity rate of £300 is more costly than a rate of £400 because less income is received in return for the same lump sum investment.

> The following formula works out how much income an annuity will provide:
>
> $$\text{Income per year} = \frac{\text{Annuity rate}}{£10,000} \times \text{Size of pension fund}$$
>
> For example, if a pension fund is £34,000 and the annuity rate is £500, the income would be $\frac{£500}{£10,000} \times £34,000 = £1700$ a year.
>
> If you divide by 100, you can see that an annuity rate of £500 per £10,000 is the same as £5 per £100; in other words, 5 per cent. This might tempt you to compare an annuity rate with the return from the other types of savings and investments discussed in Chapter 5. Yet the comparison would be misleading because, with an annuity, none of the original capital is returned as a lump sum.

To protect their income from inflation, the investor could choose an increasing annuity where the income automatically changes each year, for example, in line with inflation as measured by the Retail Prices Index (RPI), or by a set amount, say 5 per cent a year. With an increasing annuity, the annuity rate tells you how much income is paid in the first year.

Table 7.6 gives some examples of different annuity rates. You can clearly see the drawback with an escalating annuity: the starting level of income is very much lower than that from a level annuity for the same initial investment. In practice, around 80 per cent of annuities purchased in the UK are level annuities (FSA, 2003, p. 33), even though they leave pensioners vulnerable to inflation.

To see the impact that inflation could have on retirement income, let's consider the example of Elaine Jones. She reaches retirement at age 65 with a pension fund of £30,000. She checks out annuity rates and finds that she could get a level annuity paying her $\frac{£648}{£10,000} \times £30,000 = £1944$ a year, or an RPI-linked annuity paying $\frac{£436}{£10,000} \times £30,000 = £1308$ a year. Appalled at the idea of receiving over £600 a year less if she opts for inflation-proofing, Elaine chooses the level annuity. Ten years later, she still receives £1944 a year, but because prices have risen by an average 2.5 per cent every year, the income buys only the same as about £1519 would have done at the start of retirement. By age 85, although inflation is still just 2.5 per cent a year, the buying power of her pension has fallen by over one-third to only £1186.

Table 7.6 Annuity rates compared

Type of annuity	Average annuity rate[1]	Income assuming an initial investment of £30,000		
		At the start of retirement	After 10 years of retirement	After 20 years of retirement
Level annuity	£648	£1944	£1944	£1944
RPI-linked annuity	£436	£1308	£1674[2]	£2143[2]
Annuity escalating at 5 per cent a year	£362	£1086	£1769	£2881

[1]Rate for a woman aged 65. Men and older people would receive a higher income. Annuity rates are changing all the time. The rates shown are for illustration only.

[2] Assuming inflation averages 2.5 per cent a year.

Source: Moneyfacts Group, 2005, p. 51

Anyone with a partner faces another important choice: whether to buy a single-life annuity that stops when they die or a joint-life-last-survivor annuity that pays out until both they and their partner have died. Six out of ten households where the head is aged 65 to 69 (the age by which most annuities have been purchased) comprise two or more people (DWP, 2004b, Table 2.3). Yet only two out of ten people opt for a joint-life-last-survivor annuity (FSA, 2003, p. 33, Table 6.26). Unless the partner has other adequate sources of income, the absence of a joint-life-last-survivor annuity means they will be short of income if the annuity holder dies first.

If you read the footnotes to Table 7.6, you will notice that the annuity rates shown are for a person of a specific age and gender. Perhaps you wondered why men and older people would get more income than the 65-year-old woman I took as an example. An annuity pays an income for life, and so you can think of it as insurance against living too long and thus running out of money. It works like this: all the people buying annuities form a pool, and the money paid in by people who die sooner than average helps to fund the cost of paying pensions to those people who live longer than average. With all insurance, the amount the customer is charged is generally higher, the more the insurance company may have to pay out (you will be looking at this further in Chapter 9). Therefore, annuities are more expensive (in other words, the annuity rate is lower), the longer a person is expected to live.

We have already looked at life expectancy in Section 4.1. Table 7.3 showed how women on average tend to live longer than men of the same age. When it comes to annuities, this means that women receive a lower annuity rate than men of the same age. Consequently, women have to pay more for the same amount of pension each year because on average their pension is likely to be paid out for longer. For instance, in 2005, a man aged 65 could get a level annuity of £716 a year for each £10,000 lump sum, but a woman could get only £648 a year (Moneyfacts Group, 2005, p. 51).

Life expectancy is affected by other factors too. For example, the older a person is at the time they purchase the annuity, the larger the income they receive because they are expected to have fewer years left. Similarly, people in poor health and smokers can obtain better annuity rates because, on average, they are not expected to live as long as healthy people and non-smokers. Perversely, this is one area where you can benefit from unhealthy living!

In this section, the annuities I have described protect the individual from investment risk because they provide either a fixed income throughout retirement or an income which increases in a predictable way. There are other types of annuity where the income rises and falls in line with an investment fund and, with these, the individual continues to be exposed to investment risk.

Instead of buying an annuity, an individual can draw a pension direct from their pension fund. The remaining fund continues to rise and fall in line with the stock market so, again, the individual continues to be exposed to investment risk. Despite the risk, this option may be preferred, for instance, by those investors (for example, some Christian groups like the Plymouth Brethren) who are not allowed by their religion to use insurance-based products such as annuities.

Activity 7.7

How much pension will you get (to the nearest pound) if:

1 You have a pension fund of £22,000 and the annuity rate is £669?
2 You have a pension fund of £50,000 and the annuity rate is £417?
3 You have a pension fund of £50,000 and the annuity rate is £514?

Comment

The answer to Activity 7.7 is given at the end of the chapter. ■ ■ ■

6.2 Working in retirement

According to UK Government data, currently one person in eleven over state pension age carries on working (DWP, 2004a, p. 6, Table 1), usually for just a few years. Some are filling a gap until their partner retires, others boosting their finances, yet others enjoy the social side of work.

Earnings may be supplementing a pension. Many personal pensions allow the investor to start drawing just a small amount of pension, increasing to the full amount as retirement progresses. From April 2006, occupational pensions can offer the same option.

Alternatively, someone continuing to work beyond normal retirement age could put off drawing their pension. Usually that will mean that the pension is bigger once it does start because it will have had extra time to build up and will then need to be paid out for a shorter time. On the other hand, there is a risk of dying before the pension starts.

People may increasingly remain in paid employment beyond the state pension age

You'll recall from Section 4.2 that the Pensions Commission suggested that one of the choices for an ageing society is to increase the average age at which people retire, and this was incorporated in the government's proposals in 2006. The government has also encouraged a voluntary shift in retirement age by improving the terms under which starting to draw the state pension can be deferred in order to earn either extra pension or a lump sum. It also introduced legislation to outlaw age discrimination, effective from 2006. This may help older workers to stay in the labour market beyond their usual retirement age or to get part-time work. The Pensions Commission also proposed introducing financial incentives for employers to hire older workers, bringing in policies which focus on occupational health and encouraging the education and training of older workers (Pension Commission, 2005).

Such likely changes imply that in the future phrases like 'retirement' and 'pensioner' may have to be interpreted more flexibly, with people increasingly sourcing income from paid employment and pensions until well into later life.

6.3 Using a home to provide retirement income

Around four-fifths of retired couples and three-fifths of retired single people are owner-occupiers, with the majority owning their home outright (ONS, 2004b, p. 40, Table 4.6). The distribution of home ownership is uneven, with pensioners on higher incomes more likely than those on lower incomes to own their own home and more likely to own a more valuable property. However, home ownership is more even than the distribution of either pension rights or non-pension wealth other than housing (Pensions Commission, 2004, p. 200). Therefore, many people enter retirement with a valuable asset which, in theory, could be turned into retirement income.

The most obvious way to release the wealth tied up in a home (often referred to as 'equity', as we saw in Chapter 6) would be to sell the home and buy somewhere cheaper to live. Nevertheless, this will not be an option for everyone. For instance, suitable replacement properties may not be any cheaper, or the individual may not wish to move for personal reasons. An alternative approach could be an **equity release scheme**.

So far, equity release schemes are used by only about 1 per cent of retired households but it is possible that their use might grow in future (Pensions Commission, 2004, p. 194). There are two main types of scheme:

Equity release scheme
A way of unlocking the wealth tied up in a home while retaining the right to live there until death or until the home is no longer needed (for example, moving into a care home). The money released can be taken as a lump sum, as income, or as a combination of both (income is usually provided by buying an annuity).

1 *Lifetime mortgages:* The owner borrows against the value of their home. Most popular are 'roll-up' schemes where interest, rather than being paid monthly as with the normal mortgages described in Chapter 6, is added to the outstanding loan and paid only when the home is eventually sold. This maximises the amount of income or lump sum available. Yet, even at a fairly modest interest rate, the outstanding balance can increase alarmingly (see Table 7.7) because interest is charged on the interest as well as on the original loan – another example of compound interest, which you looked at in Chapter 4. Many schemes have a 'no-negative-equity guarantee', which means that the loan plus interest which eventually has to be repaid cannot exceed the value of the home.

2   *Home reversion plans:* The owner sells part of the home for a lump sum, but retains the right to carry on living in the home either rent-free or for a peppercorn rent. For example, the homeowner might sell, say, 60 per cent of their home and in return receive a lump sum equal to 30 per cent of the home's value. The precise proportion depends on various factors, including the owner's age because this determines how long the provider is likely to wait to get their money back. Any part of the home that the owner does not sell continues to belong to them and therefore they continue to benefit from at least part of any increase in the value of the home. When the owner dies (or moves permanently into long-term care), the home is sold. The provider of the home reversion plan takes its share of the sale proceeds and anything remaining is part of the estate of the former owner.

An equity release scheme is not suitable for every homeowner. The extra income and capital released can affect their entitlement to means-tested state benefits. It can also cause an increase in Income Tax. This is because the higher personal allowance for people aged 65 and over (which you saw in Chapter 2) is reduced if their income exceeds a certain amount (£20,100 in 2006/07).

Table 7.7 Example of how the amount owed under a roll-up lifetime mortgage can grow

Years since the lifetime mortgage was taken out	Balance outstanding, including rolled-up interest if the rate of interest on the loan is:			
	5% p.a.	7% p.a.	9% p.a.	11% p.a.
Initial loan	£50 000	£50 000	£50 000	£50 000
1	£52 500	£53 500	£54 500	£55 500
5	£63 814	£70 128	£76 931	£84 253
10	£81 445	£98 358	£118 368	£141 971
15	£103 946	£137 952	£182 124	£239 229
20	£132 665	£193 484	£280 221	£403 116

6.4 Inheritance and retirement income

The Pensions Commission (2004) suggested that home ownership, rather than contributing substantially towards the income of current owners, would be more likely to contribute towards the retirement income of the next generation through inheritance. With relatively high levels of home ownership becoming the norm for successive generations, the next generation could sell the inherited homes and use the wealth released to provide pensions (Pensions Commission, 2004, p. 197). Nevertheless, there are a number of reasons for treating this suggestion with caution.

Which generation will benefit from housing wealth?

First, homes may have to be sold to pay for the present owners' long-term care instead of being bequeathed to the next generation. (Long-term care is discussed in Chapter 9.) Second, recipients may use an inheritance for purposes other than retirement income. In particular, high house prices in the early 2000s, and the fact that many young people now incur substantial student debts, may be fuelling a trend towards people buying homes later in life than previously. Inherited wealth might therefore be used to pay off mortgages still outstanding or to help children pay off student debts or to get a foot on the housing ladder.

It is also hard to predict with any certainty the amount that the average person or household might inherit. The ageing of the population means that a large cohort of retired people will be passing assets on to a next generation that is relatively smaller than is the case now. Therefore, the balance of supply and demand for housing could shift and cause house prices to weaken. The value of assets passed on may also be reduced by Inheritance Tax.

In 2006/07, one in seventeen estates left on death in the UK was expected to pay Inheritance Tax (HMRC, 2006). However, this was double the proportion of that in 1998 (Inland Revenue, 1998, p. 109), and could increase further if the increase in housing wealth seen over the decade to 2005 works through to estates left on death.

Inheritance Tax at death is charged on:

- the value of everything the deceased owned, including personal possessions, home, car, investments and so on. Regarding anything owned jointly with other people, it's only the deceased's share that is included

less:

- everything the deceased owed, for example, their share of any outstanding mortgage, credit card debts, outstanding tax bills
- a reasonable amount to cover funeral expenses (typically around £2000)
- any tax-free bequests. These include gifts to a husband, wife or registered civil partner and gifts to charity. They do not include bequests to unmarried or unregistered partners or to children

plus:

- the value of gifts made within the last seven years before death.

Whatever is left is called the 'taxable estate'. The first slice of the taxable estate, called the 'nil-rate band' (£285,000 in 2006/07), is tax-free. Anything more is taxed at a single rate of 40 per cent. For example, if the taxable estate was worth £385,000, the tax charge would be: 40 per cent × (£385,000 − £285,000) = £40,000.

The nil-rate band is normally increased each year at least in line with price changes. The nil-rate bands for 2007/08, 2008/09 and 2009/10 have already been announced and are due to be £300,000, £312,000 and £325,000, respectively. Yet over the period 1995 to 2005, while the nil-rate band increased by an average of 6 per cent a year, the price of the average home rose by over 10 per cent a year. As a result, homeowners are increasingly likely to be brought into the Inheritance Tax net (Lowe, 2005).

7 Conclusion

In Sections 2 to 4 of this chapter, I looked at the policy debate around pensions, and examined how demographic factors, in particular an ageing population, affect society and the policy discussions about pensions. I considered the background to the question of who in society – individuals, employers and/or the state – should provide pensions and bear the risks.

I also looked in Section 4.3 at the choices faced by individuals and households in deciding whether to spend now or save for the future. This has helped us to understand why the UK Government offers incentives for people to save through pension schemes and plans.

Throughout this chapter, I have also been building an awareness of how individuals and households can plan for retirement. This involves trying to forecast the amount of income they might need, deciding who in the household should save, finding out what the state pension scheme might provide, and considering the range of financial tools available to help them meet this important financial goal. Section 5 worked through the financial planning model with regard to pensions. Section 6 also cautioned us that financial planning isn't something that stops at retirement – it is an ongoing process.

Answers to Activities

Activity 7.2

1   The person would receive £29.80 a week Guarantee Credit (£114.05 – £84.25 = £29.80). Their total income including Pension Credit would be £114.05 a week.

2   The person would receive £19.80 a week Guarantee Credit (£114.05 – £94.25 = £19.80). Their total income including Pension Credit would be £114.05 a week. ■ ■ ■

Activity 7.3

1   John's pension was $\frac{1}{80}$ th $\times$ 20 $\times$ £34,000 = £8500 a year.

2   Paula can expect a pension of $\frac{1}{60}$ th $\times$ 15 $\times$ £51,000 = £12,750 a year.

3   Lewis can expect 65 – 27 = 38 years in the scheme. His pension would be $\frac{1}{80}$ th $\times$ 38 $\times$ £25,000 = £11,875 a year.

Planning for later life usually means looking many years ahead. When thinking about amounts of money in the future, it is important to adjust for the impact of inflation between now and then. A yearly income of £50,000 may sound a lot, but if it is paid in thirty years' time and inflation in the meantime averages 2.5 per cent a year, the £50,000 would buy only the same as £24,000 today. Working out the pension using pay today means that the expected pension is automatically adjusted for inflation in an approximate way because we expect earnings to rise by at least as much as price inflation over time. ■ ■ ■

Activity 7.7

1 $\frac{£669}{£10,000} \times £22,000 = £1472$ a year.

2 $\frac{£417}{£10,000} \times £50,000 = £2085$ a year.

3 $\frac{£514}{£10,000} \times £50,000 = £2570$ a year.

■ ■ ■

References

Department for Work and Pensions (DWP) (2003) *Working After State Pension Age: Quantitative Analysis*, Leeds, Corporate Document Services; also available online at http://www.dwp.gov.uk/asd/asd5/rport182/Main.pdf (Accessed 15 February 2006).

Department for Work and Pensions (DWP) (2004a) *Older Workers: Statistical Information Booklet*, Autumn, London, DWP.

Department for Work and Pensions (DWP) (2004b) *Family Resources Survey*, London, Office for National Statistics; also available online at http://www.dwp.gov.uk/asd/frs (Accessed 16 May 2006).

Department for Work and Pensions (DWP) (2005) *The Pensioners' Incomes Series 2003/4*, London, Department for Work and Pensions; also available online at http://www.dwp.gov.uk/asd/asd6/pi_internet_april05.pdf (Accessed 14 February 2006).

Department of Social Security (1998) *A New Contract for Welfare: Partnership in Pensions*, Cmnd 4179, London, The Stationery Office.

Financial Services Authority (FSA) (2003) *Purchasing Annuities and an Examination of the Impact of the Open Market Option*, Consumer Research Paper 22, London, FSA; also available online at http://www.fsa.gov.uk/pubs/consumer-research/CRPR22.pdf (Accessed 15 February 2006).

Financial Services Authority (FSA) (2004) *Annual Report 2003/04*, London, Financial Services Authority.

Government Actuary's Department (GAD) (2005) *Cohort Expectations of Life* [online], http://www.gad.gov.uk (Accessed 20 June 2005).

HM Revenue & Customs (HMRC) (2006) 'Income Tax allowances, National Insurance contributions, Child and Working Tax Credit rates 2006–07 and other rates', Budget Press Release PN02, 22 March 2006 [online], http://www.hmrc.gov.uk/budget2006/pn02.pdf (Accessed 22 May 2006).

House of Lords (2004a) *Aspects of the Economics of an Ageing Population*, HL Paper 179-I, London, The Stationery Office; also available online at http://www.publications.parliament.uk/pa/ld200203/ldselect/ldeconaf/179/179.pdf (Accessed 14 February 2006).

House of Lords (2004b) *Government Response to Aspects of the Economics of an Ageing Population,* HL Paper 129, London, The Stationery Office; also available online at http://www.publications.parliament.uk/pa/ld200304/ldselect/ldeconaf/129/129.pdf (Accessed 15 February 2006).

Inland Revenue (1998) *Inland Revenue Statistics 1998*, London, Her Majesty's Stationery Office.

Lowe, J. (2005) *Giving and Inheriting*, London, Which? Books.

Moneyfacts Group (2005) 'Compulsory purchase annuities', *Investment, Life & Pensions Moneyfacts*, August, p. 51, Norwich, Moneyfacts Group.

National Association of Pension Funds (NAPF) (2004) *Thirtieth Annual Survey of Occupational Pension Schemes 2004*, London, NAPF.

Nesbitt, S. and Neary, D. (2001) *Ethnic Minorities and their Pension Decisions: A Study of Pakistani, Bangladeshi and White Men in Oldham*, York, Joseph Rowntree Foundation; also available online at http://www.jrf.org.uk/bookshop/eBooks/185935288X.pdf (Accessed 16 February 2006).

Office for National Statistics (ONS) (2004a) *Focus on Older People: Population*, London, Office for National Statistics; also available online at http://www.statistics.gov.uk/focuson (Accessed 16 May 2006).

Office for National Statistics (ONS) (2004b) *Living in Britain: Results from the 2002 General Household Survey*, London, The Stationery Office; also available online at http://www.statistics.gov.uk/downloads/theme_compendia/lib2002.pdf (Accessed 16 February 2006).

Pension Law Review Committee (1993) *Pension Law Reform, Volume 1, Report* (The Goode Report), London, HMSO.

Pensions Commission (2004) *Pensions: Challenges and Choices. The First Report of the Pensions Commission* (The Turner Report), London, The Stationery Office; also available online at http://www.pensionscommission.org.uk/publications/2004/annrep/fullreport.pdf (Accessed 14 February 2006).

Pensions Commission (2005) *A New Pension Settlement for the Twenty-First Century: Executive Summary*, London, The Stationery Office; also available online at http://www.pensionscommission.org.uk/publications/2005/annrep/executive-summ.pdf (Accessed 15 February 2006).

Smith, S. (2001) 'Fiscal policy', *Economic Review*, vol. 18, no. 3 [online], http://www.ifs.org.uk/economic_review/fp183.pdf (Accessed 16 February 2006).

United Nations (2001) Department of Economic and Social Affairs, Population Division, *World Population Ageing: 1950–2050*, New York, United Nations.

Chapter 8

Sharing and caring

Susan Himmelweit

Contents

I   Introduction

Most of us have experienced living under the same roof with other people. Often, we, or others in the household, have needed looking after: whether as a child depending on parent(s); as an adult living with a partner or with flatmates; as a parent oneself; or as an elderly parent who needs care. We are also familiar with the fact that the households in which people live change, as do the people that households care for. If you don't know this through your own life, then you can see it through the lives of families on UK TV 'soaps' such as *Eastenders* or *Coronation Street*. For instance, at the start of 2006 in *Coronation Street*, there were four generations living in the Barlow household, and over the years they have experienced births, deaths, marriages, divorces and remarriages. While TV soaps tend to concentrate on the emotional side of relationships within and between families, 'real-life' changes to households also have important financial implications that are often overlooked in such entertainment.

Four different generations of the same family could have many different 'sharing and caring' relationships

Caring
Providing a personal service to help someone who is not capable of looking after their own personal needs.

This chapter examines such financial implications. It will explain how decisions to set up or dissolve a household, and how **caring** for other household members, can both have important long-term financial effects. For most people, these issues are financially far more significant in the longer term than, say, where they bank their savings account or whether they have found the cheapest mortgage. This is because there are important opportunity costs, particularly in the long term, in the decisions that people make about sharing their household with other people, and about caring for them.

Two of the themes of *Personal Finance* – the interrelationship between individuals and households, and change over the life-course – are deeply intertwined. When looking at the financial consequences of sharing and caring, we need to keep in mind the connection between individual and household financial decision making, and to be aware of how household decisions can have an uneven impact on different members of households. This means thinking at both the individual and household level.

The social and economic context under which sharing and caring decisions are being made is rapidly changing. Families and households in the UK look quite different today from how they did thirty years ago. Moreover, there are significant differences across ethnic groups in how different generations choose to look after each other and in the types of households in which they live. Section 2 explores this diversity, and how changes in the household have important effects on expenditure.

Section 3 examines how households tend to organise caring for household members and divide up employment and caring between household members. This leads into Section 4, which looks at how individual decisions about caring are linked to employment choices. Sections 5 and 6 consider the short- and long-term implications of the difficulties of reconciling caring and employment. Finally, in Section 7, I consider what happens when a household comes to an end.

2   Families and households

Before examining the financial implications of individuals' decisions about sharing with and caring for others, it's important to put those individual decisions into a broader context. As you saw in Section 4 of Chapter 7, there has been concern – in the UK and in many other countries – about a falling birth rate leading to an ageing population and a falling support ratio. However, for children to become adults, they not only need to be born, they also need to be cared for. Similarly, many older people and people with disabilities cannot look after themselves without the help of others, and any civilised society needs to have some way of providing for their care.

In nearly all societies, **families** play an important role in the care of their members. Yet families vary across and within societies. In some societies, there are households with extended families that include three

Family
A group of people who are related and responsible for each other and comprise at least a parent and child.

or more generations. In such households, care for the young, the old and those with disabilities is shared across the generations. Across Europe, extended families are more common in Mediterranean countries than in northern Europe, where households consisting of only parents and **dependent children** are more usual. In these northern European societies, the care that families provide will often need to be supplemented by others, including non-resident family members and care from outside the family such as that provided by nurseries, residential homes for the elderly or home helps. Non-familial care may be provided by the state or bought as a service from private or voluntary sector providers.

2.1 Diversity within the UK

Within the UK, families are becoming more diverse, reflecting both changes in **social norms** and a changing ethnic and cultural composition of the population. Different cultural traditions and economic characteristics of the various ethnic groups, as well as different age structures, give rise to families and households that differ in size and composition. As Figure 8.1 shows, Asian households tend to be larger and Black Caribbean and White households smaller than those from other ethnic groups. A household's ethnicity is classified by the ethnic background of the **household reference person**.

Dependent child
A child aged 0 to 15 in a household; or a child aged 16 to 19 in either unwaged work-based training, or education or training to the end of the course or age 20 (whichever is earlier) *and* living with his or her parents.

Social norms
Accepted ways of behaving that are generally approved of in society.

Household reference person
The member of a household who brings in its highest income without regard to gender. (Before April 2001, men were usually assumed to be the head of household.)

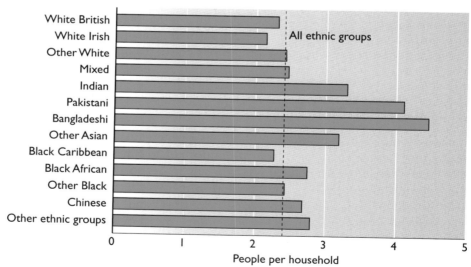

Figure 8.1 *Average household size in Great Britain, April 2001: by ethnic group of household reference person*
Source: ONS, 2004a

This bar chart shows that Bangladeshi and Pakistani households have on average over four people per household while Indian and Other Asian households have over three people in each household. The average household size for all ethnic groups is just below two-and-a-half people and the other groups that have household sizes above this are Other White (i.e. other than British and Irish), Mixed, Black African, Other Black, Chinese and Other Ethnic groups. White British, White Irish and Black Caribbean households have an average size of above two people but below the average.

The composition of households also varies. Figure 8.2 shows that White households are the least likely to contain children, while Bangladeshi households are the most likely to do so.

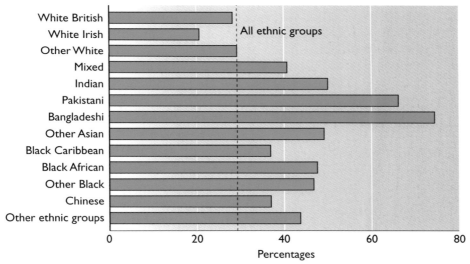

Figure 8.2 *Households with dependent children as a proportion of all households in Great Britain, April 2001: by ethnic group of household reference person*
Source: ONS, 2004a

Asian households are more likely to contain more than one family since extended families count as more than one family in one household. The highest proportion of such households in Great Britain is among Bangladeshi households, 17 per cent of which consist of more than one family that included children. White households had the lowest proportion of extended families, with only 2 per cent consisting of more than one family that included children (*Social Trends*, 2005, no. 35, p. 22, Table 2.5). (Note that this would include same-sex couples with children, as, prior to the introduction of Civil Partnerships, same-sex couples did not count as a single family.)

Figure 8.3 shows families with dependent children for the whole of the UK. From this, you can see that lone parents are especially prevalent among Black families, and least prevalent among Indian and other Asian families, where cohabitation rates are also very low. As we saw in Chapter 1, Section 3, approximately 90 per cent of lone parents are lone mothers.

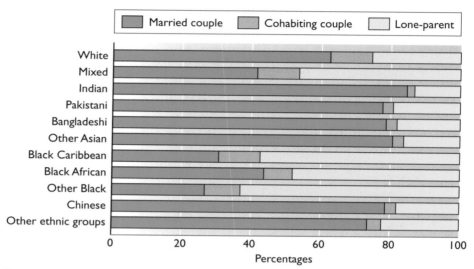

Figure 8.3 *Families with dependent children in the UK, April 2001: by ethnic group and family type*
Source: ONS, 2005a

There are also ethnic differences in the composition of households that contain older people. In 2001, less than 5 per cent of Asian and Black African households, compared with over 15 per cent of White households, consisted of pensioners living on their own, with Black Caribbean households lying in between these extremes. These differences reflect both the greater tendency for older Asian people to live with their extended family (see Chapter 7, Box 7.4) and the younger age structure of the Asian and African population (*Social Trends*, 2005, pp. 21–2).

As well as variations between ethnic groups in the UK, there are also changes to household composition across time that are part of the changing social context. Table 8.1 shows the trends over time for the UK population overall. You met a simplified version of this table as Table 1.1 in Chapter 1 – there you saw a snapshot of the position in 2004. Table 8.1 gives more detail by separating out sole pensioners from other one-person households, and separating couples with dependent children from those whose children are no longer dependent. This table enables us to look back over time and see that the proportion of households consisting of the traditional family unit of a couple with dependent children has fallen from just over one-third (35 per cent) in 1971 to under one-quarter (22 per cent) in 2004.

Table 8.1 Households in Great Britain: by type of household and family (%)

	1971	1981	1991	2001	2004
One person					
Under state pension age	6	8	11	14	14
Over state pension age	12	14	16	15	15
One-family households					
Couple					
No children	27	26	28	29	29
With dependent children[1]	35	31	25	23	22
Non-dependent children only	8	8	8	6	6
Lone parent	7	9	10	10	10
Two or more unrelated adults	4	5	3	3	3
Multi-family households	1	1	1	1	1
All households (100%) (millions)	18.6	20.2	22.4	23.8	24.1

[1] May also include non-dependent children.
Source: *Social Trends*, 2005, p. 20, Table 2.2

Conversely, there has been a steep rise in the proportion of households consisting of just one person. Most of this increase has come from the proportion of households consisting of people under pension age living on their own more than doubling. An equally significant rise has been in the proportion of lone-parent families with dependent children. One thing not shown in Table 8.1 is that there has also been an increase in step families (as it does not distinguish these from other families), who made up 10 per cent of all families with dependent children in the UK at the time of the 2001 census (ONS, 2005b).

Consider the household in which you live. How many people live in it and what is their relationship to each other? Think about how your household may differ from the households in which your parents and grandparents lived when they were your age. ■ ■ ■

2.2 Financial planning and living with others

The size and type of household in which you live has financial implications. As you saw in Chapter 3, Section 5.1, sharing a household with others results in economies of scale. This means that financial plans need adjusting with changes in a household. For example, when two people who had previously been living on their own set up home together, they will usually be able to benefit from a higher standard of living than they had previously enjoyed. This gives them the ability to make some choices. For instance, rather than letting their current standard of living rise, they may wish to save for a time when their needs are greater, thus deferring the benefits. According to the financial planning model that has been developed throughout *Personal Finance*, their first step would be Stage 1, 'to assess' how much they need to maintain their standard of living. Stage 2 is then 'to decide' on a financial plan for any spare income.

The concept of 'equivalised income' is one way in which a couple could estimate such economies of scale. Box 3.2 in Chapter 3 showed you how to use 'equivalence scales' for households of different sizes and compositions in order to calculate a household's equivalised income.

Activity 8.2

Shirley and James, who were previously each living on their own, marry and set up home together. They each earn £20,000 net income.

1   Use Box 3.2 from Chapter 3 to work out the equivalised income of Shirley's and James's households before marriage.

2   Work out how much Shirley and James can jointly save after marriage if they want to live at the standard of living to which they were previously accustomed.

Comment

Before marriage, Shirley and James were each living in households whose equivalence scale was 0.61 (the value for a single adult), so each household's equivalised income was $\frac{£20,000}{0.61} = £32,787$. That is, each single person's standard of living, from having a net income of £20,000, is equivalent to what it would be for a childless couple with a net income of £32,787. After marriage they have a joint income of £40,000 of which they require just £32,787 (since a couple's household equivalence scale is 1) to live at their previous standard of living, leaving them with £7213 (£40,000 − £32,787) that they could save. This assumes that Shirley and James were spending all their income before they started living together − if they were saving before, they can save even more once they are living together without affecting their standard of living. ▪▪▪

In practice, when people set up home together their pattern of expenditure changes. Living as a couple, they may spend more time at home and less going out, and thus more on heating and less on restaurant meals, for example.

A couple's habits and expenditure pattern may change when they set up home together

Consequently, in reality, the overall changes in the cost of achieving a given standard of living may be masked by other household changes. For example, many couples forming a household together move into better housing at the time, effectively using some of the economies of scale to finance rent or a joint mortgage that is higher than the sum of what they were paying for housing previously. There is, therefore, all the more reason for the 'Stage 4: review' part of the financial planning model to see how the benefits of the economies of scale are being applied. To obtain a more accurate picture of changes in expenditure and income, a couple could go through the budgeting process described in Chapter 3.

Besides couples getting together, there are other stages in the life-course when people change the household in which they live, sometimes for financial reasons. For instance, when starting out as students or when in their first job, many young adults cannot afford to buy or rent a place in which to live on their own, and so share a flat specifically to reap the benefits of economies of scale.

A student house share can reap the benefits of economies of scale

Older people sometimes move in with their children. As you saw in Section 2.1, there is a considerable variation among ethnic groups in the extent to which older people live with their grown-up children. One reason for older people living with their children may be financial; children may consider that asking their parents to come and live with them is one way in which they can help to raise their parents' standard of living. This is more likely to happen within families of recent immigrants, where the parents may not have been in the UK labour market long enough to build up an adequate pension.

For families, just as for couples, issues about living together are rarely purely financial. In particular, older people often need care, and their children may be better able to contribute to that care if they are all living under the same roof. Different norms concerning the care of elderly

Children asking their parents to live with them can raise their parents' standard of living

people and the responsibility of young adults to their parents, as well as different economic situations, lie behind the differences in household composition found in different ethnic groups (see also Chapter 7, Box 7.4). There are economies of scale in care too: it doesn't take ten times as many carers to look after ten people through the night as it does to look after one. This is one reason why residential homes for older people exist; someone who needs a great deal of care may not be able to afford to continue living on their own because the care costs for one are higher than they are for someone in a home that cares for many.

As you saw in Chapter 3, having children increases the income that a childless couple (or a single person) needs to maintain their previous standard of living. Figure 8.4 shows the equivalised income of four couples that each have the same household income of £20,000. Couple A have no children; Couple B have a 2-year old; Couple C a 6-year old and a 10-year old; and Couple D have three children aged 12, 14 and 16. The values for equivalised income were calculated using the scales in Box 3.2 in Chapter 3.

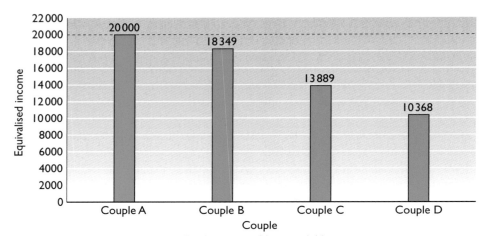

Figure 8.4 *The impact on equivalised income of having children*

In Figure 8.4, as more children are added, and the older they get, the more dramatic is the impact on the household's equivalised income. Couple D with three older children have an equivalised income of only just above half that of Couple A with no children – in other words, based on expenditure alone, their standard of living is about half that of the childless couple receiving the same (non-equivalised) income. Children make an even greater proportionate impact on the standard of living of a lone parent.

None the less, in order to take account of changes in household composition, financial planning requires considering more than just the expenditure side; it also needs to consider how much income a household can expect to earn. A household made up of employed adults will generally have a larger income than one that includes people not of working age – either children or older people. Furthermore, some of these people will need care, and this may impact on the income of the household by affecting how much time other members of the household can devote to employment.

In assessing a financial situation, it is necessary to think about the current and future care needs of household members, and the financial implications of the different ways of fulfilling these needs. One way to provide care is to pay for it by employing a carer for an older person or by sending a child to nursery, for example. Purchasing such care will increase household expenditure. Another way to provide care is for a member of the household to provide the care themselves. This usually requires forgoing some opportunities to earn money, and thus has an opportunity cost in terms of lost income. Equivalence scales only consider expenditure costs, not other opportunity costs. They also don't take account of some benefits that government provides. Consequently, they fail to capture the potentially large costs in terms of lost income that caring for members of a household may require, or all the ways in which the government may help in replacing some of that income. The next section considers the decisions households make about different ways of providing care and who should provide it.

3   The division of paid and unpaid work

Looking after the household and caring for other members of the household is a form of **unpaid work**. Some of it may be work that people do happily, and some may not be done so cheerfully, but it is work in the sense that it is a contribution to the well-being of people that would otherwise have to be paid for.

Unpaid work
Unpaid activity that contributes to the well-being of people and would otherwise have to be paid for. It includes looking after a household and caring for people.

Household members can do a variety of unpaid work

Those who live on their own have to do such unpaid work for themselves (unless they employ someone to do it from outside their household), just as they have to provide for their expenditure out of their own income. In a multi-person household, some members may contribute more unpaid work than others, just as some members of the household may contribute more income. This means that members of a multi-person household can make a variety of decisions about how to divide up paid and unpaid work between them. Chapter 3 looked at some of the ways that households plan their income and expenditure, and systems some use for managing their finances. Here, I focus on how households divide up their members' time between paid and unpaid work, especially when there are people in the household who need care.

The male breadwinner/female caregiver household is one in which the man is the sole earner and the woman stays at home to look after her husband, the household, the children, and anyone else who needs care. This model never applied to all families, but it used to be more common in the UK than it is today (Lewis, 2001).

Today, the majority of married and cohabiting women are in the labour force, even those with small children. As Figure 8.5 shows, more than half of mothers with pre-school children are in employment, and this proportion increases as the age of the youngest child increases. However, mothers often work part time; nearly 40 per cent of women with dependent children work part time, compared with only 23 per cent of those without dependent children. As their children grow up, many mothers return to full-time employment (ONS, 2004b).

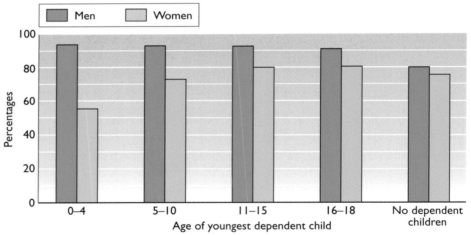

Figure 8.5 *Economic activity of men and women of working age in the UK, 2003: by age of youngest dependent child*
Source: ONS, 2004b

These patterns do not hold for all ethnic groups. Specifically, Pakistani and Bangladeshi women tend to leave the labour force when they get married, and nearly all do so by the time they have children; in 2001/02, 82 per cent with children less than 4 years old were not in the labour force. Furthermore, older Pakistani and Bangladeshi women rarely return to employment when their children are older. Nevertheless, it does not follow that women who are young now will necessarily follow the pattern of earlier generations in their community who were often first-generation immigrants with few qualifications and less than fluent English. Hours of employment also vary among different ethnic groups. Black Caribbean and Black African mothers are more likely to be employed full time than part time. Part-time employment is particularly prevalent among White mothers (Lindley et al., 2004).

There are competing social norms about the best way to look after children, with some parents feeling that full-time parental care, usually by the mother, gives a child the best start in life, while others believe equally strongly that the involvement of trained professionals and the regular contact with other children that a nursery provides are important.

There are competing social norms about the best way to look after children

Either way, the amount of unpaid work at home increases with the arrival of children, making decisions about the couple's work-life balance and the household division of paid and unpaid labour more acute. Unless the couple have made an active decision to divide everything equally, social norms and economic circumstances still mean that it is usually the woman who adjusts, increasing her hours of unpaid work and in many cases decreasing her hours of paid work, while her partner, if she has one, leaves his hours of paid work unchanged and may even increase them somewhat to compensate for the loss of her earnings.

There are also many people who devote time to caring for adults, which may also affect their employment possibilities. Most carers of adults are older people. The age group most likely to be providing unpaid care for family members, friends or neighbours are people in their fifties, with more than one in five (21 per cent) doing so, and as Figure 8.6 illustrates, the proportion declines with age. None the less, 5 per cent of those aged 85 and over were providing some form of unpaid care, and often for very long hours. (One in two carers aged 85 and over spent fifty hours or more a week caring; this figure was 24 per cent for carers in their fifties (ONS, 2005c).)

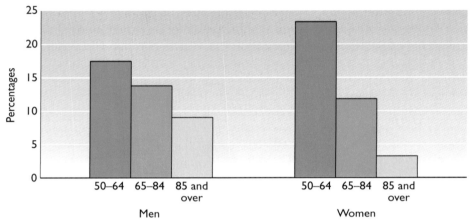

Figure 8.6 *Percentage of people in households providing unpaid care to adults in England and Wales, April 2001: by sex and age*
Source: ONS, 2005c

Among the older age groups, a man is more likely to be a carer than a woman because older carers are usually looking after a spouse and men over 65 are more likely than women of that age to have a living spouse. Among 50- to 64-year olds, a greater proportion of women than men provide unpaid care.

The most important financial consequence of being a carer arises from its effect on the carer's employment possibilities. In 2001 in the UK, as Table 8.2 shows, there were over 2 million people of working age who were not in the labour market because they had children or were caring for a dependent adult or relative. The vast majority of these were women, especially among those who were out of the labour market because of children. A larger proportion of men cared for older people than cared for children, but there were still more than twice as many women as men caring for adults. Caring is an area in which there is still a large gender difference, and within working-age couples, women are more likely to be the carers, of children or older people, and more likely to be out of the labour market as a result.

Table 8.2 Numbers of economically inactive working-age people looking after the family/home in the UK, autumn 2001: by sex and reason for inactivity

	Economically inactive		
	(000s)		(000s)
	Men	Women	All
Reason for inactivity			
One or more children below school age	39	1101	1140
One or more other children	41	606	648
Caring for dependent adult or relative	96	229	326
Other reason	13	262	276
Total	**190**	**2199**	**2389**

Source: Weir, 2002, p. 579, Table 1

For a couple, decisions about who does the caring, and the balance of unpaid and paid work need to be considered very carefully. I noted in Section 2.2 that having assessed the care needs of household members, a financial plan would then consider the financial implications of the different ways of fulfilling these needs. If it is decided that the best way to meet those needs involves reducing time in employment, there is an issue of who should do this. Often, as you have seen, couples follow traditional gender roles.

Activity 8.3

Think about some couples that you know who have children or adults to look after. Why do you think they organise things in the way that they do? Could financial reasons have entered into that decision?

Comment

Whatever other reasons enter into this decision, if one partner earns less per hour than the other, household income will fall less if the lower earning partner is the one to cut back on paid work to do more unpaid work (with the higher earner possibly putting more time into paid work to make up lost income). Since, as you saw in Chapter 2, women's wages are on average lower than men's, financial pressures will in general reinforce traditional gender roles. ■■■

There are a number of different ways in which to reduce employment to allow more time for caring, and each has different financial consequences for future earnings and pensions. Therefore, in developing a financial plan, all these factors need to be considered. Section 4 examines the alternative ways of reducing hours of employment in order to care for others.

4   Reducing time in employment

To allow more time for caring, an employee could:

- give up their current job and look for another job with hours that they prefer
- switch to working for themselves so that they can (theoretically at least) choose their own hours
- give up their current job and look for another one when they are ready to resume employment again
- take some statutory leave that, as a right, they can take from their current job
- ask for time out from their employer as a career break or sabbatical
- ask their employer to let them change or reduce their hours or to 'job-share'.

The idea of human capital that you met in Chapter 2, Section 5 is useful in looking at the financial implications of these alternatives. As you saw then, human capital is any accumulated education, training and work experience that makes a person's work worth more to an employer than that of an unskilled new recruit, and so enables that person to earn more than a basic unskilled wage.

Transferable skills
Skills acquired through training or previous employment that would be useful in other jobs.

Some human capital consists of **transferable skills** that can be used in other jobs. Yet some human capital is relevant only to a particular occupation, or even only to a particular employer, and so would not count in another occupation or for another employer. Most human capital is somewhere in between and includes some transferable skills, some skills that are specific to a particular occupation, and some skills based on experience in a current job that are of particular use to a current employer.

The effects on earnings of each of the ways of changing employment hours listed above will depend on the types of skills that employees have. Those who have easily transferable skills that can be used by many different employers may have no problems when moving between employers (though having too long a break may still lead to their human capital deteriorating – skills become rusty through being out of the rapidly changing world of work). Nevertheless, if a person's skills are specific to their current occupation and there are not many employers looking for those skills, they need to think carefully before giving up their current job. They may do better by trying to negotiate a career break or different hours with their existing employer, especially if otherwise it would mean changing occupation.

As you saw in Chapter 2, Section 5, part-time work is generally worse paid than full-time work in the UK. The **part-time pay penalty** is the difference between the hourly wage rates of full-time and part-time work. In most other European Union (EU) countries, because full-time working hours are not as long as in the UK and part-time work hours tend not to be as short, there is less of a distinction between the sort of jobs that people do part time and full time, and the part-time pay penalty is much smaller (Manning and Petrongolo, 2005). However, the long full-time working hours in the UK (and relatively expensive childcare) mean that many couples find that they cannot juggle caring responsibilities with two full-time jobs; the most common solution is for the woman to take a part-time job (see Box 8.1).

Part-time pay penalty
The difference between the wage rate that a person would receive in full-time employment and what they receive in a part-time job.

Box 8.1   A 'one-and-a-half-breadwinner' society

The UK has been referred to as a 'one-and-a-half-breadwinner' society (Lewis, 2001). This is in contrast to:

- the 'dual breadwinner' society characteristic of Scandinavian countries, in which mothers and fathers both tend to have full-time jobs but with shorter hours than in the UK
- the 'traditional male breadwinner' society that still exists in Germany and some southern European countries, in which mothers of small children tend not to be in the workforce. None the less, mothers' employment rates are rising rapidly in these countries too.

The gender gap between the average number of hours worked by women and men is greater in the UK than in any other EU country (Eurostat, 2002; Fagan, 2000).

Most part-time work is unskilled, for which many of the people doing it are overqualified (Grant et al., 2005). Part-time work, like unemployment, seems to have a 'scarring effect' on careers, so that even one year of working part time rather than full time reduces women's wage rates by, on average, 10 per cent fifteen years later, even for those who have worked full time since then. Indeed, many women working part time find it difficult to move back to full-time employment (Francesconi and Gosling, 2005).

Not all workers do badly when changing to part-time work. Under what conditions would you expect the part-time pay penalty to be smaller?

Those who do best in part-time work are often those who negotiate working hours that enable them to stay with their current employers. Those in career jobs who negotiate taking a career break, reducing their hours or job-sharing are much more likely to be able to retain their pay and promotion prospects. Others who change employers but stay in the same occupation where they can continue to use most of their skills are subject to less of a pay penalty than those who change occupations, typically into less skilled work. Nevertheless, even those who stay in their current jobs do seem to suffer some long-term penalty for working part time. Part-time workers tend to be offered fewer training opportunities and may not be as frequently promoted as full-time workers. ■ ■ ■

Over the years, various statutory rights have been introduced to help workers with caring responsibilities to stay in employment, and for the economy to retain their skills. These are outlined in Box 8.2.

Box 8.2 Employees' statutory rights to take leave for caring responsibilities

The UK Government recognises that some people need to adjust their employment around caring responsibilities, and it has given some statutory rights to paid and unpaid leave (mostly dependent on having worked for the same employer for a qualifying period). This is an area of government policy that is changing rapidly. At the time of writing in 2006, parents had considerably greater rights than workers with other caring responsibilities:

- Mothers can take one year of maternity leave at the birth of a child, with some of this leave being paid, although mostly at a low flat rate (£108.85 a week in 2006/07). The government intends to make some of this leave available to fathers if the mother does not use it all.

- Fathers can take two weeks' paid paternity leave at the birth of a child.

- Similar provisions for maternity and paternity leave apply to parents adopting a child.

■ Parents can also take thirteen weeks' unpaid parental leave during the first five years of a child's life – slightly more leave is available over a longer period for a child with a disability.

■ Everyone has a right to take unpaid leave to cope with domestic emergencies including, for example, the breakdown of usual caring arrangements.

■ Some people with caring responsibilities have a right to request a change in their working hours. Employers must consider such requests seriously but can refuse them on commercial grounds. In 2006, this right applied to parents of children under 6 (or under 18 for a disabled child), but from April 2007 will apply to carers of adults too.

The statutory right to request a change in working hours seems to be having some effect on changing employers' attitudes in the UK, and 81 per cent of such requests are granted (Grainger and Holt, 2005). In some workplaces, employers have been ahead of the government, and have been proactive in offering employees better maternity pay, carer's leave with pay, flexible working hours, homeworking and/or career breaks. Other employers, who have not previously had to face such issues, can be very supportive when asked. Some employers are not, either because it is genuinely difficult for them to make adjustments or because of (illegal) prejudice against part-time workers or employees with caring responsibilities, believing that they are less committed workers. A research project found that this was not how such workers saw themselves. In fact, many 'stressed that having caring responsibilities did not mean that they were any less conscientious at work (although [many feared] ... that that was how managers and colleagues would see them)' (Himmelweit and Sigala, 2004). Box 8.3 illustrates some of the dilemmas in which parents and carers can find themselves.

Box 8.3   The dilemmas of parents and carers

'I have always resisted going part-time, partly because of my commitment and pride in my job, partly because it is the kiss of death for female scientific researchers (I don't know of any men in similar jobs who would ever consider it) ...' (EOC noticeboard, parent and carer, submitted 31.9.04)

'I returned to work full-time for 5 months – and spent most of my weekends missing out on my son due to other homely responsibilities and 3 other children. I finally gave in and my family struggled on one income for 3 years. When I went back into the workforce I focused on something easy and half the wage and stimulation I had been used to previously and local, only part-time ...' (EOC website, mother, submitted 23.9.04).

(EOC, 2005)

Activity 8.5

Think about the two mothers in Box 8.3 and their attitudes to their jobs. Have they each faced the dilemma of reconciling employment with caring for others? Why are they so different? Think about the timescale each is considering.

Comment

The first mother clearly has a professional job with a career structure (like Peter in Chapter 2, Section 6). She is therefore worried about the long-term implications for her career of taking time out of work. Whether she is worried that she would lose skills by working part time or simply that this is how she would be perceived by her colleagues is not clear.

We don't know what sort of job the second mother had initially, but she found that working full time left her insufficient time for her family. Her family finances were too stretched living on one income, and so the solution she has found is to work part time in a job that is less skilled but is 'easy and half the wage and stimulation'. Immediate financial and time pressures have led her to this, and she does not comment on the longer-term implications. ▪ ▪ ▪

5 Short-term financial considerations in reconciling caring and employment

Now that I have looked at the sharing of paid and unpaid work, and reductions in working hours, I want to consider how to develop a financial plan that reconciles employment and caring responsibilities. The development of a financial plan in these circumstances necessitates thinking carefully about both short- and long-term financial considerations. In many families, strongly held views about what constitutes good care combine with immediate financial pressures to determine which decisions are made. None the less, there are long-term implications of such decisions, and in assessing the situation and reviewing a financial plan, it is important to be aware of these. In Section 6, I discuss these longer-term issues.

We shall start in this section by considering the immediate short-term financial effects on both the household's income through a reduction in earnings, and on its expenditure if care has to be paid for. However, in the UK the balance between these two is complicated by the fact that the government contributes in various ways to the support of children and adults needing care. The level of support from the government will vary as policies and benefits change. In this section, I explore some of the underlying financial issues. To do this I will use the example of the government support available in 2006. While the details of this support may change, the *approach* to analyse the implications of such support can be applied even when changes have been made.

5.1 Government support for parents

The welfare of children is seen as a matter of public concern and an investment in the future of society and, consequently, governments in most developed economies make a financial contribution to parents' costs in raising children. In the UK, there have been such payments since 1945, but the amount paid to poorer families has increased considerably since 1999 in an attempt to reduce child poverty rates, which were the worst in the EU in 1998, and were still well above the EU average in 2001 (DWP, 2003).

Currently, as you saw in Chapter 2, Section 7, these payments are of two types. There is Child Benefit, a universal benefit which depends only on the number of qualifying children, and Child Tax Credit (CTC), which is means-tested on family income, like Working Tax Credit (WTC) (see Chapter 2, Section 7). This means that for lower income households both CTC and WTC are withdrawn at a rate of 37 pence for every pound earned above a minimum threshold that depends on number and age of children (for CTC).

Activity 8.6

If someone in a low-income household receiving CTC or WTC decides to reduce their hours of work because of caring responsibilities, how much income do they lose for each pound less that they earn?

Comment

Those in low-income households receiving CTC or WTC will not lose a full pound for each pound less that they earn, because their tax credits will go up a little, since with lower household income less of their tax credits will be means-tested away. So their income will fall by only 63 pence (£1 minus 37 pence) for every pound that their earnings drop.

However, if any reduction in hours of employment takes a recipient below the threshold for WTC, 16 hours of employment, or below 30 hours for an individual or couple claiming the full-time element of WTC, the amount of income that would be lost through reducing hours of employment is considerably *more* than just the drop in earnings. WTC provides a strong incentive to put in just enough hours of employment to reach its thresholds. ■ ■ ■

Childcare is expensive in the UK – indeed, it is more expensive in the UK than in any other European country – because it is less subsidised by the government. However, the government does contribute to the cost of childcare for parents who are in some form of education and training. It will also pay a proportion of allowable childcare expenses, up to a maximum, if both parents or a lone parent are in employment (or have a disability) and qualify for WTC. Childcare expenses can only be claimed under WTC if the childcare is provided by a registered childcare provider, for example a nursery- or child-minder. Money for childcare is added to any other elements claimed for in WTC, and so those who claim for childcare can earn a considerable amount before it is all means-tested away, making quite a large group eligible for WTC if they can make full use of the childcare subsidies. That childcare expenses can be partially refunded under WTC goes a long way in counteracting the disincentive effect that household means-testing produces for parents who use registered childcare.

The UK Government also provides incentives to employers to help with childcare by giving them tax breaks for doing so. When employers provide nurseries or give their employees vouchers to help with the cost of childcare, this is effectively an increase in salary, but it is not generally subject to National Insurance or Income Tax for either the employer or the parent. (The childcare element of WTC referred to above cannot be claimed for costs met by an employer either directly or through vouchers.)

Sometimes, such help with childcare costs is offered through a 'salary sacrifice' scheme, by which employees give up some pay and instead take some of their salary in the form of childcare vouchers or fees. With a lower nominal salary, their tax credit entitlement might increase. Nevertheless, they will generally lose pension and other earnings-related benefits as a result of having a lower salary, and they may lose the right to return to their original salary when they no longer want help with childcare costs. This is therefore a case where short-term benefits need to be weighed up carefully against longer-term costs (see Section 6). While women may be the ones who usually think first about taking up such schemes, it may be that converting salary into childcare vouchers is worth doing for a parent who is a higher rate tax payer and already has a good pension entitlement, but not for a parent who has built up little pension entitlement so far and/or does not pay even basic rate tax.

5.2 Government help for adults who need care

There is a range of government financial support for adults who need care. Disability Living Allowance (DLA) is the main support for those under 65 who have a long-term health problem that affects their everyday activities. DLA includes a component for **personal care** and another for mobility, both paid at different levels according to the severity of the claimant's needs. Those over 65 and already receiving DLA can continue to receive it if the condition giving rise to the claim persists. New claimants over 65 can claim Attendance Allowance (AA) instead, which is also a tax-free non-means-tested benefit, but it is more limited than DLA. Both DLA and AA enable the person with a disability to pay others to look after their needs, although the money can be used in any way that the recipient wants.

Personal care
Help with personal aspects of normal living such as washing, dressing, or preparing a meal, and supervision to prevent accidents.

There is government financial support for those who need personal care

Local authorities also provide social care services directly to those needing care, or direct payments instead of those services, and help fund places in residential homes for those who do not have the means to pay the full cost themselves. Residential care will be considered in Chapter 9, so here I will focus on the care given to people in their own homes, which is more likely to impinge on earning possibilities for their carers.

Nursing care
Care that is needed because of a specific medical condition.

Those who have care needs are entitled to an assessment from their local authority to determine what type of help they need. In general, the cost of **nursing care** is met by the government. However, the amount that local authorities will contribute to the cost of any identified personal care needs is means tested on the person's income and assets, except for those over 65 in Scotland. (In Scotland, the situation is the same for those under 65 years of age, but personal care is provided free of charge up to £145 per week for over 65s with care needs, regardless of their income and assets, although they lose Attendance Allowance.) In the past, the local authority social services department would have provided that care directly, through home helps for example. Since 2003, those who qualify for help with the cost of personal care have a right to be given direct payments by their local authority so that they can organise and pay for their care themselves, but they cannot use that money to pay a carer who is a spouse or any other close relative living in the same household.

Disabilities can also affect entitlements to other benefits and occasionally reduce bills. For example, people in employment who have a disability that puts them at a disadvantage in getting a job can claim a considerably higher level of WTC, and households with a person with disabilities can sometimes obtain a reduction in Council Tax.

Payments to carers are also relevant to financial planning. Carer's Allowance (CA) is a taxable benefit for informal carers who spend at least thirty-five hours a week caring for a relative, friend or neighbour who is eligible for DLA or AA. CA can be paid to more than one person in a household, for example, to a couple caring for each other, and can be paid to the spouse or close relative of a person needing care, unlike the direct payments from a local authority. CA is not means tested but is designed to replace earnings that are lost through being a full-time carer, so is only available to carers with very low earnings (£84 per week in 2006/07). Carers who are eligible for benefits worth more than CA, including a state pension, cannot claim CA, but their other benefits may be increased, though by a smaller amount.

Activity 8.7

How might CA affect decisions about whether to reduce hours of employment in order to look after an adult needing care?

Comment

Carers who reduce their hours of employment so that they earn less than the threshold for CA will lose earnings but can claim CA. It is financially advantageous for carers whose earnings are only a small amount above that threshold to reduce their earnings to qualify for CA (especially if that also reduces the costs of providing alternative care). None the less, the impact on any other benefits received may complicate this calculation. ■ ■ ■

5.3 Assessing the immediate issues

The first step in the financial planning process is 'Stage 1: Assess' the situation. As you will appreciate, this can be quite complicated when there is someone who needs care. It involves comparing income and expenditure across a number of alternative scenarios corresponding to the different ways in which their care needs can be met by other members of their household and/or by purchasing outside care.

On the income side, this comparison would take account of the effects, if any, of people reducing time in employment to contribute time to caring, and the contribution of any relevant state benefits. On the expenditure side, this comparison would take account of the cost of alternative forms of care from outside the household; these might include nursery and day-care fees, payments to carers and home helps, and ancillary costs such as transport and heating.

The only income and expenditure items that need considering are those that vary according to the different ways of meeting the household's care needs. Such calculations are usually done at the household level, and therefore also need to consider different ways of splitting contributions between household members. Is it better, for example, to have one person giving up employment to do all the caring, or should different members of the household reduce their hours of employment by smaller amounts in order to share the caring and each retain a foothold in the labour market? For all these decisions, financial calculations won't be the only consideration. Nevertheless, it is very important to be aware of the financial implications of alternative ways of arranging care.

Activity 8.8

Do you have someone in your household needing care?

1   If so, make a list of the items of income and expenditure that are affected by the particular way in which their care is organised, and consider how these would be different if their care was provided for in another way (or ways). If you live in a household with more than one

adult, make sure that the different way(s) you consider include contributions from different members of the household.

2   If you do not have anyone currently in your household who needs care, think about a possible future situation in which that might be the case, for instance, if a parent or a spouse needed care, or if you had a young child. Make a list of the income and expenditure items that would depend on the ways in which care was provided and compare them for two different ways of providing that care.

This exercise is a good way of framing your thinking about the immediate costs and benefits of different ways of providing care, and about how responsibilities should be divided up between members of the household. However, deciding on a certain way of caring has long-term financial consequences as well as short-term ones. The next section will look at a way of assessing such longer-term financial issues. ■ ■ ■

6   Long-term financial considerations in reconciling caring and employment

The way in which care is organised may have long-term consequences for the recipients of the care. Yet there are also long-term financial consequences for those doing the caring. The main reason for this is that, as you have seen, time out of the labour market can reduce future earnings. This can be best assessed by comparing different income profiles over the life-course, like those in Chapter 2, Section 6.

Consider, as an example, Louise, who has a career – a job in which she can expect her earnings to keep rising at least until her mid forties. When she is 30, she has her first child. Figure 8.7(a) shows Louise's earnings profile if she carries on working when she has the child. By contrast, Figure 8.7(b) shows what happens to Louise's earnings profile if she decides to give up employment to look after her child for five years, and then gets an unskilled job, because that is all that is available part time, and works half time for the next five years, before moving back into full-time employment. Her earnings drop to zero at age 30 (she still has some income from Child Benefit and any CTC, but for simplicity the diagrams include only earned income). When, five years later at age 35, she starts her half-time job, her earnings are not even half as high as they would have been if she had stayed in her previous job because she is not using her skills and is subject to the part-time pay penalty. At age 40, when Louise returns to full-time work, she escapes the part-time pay penalty and her earnings more than double. None the less, her income is

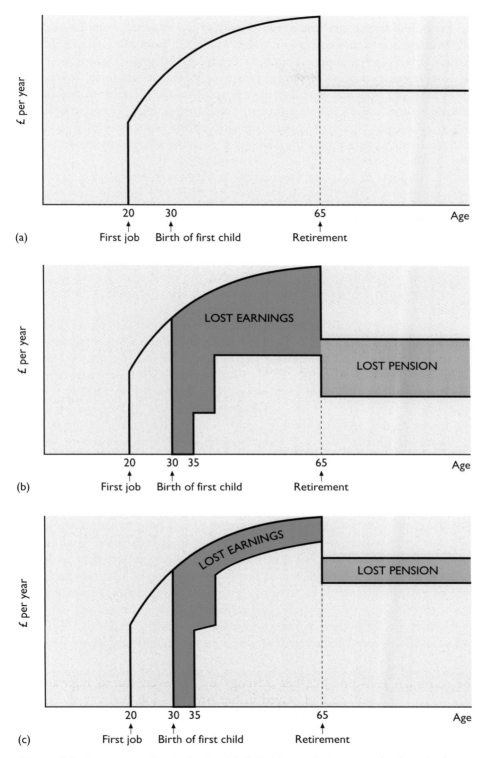

Figure 8.7 Earnings profiles for Louise (a) if she does not give up work when she has a child; (b) if she gives up work when she has a child; (c) if she negotiates with her employer to have a career break when she has a child

still far below where it would have been had she stayed in her previous job, because she is not using her skills, which are now out of date. The shaded area between the two lines on Figure 8.7(b) gives a measure of the total earnings Louise has forgone through her working life. After retirement, she will also lose a proportional amount of pension through reduced contributions to any occupational pension fund, both by herself and an employer, though her state pension will be fully or partly protected by the protection the UK state pension scheme offers to carers (see Chapter 7, Section 3.1).

We can look at this change in lifetime income in terms of opportunity cost. The opportunity cost for Louise of spending five years out of work and then five years in half-time work while looking after her child is a loss of lifetime income equal to the shaded areas in Figure 8.7 (b) minus the cost of childcare that would have had to be paid if she had stayed in employment (not shown in Figure 8.7(a)). Alternatively, another way to look at the same thing is to say that the opportunity cost of Louise having that extra net income is not having that time at home with her child.

There may be a way to reduce these opportunity costs. Think about what would have happened if Louise had followed the same pattern of five years off work and then five years part-time work, but, instead of leaving her previous employment, had negotiated a five-year career break with her employer, followed by a return to work part-time, paid at the same rate as when she left her full-time job. Her rate of pay will be a little lower than it would have been due to losing five years' experience, but much higher than it would have been in a part-time job where she was unable to use her skills. This is shown in Figure 8.7(c). Her income profile continues to rise because she is still in a career job, though it increases at a somewhat lower rate (less steeply) to reflect the disadvantages that part-timers tend to experience in training and promotion prospects. When Louise returns to full-time work (after her five years in part-time work), her pay is therefore a little lower than it would have been had she not taken any break, but nowhere near as low as it was in Figure 8.7(b). You can see the difference in lifetime earnings and occupational pension by looking at the shaded areas in Figure 8.7(c). Again, the full opportunity cost for Louise of this way of looking after her child is the difference in lifetime income minus the childcare costs that would have been incurred if she had stayed in full-time employment.

Activity 8.9

Draw income profiles for Jan, a mother who has a child at the same age as Louise and considers the same alternative patterns of employment as Louise. Jan, however, is not in a career job but in one in which she does not expect her income to rise after the age of 30. Consider how this alters the opportunity cost of the different courses of action. (Ignore any benefits or tax credits in drawing these profiles, as I did in Figure 8.7.)

Some suggested income profiles for Jan, and a commentary, are given at the end of the chapter. ■ ■ ■

The difference between Louise's and Jan's opportunity costs, outlined in the answer at the end of the chapter, impacts on the choices mothers make in reality. Mothers with high earnings from career jobs are far less likely to stop work when they have children than women who earn less or are not in career jobs. As a result, lower earning women who tend to give up work for long periods when they have children end up paying higher opportunity costs in the long run for having children than higher earning women, who do not usually give up employment (Joshi and Davies, 2000). This is one of the reasons why the UK Government subsidises childcare for low-income households on WTC, and so, if Jan were eligible for WTC childcare subsidies, her position could be different.

As you saw in Section 4, some people give up work or reduce their hours of employment in order to care for adults. The amount of time for which they will need these arrangements is generally less predictable than for children, and will often depend on the changing health of the person for whom they care. The effects on the carer's earnings profile is thus much more difficult to predict. Consider, for example, Andrew, whose mother needs full-time care after a stroke. Andrew has a good job, and like most carers he is over 50. One of Andrew's dilemmas is that he doesn't know for how long his mother will need care. She may only live another couple of years but she might live another twenty; she may need full-time care for all of that time or she may get better. This makes his decision about what to do especially difficult.

Figure 8.8(a) gives Andrew's earnings profile where his decisions about his mother's care do not affect his employment. Figure 8.8(b) shows what happens if Andrew does give up work and lives on the government support to which he would then be entitled until he can start to draw his pension (though for simplicity the diagram shows only his earned income before retirement). This assumes that Andrew does not go back into employment later. If his mother dies, or if she recovers and no longer needs him to look after her full time, it may not be easy for Andrew to find another job at his age, or he may have to accept a considerably worse paid job than he had before (despite anti-age discrimination legislation). The total effect of giving up employment on Andrew's earnings is not that different from the effect on Louise's in

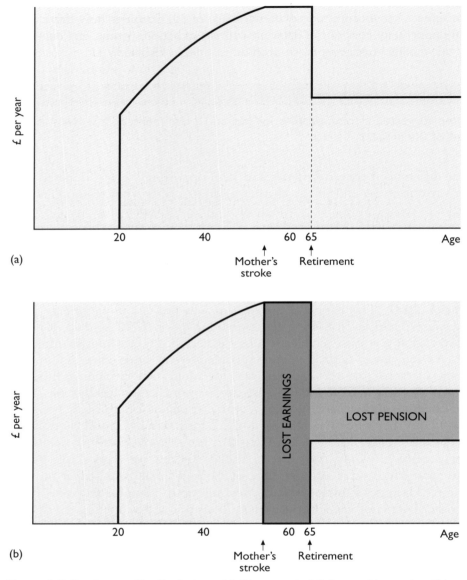

Figure 8.8 Earnings profiles for Andrew: (a) if he stays in full-time employment until he is 65; (b) if he gives up employment to look after his mother

Figure 8.7(b) – although he is affected for a smaller total number of years, the effects per year are greater for Andrew because he was better paid than Louise and gave up work entirely. The effects on his pension may be particularly severe, and depend on the type of pension he has. With a defined contribution scheme, the number of years for which he and his employer contribute to the scheme is reduced. With a defined benefit scheme, his pension will be based on fewer years in the scheme and a lower level of salary too. Furthermore, Andrew has little time before normal retirement age in which to remedy the situation.

There are relatively few Andrews. As you have seen, most carers of working age in the UK are women, and men who have caring responsibilities are less likely to give up employment and more likely to try to combine their caring with employment, however hard that may be. A greater willingness by women to become carers and a greater reluctance of men to give up employment may reflect society's expectations of women's and men's roles.

Nevertheless, this situation also has an economic explanation. If women earn less than men, they have less to lose immediately in giving up their jobs. Moreover, many women are not the main earners of their households, and so the households may be better able to forgo their earnings than those of a main or sole breadwinner. This may be better in the short term from the household's point of view, but it leaves the woman in a vulnerable long-term position herself (see Section 7). This is especially true of the many women who end up taking time off to care for others at both ends of their working lives, losing significant amounts of income as a result and leaving themselves with very poor pensions.

Many women take time off to care for others at both ends of their working lives

When the woman in a household forgoes her earnings completely, this may not be better in the long term from the household's point of view when the cumulative effects are taken into account. A couple may, in the long run, do better by each taking a small cut in pay and promotion prospects rather than one giving up the chance of using their human capital altogether. Although there are many unknowns, making it hard to consider all the long-term effects of plans, these fairly predictable effects on future employment prospects and earnings are important factors to take into account when assessing the situation and deciding on a financial plan.

7   When households come to an end

People do not stay in the same households all their lives. When they grow up, nearly everyone moves out of the household into which they were born. After a period in which they may live in a variety of different household forms, many people spend part of their life in a couple household, sharing their lives and possibly children with a partner of the same or the opposite sex. They may successively live in more than one such household.

In this chapter so far, I have implicitly focused on couple households. Yet all such households must come to an end, whether through the death of one partner, through separation or through divorce, and such endings have important financial implications that need to be considered. Consequently, financial planning for a household needs to include taking care of the long-term financial security of the members of the household as independent individuals when that household comes to an end. This is a financial goal that is frequently ignored – perhaps because people don't like to think about it. Traditionally, death of one of the partners was the most common cause of a household coming to an end. In the mid 2000s, the end of a household is almost as likely to happen through divorce, with roughly 40 per cent of first-time marriages in the UK ending in divorce, and cohabiting couples even more likely to split up.

Financial arrangements that are made during the course of a partnership will affect how people fare individually after the end of that relationship. Being aware of what would happen if the partnership came to an end is important when making financial decisions, even when that prospect seems remote. Issues that do not seem significant when a couple are together, such as what name they put their house in or which of them is bringing in the income, could have important consequences if one of them dies or the relationship breaks up. The consequences in the case of death are somewhat different from those in the case of divorce or of a relationship splitting up, and may differ according to whether the couple

Households come to an end through death or divorce or separation

are married, in a registered civil partnership, or cohabiting. However, the aim of financial arrangements needs to be the same in all cases: to ensure the long-term financial security of the members of the household.

7.1 Death

When one partner dies, a household's living costs go down, but they are not likely to be reduced by half because the economies of scale will be reduced. If the deceased was in employment, household income will be reduced, and if he or she was doing much of the household's unpaid work, household expenses will have to go up to replace the benefits of that work. In most cases, this means that a person's death leaves their household worse off, not only emotionally but financially too.

There are a number of things that can be done in advance to mitigate the effects of this. These include:

- taking out life insurance to replace the income that would be lost or to pay for the additional costs that would be incurred through having to provide a substitute for unpaid work (for example, childcare). Chapter 9 discusses life insurance in detail

- providing an inheritance that the surviving partner can use to provide extra income

- ensuring that any pension being paid will continue to pay out to the surviving partner.

There is often a difference in how these things can be done between people who are married or in registered civil partnerships and those who are cohabiting. For instance, there is tax payable on inheritances and other transfers between cohabitees, and surviving partners may not be covered by life insurance policies if there is no legal relationship. Similarly, not all pensions pay out for dependants anyway, but many of those that would pay a dependant's pension for a widow, widower or registered civil partner, will not do so for a cohabitee without a legal relationship. Prior to December 2005, same-sex couples had few of the legal rights that heterosexual couples had. However, since then gay couples who have civil partnerships can now automatically inherit from each other without a will, benefit from their partner's National Insurance contributions and pension, and make gifts and bequests to each other free of Inheritance Tax. There are complex issues involved in providing for surviving partners that will need careful thought and advice.

7.2 Divorce and separation

When couples split up, they have to decide how to split the variety of different assets that they may own. These assets may include the house in which they have lived, any other property they have acquired or inherited, any savings either has made during the time that they have been together, and also their pension entitlements. If a couple are married or in a civil partnership, the relationship will have to be legally dissolved, and if the couple cannot agree on financial arrangements between them, there will be a court ruling. This does not apply to cohabiting partners, though broadly the same issues need to be considered.

In general, the courts look at the needs of the two parties, trying to meet their needs, but recognising that each of their standards of living will normally have to fall.

Activity 8.10

Can you explain why, after a couple splits up, each partner will usually be worse off? If a couple without children splits, roughly how much extra would they jointly need to spend in order to live at the same standard of living as they did living in one household? To work this out, you will need to look back at Section 2.2 of this chapter, and the equivalence scales in Box 3.2 of Chapter 3.

Comment

The equivalence scales show that to achieve the same standard of living a single person would need to spend 0.61 of what a couple spend. That means that the couple living apart would need to spend twice 0.61, which is

1.22 times what a couple would need, that is, 22 per cent more. If that couple had been spending all or nearly all its income before they split up, then they will not be able to live at the same standard of living as before. ■ ■ ■

On divorce, the courts take various factors into account. For example, they consider the duration of the marriage (the longer the marriage, the more weight given to meeting each partner's needs); the financial resources of each partner (such as their earning power); the age of the couple (this affects career prospects and ability to save for retirement); and contributions during the marriage (including through unpaid work and bringing up children). Where there are children, their needs usually take precedence (for instance, in determining whether one parent can stay in the marital home).

The property that a couple own usually includes their pension rights and the marital home. Indeed, these are often their two most valuable assets. The courts look at all property together and can order either partner to pay a sum of money to the other, to transfer property to the other, or to sell some property and divide the proceeds. Pension rights can be split and a portion of one partner's pension rights can be allocated to the other. If the marital home is not eventually sold and the proceeds split, the partner who stays in the home will have to compensate the other financially in some way.

The courts usually presume that a clean break is desirable – that is, that the division should be a once-and-for-all situation and that there should be no continuing financial arrangement between the partners. This is not usually possible when there are children, since not only will maintenance need to be paid for the children (see Section 7.3), but if one partner has a reduced ability to take employment because they are taking care of the children, they will require maintenance payments for themselves. Maintenance payments will always be of limited duration. The partner having custody of the children may also be granted the right to continue to reside in the marital home for a fixed period, say until the children grow up, without paying compensation to the other partner.

In practice, because there are limited resources, meeting the needs of the two partners will take precedence over other goals in most financial settlements. However, where a couple are sufficiently wealthy that there is something left after meeting their needs, there remains the issue of how to divide the remaining assets. In recent court judgments, since an influential appeal case in 2000 (White vs White), there has been more of a presumption of an equal division between partners and that an income earner's contribution is no more significant than that of someone doing unpaid work looking after the home. Generally, divorce settlements in Scotland consider only assets acquired during the marriage as marital assets, but in England, Wales and Northern Ireland, especially in recent years, divorce settlements do take into account assets acquired before the marriage. This is another area where specialist advice is necessary.

The courts only become involved in financial arrangements on divorce if the partners cannot agree among themselves. If the partners are cohabiting, then the courts do not usually become involved at all. Pre-nuptial agreements about how to divide assets in the event of divorce are not binding for a divorce court's division of marital assets (though they may help specify which assets were acquired before the marriage). Between non-married partners, a previous agreement on the division of assets would be binding. A registered civil partnership is treated like a marriage; it needs legal dissolution, and recourse to the courts is available if a division of assets cannot be agreed upon.

7.3 Child support

Child Support Agency (CSA)
The Child Support Agency is an executive agency of the Department for Work and Pensions (DWP) that is responsible for ensuring that parents who live apart meet their financial responsibilities to their children.

Where there are children, a parent who is not living with the child will be expected to pay maintenance to the parent with caring responsibilities, in order to contribute to the child's living expenses. This applies to all parents irrespective of whether they have ever lived together. Parents can agree the amount that should be paid between them, or if this is not possible, the government calculates the amount that should be paid. It also does this if one parent is receiving benefits, since the government then has a stake in ensuring that fair amounts are paid and received. In the UK, since 1993, the **Child Support Agency (CSA)** has carried out this calculation, but in 2006 the government announced that it was to be replaced by a completely new system for calculating child support.

Political decisions will have to be taken about what exactly the new system should do. Any system has to decide whose responsibility it is to provide child support when one parent no longer lives with the child/children. Internationally, systems differ in how they allocate this responsibility differently between the parent and society as a whole. In countries such as the USA, the responsibility is based more on the individual, whereas in other countries such as Denmark, the welfare system provides more support through general taxation, and less importance is attached to the amount paid by the parent. The UK's system is somewhere between these two examples, with support from the government (as discussed in Section 5.1) and also a requirement that the parent who does not live with the child pays maintenance.

7.4 Long-term financial security and financial independence

Another way to ensure the financial security of both partners in the case of a relationship splitting up or if one of them dies is to make sure that each partner is financially independent; that is, that each can support themself. In Sections 5 and 6, you saw that in households where earning and caring roles are split, time out of the labour market may substantially weaken a carer's earning capacity and eventual pension rights. This may not be so serious while the relationship is intact and the other partner's income can be relied upon. Its real impact is on divorce or death, or if the income earner loses his or her capacity to earn. To prevent such events having severe effects, couples can invest in developing the earning power of both partners, ensuring that each has the resources to manage on their own if necessary – for example, by sharing caring responsibilities and time out of the labour market, or by enabling the one whose earning power has suffered to build up their human capital for the future by doing some work-related training.

Rather than relying on survivor benefits, couples may also want to ensure that both members would have access to an equally good pension if they ended up on their own. This can be achieved by one partner contributing to the other's pension, as suggested in Chapter 7, Section 3.3. Differences in amounts contributed to occupational and private pensions are the main causes of the huge inequalities between men's and women's incomes in retirement. These differences will persist so long as men and women earn different amounts and have different caring and employment histories. Yet it is something that every couple can do something about for themselves.

Other ways in which couples can influence their long-term financial security as individuals are outlined in Box 8.4.

Box 8.4 Long-term financial considerations for couples

There are a number of aspects of a couple's financial arrangements that impact on the long-term financial security of each partner as independent individuals, so couples should consider:

- in whose name the house in which they live is held and under what type of tenancy – joint tenants or tenancy in common (see Chapter 6, Section 5.3)
- in whose name any savings and investments are held. For instance, holding savings accounts in the name of the person with the lower income can both reduce Income Tax and

> ensure that this person has some independent income (see Chapter 5, Section 3.3)
>
> ■ making sure that debts are held by the person who incurs them. People are not responsible for individual debts incurred by their partner, whether married or not, but they are responsible for jointly incurred debts from a joint account or for joint mortgage repayments.
>
> It's also important to remember that whoever remains in the house after death or a separation is responsible for certain household outgoings including Council Tax.

This section has shown that when a couple splits up, it's impossible to leave each party in an unchanged financial position because two separate households cannot live as cheaply as one joint one. It has also shown that where there is or has been a division of labour in which one partner has much greater earning power than the other, the one with the lower earning power is likely to be in a significantly weaker position after death or separation. There are measures that a couple can put in place to mitigate, if not remove, the financial effects of death or separation on both partners, and especially on the more financially dependent one. Finally, despite people perhaps not wanting to think about the possibility of their relationship not lasting forever, the financial implications are best thought about and planned for while the relationship is intact and partners are getting on with each other.

8 Conclusion

This chapter has examined the financial implications of some of the most significant personal relationships people have: those that lead us to want to live with others and to care for them. In Section 2, I looked at diversity and change in the UK's household living arrangements – a major component of the theme of the changing social and economic context. The chapter has also explained how changes over the life-course that affect with whom we live and the way in which we care for others have significant and long-term effects on the financial situation of households and their individual members. You'll recall that change over the life-course and the interrelationship of individuals and their households are also both key themes of *Personal Finance*.

I have also stressed how financial planning needs to take account of such life-course changes, adjusting and reviewing plans as things change. In Sections 5 and 6, I looked at the short- and long-term financial implications for household members undertaking caring responsibilities. Section 7 highlighted the financial implications of the dissolution of a household, and the need to think about and put in place arrangements that would mitigate the worst financial consequences of households coming to an end.

Knowing what the future holds is a luxury that we do not have, and it is not only changes in relationships that can have financial implications: there are many other life events that can impact on household finances and financial plans. We shall consider some of these, and how to prepare for them, in Chapter 9.

Answer to Activity

Activity 8.9

Figure 8.9(a) shows Jan's income profile if she does not interrupt her employment when she has a child. Figure 8.9(b) shows her income profile if she leaves her current job when she has a child and then five years later gets a part-time job for five years before returning to full-time employment. Her earnings remain a bit less than they would have if she had not left her original job, but the total loss, including to her pension, is much less than it was to Louise following the same strategy, because Jan's income would not have kept rising had she stayed in employment. Indeed, if Jan manages to negotiate a career break with her employer, as in Figure 8.9(c), she may lose relatively little – just the amount of the earnings that she would have made during the period she is out of employment or working reduced hours (and the corresponding loss of pension). Not surprisingly then, less educated women who are less likely to have career jobs, therefore have less to lose from taking time out of employment when they have children. They are therefore more likely to do so than more educated women.

However, there is another major potential problem for Jan. If she has to pay for childcare, her remaining earnings may not be enough to cover the cost of that childcare. In this case, she may not be able to follow either of the strategies in Figures 8.9(b) or 8.9(c). In that case, she may have to give up employment for longer, say for 10 years, and then go back to part-time employment for the rest of her working life. This is currently a common pattern for less well-educated mothers. As Figure 8.9(d) shows, this turns out to have huge opportunity costs, both in terms of lost earnings and lost pension.

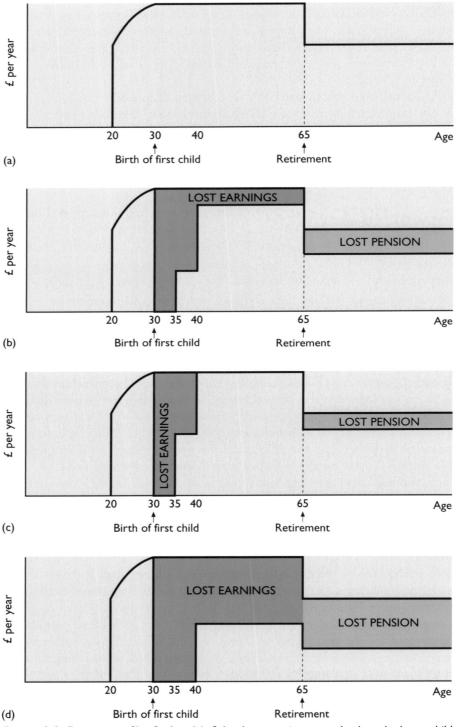

Figure 8.9 *Earnings profiles for Jan: (a) if she does not give up work when she has a child; (b) if she gives up work when she has a child; (c) if she negotiates with her employer to have a career break when she has a child; (d) if she gives up work when she has a child and stays out of work for ten years and then returns to part-time work for the rest of her working life* ■ ■ ■

References

Department of Work and Pensions (DWP) (2003) *Measuring Child Poverty* [online], http://www.dwp.gov.uk/consultations/consult/2003/childpov/final.asp (Accessed 31 March 2006).

Equal Opportunities Commission (EOC) (2005) *Part-time Is No Crime – So Why the Penalty?*, Manchester, Equal Opportunities Commission.

Eurostat (2002) 'Labour force survey – principal results 2001 – EU and EFTA countries', *Statistics in Focus, Population and Social Conditions*, Theme 3 – 19/2002; also available online at http://www.eds-destatis.de/en/downloads/sif/nk_02_19.pdf (Accessed 9 May 2006).

Fagan, C. (2000) 'Men's long work hours and women's short work hours: the case of Britain' in Peltola, P. (ed.) *Working Time in Europe: Towards a European Working Time Policy*, Finnish EU Presidency Conference Report, Helsinki, Hakapaino Oy.

Francesconi, M. and Gosling, A. (2005) *Career Paths of Part-time Workers*, EOC Working Paper Series, Manchester, Equal Opportunities Commission.

Grainger, H. and Holt, H. (2005) 'Results of the second flexible working employee survey', *Labour Market Trends*, vol. 113, no. 7, July, pp. 297–302.

Grant L., Yeandle, S. and Buckner, L. (2005) *Working Below Potential: Women and Part-time Work*, Manchester, Equal Opportunities Commission.

Himmelweit, S. and Sigala, M. (2004) 'Choice and the relationship between identities and behaviour for mothers with pre-school children: some implications for policy from a UK study', *Journal of Social Policy*, vol. 33, no. 3, July, pp. 455–78.

Joshi, H. and Davies, H. (2000) 'The price of parenthood and the value of children', in Fraser, N. and Hills, J. (eds) *Public Policy for the 21st Century: Social and Economic Essays in Memory of Henry Neuberger*, Bristol, Policy Press.

Lewis, J. (2001) 'The decline of the male breadwinner model: the implications for work and care', *Social Politics*, vol. 8, no. 2, pp. 152–70.

Lindley, J., Dale, A. and Dex, S. (2004) 'Ethnic differences in women's demographic, family characteristics and economic activity profiles, 1992 to 2002', *Labour Market Trends*, vol. 112, no. 4, April, pp. 153–65.

Manning, A. and Petrongolo, B. (2005) *The Part-time Pay Penalty*, London School of Economics and Women & Equality Unit; also available online at http://www.womenandequalityunit.gov.uk/research/part_time_paypenalty.pdf (Accessed 31 March 2006).

Office for National Statistics (ONS) (2004a) 'Focus on ethnicity and identity: households' [online], http://www.statistics.gov.uk/cci/nugget.asp?id=458 (Accessed 29 January 2006).

Office for National Statistics (ONS) (2004b) 'Focus on gender: work and family' [online], http://www.statistics.gov.uk/cci/nugget.asp?id=436 (Accessed 29 January 2006).

Office for National Statistics (ONS) (2005a) 'Focus on families: ethnicity' [online], http://www.statistics.gov.uk/cci/nugget.asp?ID=1167 (Accessed 29 January 2006).

Office for National Statistics (ONS) (2005b) 'Focus on families: stepfamilies' [online], http://www.statistics.gov.uk/cci/nugget.asp?ID=1164 (Accessed 29 January 2006).

Office for National Statistics (ONS) (2005c) 'Focus on older people: health and social care' [online], http://www.statistics.gov.uk/cci/nugget.asp?id=1268 (Accessed 29 January 2006).

Social Trends (2005) no. 35, Basingstoke and New York, Palgrave Macmillan for The Office for National Statistics (ONS); also available online at the ONS website, http://www.statistics.gov.uk/downloads/theme_social/Social_Trends35/Social_Trends_35.pdf (Accessed 28 March 2006).

Weir, G. (2002) 'The economically inactive who look after the family or home', *Labour Market Trends*, November, vol. 110, no. 11, pp. 577–87; also available online at http://www.statistics.gov.uk/downloads/theme_labour/LMT_Nov02.pdf (Accessed 30 March 2006).

Insurance and life events

Chapter 9

Ian Fribbance

Contents

1 Introduction

A famous saying asserts that 'the only certainties in life are death and taxes'. Other than the certainty of our own mortality and paying taxes, there are the many vagaries of fate, fortune and 'luck', producing sometimes unexpected or major events with which everyone has to contend over their life-course. These 'life events' are relevant and important in *Personal Finance* because they can have major financial impacts. A list of major life events that could significantly affect anyone and their financial position can be quickly constructed. For example, thinking about my own life, I *might* fall seriously ill; I *might* have my house burgled; I *might* have an accident – or to be rather more positive – I *might* win the Lotto. I'm sure you could quickly come up with a long list of events that might happen to you in the future too.

The potentially major financial impacts of events like these can derail otherwise carefully constructed financial plans. Such events may initially impact on individual or household budgets (for example, if someone becomes too ill to work and loses their income) or on a person's financial balance sheets (for example, with the unexpected destruction of assets). Yet in either case, planning to cope with such major eventualities is necessary. Therefore, an important component of developing financial capability is thinking about preparing for these life events. In order to do that, we need to revisit material that you have come across earlier. Consequently, Section 2 uses a diagram of income and expenditure over time, and Section 3 revisits risk and develops the related idea of probability: crucial factors in financial planning for major life events.

How people prepare for the financial implications of major life events is shaped – like so many things in *Personal Finance* – by the society and economy in which they live. You've seen how, in the UK, the greater emphasis in recent times on individual responsibility and financial self-reliance means that individuals now have to bear more risk themselves, rather than sharing it collectively through the state. As a result, it has become even more important to understand how to manage risks and prepare for the possibility of unexpected events.

Many of the risks that you've come across earlier in *Personal Finance* are 'speculative' risks – ones that have a chance of *either* a loss *or* a gain – such as the changing value of share prices seen in Chapter 5, or the house price changes discussed in Chapter 6. The risks considered in this chapter are somewhat different; they are of events that cause a financial loss. People have to find ways in which to prepare for the possibility of these events, for instance, taking out insurance, which I look at in detail in Sections 4–7. Finally, Section 8 looks at how the changing social and economic context could impact on the insurance market in the future.

2 Life events and their financial consequences

The events that unfold over the course of a life can take many different forms. One expected life event is death itself, but even then, generally, we cannot be certain about its timing. The financial impact of someone's death – leaving aside other kinds of impacts – will vary according to the circumstances of the individual concerned, such as whether they have dependants or not, and at what stage of life death occurs.

Nevertheless, most other events in life are essentially unexpected, in the sense that we can't be certain *if* they will happen, nor can we be certain of their timing. Of course, unexpected events can have both positive and negative financial effects. An unexpected event with a positive financial outcome would be that elusive Lotto jackpot win. There may be other events that are also good news in themselves, but where the financial impact is negative, for instance, when delighted parents find that they are expecting twins, and then realise the future financial implications. Conversely, there can be negative life events with positive financial effects – terrible news, such as the unexpected death of a loved relative, may later bring an inheritance. Chapter 8 discussed other unexpected events affecting relationships between individuals that can have important financial implications, for example, forming a new household, having children, an elderly parent needing care, the death of a partner, and separation or divorce. Some, but not all, of these can be prepared for.

The unexpected events that concern us in this chapter are those where there is a **peril**: a contingency (or event) causing a financial loss. The reason to focus on these events is that they have the potential to throw out our financial plans and therefore make our goals harder or impossible to attain. The potential significance of such events for financial planning can be illustrated quite starkly with the use of the income and expenditure over time model. Let's briefly return to the case of Jenny, from Chapter 3. You may recall that Jenny had a very tight budget, but managed to generate an excess of income over expenditure after she had done some careful budgeting. However, what would happen to Jenny if she fell ill?

Peril
An event that causes a financial loss.

As you can see from the income and expenditure diagram in Figure 9.1, if Jenny's salary were lost because she was too ill to work after 2009, her expenditure would soon far exceed her income. This is because if she has to rely on state benefits, her income would drop far more than she could easily adjust her expenditure. Therefore, she would have to run down her assets if she has any, and/or increase her liabilities by taking out debt.

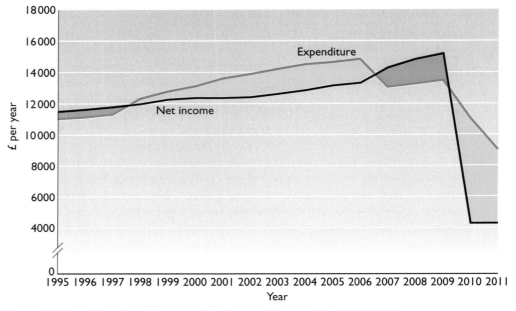

Figure 9.1 *Jenny's real net income and real expenditure profile, 1995–2011*

Activity 9.1

What 'perils' might you and/or your household face? Think about one event that might affect your income and one that might affect your expenditure.

1   Try sketching two income and expenditure diagrams to illustrate the potential effects of these two perils.

2   Would you be able to cope with the perils by adjusting your income and/or expenditure? Or would the perils have an impact on your financial balance sheet through having to run down assets or borrow money to cope with the effects of the perils?

Comment

You may have thought of perils that impact on *income*, such as losing your job, or an accident that means you have to change your work or reduce your hours of work to care for someone. You may also have thought of perils that impact on your *expenditure*, such as finding dry rot in your house, writing off your car, or having an accident that means you have to pay for personal care. Hopefully, you will have given yourself an impression of the potential impact of these events on your income and expenditure. In many cases, sufficient adjustments of income and expenditure cannot easily be made, and so the peril will also impact on the personal balance sheet through savings having to be run down or debts taken out. ■ ■ ■

Activity 9.1 should make clear that the financial impacts of major perils can be crucial, either by worsening a budget via income reductions or expenditure increases, or by impacting on the financial balance sheet, such as if a sudden loss of assets is involved. Any or all of these impacts could adversely affect financial plans and standards of living, and perhaps make some goals for the future difficult or impossible to attain. It can be tempting to ignore the possibility of perils actually happening: after all, most people don't like to have to think about what are usually unpleasant events. None the less, financial capability includes thinking about the chance that such events *might* occur, their potential impact if they do, and, crucially, how to protect against that impact. Perils have different chances of happening, different financial consequences, and can be protected against in different ways. We first need to examine the concepts of risk, uncertainty and probability that underlie this idea of what *might* happen.

3 Probability, uncertainty and risk

Probability is the likelihood of an event occurring. It is represented by a number between 0 and 1: at 0 probability there is no chance whatsoever of an event occurring, whereas at a probability of 1 the event definitely will occur. Thus, as death is certain, the probability of dying *at some point* is 1 (it is inevitable and there is a 100 per cent chance it will happen), but the chances of living forever are 0 (or 0 per cent) because it definitely will not happen. The closer the number is to 1, the *greater* the probability of an event happening. The closer the number is to 0, the *smaller* the probability of an event happening. We use the idea of probability in everyday speech: a 'one-in-ten chance' is another way of saying 0.1 probability (or a 10 per cent chance), and the expressions 'evens' and '50:50' are both alluding to a probability of 0.5 or 50 per cent. We touched on probability in Chapter 5, Section 6 when we looked at the probabilities of equities outperforming savings or gilts by referring to historical data.

Probability
A measurement of the likelihood that an event will occur. Probabilities are expressed as numbers between 0 and 1.

The probabilities of different events happening to someone

It's easy to calculate precise probabilities in a limited number of situations such as fixed odds or mechanical gambling games. For example, the probability of getting a 'tail' on the toss of a coin can be worked out as 0.5 (or one half), or it can be calculated that rolling a 'four' on a throw of a die has a probability of one-sixth (or 0.167). There are no such precise probabilities for most life events because there is no finite range of outcomes with an equal chance of each one occurring. In most real-life situations, you need further information to help you to assess how likely each of the possible range of outcomes is to occur. Ascribing probabilities to individual life events is therefore hard – if I had no data or statistical evidence to refer to, I could only know that, say, my chance of dying *at a particular time*, such as this year, or in the next decade, is somewhere in between 0 and 1.

Actuaries
Professionals who analyse risk and its financial impact.

However, there are statisticians known as **actuaries**: people who use mathematical, statistical and economic analysis to estimate the probabilities of various events happening. They cover a number of fields, including mortality and health, and general events such as property loss. When actuaries estimate the probability of potential events, they are doing so on the basis of carefully analysing past statistical information to forecast the future. It's not necessarily a case of simply extrapolating (or carrying forward) trends from the past into the future; it may be that predictions about the likelihood of potential events have to adapt by incorporating new and emerging knowledge about how things may change in the future. This is so that predictions about the future are made on the basis of the best available evidence. Box 9.1 looks at an example of one area in which actuarial predictions about the future are changing in response to new knowledge.

Box 9.1 Actuarial predictions and climate change

Big rise in cost of storms over next 70 years forecast by insurers

The cost of big storms, which will become more frequent owing to climate change, is likely to rise by two thirds to £15 bn a year in the next seven decades, the Association of British Insurers (ABI) will warn today. Nick Starling, director of general insurance at ABI, will urge the leaders of the Group of Eight indus-trialised nations to take action on emissions when they meet to discuss climate change next week.

By 2040, the average annual cost of hurricanes in the US will rise from $9.5 bn (£5.2 bn) to $11.4 bn. In a bad year, hurricanes in the US will cost $71 bn in 2040 and $104 bn in 2080 in insured costs. ...

Although scientists cannot say *exactly* what will happen as the climate changes under the influence of an increased burning of fossil fuels, they estimate that the incidence of extreme weather such as storms, floods, droughts and heatwaves will increase. ...

The report will be published today at a conference on the financial risks of climate change, organised by the ABI. Allianz Global Investors, the combined funds group, and WWF, the environmental campaign group, will urge financial managers and analysts to evaluate client portfolios for climate change risk.

(*Financial Times*, 29 June 2005, p. 4)

Events such as Hurricane Katrina change actuarial forecasts of future financial risks of climate change

So, what are the sorts of life events whose probabilities can be calculated on the basis of best available statistical evidence? One example is the probability of dying for each subsequent year of our lives, which has been calculated by government actuaries. They produce 'life expectancy tables' from which I can work out that, for instance, because I am a 40-year-old male, on average I will live for another 37.9 years, or almost to the age of 78. Nevertheless, men of my age also have approximately a 0.0017 probability of dying in the *next* year – or, expressed differently, for every 10,000 males aged 40 in the UK, approximately 17 will die this year (GAD, 2005). From such life expectancy tables, if I wished I could work out the chances of dying before age 78, or perhaps of dying before retirement age, for an average person of my age and sex. Another unhappy prospect is the approximately 0.003 probability of me being burgled in the next year – apparently, an almost twice as likely event as my death (Home Office, 2004). At opposite extremes, there is only a 0.00000033 (1 in 3 million) probability that I might be struck by lightning (BBC, 2005), but an approximately one-third (1 in 3) chance of suffering cancer at some point in my life-course (ONS, 2005).

Activity 9.2

Would it be possible to estimate (or find an estimate for) the probability of the following?

- death in the next year for someone of your age and sex
- tossing a coin and calling 'heads'
- falling in or out of love next year
- Tottenham Hotspur winning the European Champions League in the next three years
- UK house prices falling next year
- being burgled in your area.

Comment

You could find or make some estimates of the probabilities, but not all. Getting a 'head' has a 0.5 probability. You could also find out the probability of death of an average person of your age and sex from the Government Actuary's Department (GAD) life tables, and of the burglary chances using the Home Office data, as I did. Yet the three remaining events are rather hard to find probabilities for: there may be some figures available for the chances of house prices falling, but estimates could vary according to who is making them because they rely on many unknown factors and a person's 'feel' about how to extrapolate from the past to the future. Football (and similar events on which there is gambling) often has published odds, but these will be determined by the money already bet, and hence will reflect the subjective feel of those punters laying bets. It would be almost impossible to find a sensible estimate of the probability of falling in or out of love in the next twelve months: though some fortune-tellers, astrologers or some kind of wild survey statistic may suggest otherwise. ∎∎∎

This leads us to a distinction that is sometimes made between uncertainty and risk. **Risk** can be defined as a situation where the probability of something happening is known or where the probability can be estimated. It isn't possible to do this for all kinds of events, and if the likelihood of an event can't really be estimated then the event is said to be subject to **uncertainty**. There is something of a continuum between the two, and the distinction is sometimes not clear-cut – indeed, this is an area of economic research. Even when risks are theoretically measurable, they won't tell the whole story, for example, the statistical risk to a whole group won't equate to the risk to one member of it. An individual's chance of death in a particular year won't be quite the same as those described in the GAD tables for people of the same age and sex because it will be affected by other factors – occupation, income, location, health, genetic inheritance and so on. The more precise the information we have on which to estimate the probability, the further it will move along the spectrum from an 'uncertainty' towards a 'risk'. None the less, because so many of these factors are unknowable, no such risk can be quite like the definite probability of the coin-tossing example. Also, most people don't have sufficient resources, interest or the ability to access information to investigate the probabilities of unexpected events: this is another example of the idea of a 'trade-off' that we have seen in earlier chapters of

Risk
Where the probability of something happening is known or where the probability can be estimated.

Uncertainty
Where the probability of an event cannot be estimated.

An individual's chance of death in a particular year may not be quite the same as those described in the GAD tables

Personal Finance. Consequently, individuals and households will usually operate under conditions of uncertainty when it comes to the perils that they may face.

The risks that give rise to possible perils are often called **pure risks.** These are risks that give rise to a definite loss, and where the occurrence of the event is not under the control of the person(s) that might suffer the loss. These are the kinds of risks against which insurance can usually be taken out. Let's look next at the principles and issues surrounding the provision of insurance.

Pure risks
Risks that give rise to a definite loss, and where the occurrence of the event is not under the control of the person(s) that might suffer the loss. Such risks can usually (but not always) be insured against.

4 The provision of insurance

4.1 The principles and problems of insurance

Insurance is a method whereby individuals or households (or organisations) pay a sum of money called a 'premium' to an insurer in exchange for being 'indemnified', or protected against, the losses that result from specific perils, under conditions specified in a contract. This contract is called an 'insurance policy'. Those taking out an insurance policy are transferring the risk of the financial loss arising from the peril to the insurer, and thus reducing the potential consequences on an individual person or household.

Insurance
A system by which individuals or households, in exchange for payment of a sum of money (called a 'premium'), are guaranteed indemnity for losses resulting from certain perils, under conditions specified in a contract.

Actuaries provide statistics to insurers to help quantify the risks that insurers are taking on. Insurers need data on the probabilities of the perils for which they offer insurance – death, illness, disease, burglary, accidents and so forth – and data on people of different ages, genders, locations, postcodes and households so that they can estimate what their risks of paying out are. Actuarial data will give an approximation of the future claims that the insurer might face across the range of perils they insure. Insurers will then aim to set premiums so that, on average, total premium income will cover the cost of paying out for claims, building up reserves *and* making a profit.

Insurers spread their risk by insuring many individuals and households against various different risks. By insuring a large number of risks, the average number of times that insurers have to pay out will be more predictable, and thus so will be the total amount that they have to pay out in any given year. In taking on the risks of many and aggregating them, the insurer faces a more predictable future than the individual policy holders would if they had to face their risks themselves. As you saw in Chapter 5, people are generally risk averse and many will be prepared to pay money to have risks taken from them. By aggregating and therefore reducing risks, the insurance company can, without taking on too much risk itself, charge a premium that is attractive to risk-averse individuals and still make a profit.

Note, however, that the predictability that comes from aggregating risks only applies to **independent risks**; these are risks whose occurrence is completely unrelated to one another. This applies to car insurance, for example. The risk that I will have an accident in London is completely unrelated to the risk that you will have an accident in Edinburgh. Insurers can cope with such unrelated perils; conversely, an enormous pile-up on a motorway might be a problem. Large-scale natural disasters can result in a great number of insurance claims at the same time, which is one reason why insurers are concerned about the effects of climate change, as you saw in Box 9.1. In fact, some insurance policies exclude the effects of natural disasters and acts of war precisely because in these cases risks are *not* independent and so they can give rise to such a large number of claims that even the biggest insurance companies would be in danger of insolvency.

One long-recognised problem in providing insurance is that of **moral hazard**. This is the tendency for people to increase the risk when the cost of the peril will be borne by others such as an insurer. To illustrate, when a home is insured, people may become less prepared to spend money on securing its contents with locks and alarms because the value of any loss could largely be reclaimed from an insurer, compared to a situation where the contents were uninsured and any loss would be borne by the householders. Behaviour becomes more careless because of the insurance safety net. Insurance companies are used to the problem of moral hazard and so most insurance policies include features designed to combat it. This includes: measures to deter people behaving in a more risky manner, such as requiring an **excess** on insurance claims (for example, requiring policy holders of a home contents insurance policy to pay the first £100 of a claim after a burglary); rewarding those taking risk-avoidance measures (for example, by offering 'no-claims discounts' to those who don't need to make a claim, and offering lower household insurance premiums to those fitting house alarms); and wholly excluding cover for those who don't take precautions (for example, a car theft wouldn't be covered if you left the car door unlocked and the keys in the ignition). The problem of moral hazard occurs only because most risks are *not* in fact pure risks but risks that we can influence to some extent. If we can influence the risks too much, then we will not be able to get insurance for them, for instance, many travel insurance policies exclude claims for suicide, self-inflicted injury and deliberate exposure to exceptional danger.

Independent risks
Risks whose occurrence is unrelated to one another.

Moral hazard
The tendency for an insured person to become willing to take on more risk because they are covered by insurance.

Excess
An initial monetary amount of an insured loss that the insured will have to pay out themselves.

Adverse selection
The tendency for people who have a greater than average likelihood of suffering a peril to apply for insurance to a greater extent than other people.

Asymmetric information
Where one party knows something that another does not. It's frequently used to refer to information that people wanting insurance might know about their own risks that they do not reveal to their insurers.

There is also the problem for insurers of **adverse selection**. This is where the people who take out an insurance policy are those at the greatest risk of suffering the peril. This can happen in situations of **asymmetric information**, where one party, the person wanting to take out insurance, has better information about the precise individual risk that they face than the other, the insurer, who might merely know the statistical evidence for the wider group of people facing that risk. For example, if insurance were offered against ill health, those who might know they have some predisposition to particular health problems would be more likely to take out the insurance than those who do not. The same principle applies to other insurances such as redundancy (where those with the least secure jobs would be most likely to take it out), property loss and so on. Two related problems arise for insurers from adverse selection. First, insurers, realising that they don't know the risks as accurately as individuals, will build in higher premiums to compensate for the problem of adverse selection. Second, individuals who know themselves to be low risk will then find the insurance premiums not worthwhile and will become less likely to take out insurance, while those who know themselves to be high risk will continue taking out insurance. This will raise the average risk and, in turn, the premium charged, which will further deter those at low risk from taking out insurance, and so forth. Thus, sometimes, the problem of adverse selection can mean that particular kinds of insurance will not exist, and it can become impossible to insure against particular perils.

Insurance companies have strategies to try to address the problem of adverse selection. The most common one is to discriminate between different groups of people with different risks. In order to find out which risk categories people fall into, insurance companies may ask potential customers questions to establish the risk faced by different individuals and, hence, assess an appropriate and individual insurance premium using an appropriate 'loading' for a customer's particular risk factors. Consequently, the law requires **utmost good faith** in telling the truth to insurers, and failure to comply means the insurers could reject liability in the event of a claim.

Utmost good faith
A legal obligation to disclose any detail that may be of some importance to insurers, whether or not it is requested.

Your life insurance quote

To allow us to calculate how much your life insurance might cost, please answer these questions.

Plan details		
Life insurance is for:	○ Only you ⦿ You and your partner	

Your details	You	Your partner
Sex:	⦿ Male ○ Female	○ Male ⦿ Female
Date of birth:	☐ (dd/mm/yyyy)	☐ (dd/mm/yyyy)
Have you used any tobacco products in the last 12 months? (including cigarettes, cigars, pipes or nicotine replacements)	⦿ Yes ○ No	○ Yes ⦿ No

Your life insurance		
Amount of life insurance:	£ ☐	
For how many years?	☐ Years	
Enter	☐ Title	
	☐ First name	☐ Surname

Figure 9.2 *A question about use of tobacco is one of the most common ways for insurers to establish the risk faced by an individual applying for life or health insurance*

Alternatively, the insurer could charge everyone the same premium but exclude some types of claim – this is called 'post-sale discrimination'. For instance, a health insurance policy may be open to all but not cover claims arising out of any existing health problem when the policy was bought. The sellers of insurance are required to draw customers' attention to any particularly onerous or unusual exclusion.

These approaches do not provide a complete solution to the issue of adverse selection. If insurers cannot find out sufficient information, and there is still asymmetric information, then the market for a particular insurance product may still not develop. We shall see some examples related to this in Sections 7 and 8. It's also interesting that the problem of adverse selection disappears when insurance is compulsory, such as in state insurance schemes (like National Insurance in the UK) that insure the whole of a population. This is because, by definition, everyone is included regardless of their risk category.

Activity 9.3

1   Take a look at one insurance policy that you have. Read the policy including its 'small print' and try to remember the questions that you had to answer when you took the policy out. Jot down some points from the small print relating to 'moral hazard' and some questions relating to 'adverse selection'.

2   If you don't have any insurance, think of some examples of the type of restrictions related to moral hazard that you would expect to find in such policies, and some questions that relate to adverse selection that you might expect to have to answer in order to take out insurance.

Comment

You may have come up with many different examples. It is likely that you found some policy restrictions to limit the effect of moral hazard, for example, both motor and home insurance policies may require you to use locks; insurance for ill health won't cover self-inflicted injuries; and insurance that provides for loss of income won't pay out if you intentionally make yourself unemployed. Some questions that you may have had to answer relating to adverse selection on car insurance include your age, sex, and claims history. Similarly, postcode is used to assess risk for a wide range of insurance policies, in particular, home contents insurance. ■■■

Insurers can never be certain of the pay-out amounts arising from insurance policies because the estimate of the risks is based on actuarial data that may have to be revised in the light of the reality of future events. If insurers are caught out by major disasters or cataclysmic events, then they can, and often do, make losses. The terrorist attacks in the USA on 11 September 2001, and the 2004 and 2005 Caribbean hurricanes all cost insurers enormous and unexpected sums. Therefore, insurers usually prefer to *diversify* their risks by ensuring that the risks they cover are independent, and offering different kinds of insurance policies covering many different perils to try to avoid major losses. Insurance companies also use what is called 'reinsurance'. This is provided by a few very large companies with huge reserves, who sell policies to other insurance companies, allowing the latter to reduce their risks and protect themselves from exceptionally large losses.

4.2 The development of insurance

Insurance-type schemes have existed for a long time: early forms existed in ancient Greek, Roman and Hebrew societies. In the UK, insurance began to take on recognisable forms during the seventeenth century, with the development of home insurance in response to the Great Fire of London, and the development of Lloyd's of London in response to the demand for marine insurance as London grew as a shipping centre. London remains a major centre of the world insurance industry today, and Lloyd's remains at the hub of London's financial centre, offering reinsurance and specialist marine insurance, as well as personal and commercial insurances.

LLOYD'S COFFEE-HOUSE

Inside the Lloyd's coffee house where insurance in the UK took on recognisable forms; and the inside of Lloyd's of London as it is today

The roots of many UK insurance companies also go back a long way. In many cases, their origins lie in mutual organisations, in which people came together to pool their risks of, for example, their house burning down, or to provide insurance against sickness, inability to work, or death. Mutuals often provided their own fire brigades to protect policy holders' properties. Many mutual societies later merged, 'de-mutualised', or were taken over by limited companies. For instance, the Hand-in-Hand Fire & Life Insurance Society that was founded in 1696 in a London coffee house (under the title of Contributors for Insuring Houses), and operated its own fire brigade, eventually merged with the Commercial Union company in 1905. In 1998, the Commercial Union and General Accident companies merged, and this business combined with Norwich Union (itself once a mutual organisation) in 2000, and became known as Aviva PLC (although retaining the Norwich Union brand for UK insurance business) (Aviva, 2005).

A nineteenth-century Norwich Union firemark, used to identify buildings it insured to its fire brigade, and a twenty-first-century Norwich Union advertisement

Many of the mutual organisations that traditionally provided insurance were 'friendly societies' – you came across these in Chapter 5, Section 7. Membership of mutual societies providing insurance peaked in the middle of the twentieth century. Since then membership has dropped, and many friendly societies have merged or disappeared. The decline of the friendly societies in insurance is often argued to be due to the creation of the welfare state in the 1940s, when the state took over many of the insurance functions previously provided by these mutuals. Nevertheless, a number of friendly societies and other mutual organisations still thrive in the UK insurance market. For example, the Liverpool Victoria Friendly Society, the Scottish Friendly Assurance Society and Royal London Mutual Insurance Society still provide various types of insurance, along with a significant cooperative called the Co-operative Insurance Society.

As a result of mergers and takeovers, large corporate insurance companies have come to dominate the UK insurance market. These

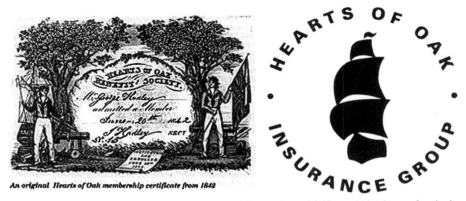

An original Hearts of Oak membership certificate from 1842

Hearts of Oak friendly society membership certificate from 1842; and the logo of today's Hearts of Oak friendly society

companies, such as Aviva, Royal & Sun Alliance and Legal & General, sell policies in order to make a profit for their shareholders. In recent years, there have been some new entrants to the insurance market with companies selling exclusively over the internet or over the phone, or specialising in certain types of insurance or in insurance for certain groups such as women. However, most of these are brand names owned by existing companies: Direct Line insurance is part of the Royal Bank of Scotland group, as is Churchill insurance, another well-known brand name. Meanwhile, Royal & Sun Alliance has become known as the 'More Than' brand in the UK.

The Royal Bank of Scotland Group

Churchill Insurance and Direct Line are part of the Royal Bank of Scotland Group

Because of the UK's role as a centre of the finance industry, its historical development of insurance, and its economic liberalisation, the UK insurance market today is well developed; measured by total premiums paid, it is the largest insurance market in Europe and the third largest in the world, exceeded only by the USA and Japan. Almost 1200

European Economic Area (EEA)
A free trade area consisting of the European Union (EU) members, plus Iceland, Norway and Liechtenstein.

insurance companies are authorised by the UK or another **European Economic Area (EEA)** member state to carry out insurance business in the UK. In 2004, the UK insurance industry was employing 339,000 people, around one-third of all financial services jobs (ABI, 2005).

Some of the historical changes in insurance provision highlight a fundamental question: how should a society best handle the management of the risk facing individuals? We've seen that insurance has existed in many societies for some time, but some belief systems generally reject the use of insurance. Islam has traditionally seen conventional insurance as akin to gambling, and as such against most interpretations of shariah law. Muslims (and some Christians such as the Amish and Plymouth Brethren) have therefore usually avoided conventional insurance, and instead depended on support provided by their communities when disasters strike. This can be thought of as a particular form of 'social insurance' – an individual's risk is taken on collectively by the community who will share the cost of rebuilding. Shariah law does allow for a particular kind of cooperative, pooling-of-resources type of insurance called 'Takaful', which has only very limited availability in the UK. Less 'collective' societies cannot generally effectively support this type of system, and a reliance on community action would be unlikely to work for the large-scale financial risks common in an advanced economy.

Assuming that the principle of insurance is accepted, there is then the question of whether it should be through the state, through private provision, or through private but collective action such as the mutual movement. A major argument in favour of state provision is that this creates the largest possible pool of people that is collectively insured. To illustrate, a system of 'National Insurance' allows substantial 'pooling' of risk by including everyone of working age within its scope. The costs of arranging insurance should be lower per head when they are shared out as widely as possible. In addition, making insurance compulsory, as National Insurance is for UK workers, will eliminate the problems of adverse selection. This should also help lower the costs of insurance, and therefore make possible some kinds of insurance that would not otherwise exist if it was left up to the private insurance market. Another argument in favour of state provision of insurance is about fairness. Many believe that concepts of fairness dictate that everyone should have access to certain supporting services or benefits, such as health care or financial support in times of misfortune, regardless of whether the individual would have been able to afford the insurance premiums necessary to provide this privately.

During the course of the twentieth century, as belief in collective provision grew, the UK state took on major aspects of an insurance role. As we saw in Chapter 2, there are state benefits that are paid out in adverse circumstances such as unemployment or incapacity. Some of these are still based on a National Insurance system, and eligibility for some benefits depends on previous contributions. The state also provides services, such as the National Health Service (NHS), that are free at the point of use, and are funded out of general taxation. In many other EU countries, social insurance schemes refund some or all of incurred health treatment costs. State services, such as the UK's NHS, can be seen as a type of insurance against the adverse circumstance of falling ill – without the NHS, there would have to be greater household expenditure on health, and private insurance against ill health would be much more widespread.

There are arguments opposing state provision of insurance, where it is believed that insurance is often better arranged either privately or through collective mechanisms such as mutual societies. One argument is that state provision undermines ideas of self-reliance and personal responsibility that organisations like the friendly societies were trying to promote. In fact, some might argue that state provision simply 'crowds out' the private provision that might otherwise have existed, as happened with the decline in friendly societies. Some also claim that private insurance systems, by having to respond to market forces, are more likely to provide the type of provision that people want. Some would also maintain that the pooling of risks in a state system is in fact *unfair*: that lower risk people should not have to pay more to support higher risk people.

We have seen throughout *Personal Finance* that, in recent decades, political support for state collective provision has waned, and a belief in economic liberalisation has increased. As part of this, some aspects of the state's insurance role have declined too. For instance, some benefits have been reduced, abolished or have simply lost value in real terms. An example of this was in 1995 when the UK Government reduced the help available to people who were not working but were paying a mortgage – the 'waiting period' before a claim to cover mortgage interest payments could be made was increased substantially to nine months, enough time to fall behind with payments. This process is another example of the transference of risk from the collective, back to the individual, and then, for people who pay a premium to insure against such a risk, on to an insurance company.

5 Decisions about insurance

We can now look at how to make insurance decisions. There are a number of ways of approaching the management of the risk and the uncertainty surrounding perils. One approach might be to ignore the risk but, as we've seen, if the peril then materialises there may be major negative financial ramifications, and so this would be a high-risk strategy. Another approach is to try risk elimination or risk reduction. For instance, by not flying (to eliminate a risk of death in an air crash); eating healthily (to reduce the risk of premature death); fitting house alarms (to reduce the risk of burglary or fire) and so on. These things may be beneficial in themselves – although they may have costs attached too – but they cannot eliminate all of life's risks and uncertainties.

Self-insurance
The process of establishing a fund to cover the costs of any potential financial loss.

Therefore, other strategies will be needed. One such strategy might be that of risk assumption, or taking on the potential financial impact of the peril materialising. This implies a policy of **self-insurance**: establishing a fund using saving products to cover the costs of any potential financial loss. This can be a strategy adopted by choice by people who are risk takers or who have enough income or savings to cover possible losses, but it can also be adopted by default when other types of insurance are not available or are too expensive. Yet where the financial impact of a peril is large and beyond the financial resources of most individuals, many people who can afford to do so pursue a policy of transferring the financial risk, by using insurance to pass it on.

We can see the actual uptake of various types of insurance in the UK in Table 9.1. This table also shows the average expenditure on each type of insurance policy by those households that buy them, although it doesn't include insurance cover provided through employers, so it understates total insurance expenditure. We shall look at the different types of insurance listed in Table 9.1 in detail in Sections 6 and 7.

Table 9.1 Household expenditure on insurance in the UK, 2004

	Percentage of households purchasing insurance policy	Average annual expenditure on each insurance product per household buying
Home contents	77	£159
Home buildings/structure	64	£188
Motor	72	£556
Life insurance	47	£807
Medical	11	£630
Mortgage protection	21	£407
Income protection	2	£485

Source: adapted from ABI, 2005, pp. 3–4

Only three types of insurance are held by the majority of households. The percentage of households with some policies, such as income protection insurance, is small. None the less, these may still need to be considered, depending on household and individual circumstances.

Individuals and households need to make judgements about what insurance to buy in the light of their own personal circumstances. How might such decisions be made? Some types of insurance are compulsory: in addition to National Insurance for all workers, the UK Government requires drivers to have insurance, and for mortgage borrowers the lender will insist on buildings insurance (although the borrower does not have to take out the insurance offered by the lending organisation). Beyond compulsory insurances, decisions need to be made about what insurances to take out. We can use the financial planning model that you have become familiar with as a way of considering these decisions; Figure 9.3 shows how to apply the model to insurance.

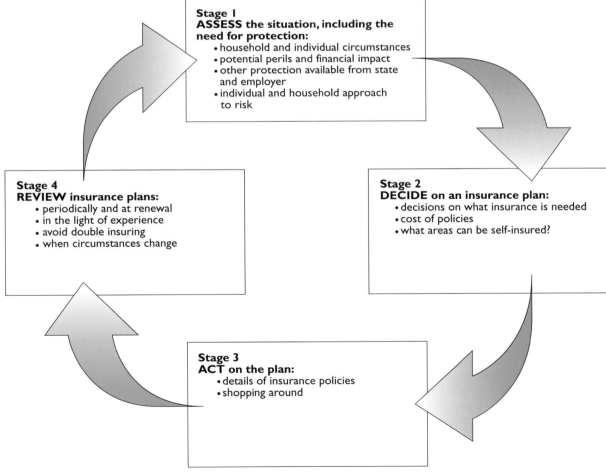

Figure 9.3 *A financial planning approach to insurance decisions*

Let's look at the stages in Figure 9.3 in turn, while remembering that in practice financial planning needs to be a flexible process, with movement back and forwards between the stages. For 'Stage 1: Assess', we've already looked in Section 2 at the perils that may be faced by different individuals or households. It's worth stressing that the importance of these perils and related insurance policies will vary according to individual circumstances: life insurance is likely to be especially important in a family with children and with one income earner, but it may be irrelevant to a single person with no dependants. An important factor to consider is what other protection is available. State National Insurance is part of this equation, as are any benefits available from an employer. With large employers, benefits may include sick pay above the statutory minimum, 'death in service' benefits, and private medical insurance (PMI). Individuals need to find out what their entitlements are as part of Stage 1. These entitlements may not completely replace the need for additional private insurance, but it's important to know what entitlements there are: the combination of what the state and an employer provides could eliminate the need for some types of private insurance, or reduce the amount of additional cover needed. The private insurance element can be seen as building upon the state and employer provisions, as illustrated in Figure 9.4.

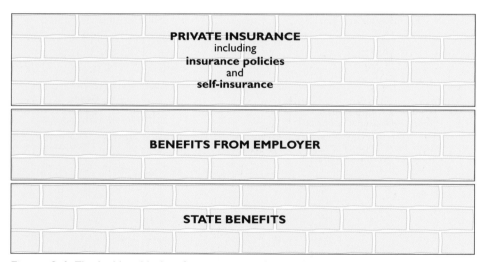

Figure 9.4 *The building blocks of an insurance plan*

In Figure 9.3, the next step is 'Stage 2: to decide' which additional insurance policies are appropriate for the individuals or households concerned. The most important cases to consider are where the financial loss from a peril would be beyond the individual's or household's financial capability to restore. The obvious example of this is insuring the home – rebuilding costs would be far beyond most people's means, and so most people decide that risk shifting makes sense (or have to do so as a condition of their mortgage). But where the costs of the loss would be smaller, self-insurance may be considered a better alternative. To illustrate, paying the cost of domestic appliance repairs may make more sense than taking out an extended warranty. As a rule, the greater the potential financial impact of the peril, the more likely it is that insurance should be considered.

Another factor in deciding on insurance is the cost of the insurance policy. Normally, the higher the premium, the less likely someone is to take out an insurance policy. It would be theoretically possible to calculate the expected benefit from an insurance policy, taking into account the financial impact of a peril and the probability of it occurring. However, such calculations are extremely hard to perform in practice – Section 3 gave some reasons why. A further factor that would be assessed in Stage 1 of the financial planning process, and then used in deciding on insurance, is an individual's approach to risk. Aversion (or otherwise) to risk will, as we saw in Chapter 5, be affected by a variety of factors such as age, tastes and preferences. The more risk averse someone is, the more likely they are to consider additional insurances.

Decisions about whether to take out insurances will have a direct impact on household budgets – taking out more policies will increase expenditure. Conversely, for any insurance policies already held, ways of reducing the premium paid will reduce expenditure. This feeds directly back into the budgeting process discussed in Section 3 of Chapter 3. Yet one way of thinking about insurance is that its impact on the household budget through raising expenditure now is in order to protect the future household budget from bigger claims on its expenditure in the future.

Stage 3 in Figure 9.3 is about *acting* to put the insurance plan into effect. This involves looking at the details of policies (discussed in detail in Sections 6 and 7) and shopping around for the best deal. As we have seen for other aspects of financial planning, there is quite a bit of going backwards and forwards between Stages 1–3; trying to put some plans into action may not work, or the plans may turn out to be more expensive than you first thought, and so the plan will need to be remade.

As the UK's insurance market is so developed, taking out insurance is relatively easy. Insurance policies can be bought either directly from an insurance company or through an intermediary (usually called a 'broker') who can select a policy from different companies. Brokers, such as members of the British Insurance Brokers Association, deal with insurance such as home, motor, and travel insurance (which we look at in

Section 6), as well as term life insurance (covered in Section 7).
Independent Financial Advisers (IFAs) are the intermediaries who
can give advice on life insurance and the more complex health insurances
(covered in Section 7) as well as savings and investments (covered in
Chapter 5) and pensions (the subject of Chapter 7). In all cases, unless
simply 'executing' a client's instructions, the company or intermediary is
required to recommend a product that meets individual circumstances
and needs. Insurance is also sold by third parties, such as shops that
sell extended warranties on their goods, travel agents that sell holiday
insurance, and so forth. Generally, the more complicated the insurance,
the more an intermediary can be useful in helping people to assess their
situation and their needs, in recommending and explaining policies, and
in assisting in the event of a claim.

Stage 4 in Figure 9.3 is to ensure that decisions about insurance are
regularly *reviewed*. This feeds back into regularly assessing the need for
insurance, and into the other stages too. Insurance needs can be reviewed
when policies come up for renewal and when personal circumstances
change (for example, when the composition of the household changes,
or when new assets are acquired). As with any plan, periodic reviews
are also needed to check how things have worked out in the light
of experience. Further, this provides the chance to remove 'double
insuring' – to check that the same risk is not insured twice (for instance,
with a travel and a home insurance policy), which would be unnecessary
expenditure.

It is also important to remember that the financial planning process
takes place inside the social and economic context. One part of this is
that insurance is heavily marketed, with adverts for various insurance
policies on television and in many other media, and with promises of
cheaper quotes. This reinforces the need to approach decisions about
insurance in a methodical manner, such as through the four-stage
financial planning process detailed above.

In Sections 6 and 7, I consider the specifics of insurance policies,
starting with 'general insurance' in Section 6, which, since January 2005,
has been regulated in the UK by the Financial Services Authority (FSA).
General insurance covers home, motor, travel and other similar insurance.
Section 7 will then look at life and long-term protection insurance. You
should note that most general insurance premiums are subject to
Insurance Premium Tax (IPT) which is collected with the premium.
In 2006, this was 5 per cent for most general policies, but 17.5 per cent
for travel insurance and policies purchased as add-ons to other products
(such as an extended warranty); life insurance and other long-term
insurance policies have no IPT.

Insurance is heavily marketed in the UK

6   General insurance

6.1   Home

Given the size of the potential losses, home insurance is one of the first types of insurance considered when a household comes into being, and most households, as you saw from Table 9.1, decide to take it up. Home insurance includes buildings insurance for the actual structure (for those that own their own home), and contents insurance for household possessions. Buildings and contents insurance don't have to be taken out with the same company, and it can be cheaper to shop around for the lowest costs of each separately. However, using one company for both may obtain a small premium reduction, and speed up any claims in the event of damage to both home and contents. Mortgage borrowers do not have to take out the home insurance offered by a mortgage company and can make their own (often cheaper) arrangements.

The costs of both elements of home insurance are determined by the risk factors associated with the particular policy and circumstances. You will recall from Section 4 that insurance companies ask questions to try to ascertain the risk as accurately as possible. For example, the location of the property will enable judgements about whether it is subject to flooding or subsidence or other natural perils (and thus whether it will require a higher buildings insurance premium), and the rate of burglary in the area will be one of the main risk factors considered for contents insurance.

Box 9.2 lists many of the main variables to think about in assessing exactly the kind of contents insurance needed – adding them will increase the cover but also the premium. When possessions are limited (for instance, when setting up home), a basic policy offering only a small amount of cover may suffice, which keeps the premium low. Paying for cover for £30,000 of contents insurance when there is only £15,000 worth of items would be wasting money. Yet having cover that does not equal the actual value of the possessions will mean that only a proportionate amount of any actual claim is paid. Note that accepting a higher excess in return for a lower premium is like a small element of self-insurance, and you may assist in building up a no-claims discount by paying for small claims yourself. Different insurers may charge different premiums for the same cover, and so, having decided exactly what kind of cover is needed, people can gain by shopping around.

Box 9.2 Home contents insurance: some variables and some strategies to keep the premiums down

Variables that will influence the level of home contents insurance premiums include the following, each of which will increase the level of premium:

- cover for accidental damage
- special provisions relating to jewellery, antiques or fine art
- higher limits for the value of individual items
- cover for items kept in the shed or garden
- students' and holidaymakers' possessions when away from home
- 'new for old' – the replacement of used and perhaps out-of-date domestic items with newer models
- bicycle cover
- protection for business equipment for homeworkers
- legal expenses insurance. This is cover for legal costs incurred in civil actions arising out of the use and ownership of the property (for example, with a neighbour, or a dispute with a supplier of goods). Policies often cover claims relating to personal injury, consumer protection, residential matters, employment and taxation, and often provide access to legal documents and helplines. Not usually covered are claims to help defend against criminal prosecutions, claims arising from anything done deliberately or negligently, or where the insurance company would find the claim to be expensive or trivial, or where other specific insurances may be better.

There are also some common strategies for reducing premiums:

- fitting higher standard locks
- fitting burglar alarms (those connected to the police save more, but these systems can be rather expensive)
- 'Neighbourhood Watch' membership
- taking on a higher policy excess
- building up a 'no claims' discount (a reduction in the premium that applies when 'no claims' have been made).

6.2 Motor

The UK Government – like almost all others – legally requires car drivers to take out insurance. The legal minimum obligatory insurance is third-party insurance which, as its name suggests, insures against the damage inflicted by the insured on another person or their property (for example, your passengers, other drivers and their cars), but doesn't cover the costs of the insured. Higher levels of cover include: third party, fire and theft insurance, which will also pay for repairs or a new car if the insured's is a **write-off** from theft or fire; and comprehensive insurance, which means that claims for damage to one's own car can be made, whatever the cause of damage or loss. Some policies may include the offer of roadside assistance or a replacement car. Box 9.3 provides practical details on motor insurance, as well as some suggestions on how premiums may be kept down.

Write-off
A damaged or stolen car that insurers decide to pay an agreed value for rather than paying for the cost of repairs.

Box 9.3   Motor insurance: some cost factors and some strategies to keep the premiums down

The first decision that needs to be made is on the type of cover needed, for example:

- third party, or third party, fire and theft, or comprehensive insurance
- whether additional features such as roadside assistance or a replacement car are needed.

Insurance premium costs are normally determined by these risk factors:

- driver's characteristics (i.e. age and sex). A young male driver will have to pay a higher premium than a middle-aged woman due to the higher probability of a claim
- previous convictions for traffic offences
- previous accident and claims history
- expense and power of car. More expensive and higher powered cars often have a higher probability of theft or accident (as well as a higher repair cost)
- the location and its crime rate.

Common strategies for reducing premiums:

- ability to park your car 'off-road' or in a garage
- locking your car with an immobilising device (if you promise to do this, you must actually do it)
- taking on a higher policy excess

- building up a substantial no-claims discount
- changing your car to one in a lower insurance 'group' (a categorisation for motor insurance purposes)
- trying new providers – online, telephone, motor insurance brokers, insurers specialising in market segments (for example, women drivers, older people)
- shopping around extensively
- where a household has multiple cars, investigating a 'family' motor insurance policy that allows any household member to drive any car
- taking an advanced driving qualification.

Motorbike insurance is often more expensive than that for cars because the probability of accident and injury is higher, but the same practical principles apply. Boat insurance is also similar to that for cars as it is necessary to have at least third-party insurance (this is a specialised area of insurance often requiring a broker). Holiday caravan owners may also want to consider insurance and the risk attached to the loss or theft of the caravan from home or while on holiday. Some insurers may include caravan insurance as part of a main household policy.

6.3 Travel

Insurance for travel is an area of insurance that has changed radically since the 1990s – partly due to an increase in foreign travel, but also because of changes in the insurance market itself. Travel insurance covers the risks of disruption to the holiday; theft of belongings; the traveller causing injury, damage or loss to others; and the risk of medical problems while abroad. Medical emergencies can lead to significant health-care bills being incurred in the country visited, or large costs in repatriation to the home country. Note that a European Health Insurance Card (EHIC), available through UK post offices, allows access to emergency medical services throughout the EEA and Switzerland on the same basis as local nationals, which may require the patient to pay towards the cost of those services in some countries.

Traditionally, travel policies were often offered for a single trip as part of the purchase of a foreign holiday, or people made their own insurance arrangements for each trip they were undertaking. However, the market has recently been revolutionised, and increasingly people make insurance arrangements for their travel generally (rather than for a single trip) through the purchase of insurance for a fixed period of time. This trend was enhanced by changes to the law in the UK which prevented holiday firms from forcing customers to pay over the odds for compulsory

The large expansion in foreign travel in recent years has helped to build a much more competitive market for travel insurance

single-trip insurance. Since then, the market has expanded with the entry of new insurers and brokers, and new products have become available. As with all other types of insurance, shopping around for the precise cover required may reduce costs. To illustrate, different policies cover different parts of the world, they may or may not include winter sports (an activity with a rather high probability of accidents), and they vary as to how long any individual trip may be within a given time period.

6.4 Other general insurance

It may seem as though every time you buy a consumer item, you are offered an extended warranty for it. This is a form of insurance policy offered by retailers who earn commission from the insurers whose policies they sell. Typically, this insurance costs a large amount relative to the actual item, and does not pay out as often as that ratio might suggest. Therefore, buyers need to examine this type of insurance with great caution, and perhaps consider self-insurance for items such as televisions and music centres.

Payment Protection Insurance (PPI) offers to protect credit card debt payments, or payments on a loan. The fact that it is offered as a product directly connected to the loan repayment or the credit card should suggest caution is needed because the lenders earn commission from the insurers whose policies they sell. Such cover may be superfluous and replicate existing cover if you have one or some of the protection policies that are considered in Section 7. PPI policies are often heavily marketed too. As we saw in Chapter 1 (Box 1.2), Citizens Advice has issued a 'super complaint' about PPI to the Office of Fair Trading.

General insurance is an almost endless topic: if there is a risk of a peril, there is probably an insurance out there that could cover it. It has been reported that US rock musician Bruce Springsteen insured his voice for £4 million and England footballer David Beckham insured his legs for £40 million. There is insurance covering the risk of rain at outdoor events, weddings insurance, and insurance against the unexpectedly large costs of twins. Pet insurance is one of the UK's fastest growing areas of insurance, with now almost 2 million pet insurance policies. Decisions on pet and any general insurance should be considered using the financial planning process.

Activity 9.4

Go through a financial planning process for the general insurance needs of you and/or your household, and decide on an insurance plan. If this seems too big a task, just concentrate on one particular area of insurance, for example, home or travel insurance.

Try to be precise, for instance, in terms of the amount of cover needed, and what excess you will accept. Having made the plan, obtain the information needed to act on it by asking for quotes for insurance products from different companies. You may want to use the telephone or internet for this.

Now look at your current insurance in the area(s) you have selected:

- Do you find that you can make any savings over current insurance costs?

- Have you checked that you haven't got double insurance for any particular risks?

- Can you revisit your budgeting process (from Chapter 3, Section 3) in the light of any savings you identify?

Comment

This exercise may show the potential benefits of taking a structured approach to financial planning. If you have been able to identify any savings, you can reduce your expenditure. ■ ■ ■

7   Life and long-term protection insurance

There is a well-developed insurance market offering a range of personal 'protection' policies dealing with the consequences of death or ill health. For all these types of insurance, the 'Stage 1: Assess' part of the financial planning process requires thinking about at both the level of the individual and the household. What would the effect of the peril be on other members of the household? This may depend on what that person contributes to the household, be it income or unpaid work. As Section 5 suggested, it is vital when assessing the need for these types of insurance to be clear about what benefits would be available from the state, or possibly an employer, if the peril occurred. State benefits are generally provided in the same circumstances as private insurance, and having private insurance may reduce the value of means-tested state benefits, and this needs to be taken into account. Moreover, you need to consider the provision of payments for absence during sick leave by employers, and the provision for dependants of deceased members by pension schemes.

7.1 Life insurance

The financial effects on others of premature death vary greatly between people in different family circumstances: for example, a single person with no dependants; two co-dependent income earners sharing household costs; a married person with four children who is the sole earner of the household; or someone who is the sole carer of an elderly parent. Where someone's income is the major (or sole) part of household income, or their unpaid work is necessary to the care of others, the death of that person would risk making the dependants or co-dependants suffer serious hardship as well as the sad death of a loved one. So protection insurance, such as term life insurance, may be important. However, life insurance may be irrelevant to a single person with no dependants.

As we saw in Table 9.1, almost half of all households do decide to take out life insurance. Many life insurance products take the form of term insurance, which insures against the financial consequences of death within a specified term of perhaps five, ten or twenty years. The length of the term may be chosen to mirror the length of a large debt such as a mortgage, so that if the major income earner dies, that debt will be cleared. This is why mortgage providers often insist on life insurance and why for many people it will make sense to have it – it enables surviving family members to remain in their home, despite the death of the person whose income was paying off part or all of the mortgage debt. Term insurance can be level term insurance (where the amount covered will remain the same during the whole of the cover term), or 'decreasing' term insurance when the amount covered will fall over the length of the term. This is typically used to protect against a debt that declines over time such as a repayment mortgage. There is also a type of term life insurance that will pay out an income rather than a capital sum to family members. This might be used where there is no substantial debt to be covered. It could be used, for instance, to provide an income that replaces that of the person who died, or an income that can be used to buy replacement childcare or elderly care if a parent or a carer dies.

Some life insurance is not for a specified term, but it is open-ended, or whole of life, cover. You won't be surprised to read that this is rather more expensive than term insurance, and is primarily designed to build up an investment, rather than dealing with the consequences of an untimely death. Naturally, the cost of whole of life cover will depend at what age and state of health it is taken out.

Endowment policies are another variant of life insurance linked to investment. As we saw in Chapter 6, these kinds of policies were traditionally commonly associated with house purchases. Endowment policies have life insurance cover built in; where the policy was purchased along with a mortgage, the insurance cover was intended to be sufficient to clear the outstanding mortgage debt. Endowment policies, being a stock market-linked investment, were not guaranteed to grow enough to pay off the mortgage in full. Following controversies over their 'mis-selling', and poor stock market performance in the early 2000s, the use of endowment policies for mortgages has been in sharp decline.

You should also note that in the UK (and Canada), whole life insurance and the insurance element of endowment policies have often been referred to as 'life *assurance*' rather than insurance – essentially, this is because there is an assurance of a pay out, unlike with other forms of insurance. However, the term is not used in most countries, and increasingly the term 'insurance' is used even for these types of policies.

Box 9.4 discusses some useful 'tips' about life insurance.

Box 9.4   Some life insurance tips

- Life insurance is often written 'in trust', so that any pay out goes straight to the beneficiary rather than into the deceased's estate. This avoids the danger of having to pay Inheritance Tax, and avoids delays that can be caused by legal processes.

- The amount of cover required by an individual should be calculated *before* buying life insurance. This might include paying off debts (including a mortgage), and providing capital from which to produce some income for surviving household members. No one should take the level of cover offered without assessing their personal needs.

- The new UK pension rules from April 2006 allow term life insurance to be part of a pension plan, thus receiving tax relief on payments. This is a complex area and advice could be taken from an IFA.

7.2 Income protection insurance, critical illness cover and accident, sickness and unemployment insurance

If the ability to work and earn income is impaired or lost, there is a major risk to the financial well-being of an individual and their household. The long-term illness or disability of someone providing care can also cause major financial loss to a household if an alternative form of care has to be found and paid for. Private insurance policies in this area are a complement to the protection that may be offered by employers and by the state. For example, in the case of serious illness, in the UK the state will offer some support through the National Insurance and benefits system, and some employers may do so too. Yet as we saw in Jenny's case in Figure 9.1, state benefits will produce only a well below average income, and therefore may be insufficient to sustain an existing standard of living. In addition to finding out what is available from an employer, it is also important to consider what self-insurance is available, for instance, for how long assets could produce an income, or be used up, to sustain someone in a medical crisis.

Income protection insurance (also known as permanent health insurance or PHI)

This is designed to pay an income (sometimes tax-free) when a person is unable to work due to serious illness or injury, if necessary through to retirement. Its take-up has proven limited as can be seen in Table 9.1, perhaps because it is a complex product and subject to adverse selection, so that the premium can be too high for the people most interested in taking it out, such as those in poor health.

Critical illness cover (CIC)

This is a simpler product than PHI that pays a lump sum tax-free payment if the insured is diagnosed with a restricted range of major disabilities or serious illnesses, such as cancers, organ failures, or nervous diseases, or if permanently disabled and unable to carry out basic tasks. Assessment often revolves around whether the insured is able to undertake certain basic tasks of daily living without assistance. Once payment has been made against such a policy, the insurance ceases and the insured is free to spend the money as they wish, for example, to make adaptations to the home, or pay for private nursing care.

It's important to appreciate that only a precise list of conditions is covered in CIC. In reality, the most common reasons for being unable to work are back problems and mental stress – neither of which would trigger a CIC pay out. Similarly, rare or undiagnosed conditions result in no pay out. Consequently, CIC could not meet an assessed need of providing protection against any loss of income from being unable to work. Many insurers offer CIC in combination with life assurance, which can be on a level or, in the case of mortgage cover, a decreasing basis. CIC can be added on to an endowment policy when arranging a mortgage. Once again, these combinations should be considered carefully according to need, particularly if taking them out together would produce a discount. In this case, it is important to think about why such a discount is being offered.

Accident, sickness and unemployment (ASU)

This insurance covers these three named eventualities. It can be a stand-alone policy, it can be sold as loan payment protection insurance or, as mentioned in Chapter 6, Section 5.4, it can be sold when connected with a mortgage, as mortgage payment protection insurance (MPPI). The distinguishing feature of ASU insurance is that the pay out is (normally) limited to a maximum of two years, whereas PHI pays out until recovery or retirement. MPPI needs to be considered as part of the decision on an overall 'insurance plan', not just in terms of state benefits and assets but also in terms of other insurance arrangements and policies. For instance, it might be duplication to have both income protection insurance and MPPI, depending on circumstances. Normally, MPPI policies are offered at a particular rate and pay up to a maximum of approximately 125 per cent of monthly mortgage outgoings, with payment normally starting a short period after the peril happens.

7.3 Private medical insurance and health cash plans

Private medical insurance (PMI)

A decision about whether or not to supplement the care on offer in the UK from the NHS with PMI will depend on individual factors. For example, someone running a business that may lose trade while they wait for an operation may have a greater need for PMI than someone who is not in that position. Other factors to consider may include your perception of local NHS waiting lists and facilities, or ancillary aspects of care such as being looked after in a private room, or being able to exercise more choice over where and when treatment takes place. However, PMI is expensive, and there have been questions raised about the lack of facilities in some private hospitals, such as the absence of accident and emergency facilities. Some people have political or moral objections to paying for private health care in a society with an NHS system.

PMI is sometimes offered through an employer, in which case it is a taxable benefit. PMI varies tremendously – some medical insurance companies provide their own network of hospitals, whereas others may use other private hospitals or private facilities in an NHS hospital. (Some people may use private medicine by paying for it directly – a kind of self-insurance.) An important reason for wanting PMI is the fact that it will pay the fees that medical professionals charge for private health care, often resulting in seeing a consultant faster than through the NHS. PMI usually covers hospital charges, treatments, drugs, diagnostic tests, outpatient treatments, and pays cash for hospital stays when the insured opts for the NHS rather than private health care. Conversely, there are substantial exclusions, such as all long-term and degenerative illnesses common in old age, AIDS, pregnancy, having vaccinations, and alcohol and drug misuse. PMI premiums have risen substantially in recent years for the same reason that term life cover premiums have been falling – advances in medical technology, procedures and available drug treatments. PMI can be very expensive in later life, although there are budget plans and policies with a larger excess that can limit the cost.

NHS dental provision still exists on a patchy basis. While most people will have to pay 80 per cent of treatment costs on the NHS, there are still some categories of people who are entitled to free treatment, such as children, people in receipt of certain benefits, pregnant women and people on a low income (including students), who can obtain an HC2 certificate by completing a form available from the dentist or local social security office. Being a pensioner does not guarantee access to free dental care. There are specific dental insurance policies available, as well as dental health plans. The latter require a monthly subscription in return for access to dental work – usually for no additional charge, or the subscription perhaps covers 75 per cent of the costs incurred for certain 'routine and restorative' work. An individual's monthly subscription will vary according to the condition of their teeth, although some schemes may be available through an employer on a group basis.

Health cash plans

These are different to PMI in that they offer small, direct cash payments in the event of certain medical circumstances, in return for a monthly payment that is effectively a subscription to belong to the plan (rather than an insurance premium). Health cash plans are offered by not-for-profit, mutual organisations like the Simplyhealth Group, whose subsidiaries include HSA and HealthSure. These plans enable policy holders to claim cash if they undergo common medical treatments such as dental and optical care, physiotherapy and sometimes complementary medicine, which PMI often does not cover. Health plan providers generally offer a number of types of plan, ranging in cost and in the potential level of cash to be paid back to customers. Such plans are often available through employers who may operate a scheme whereby they obtain a discount for their employees. People take out these plans because they are seen as affordable and very simple. Over 4.7 million people in the UK had a health cash plan, either individually or through their employer, in 2005 (Health Insurance & Protection, 2005).

7.4 Care and insurance

As we saw in Chapters 7 and 8, retirement and care needs have to be planned for carefully. The increased risk of ill heath in old age means that many of us may need care in some form or other, for instance, daytime personal care for those who can live at home but need assistance with daily tasks, or possibly care in a residential or nursing home. For example, in 2001/02, 14 per cent of people aged over 65 living in a private household were unable to walk down the road on their own. These people are therefore much more likely to need assistance; 19 per cent of this group had private home help and a further 16 per cent had local authority home help (*Social Trends*, 2005, pp. 117–18). Whereas only 0.9 per cent of 65- to 74-year olds live in a care home (or long-stay hospital), this increases to 20.7 per cent of those over 85 (Age Concern, 2004). The demographic changes we saw in Section 4 of Chapter 7 are making long-term care a more important issue in personal finance, where longer life expectancy makes thinking about planning ahead more vital, and for government, where the question of care for the elderly is becoming more politically significant. For younger people, thinking about how to meet long-term care needs is a necessary part of financial planning. This is specifically an issue for those likely to enjoy assets or incomes that will make them ineligible for much state financial help as they grow older.

Financial planning for care in one's own home was considered in Chapter 8. Here we will concentrate on residential care, which can be particularly expensive: £20,000 per annum for private nursing home fees in the UK is common. As you saw in Chapter 8, Section 5.2, the situation with personal care is different in Scotland from the rest of the UK. One of the most significant changes brought in by the devolved administration in Scotland was the abolition of personal care charges for people aged 65 and over. As well as making personal care in the home free, those living in residential homes who would otherwise pay their own fees (those with assets over the 'upper limit' in Table 9.2), now receive £145 a week towards personal care. (Note that the net financial gain is less, as those in homes lose Attendance Allowance if they become eligible for free personal care up to £145 per week.) The UK Government has so far rejected proposals to do the same in the rest of the UK.

Government assistance towards residential care costs is treated differently from assistance with health costs, and is available through local authority social services – but typically only on a means-tested basis. That is to say, assets that have been accumulated (including your home if you live alone), and income, will be taken into account in determining whether or not the local authority will pay for such care. With assets over the 'lower limit' identified in Table 9.2, some contribution towards the costs will be required, with the local authority paying the difference. Only those with assets under that lower limit figure will be paid for by local authorities, and even then just on the basis of a standard pay out that may need to be 'topped up' privately if the charges for the particular home are higher than the local authority deem normal for the area. With assets over the 'upper limit', there is no state support (except for the £145 contribution to personal care for those over 65 in Scotland).

Table 9.2 Upper and lower limits of assets for state funding of long-term care in the UK, 2006/07

	Lower limit	Upper limit
England	£12 750	£21 000
Scotland	£12 250	£20 000
Wales	£16 000	£21 500
Northern Ireland	£12 750	£21 000

As a result of these limits on assets, less than 20 per cent of the 480,000 people in UK residential or nursing homes are paid for by local authorities (CareAware, 2005). There has been controversy over this means-tested system because it could be argued that it penalises those who have saved, bought their own home and taken out a private pension, and that it perhaps acts as a disincentive to lifetime saving. It can also be claimed that the system unfairly penalises those who suffer from certain types of illness: dementia and physical disability may result in needing means-tested personal care, whereas those suffering from cancer or heart attack are treated free in the 'universal' NHS system. Long-term care can quickly diminish the value of assets built up before old age. This may hinder financial plans developed for later life, and reduce or eliminate inheritances. If leaving a financial legacy is a personal goal, then long-term care will be a serious concern. For example, over 70,000 homes are sold every year to fund the costs of long-term care (CareAware, 2005). However, it could be counter-argued that running down assets accumulated during a lifetime in order to pay for care costs towards the end of someone's life-course is a perfectly reasonable and rational use of those assets.

There are a number of possible approaches to making private provision in the area of care. One way to cope with the uncertainty of the length of time for which care will be needed is to purchase a plan to pay for care. A lump sum investment is made in return for a regular income, often paid directly to care providers. Special rates apply because the purchaser often has a limited life expectancy. An 'Immediate needs care fee payment plan' is an annuity that can be purchased for an elderly person already in or about to enter a residential care home, and pays a certain amount per year directly to the care provider. Such plans are often purchased with some inflation protection. A 'Deferred immediate needs plan' is one that starts to pay the residential home from one to five years after the date at which the annuity is purchased. This type of plan can reduce the cost of the annuity compared with an immediate needs one.

Another way to cover the costs of care is through an equity withdrawal scheme based on the value of a property. These were considered in Chapter 7, Section 6, and are especially useful to people who would like to stay in their own home but where doing so would entail extra care costs.

Long-term care insurance is another possibility. This usually consists of the payment of a one-off lump sum premium that is invested to fund care that might be needed in the future – it also means that, should circumstances change, the investment can be redeemed. (Long-term care policies can also be bought with a monthly premium.) The benefit (generally index-linked) from such a policy needs to reflect the likely cost of personal care. As with CIC, standard tests assess whether certain daily tasks, such as dressing, eating, using the toilet and so on, can be performed in order to determine if a claim for a payment can be made. This area of insurance is very complicated, as are the rules governing the various state benefits, and it's an area where financial advice from an IFA is often sought.

The market for long-term care insurance policies has shrunk substantially: insurers have had little data on which to base their risk calculation and, fearing adverse selection because people know more about their needs for long-term care than insurers, have tended to set unacceptably high premiums. Should political changes bring in greater state financial support for personal care, the market is likely to shrink even further.

Activity 9.5

Consider 'Stage 1: Assess the need' of the financial planning process with regard to protection insurance:

1   How would you prioritise your current needs for protection insurance?

2   What events might cause your priorities to be reviewed in the future (as part of 'Stage 4: Review the outcome' of financial planning)?

Comment

Your current priorities will depend on your individual, household and family circumstances, and the way in which you earn your living. Events that may cause some re-evaluation in the future include: setting up or dissolving a marriage or partnership; having children; changing your line of work, and so forth. ■■■

8 Insurance and social and economic change

Let's now return to a wider discussion of insurance that picks up from some of the changes to the industry that I discussed in Section 4. Continuing rapid social and economic changes throw up major questions for the insurance industry, and therefore for future personal decisions about insurance plans. To illustrate, the gender pattern of the take-up of insurance may be changing over time; as women have increasingly become income earners (as you saw in Chapter 2), so it has become relatively more important to protect these earnings than when men were typically the sole household breadwinners. Box 9.5 is a good illustration of this.

Box 9.5 Gender gap narrows in life insurance

It has been revealed that more and more women are buying life insurance after research by LifeSearch showed that women are buying policies in much greater numbers to protect relatives should the worst happen. Figures for 2004/05 show that the number of female customers on LifeSearch's books has risen from 0.2 per cent in 1999, to 39 per cent, a rise attributed to changing financial positions among women. 'We attribute this increase to the growing awareness of the importance of protecting the financial stability of the family,' said LifeSearch policy adviser, Linda Tyson. 'More and more women are either the main or the only breadwinner and are realising the importance of protecting their incomes.'

(PrudentMinds.com, 24 May 2005)

Another interesting question facing the insurance industry is that of sex discrimination. Currently, it is possible for insurers to charge different rates for males and females according to the differing actuarial risk. This is common practice in the UK but not in some other EU countries where the insurance industry is less developed. For example, men are charged significantly more than women for motor insurance (to reflect their greater likelihood of having a crash); men are also typically charged more for life insurance (as their life expectancy is less), but conversely women are often charged more for health-related insurances such as IPI (because they tend to make more claims than men). In 2004, the EU's draft Gender Equality Directive suggested outlawing such 'sex discrimination' in insurance. In the end, an exception was made for insurance where it can be shown that sex is a decisive factor in assessing risk. This decision will be reviewed in 2010, and a move to outlaw such price discrimination could have a significant impact on premiums. In the meantime, some firms can continue to specialise in insurance policies for women.

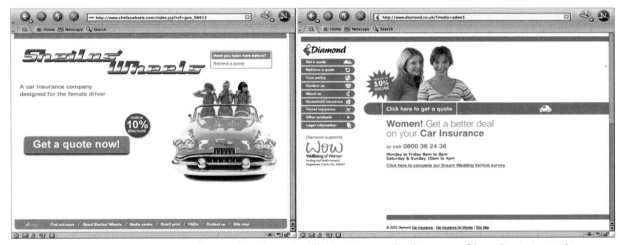

Women-only insurance companies advertise heavily in the UK, but they might disappear if 'sex discrimination' in insurance were outlawed by the European Union

Another major area of impact on insurance is recent major technological advances. It is becoming increasingly possible to assess risk on a much more individual basis. This threatens to undermine the risk pooling element of insurance, perhaps leaving some people, or properties, unable to obtain insurance. For instance, in late 2004, the Environment Agency released a new detailed 'flood map' of England and Wales, giving precise details about which properties are subject to flooding (a Scottish 'flood map' should follow in 2006). This could be used by insurers to vary their premiums more widely (making it much more expensive and perhaps unaffordable for the most 'at risk' households), or even to deny insurance altogether in some cases. In turn, this may make the 'at risk' homes much less valuable, but it may have the positive effect of discouraging future building in flood-risk areas. A further example of major technological advances affecting insurance is that of the technological advances in the field of genetics and genetic testing. This may raise fundamental questions about life insurance and health insurance. Box 9.6 contains an interesting article that gives more details on this fascinating issue.

Box 9.6   Case study: genetic testing and its insurance implications

Life; it's all in the genes

Keith Sankey

While there is no denying that the science of genetics made rapid strides through the 1990s and into the current millennium, movement was faster in some fields than in others. Progress in the project to map the human genome outstripped all but the most optimistic of expectations. However, the use of genetic epidemiology in the diagnosis and treatment of disease lagged some way behind. In the context of life and health insurance, genetic testing as a means of predicting the future development and progress of serious illness is a highly controversial topic.

On the one hand there are those who argue that applicants for cover should not have to disclose test results. One of their concerns is the risk of creating a genetic underclass, many of whom might not be insurable on any terms. Another is the possibility of developing a 'superclass' of people, with positive genetic characteristics who could obtain cover at preferential premium prices. This could herald a major shift away

from the principle of pooling risk across a wide and fairly diverse group of people to a more detailed form of classification somewhat akin to the use of postcodes in the rating of motor and property insurance.

On the other hand, life and health insurers want the ability to take all risk factors (including those of the genetic kinds) into consideration when assessing applications for life and health cover. Of particular concern to them is the clear anti-selection risk that would be present if applicants were to have the right to keep genetic-based material facts to themselves without disclosing them to their insurer.

In the UK, insurers, through their trade body, the Association of British Insurers (ABI), agreed in 2001 to abide by an extended moratorium on the use of adverse results from predictive tests for genetic illnesses in setting their premium rates for the various kinds of life and the health cover. The moratorium, which will run at least until November 2006, has strict monetary limits. Applicants for life assurance cover of up to

£500,000 do not have to disclose the results of any genetic tests they have had. For health insurance (critical illness cover, income protection and long-term care), the threshold is pitched rather lower – at £300,000). Where more substantial cover is required, an insurer can ask for the results of a test that has been approved by the Government's Genetics and Insurance Committee (GAIC). So far only one such test has been given the GAIC nod: that for Huntington's disease where the application is for life assurance cover. Although insurers are still free to ask questions about an applicant's family history, there is one step they must never take. They cannot ask an individual to undergo a genetic test. In its second report published in December 2003, the GAIC revealed it has so far received 18 applications for approval for insurers to use genetic test results in the assessment of applications for life and health cover. While one, that for Huntington's disease for life assurance, was given the go ahead some years ago, the other 17 remain outstanding. These involve Huntington's disease (critical illness cover, income protection and long-term care), autosomal dominant early onset Alzheimer's disease (eight applications) and hereditary breast and ovarian cancer (six applications).

The GAIC report highlighted particular problems with critical illness cover, which has been the fastest growing form of health insurance in the UK since its introduction in the late 1980s. Alan Tyler, health and welfare strategy manager at Swiss Re Life & Health, is a member of the GAIC. He comments: 'Critical illness requires regular product design and pricing reviews against the background of advances in medical diagnostics and methods of treatment. Genetic knowledge is advancing particularly rapidly and will change clinical practice for many of the conditions

critical illness covers. As people acquire more information about their susceptibility to disease, any long-term extension of the moratorium, which denies insurers access to information known to the applicant, is likely to impact on price. Indeed, it may throw the very viability of the product itself into question, particularly if the moratorium were to be extended to family history information as some have suggested.'

The 1997 Convention on Human Rights and Biomedicine covers genetic testing. Article 11 prohibits any form of discrimination against a person on the grounds of genetic heritage, while article 12 limits predictive testing or diagnostic genetic testing to health purposes or scientific research linked to health purposes and makes this subject to genetic counselling. However, the countries that

have both signed and ratified the convention are mainly the smaller ones with less developed insurance markets. Some of the bigger players (including France, Italy and the Netherlands) have signed but not ratified. Others (including Belgium, Germany and the UK) have done neither.

Genetics is an issue that is here to stay. Its power as a predictor of future morbidity and mortality is sure to increase over the years ahead as medical science marches on. Insurers are right to be concerned about the anti-selection risk. In the UK, the moratorium agreed in 2001 is due to come to an end in November 2006. Some might argue that it is merely a stopgap palliative measure. The industry waits with interest to learn what is to replace it.

(adapted from *Reinsurance*, 1 May 2004, p. 22)

Activity 9.6

Having read the article in Box 9.6, answer the following:

1   What classic insurance problem is the phrase 'the clear anti-selection risk that would be present if applicants were to have the right to keep genetic-based material facts to themselves' referring to, and how would this come about?

2   Why does Alan Tyler argue that the increased availability of genetic tests, which cannot be used by insurers, may 'throw the very viability of the product itself [critical illness cover] into question'?

3   What would be the dangers of a change to Article 11 of the Convention on Human Rights and Biomedicine that would allow insurers to use genetic testing?

1   This refers to the problem of asymmetric information leading to adverse selection. Insurers fear that it would come about in this case if people could know the results of genetic tests without having to disclose them to insurers. Those wanting insurance would have more information than the insurers, and those who knew they were genetically predisposed to serious illness would be more likely to take out insurance than those who knew they were not so disposed.

2   CIC may be under threat because of the problem of adverse selection. The insurers are arguing that once genetic information is available, if they are not allowed to know and use it to discriminate in premiums between people, then the market will collapse. Insurers will have to put up the price of cover significantly for everyone, which will mean that people of low risk won't take out the insurance, and so the price of cover will have to rise again, discouraging more people from taking it out, and so on.

3   If it became possible to discriminate on the grounds of genetic inheritance, then, as the article in Box 9.6 points out, we might see the development of a 'genetic underclass' that finds it impossible to get insurance and even jobs if employers consider it to be a risk. This would have serious financial implications for anyone in that position. ■■■

The only way around the problems discussed in Activity 9.6 would be to have compulsory insurance such as that provided by the state. This is the solution effectively adopted in the UK for health care and in some other countries, such as Sweden, for elder care. Different countries have travelled along different paths on these issues, so that they now have significant differences regarding which areas it is considered appropriate for the state to cover risks and in which areas individuals are expected to make private insurance provision.

A final area to consider is the changing perception of risk. An academic, Ulrich Beck, has argued that we are now living in a **risk society** (Beck, 1992). He argues that this is a society where a new political battleground is the extent to which people and society wish to see risks reduced or eliminated; and where many of those risks are often created by human activity. In the context of this discussion, this implies that the balance between risk taking and risk-aversion may be changing towards the latter. As Professor Nick Pidgeon of the University of East Anglia in the UK puts it:

> It may ... be the case that we have indeed entered a new era or 'risk society' where, despite living longer and healthier lives than ever

Risk society
A society that is preoccupied with ideas of safety in response to the perception of increased risk brought about by the modern world.

before, expectations of greater regulatory protection that come with affluence, and a change in the processes that generate hazards (such as globalisation, large-scale production, and uncertain technological implications), have brought with them anxiety about the future.

(HERO, 2001)

We could be becoming an increasingly risk-averse society as we seek to minimise dangers and seek litigation or demand action from regulatory bodies when things go wrong. If we *are* living in an increasingly risk-averse society, it seems likely that our fascination with insurance can only increase. This may mean more insurance products becoming available, and even greater marketing of those already offered.

9   Conclusion

In this chapter, I started in Section 2 by considering the possibility of unexpected events and why planning for them is needed as part of a comprehensive financial planning process. This planning includes risk shifting through the use of insurance. You saw in Section 3 how an insurance market comes about in the face of risk and uncertainty, and in Sections 4 and 8 how it may develop, or decline, in response to changes in the protection offered to us by government, or in response to other social and economic change. In Sections 6 and 7, I looked at the main types of insurance that might form a portfolio of protection, and you saw that it was important to view these in the context of the protection offered by the state and by employers, and as part of a wider insurance plan. In Section 5, I examined some of the factors relevant to deciding what insurance can be taken out, including personal circumstances, risks and financial impacts.

References

Age Concern (2004) 'Older people in the United Kingdom: some basic facts 2004' [online], http://www.ace.org.uk/AgeConcern/Documents/factcard2004.pdf (Accessed 20 March 2006).

Association of British Insurers (ABI) (2005) '2005 UK insurance – key facts' [online], http://www.abi.org.uk/BookShop/ResearchReports/Key%20facts%202005_LR.pdf_(Accessed 20 March 2006).

Aviva (2005) 'Education: history' [online], http://www.aviva.com/index.asp?pageid=67 (Accessed 28 November 2005).

BBC (2005) 'Weather basics – lightning' [online], http://www.bbc.co.uk/weather/features/basics_lightning.shtml (Accessed 24 February 2005).

Beck (1992) *Risk Society: Towards a New Modernity*, London, Sage.

Care Aware (2005) 'The statistics of care' [online], http://www.careaware.co.uk/statistics_of_care.htm (Accessed 22 November 2005).

Government Actuary's Department (GAD) (2005) 'Interim life tables 2002–2004' [online], http://www.gad.gov.uk/Life_Tables/Interim_life_tables.htm (Accessed 11 November 2005).

Health Insurance & Protection (2005) 'Filling the gap' [online], May, http://www.hi-mag.com/healthinsurance/article.jsp?articleid=1117022512548 (Accessed 27 April 2006).

Higher Education & Research Opportunities in the United Kingdom (HERO) (2001) 'Making sense of the risk society' [online], http://www.hero.ac.uk/uk/research/archives/2001/making_sense_of_the__risk1007.cfm (Accessed 11 March 2006).

Home Office (2004) *Crime Statistics for England and Wales* [online], http://www.crimestatistics.org.uk/output/Page1.asp (Accessed 24 February 2005).

Office of National Statistics (ONS) (2005) 'Health: cancer' [online], http://www.statistics.gov.uk/cci/nugget.asp?id=915 (Accessed 20 March 2006).

PrudentMinds.com (2005) 'Gender gap narrows in life insurance' [online], 24 May, http://www.prudentminds.com/newsarticle8579310.html (Accessed 11 March 2006).

Social Trends (2005) no. 35, Basingstoke and New York, Palgrave Macmillan for The Office for National Statistics (ONS); also available online at the ONS website, http://www.statistics.gov.uk/downloads/theme_social/Social_Trends35/Social_Trends_35.pdf (Accessed 7 April 2006).

Personal finance: the changing context

Chapter 10

George Callaghan and Martin Higginson

Contents

1 Introduction

Thursday October 24th

My mother phoned me at work and told me that a letter from Barclays had arrived. I asked her to open it and read what it said over the phone. After an agonising wait ... my mother told me ... the communication from Barclays was my Visa statement. However, there was a blank cheque attached to the statement and a letter, saying, 'Dear Mr Mole, The attached cheque can be used where your Barclaycard may not be accepted: e.g. payment of utility bills, local tradesmen, home improvements or school fees. Cash rate applies. Please see conditions on reverse of this statement.' ...

I asked her what the interest would be on the cheque. She said, 'It's 2 per cent for cash advances.' She went on, 'It says here your credit limit is £10,000. How did you wangle that?' ...

Friday October 25th

... I read for myself the letter from Barclaycard inviting me to cash their cheque. I was astounded, appalled and horrified to read the interest rate charged on my cheque is 21.4 per cent, and not 2 per cent as my mother had erroneously told me on the phone. The 2 per cent is the charge they will make for processing the cheque (£160).

There has been no sun in the last few days so, rather than trust my calculator, I phoned my friend Parvez, who has just passed his accountancy exams.

He said he charged £25 for the first ten minutes of phone advice and thereafter £2 a minute. I hurriedly gave him the figures and asked him how much I would end up paying for my £8000.

After eleven minutes, during which Parvez asked me a lot of time-consuming and unnecessary questions, he said, 'It's gonna cost you an arm, a leg and a torso. A minimum of £162.34 a month. If you pay the minimum each month, it's going to take thirteen and three-quarter years to pay off and it will cost you £26,680.88 if interest rates don't go up. You've fallen into the compound interest trap, Moley, innit?'

(Townsend, 2005, pp. 41–3)

The unsolicited receipt of a credit card cheque (of the kind you saw in Chapter 1, Figure 1.3) by Adrian Mole, Sue Townsend's fictitious diarist, provides a humorous example of some of the financial offers that can be received by UK citizens. It also suggests what *could* happen to those who are unwary. *Personal Finance* has shown how, largely as a result of the policy of liberalisation, financial choices have to be made across an increasing number of important areas. From retirement planning to decisions about care, from spending to taking out debt, and from insurance choices to selecting savings and investment products, UK citizens are increasingly required to make important financial decisions. Perhaps if Adrian Mole had gained knowledge of the four themes of *Personal Finance*, he would have been able to make an effective decision about the potential use of the credit card cheque, without having to resort to phoning his accountant friend Parvez for some rather expensive advice!

This last chapter opens, in Section 2, by revisiting the main themes and issues that have run throughout *Personal Finance*, emphasising the interconnections between them, and demonstrating how financial knowledge and understanding are essential when making informed financial choices. The chapter then moves on to explain what social scientists call 'agency'. As you will see in Section 3, you have already come across a number of examples of agency in the book: in this last chapter we explain and explore the concept more fully. Section 4, which takes up the bulk of the chapter, uses the two issues of demographic change and technological change to investigate how ongoing social and economic change could impact upon the type of personal financial choices that may be faced in the future.

2   Themes

The first theme running throughout this book has been that financial choices, and the decisions that flow from them, all take place within a wider – and changing – social and economic context. This context has a number of elements, including not just social and economic changes but also political, demographic, cultural and technological changes. *Personal Finance* has emphasised the changes that have financial implications. So, for instance, changes in household size, an ageing society, an increasingly 'consumer society', changing government policies towards the support of families, and the impact of different cultural values have all been discussed at different points throughout the book. A particularly important aspect has been the economic and political process we have described as 'liberalisation', a process which emphasises free markets and increased competition, and limiting the direct role of the government in the economy. Liberalisation gathered momentum in the UK in the early 1980s under the Conservative Government of Margaret Thatcher, and has been continued and extended (in some aspects at least) under subsequent Conservative and Labour governments. We focused in Chapter 4 on the liberalisation in the financial services industry.

In addition, in Chapter 6 we looked at how local authority housing had been sold off; in Chapter 7 you saw that the relative importance of the state pension had declined; and in Chapter 9 that the reduction in the real value of some government benefits might influence insurance decisions.

The process of liberalisation gained momentum under the Conservative Government of Margaret Thatcher

One important result of this process of liberalisation is that individuals face a greater number of financial choices than in the past, and that they have to take more responsibility for the outcome of the financial decisions that are made. On the one hand, this has certainly helped to lead to a greater range of financial products and financial providers for most consumers. Moreover, many people would argue that it has brought some important benefits, such as contributing to the growth in home ownership by helping to make mortgages more readily available, and that it has enabled more people to own investments such as shares.

Yet, as *Personal Finance* has also shown, another outcome of liberalisation is that the risk associated with making financial decisions is increasingly borne by individuals and households rather than collectively. This is very clear in areas such as planning the finance for studying in higher education, or ensuring financial security in retirement. Therefore, faced with greater choice *and* greater responsibility, the type of knowledge and understanding of personal finance that you have built up throughout this book is becoming increasingly important.

Activity 10.1

Think back to Chapter 4 on debt, and identify some examples of liberalisation in the UK financial services industry, and some examples of the effects of this on consumers.

Comment

Chapter 4 explored a number of aspects of liberalisation in the financial services industry. The Financial Services Act 1986, the Building Societies Act 1986 and the Banking Act 1987 all helped to lead to rapid subsequent changes in the financial sector, and prompted increased diversification and competition between financial institutions. This led to a number of outcomes for consumers, including being given more choice in a whole range of financial products, but also facing more forceful marketing techniques. Combined with other economic and social changes, such as rising real income for UK citizens, the financial services industry has been radically changed. For instance, as you may know from your own experience, it is now possible for customers to shop in a supermarket not only for groceries but also for credit cards, insurance and mortgages. As part of this liberalised financial environment, unsolicited offers for financial products, including the type of blank credit card cheques received by Adrian Mole, are increasingly common, a situation that requires individuals to make more financial choices. ■ ■ ■

Accompanying and following in the wake of the liberalisation of financial services has been a growing emphasis on the regulation of the financial services industry. As you have seen, the Financial Services Authority (FSA) is the primary organisation that Parliament has established to regulate the financial services industry. The FSA also has a statutory duty of promoting public understanding of the financial system. Hence it is concerned with ensuring that good information is available to consumers and that citizens are sufficiently financially capable to make financial decisions. To this end, the FSA requires firms to provide key product information to consumers (for example, in the form of comparative tables and a consumer website) and works with a variety of partners to improve financial capability. Indeed, the FSA, along with educational organisations, has suggested that increased financial education is essential if UK consumers are to avoid storing up some serious problems for the future. Reading and studying *Personal Finance* is an excellent example of the way in which public knowledge and financial capability can be increased. We hope this can be illustrated by revisiting an Activity that you met at the start of the book.

Activity 10.2

Activity 1.2 in Chapter 1 asked you to consider how confident you were in handling your financial affairs. Let's return to the five questions in that Activity and see if what you have learned during the course of reading *Personal Finance* allows you to answer with more confidence.

1   Can you explain what 'APR' is?

2   Do you understand:

    (a) the difference between a repayment and an interest-only mortgage?

    (b) what an ISA is?

3   Can you explain what inflation is and why it matters?

4   Can you explain what the principle underlying insurance products is?

5   Can you calculate 4 per cent interest on £2000 over two years?

Comment

I hope you can now answer these questions. If you need to refresh your memory, the answers can be found in the following chapters:

1   Chapter 4 explained that the APR is the Annual Percentage Rate of interest charged on debt products.

2   Chapter 6 explained the different types of mortgages, and Chapter 5 explained that ISAs are tax-free individual savings accounts (and not an iPod accessory or energy drink which, as you saw in the book Introduction, are both common ideas among the 18–24 age group).

3   Chapter 2 defined and explained inflation, and the importance of 'real' values was discussed a number of times in later chapters (for example, the idea of real interest rates in Chapters 4 and 5, real returns in Chapter 5, and real property prices in Chapter 6).

4   Chapter 9 discussed insurance products and the principles underlying them.

5   Chapter 4 explained how interest payments can be calculated.

After reading *Personal Finance*, you should be able to answer specific questions like these, *and* have the confidence to ask questions of your own. To illustrate, the knowledge you gained from Chapter 4 may prompt you to ask for further information about question 5 in Activity 10.2: Are there any repayments over the two years? If so, when did these take place? Is compounding applied? By thinking like this, and by having the knowledge and confidence to ask for further information, you are demonstrating financial capability. ■ ■ ■

A second theme running throughout *Personal Finance* concerns the interrelationship between individuals and their households. This is closely related to the changing social and economic context because, as you saw in Chapters 1 and 8, the number, size and type of households has been changing in recent decades, and this is connected to demographic and other forms of social change. Household change also affects the nature of household relationships, so that, for instance, some people have financial responsibilities for more than one household such as supporting elderly relatives (in the UK or overseas), or providing financial support for children or ex-partners even though they are part of a separate household. Such extended families mean that there can be quite complex financial interrelationships both within, and between, different households.

Consequently, it is important to recognise that individual financial decisions often involve discussion and debate with other household members and, possibly, consultation with family members living in other households. In such circumstances, social and cultural factors come into play because these can influence the outcome of financial decisions. And the decisions of one person have implications for other members of the household. There are a number of examples of this within *Personal Finance*. For example, you saw in Chapter 3 how different types of household money management systems influence spending and budgeting, and in Chapter 8 we explored the short- and long-term implications of different decisions on sharing and caring. You've also seen that there can be important financial implications depending on who in a household has the pension entitlements, the savings and investments, or the responsibility for a debt agreement.

The third theme of the book relates to change over the life-course and, in particular, the financial planning implications of that change. This could include commonly anticipated events: for instance, forming a household or partnership, living together in a property, bringing up and caring for a family, or retiring. We looked at these throughout various chapters, especially Chapters 6 to 8. However, there are also unexpected events, such as getting divorced, being made redundant, or suffering a change in health, and these were discussed in Chapters 8 and (particularly) 9. This theme is important because it highlights the issue of thinking over a number of different time frames, and considering what might happen over five years, ten years and in the longer term. *Personal Finance* has shown that effective financial planning means *regularly reviewing personal finances in the light of changing circumstances.*

This brings us to the fourth theme: financial planning. This theme provides a systematic way of thinking through financial choices and making decisions. As a starting point, Chapter 1 asked you to consider the financial implications of goals, which might include matters as diverse as planning for retirement, budgeting for a mortgage, or expressing a concern for social fairness. What is important in financial planning are the financial implications of each goal. For example, what savings are required to meet a specific goal? Is reaching such a level of savings possible given existing spending commitments? Might striving to attain one goal mean that another goal is unaffordable? Which financial product is best suited to meet which goal?

In order to provide a framework to think through these issues, Chapter 1 introduced the four-stage model of the financial planning process which, along with its diagrammatic form, has featured throughout *Personal Finance*. This financial planning model describes how financial decisions can be thought about in four different stages: Stage 1: Assess; Stage 2: Decide; Stage 3: Act; and Stage 4: Review. This approach to financial planning has been applied in all the chapters.

Activity 10.3

Think about the tracking and managing of individual or household finances. What important tools in the 'Stage 1: Assess' part of the financial planning process did you learn about in Chapters 2, 3 and 6?

Comment

In Chapter 2, you learned how cash flow statements can be used to record the sources of household income. Chapter 3 built upon this by adding the spending side of the cash flow statement; it also explained how budgeting is an essential tool in managing household finances. Chapter 6 then introduced the financial balance sheet, and explained that it can provide a snapshot of liabilities and assets, enabling calculations such as of net worth and the current asset ratio. All of these are useful in the *assess* stage of any financial planning process when it is necessary to work out financial constraints and the current position. ▪ ▪ ▪

A crucial aspect of the model of the financial planning process is integrating the interconnections between individual financial planning and the broader social and economic context. These interconnections are shown by the arrows in Figure 10.1. They illustrate how individual decisions are shaped by the wider context, and that the wider context is, in turn, shaped by individual decisions. This is the same diagram of the stages in the financial planning process first introduced in Chapter 1 as Figure 1.3, but this time we have added some examples, drawn from different chapters of *Personal Finance*, of the interaction between financial planning and the economic and social context.

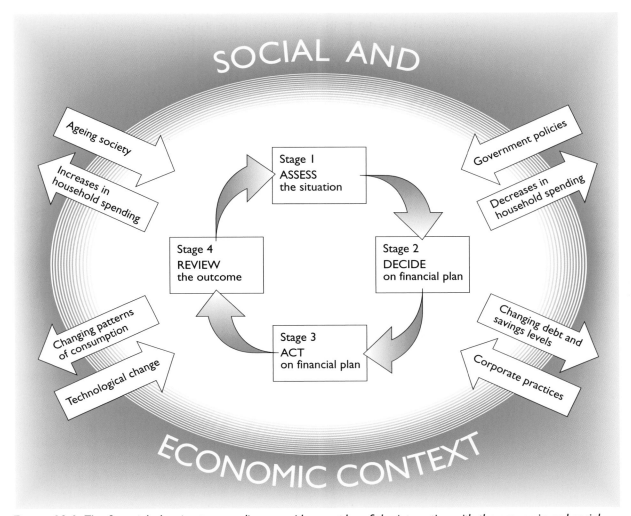

Figure 10.1 *The financial planning process diagram with examples of the interaction with the economic and social context*

An example of the way in which the broader social and economic context influences individual financial decisions is through specific government policies, such as changes to state pensions or the financing of university study. Another example is how corporate practices, such as the development and heavy marketing of new financial products, can influence individual choices and decisions by encouraging people to act and behave in a certain way. But influences can also work the other way, with individual decisions having a cumulative impact on the whole economy. To illustrate, if many people decide to cut spending, then demand for goods and services will fall which, in turn, may lead to higher unemployment. This outcome might not be intended by any individual but, taken together, such decisions can change the broader economic context.

3 Changing the context

Financial capability implies that individuals can manage their finances in order to influence outcomes and events in a beneficial way for themselves and others. Social scientists call this ability to exercise influence **agency**. So an aspect of individual agency is using choices and decisions to influence one's own financial circumstances. You have seen many examples of individual agency throughout *Personal Finance*. These include decisions about employment; the choice of how much to spend and on what things; decisions on taking out debt, or saving and investing; decisions on planning for old age; and decisions on caring and insurance. In each case, individuals can use financial planning to shape and change their financial circumstances. (This social scientific meaning of agency is not to be confused with the legal and business use of 'agency' where a person or organisation acts on behalf of another person – such as an estate *agency*.)

It is also possible for individuals to act collectively in order to influence the broader social and economic context. You have seen some instances of how individual actions can have an unintended cumulative impact. For example, at the end of Section 2 it was mentioned that individual decisions to cut spending may lead to an increase in unemployment. In addition, it's also possible for individuals to act with the *intention* of causing a cumulative impact. For example, if many individuals act so as to reduce the environmental impact of their consumption, then together they might have a significant effect. Here, individual actions can have an intended cumulative impact. This can also happen if people group together and act with others in order to influence the social, economic and political environment, thus *creating* change. This is known as 'collective agency'. Collective agency involves active engagement with others.

Agency
Attempts to respond to and influence circumstances and the broader social and economic context.

Activity 10.4

Drawing on your own experience and the previous chapters of *Personal Finance*, can you think of examples of both (a) intentional individual action to cause a cumulative effect, and (b) collective agency?

Comment

There have been examples of both intended individual action and collective agency in *Personal Finance*.

For instance, in terms of individual action, there was the discussion of ethical investment in Chapter 5, where investors use their own financial power to encourage ethical corporate practice. Another example might be that savers could choose, as a matter of principle, to save with mutual building societies, which are members' organisations, rather than banks, whose purpose is to make profits for their shareholders.

You have also come across examples of collective agency in *Personal Finance*, involving active engagement with others to effect change. For instance, Chapter 7 noted that pensioners have sometimes expressed a collective voice about the declining relative value of state pensions. Thinking more widely, many workers are also members of trade unions – which are still major and important voices for the expression of collective agency. For example, they may seek wage increases, or better terms and conditions for their members, or might mobilise to defend existing pension scheme entitlements.

Some agency can involve both individual and collective elements. For instance, individuals can use their buying power to boycott a particular good or service, corporation, or even country, or – perhaps more positively – to focus their consumption on particular aims such as shopping locally or buying organic produce. Such efforts may be reinforced by expressions of collective agency encouraging others to do the same thing.

I hope you will have come up with one or more of these examples or, perhaps drawing on your own experience, you may have added some additional ones. Perhaps the crucial point here is that individual financial choices can also be part of a deliberate attempt to press for social and economic change. ■ ■ ■

Collective agency and individual actions can change both the social and economic context

A thought that may have occurred to you is that people are not free to make *any* financial choice they want. Influencing your own financial circumstances, or changing the broader context even when acting collectively, can be difficult. In other words, both individual agency and collective agency are subject to certain constraints. One of these constraints is financial; a person's financial position, in terms of income and wealth, clearly limits financial choices and options. These financial constraints are effectively included in the financial planning model – when *assessing* the situation, an existing financial position is one of the things that has to be assessed. Thus, to illustrate, someone whose low income excludes them from mainstream finance may have to turn to the alternative credit market for debt – and pay higher interest rates as a result. Similarly, someone from a low-income household might be outraged by, say, the commercial logging of native hardwoods in Brazil but be unable to use ethical investment as a way of changing corporate behaviour because they don't have any money to invest. They may be able to use other avenues, but their existing financial position acts as a financial constraint.

Another type of constraint is given by social norms. Issues such as someone's gender, age or cultural background may influence the financial choices open to them. For example, some women may find that prevailing social norms as to which partner has more responsibility for childcare can influence their participation in the labour market – a decision with important financial implications. Elderly people may find that, despite legislation to the contrary, age discrimination limits their employment opportunities, and religious guidelines and rules can influence attitudes to borrowing and saving.

Despite these constraints, the concept of agency is still useful. Individuals *can* engage with and influence their financial circumstances, and the broader social and economic context. In fact, one of the most important things about *Personal Finance* is that the learning it provides will mean that you have more knowledge and confidence to help you understand the financial choices available, and to help you make the financial decisions most appropriate for you. In addition, it is possible to use both the cumulative impact of individual financial decisions, and other forms of collective agency, to press for social and economic change. Financial and other social or economic constraints can limit agency, but agency can also influence and transform the social and economic context.

4 The challenge of change

By now, it should be evident that the UK's financial environment in the early years of the twenty-first century is characterised by a high level of choice and by greater individual responsibility for the outcomes of financial decisions than was the case in earlier decades. While looking to the future always involves uncertainty, the prevailing trend would suggest that such choice and responsibility will, if anything, continue to grow. This means that the ability to cope with change, to plan ahead and demonstrate the type of agency described in Section 3, will become even more important in the future. Financial capability includes being able to respond appropriately to future change. The purpose of this section is to explore how what you have learned so far in *Personal Finance* can help you to meet the challenge of such future change. This is done by using two issues as examples that illustrate different elements of social and economic change.

The first issue, closely related to the theme of change over the life-course, involves considering the personal financial impact of demographic change and an ageing society. It introduces data on demographic change, and investigates what this might mean for the type of personal finance choices people may have to face in the future. The second issue, closely connected to the theme of the wider social and economic context, is the ongoing growth of digital technology. Sophisticated software developments and other technical innovations in the world of personal finance are increasing rapidly. What will this mean in practical terms? Might it mean more choice and more opportunity, or will it simply mean the same set of decisions dressed up in a new technological format?

4.1 Demographic change and an ageing society

Chapter 7 showed that the UK has an ageing population. Between 1901 and 2003, the proportion of the population aged 50 and over increased from 15 per cent to 33 per cent, and is projected to grow to 41 per cent by 2031. Figure 10.2 shows the actual number of people aged 50 and over, and shows an increase from 5.7 million people in 1901 to 13.8 million in 1951, and to 20 million people in 2003, with a projection of 27.2 million by 2031 (ONS/DWP, 2005, p. 2).

One implication of these changing demographics is an increase in the proportion of the population in the oldest age ranges. Therefore, for example, the proportion of the population aged 85 and over is forecast to grow from 5.5 per cent in 2003 to 9.1 per cent by 2031. Another interesting indicator of the ageing population is the number of people who live to reach the age of 100 years. In 1911, there were only 100 centenarians in England and Wales; by 2031 there will be 48,000 (ONS/DWP, 2005, pp. 3–4).

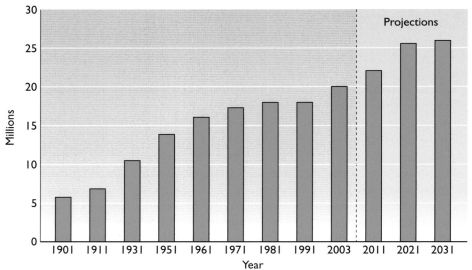

Figure 10.2 *Number of people aged 50 and over in the UK*
Source: ONS/DWP, 2005, p. 2, Figure 1.1

Many more people are living to older ages

Chapter 7 introduced data showing the increasing life expectancy of the UK population; it is important again here. Table 10.1 shows that life expectancy is rising rapidly in the UK. For example, a male aged 20 in 1981 could expect to live a further 61.8 years (to age 81.8); but a male aged 20 in 2001 could expect to live until aged 84.1.

Table 10.1   UK life expectancy at age 20

Someone aged 20 in the year ...	... could expect on average to live for this many more years	
	Men	Women
1981	61.8	65.9
1991	62.9	66.9
2001	64.1	68.0
2011	65.4	69.0
2021	66.6	70.1

Note: Table 10.1 shows 'cohort' expectations of life that are based on how long people have lived in the past but are adjusted for known or expected changes that improve or reduce life expectancy.
Source: GAD, 2005

Another pattern usually associated with demography and ageing is a greater number of older women than men because of women's greater life expectancy. Yet as mortality rates among men decline, this pattern is changing and the gap is closing; projections show that by 2031 there are expected to be 90 men per 100 women over the age of 50 compared with only 85 men per 100 women over 50 in 2003 (ONS/DWP, 2005, p. 4).

What are the personal finance implications of such significant demographic changes? Perhaps the most obvious relates to financial planning. We discussed the importance of planning ahead over different time horizons when looking at the theme of change over the life-course in Section 2, and the data and forecasts discussed above give clear indications that *the typical life-course will be longer in the future*. This, in turn, has implications for financial planning. While living longer is, of course, something to be celebrated, it does mean that what happens to pensions is going to become increasingly important. You know from Chapter 7 that, by retirement, most people rely on pensions to provide income. Indeed, from the age of 60 onwards, pensions make up the majority of weekly household income (ONS/DWP, 2005, p. 67). However, if the current trends continue – for the value of occupational pension provision to decline and for the state pension age to increase as it does after 2010 for women and may do for everyone if government proposals become law –younger people might expect to be faced with a financial environment rather different from that experienced by previous generations.

What might the demographic changes in the UK mean for your own income in old age?

Obviously your answer will depend on such factors as your current age, employment position, gender, the composition of your household, and your existing pension provision. In most cases, it is likely that you will at least have to think carefully about planning for your retirement, including your pension, savings and investments, and perhaps working for longer. Chapter 7, Section 3 contains a detailed examination of the different pension options (so now may be a good time to go back and have a look at that chapter). It's possible that you may have to budget for increased payments into a pension scheme, and think about the possibility of making these payments for a greater number of years. You may also want to consider additional forms of saving and investing. You may have to stay in your job for more years than you thought, or you may have the option of mixing part-time employment with semi-retirement, rather than retiring fully at a particular time. Another option after retirement, for those who own their own property, may be to release some of the equity in their property. ■ ■ ■

In addition to retirement planning and pensions, the ageing population throws up a second issue with important financial implications – namely, caring relationships. As Chapter 8 pointed out, one aspect of decisions about caring is the opportunity cost of looking after other people. In old age, this may mean looking after partners, grandchildren or other household members; clearly, time spent caring for others is time that cannot be spent in paid employment. UK Government data shows that, in April 2001, 625,000 men and women aged between 65 and 74 provided unpaid care, and that in over 30 per cent of these cases, carers were working fifty or more hours a week (ONS/DWP, 2005, p. 63). If the government wishes to encourage people to work into old age, then perhaps one area of future policy development will be to provide assistance for elderly carers.

As you saw in Chapters 8 and 9, another aspect of caring involves paying for either residential or home care. In 2001, 27 per cent of those aged 90 and over were living in medical and care establishments in England and Wales and, as the population ages, the number of people requiring such care is likely to grow. Similarly, the number of home-help hours, estimated at 3.4 million for England in 2004, is likely to increase

(ONS/DWP, 2005, pp. 57–8). As you saw in Chapter 9, care in residential homes can cost £20,000 per annum – and even two to three hours of assistance in someone's own home can cost as much as £9000 per year. How such care is paid for is already a politically important topic with, for example, people in Scotland benefiting from free personal care up to £145 per week for the elderly, compared with just Attendance Allowance to pay for care in the rest of the UK. It remains to be seen how government policy develops in this area, both in Scotland and in the rest of the UK. For instance, if policy in the rest of the UK continues to follow the trend towards greater individual financial responsibility, then individuals will have to take into account the potential financial costs of caring in old age in their future financial planning. If, on the other hand, the rest of the UK follows the new policy in Scotland, there would be different implications for future financial planning.

A third issue thrown up by an ageing population, related to both income in retirement and caring, is what the increasing number of older households decide to do with the wealth that they hold. Apart from the contributions tied up in any pension schemes, the two main sources of wealth are financial assets, such as savings and investments, and non-financial assets such as housing. Of these, housing is more evenly spread throughout the population, with 66 per cent of households where the household reference person is aged 65 to 84 owning their property outright. This opens up the possibility for more elderly citizens to use their homes to help provide retirement income or to meet caring or other expenses. They could do this by selling and buying somewhere cheaper, or by using one of the equity release schemes described in Chapter 7, Section 6.3. The evidence so far, however, indicates that the majority of older people do not wish to do either. To illustrate, a survey of English households in 2003/04 found that of the 6 per cent of households where the household reference person was aged between 65 and 84 who moved home in the previous three years, only 23 per cent did so because they wanted a smaller or cheaper house or flat, and this only rose to 27 per cent among the movers aged over 85 (ONS/DWP, 2005, p. 23). In addition, evidence from the Council of Mortgage Lenders showed that the equity release market in 2005 was less than 1 per cent of the residential mortgage market (CML, 2005). While only a minority of elderly households are moving or releasing equity in the mid 2000s, it could be the case that changing policy on pensions and caring means that many more people will have to consider this option in the future.

Activity 10.6

For what reasons might elderly people be reluctant to move to a cheaper or smaller property, or to participate in equity release?

Comment

Elderly people may be reluctant to leave a geographical community with which they feel familiar. They may also have concerns about the costs and risks associated with equity release, which were discussed in Chapter 7, Section 6.3. A further factor could be connected to inheritance, with elderly people wishing to leave their major form of wealth to their family. ■ ■ ■

In purely financial terms, many of the changes associated with an ageing society appear to produce more worries and problems for financial planning. None the less, there may be positive outcomes, often with indirect financial implications. For example, not only are many people living longer, but the majority of those aged 65 and over report that they are either in good or fairly good health (ONS/DWP, 2005, p. 42). This may mean that they will be able to pursue employment opportunities, giving potential benefits in the form of higher household income. Some older people also feel that paid (and unpaid) work can have a positive effect on their health and well-being.

Another likely development, with a possible indirect impact on personal finance, is that elderly people will use the political process (a form of collective agency) to press for changes in government policy. Box 10.1 contains an extract from the pressure group Age Concern, published in the run-up to the UK General Election in 2005, to illustrate what some of the changes in government policy might involve, including increases in the basic state pension, an end to age discrimination, and an improvement in public services for the elderly. Evidently, if there were such changes in policy, elderly individuals and households would be in a better financial position: pensions would be increased, employment opportunities improved, and the costs of caring reduced. This would consequently change the financial planning of those thinking ahead to retirement.

Box 10.1 Age Concern briefing on older voters

Age Concern research shows that the over 50s are a powerful electoral force, a higher than average percentage of whom will always turn out to vote.

Winning in 2009
The importance of the Baby Boomers

Age Concern's Agenda for the UK general election

- **Ending the scandal of pensioner poverty** – Age Concern wants the next government to increase the Basic State Pension to £109 a week and keep the State Pension Age at 65. The Government must persuade employers to do more towards our pensions and it must provide better information and advice about income in later life. The important work of carers should also be rewarded.

- **Stopping age discrimination** – Age Concern wants the next government to end the discrimination older people experience in health and social care, end mandatory retirement ages and create a powerful Commission for Equality and Human Rights that would promote age equality.

- **Improving public services** – Age Concern wants the next government to increase resources and provide more choice in care, housing and support services. The government must put more emphasis on prevention. It must protect the most vulnerable and improve services for older people with mental health problems.

(Age Concern, 2005)

Changes in the social and economic context associated with an ageing population, then, will have important consequences for personal finance. It's probable that the society of the future will be characterised by people staying in employment for longer; more elderly households obtaining income from a mixture of paid employment and pensions and other benefits; and households having to balance providing care for others with planning ahead to cover the costs of their own caring. It is also the case that decisions made by elderly citizens acting together could, in turn, change the social and economic context. All this means that the knowledge and skills that you have been building up throughout *Personal Finance*, such as an understanding of the social and economic context, an awareness of the interrelationships between individuals and other household members, and the need for financial planning over the life-course, are likely to grow in importance. The ability to demonstrate agency, to make the most appropriate financial decision from the choices available, is likely to be required well into old age.

4.2 The digital age and personal finance

An element of the social and economic environment that has changed rapidly in recent years is technology. Let's explore some of the implications for personal finance arising from changes in digital technology.

We are in the middle of an 'internet revolution'. In Great Britain, the proportion of households with a broadband connection almost quadrupled from 8 per cent to 31 per cent between April 2003 and July 2005 (*Social Trends*, 2006, p. 191, Figure 13.3). Figure 10.3 illustrates the size of total growth in internet access, with 64 per cent of adults in Great Britain, some 29 million people, having accessed the internet in the three months prior to October 2005 (ONS, 2006).

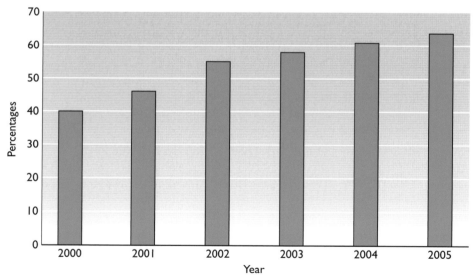

Figure 10.3 *Internet access: adults who used the internet in the three months prior to October 2005, Great Britain*
Source: ONS, 2006

The internet has already had quite an impact on personal finance matters. First, online shopping has been growing rapidly. The ONS survey cited above also found that 61 per cent of those using the internet had bought or ordered goods, tickets or services. It also showed that people aged 25–44 were most likely to buy online (67 per cent), while people aged over 65 were least likely to buy online (41 per cent) (ONS, 2006).

Another finding, this time from e-commerce trade body Interactive Media in Retail Group (IMRG), found that some 24 million UK consumers shopped online in 2005, spending an average of £816 each during the year. The pace of change was also quite striking, with spending over the internet totalling £19.2 billion in 2005, up 32 per cent from just one year earlier (BBC, 2006). An indication of the percentage of online shopping as a proportion of total retail sales is provided by IMRG who estimate that, in the run-up to Christmas 2004, online spending was around 7 per cent of total UK retail sales (Easynet, 2004).

Activity 10.7

Which, if any, online purchases have been made by you or others in your household in the last three months? What impact do you think such purchases may have on the corporate sector?

Comment

You are most likely to have purchased books, music and videos. In fact, market analysts Verdict and e-commerce trade body IMRG (BBC, 2005, 2006) suggest that the levels of online sales are putting competitive pressure on retailers of books, music and videos, and on music retailers in particular. The next most popular online purchases were electrical goods and clothing, with Verdict indicating that high-street retailers specialising in these products could also be under threat in the future. This is a good example of the way that financial decisions by households can affect the economic environment. ■ ■ ■

A second trend with personal finance implications is the popularity of internet banking. ONS noted a gender difference here, with 48 per cent of men who used the internet doing so for internet banking, compared with 39 per cent of females (ONS, 2006). Research carried out for the Alliance & Leicester bank in 2006 found that 59 per cent of the adults surveyed do most of their banking online, and 61 per cent said that they used internet banking a lot more than they did two years before. The bank's research has also shown that the most popular reasons for customers accessing their internet banking site are to check balances, make payments and transfer money, and the research predicts that, by 2020, 80 per cent of adults (42 million) will be using internet banking (Alliance & Leicester, 2006). Banks are able to operate internet-based accounts and services more cheaply than those requiring a full high-street presence. That's the reason, as you saw in Chapter 5, Section 4.3, why internet-based savings accounts usually pay higher rates of interest. The internet is also likely to have an increased impact on the various investment products described in Chapter 5, Section 5, with online trading of shares and funds increasingly common. All of this could have a major impact on the way that households manage their money in the future, with the more immediate and easily and freely accessed financial information provided by digital technology potentially allowing households to track their flows of income and expenditure, and their stocks of assets and liabilities, more effectively and quickly.

A third important impact of the internet revolution is that the addition of a new medium for shopping and banking also has implications for the marketing of goods and services, with corporations being likely to use the greater access that digital technology provides to try to increase their sales and profits. Advertisements via text message and email are becoming increasingly common. Although corporations sending email or text message adverts are supposed to receive the permission of recipients first, this doesn't always happen, and 'spam' emails and unsolicited text messages from unscrupulous firms are rife. Legitimate businesses have encouraged people to sign up to receive message alerts of offers, events and promotions such as pubs and clubs sending texts advertising drinks promotions. With the development of picture messaging and personal digital assistants, such opportunities seem set to increase.

Another aspect of this targeted marketing is where financial organisations create databases and other knowledge management systems to target individuals with products at particular times. So, for instance, customers may receive emails after Christmas offering extended overdrafts, or texts offering a new personal loan immediately following final repayment of an existing loan. An interesting real-life example is contained in Box 10.2, which describes how a pizza delivery chain makes use of digital technology.

New communications media create new, more individualised marketing opportunities

---

Box 10.2   Digital marketing strategies

Interactive marketing

By being constantly connected, consumers are allowing marketers access to parts of their lives that not long ago would have been more difficult to penetrate. Digital technologies, and the content they deliver, have added dynamic segmentation and targeting capabilities to more traditional methods. ...

A good example is Domino's Pizza who is deliberately associating its brand with specific content (The Simpsons, family show), at a particular time of day (dinnertime) with a highly distinctive signature (jarring, loud sounding siren to denote heat).

The pizza delivery service must surely rank as a perfect real life example of Pavlov's conditioned reflex experiment. Just the sound of the siren most likely suffices today to have masses across Britain salivating for 'hmmm ... Simpsons ... dinner ... Domino's'.

The campaign simultaneously creates awareness, an impulse and the opportunity to purchase. The red interactive button on the television remote allows viewers to act on their impulse immediately, minimizing the opportunity to change their mind.

Moreover, Domino's administers the marketing *coup de grÐce* by making it easier over time to use the service. [Internet] cookies keep track of the previous orders and choices and literally allow customers to have dinner delivered to their door at the touch of a button ('same as last time?'). For Domino's, the interactive television remote control has proven to be a magic wand. Not surprisingly, sales through online channels now reach a significant £300,000 per month from 20,000 orders.

The pizza delivery service could go further still, though, by extending its presence to additional digital platforms. Mobile phones come to mind immediately as a channel that can prove as sticky as American cheese. Using SMS (Short Message Service), the text messaging service to offer electronic coupons would, for example, allow Domino's to further increase loyalty and pervasiveness in its customers' lives. Learning how to capitalize on obvious synergies between the various channels is key to getting the most out of digital marketing campaigns!

(adapted from National Computing Centre, 2006)

This discussion of marketing relates to the discussion in Chapter 3, Section 3 about how marketing and advertising in particular can pressurise people to increase consumption. Yet, as you may remember from Chapter 3, advertising, at least in principle, has the function of improving the quality and quantity of information flowing to citizens. One challenge in our consumer society is to make an informed decision when faced with an increasing number of choices.

A fourth change to emerge from the growth in digital technology is the development of person-to-person transactions that bypass traditional corporations. Perhaps the best-known of these is eBay where transactions take place directly between individuals, often using direct payment systems such as PayPal. Both eBay and PayPal earn their revenue by charging a small fee on certain transactions and services. One industry report estimated that, by 2006, 10 per cent of the UK population had become PayPal customers, representing some 10 million user accounts (Ilett, 2006).

eBay and PayPal are both rapidly increasing in popularity

Another report noted the development in 2005 of an online loan service called 'Zopa'. The idea behind this is similar to eBay, except, rather than buyers and sellers of goods coming together, those wishing to lend money are put in touch with those wanting to borrow money. Lenders set the interest rates at which they will lend money, and credit ratings are used to distinguish between borrowers. Those interested in taking out a loan, meanwhile, choose between different rates, and Zopa sets up the transaction, charging 1 per cent of the amount borrowed (Duffy, 2005). Zopa is licensed by the Office of Fair Trading (OFT). The long-term implications of this development for some traditional financial organisations offering saving and debt products remain to be seen.

The rapid increase in the number of financial transactions that involve credit card and other financial details being provided online has led to growing concerns about fraud and security. This, in turn, has led to new developments in regulation and consumer protection, with the OFT giving detailed guidance on online shopping. Box 10.3 gives an example of the consumer advice provided by OFT.

Box 10.3 Online shopping – before you buy

Many tips on buying on the internet are the same as for buying from a shop, such as:

- shop around! That great deal might well be on offer somewhere else – and cheaper
- use retailers and services you know about – or ones that have been personally recommended to you.

But there are also extra things to remember when shopping online:

- a company might have a great website but that doesn't mean it's law-abiding
- make sure you know the trader's full address – especially if the company is based outside the UK
- don't assume an internet company is based in the UK just because its web address has 'uk' in it – check out the physical address and phone number
- look for websites that have a secure way of paying (known as an encryption facility) – these show a padlock at the bottom of the screen when you are filling in the payment details
- check whether the company has a privacy statement that tells you what it will do with your personal information.

Look for firms that are part of an independent approval scheme such as TrustUK. These are companies that have signed up to particular standards. These include measures to:

- protect your privacy
- ensure your payments are secure
- let you know what you've agreed to
- tell you how to cancel orders
- deliver goods or services within agreed timescales
- protect children
- sort out complaints – regardless of where you live.

Please note: There are many different trader approval schemes worldwide – so check out what their particular approval means.

(OFT, 2006)

Activity 10.8

What impact do you think the rise of internet technology will have upon the kind of financial exclusion described in Chapter 1, Section 2?

Comment

One possibility is that the rise of internet technology could add to financial exclusion because low-income households may not be able to afford the costs of computer equipment and broadband rental, excluding them from the lower prices associated with the online marketplace. For instance, in 2004/05 in the UK among households in the top 20 per cent for income, 87 per cent had an internet connection; this compared with only 18 per cent of households in the bottom 20 per cent for income – a difference of 69 per cent (*Social Trends*, 2006, p. 191, Figure 13.5). However, one counter-argument is that the internet improves financial *inclusion* by making it easier for people who may be at home for much of the time, for example, carers, the elderly and the less mobile, to have access to the range of financial choices available through the internet. ■ ■ ■

Without doubt, the growth of digital technology has significant implications for personal finance. Perhaps the most important of these relates to information: there will be more of it and it will be available all the time. This will mean that the citizens of the future may face an even wider variety of financial choices than in the past, and that these will be presented through increasingly sophisticated personalised marketing techniques. Moreover, these citizens will also have access to more information about the quality of goods and services, and instant access to details of their bank accounts, savings accounts and investments. The second of these may mean that tracking and managing flows of income and expenditure, and keeping track of the value of assets, becomes easier and more transparent. Conversely, online accounts could make it harder to keep track, since, instead of being prompted regularly by statements arriving through the post, the onus may be on the consumer to log on and seek out information, requiring more pro-active engagement. There may also be implications in terms of who in the household has access to the information. The challenge for individuals and their households, as they are presented with more and more information, is to make sense of the important information. In this process, the knowledge and skills you have learned in *Personal Finance*, especially using the financial planning process to make informed financial decisions, will become increasingly relevant.

Looking back over the content of *Personal Finance*, what other changes in the economic and social context can you think of that would have a substantial impact on personal finance matters?

There are *many* different examples you might have thought of. Here are three other examples of changes in economic and social context that could have an impact on personal finance in the future:

1   Changes in government social policies, such as changes in policies on care, or changes to the National Health Service (NHS). If, for instance, more charges were to be introduced into the NHS, this might change financial decision making about private medical insurance.

2   Taxation changes, such as changes to the rates of Income Tax or changes to the thresholds for Stamp Duty Land Tax or Inheritance Tax. If, for example, Stamp Duty Land Tax were to be abolished or, alternatively, increased substantially, this would have significant impacts on decisions about property purchase. In turn, such changed decisions could affect property prices.

3   Economic changes, such as changes in the rate of inflation or the level of interest rates. To illustrate, if inflation were to rise rapidly, this could affect many financial decisions such as how much to save, whether to buy or rent property, and ensuring that planning for retirement was inflation proofed. ■ ■ ■

5   Conclusion

The two issues of demographic and technological change in Section 4 of this chapter offer specific examples of how the themes covered in this book can be applied to working through some of the financial implications of future change. As you encounter and engage with change in the future – whether it is economic, social, cultural, demographic or technological – the knowledge and understanding you have built up through reading *Personal Finance* will improve your ability to make informed financial decisions. This doesn't necessarily mean that you'll be satisfied with the outcome of every financial decision that you take, but it does mean that you will be able to respond better to different and developing financial situations. That's because you have developed greater financial capability, enabling you to ask the right questions – and better judge the quality of the answers.

References

Age Concern (2005) 'Briefing on older voters' [online], http://www.20millionvotes.org.uk/briefing_older_voters.html (Accessed 8 February 2006).

Alliance & Leicester (2006) 'Britons banking on an online future' [online], 1 March, http://www.alliance-leicestergroup.co.uk/html/media/non-indexed/release.asp?txtTable=pressreleases&txtCode=PR0103061 (Accessed 23 March 2006).

BBC (2005) 'Online shopping "soaring in UK"' [online], http://news.bbc.co.uk/go/pr/fr/-/1/hi/business/4281927.stm (Accessed 23 March 2006).

BBC (2006) 'Festive boom for online shopping' [online], http://news.bbc.co.uk/go/pr/fr/-/1/hi/business/4630472.stm (Accessed 23 March 2006).

Council of Mortgage Lenders (CML) (2005) Table MM7, 'Equity release market summary: annual' [online], http://www.cml.org.uk/cml/statistics (Accessed 14 May 2006).

Duffy, J. (2005) 'If the world was run like eBay' [online], http://news.bbc.co.uk/go/pr/fr/-/2/hi/uk_news/magazine/4334391.stm (Accessed 23 March 2006).

Easynet (2004) 'Ecommerce boom' [online], http://www.uk.easynet.net/corporate/retail_newsletter/article_2.asp (Accessed 23 March 2006).

Government Actuary's Department (GAD) (2005) 'United Kingdom males: cohort expectations of life' [online], http://www.gad.gov.uk/Life_Tables/docs/2004/20045yrUKcohort1981web.xls_(Accessed 14 May 2006).

Ilett, D. (2006) 'Where next for PayPal?' [online], 21 March, http://www.silicon.com/financialservices/0,3800010322,39157275,00.htm (Accessed 23 March 2006).

National Computing Centre (2006) 'Digital marketing strategies' [online], http://www.nccmembership.co.uk/POOLED/articles/bf_webart/view.asp?Q=bf_webart_113188 (Accessed 23 March 2006).

Office for National Statistics (ONS) (2006) 'Internet access' [online], http://www.statistics.gov.uk/cci/nugget.asp?id=8 (Accessed 23 March 2006).

Office for National Statistics (ONS)/Department for Work and Pensions (DWP) (2005) *Focus on Older People*, Basingstoke and New York, Palgrave Macmillan; also available online at http://www.statistics.gov.uk/

downloads/theme_compendia/foop05/Olderpeople2005.pdf (Accessed 19 April 2006).

Office of Fair Trading (OFT) (2006) 'Online shopping – before you buy' [online], http://www.oft.gov.uk/Consumer/Your+Rights+When +Shopping+From+Home/Online+shopping/Before+you+buy.htm (Accessed 23 March 2006).

Social Trends (2006) no. 36, Basingstoke and New York, Palgrave Macmillan for The Office for National Statistics (ONS); also available online at the ONS website, http://www.statistics.gov.uk/downloads/ theme_social/Social_Trends36/Social_Trends_36.pdf (Accessed 20 April 2006).

Townsend, S. (2005) *Adrian Mole and the Weapons of Mass Destruction*, London, Penguin.

Glossary

Actuaries: Professionals who analyse risk and its financial impact.

Adverse selection: The tendency for people who have a greater than average likelihood of suffering a peril to apply for insurance to a greater extent than other people.

Agency: Attempts to respond to and influence circumstances and the broader social and economic context.

Annual Equivalent Rate (AER): AER or Annual Equivalent Rate is the rate of interest on savings products calculated to take into account different payment patterns.

Annual Percentage Rate (APR): APR or Annual Percentage Rate is a summary figure for comparing debt costs which brings together interest rates and other charges.

Annuity: A type of investment where the investor pays a lump sum and in return receives an income paid either for a set period or, as in the case of most pensions, for the rest of their life. Once the investment is made, they cannot change their mind or get their lump sum back.

Asset allocation decision: The choice of how to divide a savings and investments portfolio across cash deposits, bonds and equities.

Assets: Everything that a person owns that has a monetary value (e.g. property, investments or cash).

Asymmetric information: Where one party knows something that another does not. It's frequently used to refer to information that people wanting insurance might know about their own risks that they do not reveal to their insurers.

Bankruptcy: A process that happens when an individual cannot pay their debts, and all their property is distributed to the people to whom they owe money.

Bear market: A market in which prices are falling. A 'bear' is a person who expects that the market or the price of a particular share will fall and so sells – perhaps in order to buy the shares at a lower price later on.

Bond: A certificate of debt that is issued by a government or corporation in order to raise money.

Bridging loan: A temporary loan to extend further funds during the selling of one property, when the seller has already acquired another.

Broker: A person who buys and sells securities on behalf of others in return for brokerage or commission.

Budget: A detailed plan of income and expenditure expected over a certain period of time.

Bull market: A market in which prices are rising. A 'bull' is a person who expects that the stock market or the price of a particular share will rise and so buys in the hope of making a profit on selling at a higher price.

Capital Gains Tax: A tax on capital 'gains'. If an asset has increased in value when it is sold or given away, the 'gain' (profit) above a certain threshold (£8800 in 2006/07) may be taxable.

Caring: Providing a personal service to help someone who is not capable of looking after their own personal needs.

Cash flow statement: A record of income and expenditure over a certain period of time.

Child Support Agency (CSA): The Child Support Agency is an executive agency of the Department for Work and Pensions (DWP) that is responsible for ensuring that parents who live apart meet their financial responsibilities to their children.

Compounding: The process by which interest repayments are added to the original amount borrowed to give a higher total figure which, in turn, attracts interest rate charges.

Conspicuous consumption: The ostentatious display of wealth in order to gain recognition by others of an increase in one's status.

Consumer society: A society in which people place a high value on possessions, and are continually encouraged to purchase more.

Consumer sovereignty: An assumption that consumers have the power to dictate the types, quality and quantity of the goods and services provided in a market place.

Council Tax: A domestic property tax collected by local authorities based on the estimated property value so that the bigger the property, the higher the tax. Some adults such as full-time students and carers are 'disregarded' for Council Tax; a 25 per cent discount is applied to households with only one adult who is not disregarded; a 50 per cent discount is applied to households where *all* the residents are disregarded (such as a household consisting only of full-time students).

Credit: An arrangement to receive cash, goods or services now and to pay for them in the future.

Cross sectional: Data relating to different variables at the same time period.

Current asset ratio: Total liquid assets divided by total short-term liabilities.

Cyclical: A recurring pattern of a variable over time showing peaks and low points at regular intervals.

Defined benefit: Describes a pension scheme where the pension is worked out according to a formula, usually linked to pay and length of time in the scheme.

Defined contribution/Money purchase: Describes a pension scheme where the pension depends on the amount paid in, how the invested money grows, and the amount of pension that can be purchased from an insurance company at retirement.

Dependent child: A child aged 0 to 15 in a household; or a child aged 16 to 19 in either unwaged work-based training, or education or training to the end of the course or age 20 (whichever is earlier) *and* living with his or her parents.

Diversification: An investment strategy that aims to reduce market risk by combining a variety of investments, such as stocks and bonds, that are unlikely to all move in the same direction at the same time.

Dividends: The part of a company's post-tax profits distributed to shareholders, usually expressed as an amount per share.

Economies of scale: Decreases in the unit cost of production or consumption associated with increasing scale.

Equity release scheme: A way of unlocking the wealth tied up in a home while retaining the right to live there until death or until the home is no longer needed (for example, moving into a care home). The money released can be taken as a lump sum, as income, or as a combination of both (income is usually provided by buying an annuity).

Equity withdrawal: The process whereby mortgage levels are increased to release funds for additional spending.

Equity: Equity in a property is the excess of the market value of the property over the outstanding mortgage debt secured against it.

Equivalised: Household income adjusted to take account of household size and composition. For example, a household of three would require a higher income than a household of one.

Ethical investment: Investments made in companies that are deemed to be socially responsible. Ethical investments tend to exclude companies involved in tobacco, gambling and the arms industry.

European Economic Area (EEA): A free trade area consisting of the European Union (EU) members, plus Iceland, Norway and Liechtenstein.

Excess: An initial monetary amount of an insured loss that the insured will have to pay out themselves.

Family: A group of people who are related and responsible for each other and comprise at least a parent and child.

Financial balance sheet: A financial tool that records household or individual assets and liabilities at a particular point in time.

Financial constraint: Inadequate resources which limit achievable goals.

Financial exclusion: Lack of access to mainstream banking and financial services.

Financial intermediaries: Persons and institutions who arrange investments (and other products) on behalf of others, such as financial advisers and brokers.

Fixed costs: Costs that remain the same regardless of how much is consumed or produced.

Flat rate: Describes an amount of pension where the value is not linked to a person's earnings.

Friendly Societies: Mutual organisations that provide savings and life insurance plans to their members. They benefit from special tax treatment but investors can only put in small amounts, currently £25 per month.

Funded scheme: Pension scheme where an investment fund is built up from which to pay pensions and other benefits as they fall due.

Gilts: Gilts raise money for the UK Government by offering a secure investment, usually over a fixed period with a fixed rate of interest. Gilts can be bought and sold on the London Stock Exchange. At the end of the term, the holder is repaid the original purchase price.

Graduate earnings premium: The extra earnings received by virtue of having a university degree.

Gross Domestic Product (GDP): The value of all goods and services produced by an economy over a set period of time, usually a particular year.

Gross income: Total income before any deductions have been made.

Heuristics: Rules of thumb used to guide one in the direction of probable solutions to a problem.

HM Revenue & Customs (HMRC): HMRC is the department responsible for the business of the former Inland Revenue and HM Customs and Excise – and collects the bulk of tax revenue as well as paying tax credits and Child Benefit.

Household reference person: The member of a household who brings in its highest income without regard to gender. (Before April 2001,

men were usually assumed to be the head of household.)

Household saving ratio: The savings ratio measures the percentage of annual total household disposable that is saved (in the UK, this does not include employees' contributions to pension schemes).

Household: A person living alone or a group of people who have the address as their only or main residence and who either share one meal a day or share the living accommodation.

Human capital: The accumulation of a person's knowledge and skills, built up through formal or informal education and training.

Income Tax: A tax which is payable on almost all sources of income within a given tax year from 6 April to the following 5 April. There is no minimum age at which a person becomes liable to pay income tax.

Income: Money *flows* received over time.

Independent Financial Advisers (IFAs): Advisers who can select from all available products, and are authorised and regulated by the Financial Services Authority (FSA), which means complying with FSA rules, including giving 'suitable advice'.

Independent risks: Risks whose occurrence is unrelated to one another.

Individual Savings Account (ISA): An ISA allows up to £7000 savings per tax year, with no tax on the capital gain or interest received (dividend and share-based income is taxed at 10 per cent). In each tax year you can either save in one Maxi ISA, which can include both cash (up to £3000) and shares, or you can have two Mini ISAs – one for up to £3000 cash, and one for up to £4000 shares. You cannot invest in both a Mini ISA and a Maxi ISA in the same tax year, and you can only open one Maxi ISA in each tax year.

Inflation: A continual increase in the general level of prices. The rate of inflation is expressed as a percentage figure and measures how much a typical 'basket' of goods changes in price from one year to the next.

Informal economy: Paid employment that is hidden from the state.

Inheritance Tax: Tax on the value of a deceased person's net assets (also known as the person's 'estate') above a tax-free threshold. Tax may also be levied on any gifts made during the seven years before death, and on a few lifetime gifts.

Insolvency: When someone is unable to pay the debts they owe.

Insurance Premium Tax (IPT): A tax levied by the UK Government on some insurance premiums.

Insurance: A system by which individuals or households, in exchange for payment of a sum of money (called a 'premium'), are guaranteed indemnity for losses resulting from certain perils, under conditions specified in a contract.

Interest rate: The exact price that a borrower pays for debt, normally expressed as an annual percentage.

Interest: The charge a borrower pays for the use of someone else's money.

Interest-only mortgage: A mortgage where the periodic repayments made by the borrower to the lender are solely the interest due and where the capital or principal sum borrowed is paid off in full at the end (or 'maturity') of the mortgage.

Intestate: Dying without a valid will, meaning that law determines who benefits from the deceased's property.

Inverse relationship: A relationship between two variables that move in opposite directions.

Joint tenants: Two or more people who own a property together. The joint tenants do not own distinct shares in the property.

Key Facts Illustration (KFI): Details the features, terms and conditions of a mortgage on a standard basis, enabling comparisons to be made between different lenders' products.

Liability: An amount of money owed at a particular point in time.

Liberalisation: Government policy to promote free-markets and competition.

Life-course: The time profile of various stages in a person's life.

Liquid assets: Those assets that can be quickly converted into cash.

Loan-to-value (LTV): A measure of a loan (or mortgage) as a proportion of the lender's valuation of the property on which the loan (or mortgage) is secured.

Manufacturing: Manufacturing jobs are those in industries that convert raw materials and components into goods (e.g. textiles, steel, cars).

Market timing: A technique of buying and selling stocks in conjunction with the ups and downs of the market.

Means tested: Means tested refers to payments that are made only to those who are assessed to have a certain level of income or less, and in some cases, a certain level of assets or less.

Mis-selling: High-pressure or misleading sales techniques inducing people to buy inappropriate financial products.

Moral hazard: The tendency for an insured person to become willing to take on more risk because they are covered by insurance.

Mortgage indemnity guarantee (MIG): An insurance policy which insures the lender for any losses on lending above a defined minimum loan-to-value sum. This is charged to the borrower.

Mortgage: A loan secured on property or land.

National Insurance: Contributions from both employees and employers which form the basis for paying state benefits related to unemployment, sick pay and pensions.

Negative equity: Where the market value of a property is exceeded by the outstanding mortgage debt secured against it.

Net income: Income after deductions such as Income Tax and National Insurance.

Net saving: Household net income minus household expenditure.

Net worth/net wealth: The value of all assets minus all liabilities.

Nursing care: Care that is needed because of a specific medical condition.

Occupation: A group of similar jobs found in different industries or organisations.

Occupational pension: Pension from a scheme provided by an employer for workers and their dependants.

Opportunity cost: The cost of doing or having something measured in terms of the best alternative forgone.

Other things being equal: A term used by economists and others to indicate that while changing one factor, other factors remain unchanged.

Overdraft: A facility provided by banks and some building societies which allows customers to go into debt on their current account.

Owner-occupation: To own outright, or to be in the process of buying, the property you are living in.

Paid employment: Work that receives a financial payment.

Part-time pay penalty: The difference between the wage rate that a person would receive in full-time employment and what they receive in a part-time job.

Pay-as-you-go (PAYG) scheme: Pension scheme where pensions and other benefits paid out today are paid for out of tax revenues collected today.

Pension: A regular payment that forms part of financial support in old age.

Pensioner: A person who has started to draw a pension whether or not they continue to do some paid work.

Peril: An event that causes a financial loss.

Personal care: Help with personal aspects of normal living such as washing, dressing, or preparing a meal, and supervision to prevent accidents.

Personal pension: Pension from a retirement savings scheme taken out by an individual to provide for themselves and their dependants.

Portfolio: A set of financial assets held by an individual (or a bank or other financial institution).

Pound cost averaging: The investment technique of allocating a fixed sum for the purchase of particular investments on a monthly (or other periodic) basis. When prices fall, the fixed amount will buy more shares/units, and when prices rise, fewer shares/units are bought.

Premium Bonds: A Premium Bond is a bond issued by the UK Government's National Savings & Investments scheme. The government pays interest on the bond, but instead of the interest being paid into individual accounts, it is paid into a prize fund, from which a monthly lottery distributes tax-free prizes.

Principal sum (or capital sum): The original amount of debt taken out.

Private pension: Used collectively to refer to occupational pensions and personal pensions as opposed to state pensions.

Probability: A measurement of the likelihood that an event will occur. Probabilities are expressed as numbers between 0 and 1.

Productivity: The amount of output (of goods and services) per unit of inputs used to produce it. If productivity increases, there will be more output from the same inputs.

Progressive taxation: A tax whereby the proportion of a person's income paid as tax increases as their income increases.

Public good: A good or service that can be consumed simultaneously by different people, and from which each person can benefit, and cannot be excluded.

Pure risks: Risks that give rise to a definite loss, and where the occurrence of the event is not under the control of the person(s) that might suffer the loss. Such risks can usually (but not always) be insured against.

Recession: A reduction in the level of economic activity measured by two consecutive quarters of negative economic growth.

Redistribution of income: The process of re-allocating income to achieve social objectives, usually the creation of a 'fairer society' through a more equal distribution.

Registered civil partner: A same-sex partner treated in the same way for tax, benefit and most legal purposes as a husband or wife. Two people of the same sex can form a civil partnership by signing a registration document.

Registered Social Landlords (RSLs): Providers of rented social housing who are registered with, and regulated by, the relevant national body in the four nations of the United Kingdom (such as the Housing Corporation in England). Most RSLs are housing associations, but others include trusts and cooperatives.

Renting: A form of housing tenure where the person who lives in the house is a tenant, paying rent to the landlord, who owns the property.

Repayment mortgage: A mortgage where the periodic repayments made to the lender are the sum of the interest due and an amount of the original capital (or 'principal') sum borrowed.

Retirement: The period of life after (the main source of) paid employment ends.

Right-to-buy: The entitlement of the tenant of a rented public sector property to buy that property from the owner.

Risk society: A society that is preoccupied with ideas of safety in response to the perception of increased risk brought about by the modern world.

Risk: Where the probability of something happening is known or where the probability can be estimated.

Risk-aversion: Preferring a lower but more certain financial return rather than a higher but less certain return.

Saving: A flow of money that contributes towards a household's savings.

Savings: The total value of all financial assets (including investments) that a household has at a particular point in time.

Secured debt: Debt secured against an asset such as a home. If the debtor fails to make adequate repayments, the lender has a right to obtain money by selling the asset.

Self-insurance: The process of establishing a fund to cover the costs of any potential financial loss.

Services: Service sector jobs include those in business services and finance, education, hotels and restaurants, the health sector and most public sector work.

Shares (or equities): A part ownership in a company.

Small print: A product's terms and conditions, typically written in small letters and/or technical jargon.

Social class: An informal ranking of people in a society based on their income, occupation, education, and other factors.

Social norms: Accepted ways of behaving that are generally approved of in society.

Social status: A social position within a society; or the social honour or prestige that a particular individual or group is accorded by other members of a society.

Stamp Duty Land Tax: A tax payable by the purchaser when a property is bought and its price is over a certain threshold, the amount payable being calculated as a percentage of the total purchase price.

Standard of living: The quality of life enjoyed by an individual or household, depending on factors such as income, housing condition, the environment, and public services such as health and education.

State additional pension: A state pension available mainly to employees. The amount received varies from one person to another depending largely on their average earnings while the pension was building up.

State pension age: The age at which a person becomes eligible to draw a state pension. In the UK, this is 65 for men and, until 2010, 60 for women but then rises to 65 for women born after 5 March 1955. In 2006, the Government proposed raising the state pension age in stages to age 68 by 2044.

State pension: Pension provided by the government to everyone in the UK who qualifies.

Status symbol: A status symbol is something that indicates the social status of its owner. Usually a status symbol is a mark of high status.

Support ratio: The number of people of working age divided by the number of people over state pension age.

Symbolic consumption: Consuming products or lifestyles for social meanings attached to those products or lifestyles for others to see

Tenants-in-common: Two or more people who own a property together. Each has a distinct share.

Term: The period of time over which a debt is to be repaid.

Time preference: The tendency of people to prefer 'present goods and services' (those available for consumption now) to 'future goods and services' (those expected to be available for consumption at a future date).

Trade-off: A sacrifice of something in order to have something else.

Transferable skills: Skills acquired through training or previous employment that would be useful in other jobs.

Uncertainty: Where the probability of an event cannot be estimated.

Unit trusts: Collective funds that allow private investors to pool their money in a single fund.

Unpaid work: Unpaid activity that contributes to the well-being of people and would otherwise have to be paid for. It includes looking after a household and caring for people.

Unsecured debt: Debt not backed by any asset.

Utmost good faith: A legal obligation to disclose any detail that may be of some importance to insurers, whether or not it is requested.

Welfare state: A system whereby the state funds or provides public services and redistributes income to provide a 'safety net' for its citizens.

Working life: An official definition meaning the tax years from age 16 to state pension age. For a person whose state pension age is 65, working life is 49 years.

Write-off: A damaged or stolen car that insurers decide to pay an agreed value for rather than paying for the cost of repairs.

Index

Acknowledgements

Grateful acknowledgement is made to the following sources:

Chapter 1

Text: Box 1.1: Courtesy of the Citizens Advise Bureau; *Box 1.3: Personal Finance and One Parent Families: The Facts (summary),* 2004. By permission of One Parent Families.
Photographs: Page 11 top left: Copyright © Charles Hewitt/Hulton Archive/Getty Images; *Page 11 top right:* Copyright © Harold M. Lambert/Getty Images; *Page 11 bottom left:* Copyright © Image Source/ Rex Features; *Page 11 bottom right:* Copyright © Daniel Sambraus/Science Photo Library; *Page 24 top left and bottom left:* Copyright © John Birdsall www.JohnBirdsall.co.uk; *Page 24 top right:* Copyright © Bubbles/Ian West; *Page 24 bottom right:* Copyright © Paul Brown/Rex Features.

Chapter 2

Text: Box 2.3: 'Young people set to miss out on £4,000 a year by dropping out', Learning Skills Council. Crown copyright material is reproduced under Class Licence Number C01W0000065 with the permission of the Controller of HMSO and the Queen's Printer for Scotland; *Box 2.5:* MacErlean, N. (2004) 'Six million say: it's no credit to the government', *The Observer,* 5 December 2004. Copyright © Guardian Newspapers Limited 2004.
Photographs: Page 47 top left: Copyright © Andrew Holt/Alamy; *Page 47 top right:* Copyright © David Cole/Rex Features; *Page 47 bottom right:* Copyright © Don Carstens/Rex Features; *Page 62:* Copyright © Robert Judges/Rex Features; *Page 67:* Copyright © Image Source/Rex Features; *Page 68:* Copyright © Ingram Publishing/Alamy; *Page 75 right:* Copyright © John Birdsall www.JohnBirdsall.co.uk; *Page 78:* Copyright © Jonathan Banks/Rex Features.

Chapter 3

Figures: Figure 3.4 left: By kind permission of Citroen UK Ltd, image courtesy of The Advertising Archives; *Figure 3.4 right:* Image courtesy of The Advertising Archives.
Photographs: Page 91: Science Photo Library; *Page 94 left:* Copyright © Chris Ison/PA/Empics; *Page 94 right:* Copyright © Jonathan Hordle/Rex Features.

Chapter 4

Photographs: *Page 138 left:* Copyright © Toby Melville/PA/Empics; *Page 138 right:* Copyright © Martin Higginson; *Page 145:* Copyright © Des Jenson/Photoshot; *Page 156:* Copyright © Justin Pumfrey/Taxi/Getty Images; *Page 160:* Courtesy of the Advertising Archives; *Page 163 top:* By permission of Consumer Credit Counselling Service; *Page 163 bottom:* Copyright © TopFoto.co.uk.
Cartoon: *Page 139:* Stan McMurty, *Daily Mail*, 11 May 2005. Copyright © Solo Syndication. Centre for the Study of Cartoons and Caricature, University of Kent.

Chapter 5

Text: *Box 5.1:* Press Association (2005) 'Savings hit record high as concerns mount over debt', *The Guardian*, 14 December 2005. Copyright © Press Association; *Box 5.5:* National Savings & Investments www.nsandi.com; *Box 5.7:* 'What is ethical investment?' (2006) The Ethical Investment Partnership Ltd.
Tables: *Table 5.4: Social Trends* 2005. Crown copyright material is reproduced under Class Licence Number C01W0000065 with the permission of the Controller of HMSO and the Queen's Printer for Scotland; *Table 5.7:* Cowie, I. (2005) 'Take a hundred years and £100 and equities could make you a millionaire', *Daily Telegraph*, 25 February 2005.
Figures: *Figures 5.2, 5.3 and 5.4:* Halifax plc; *Figure 5.5 top right:* Courtesy of The Advertising Archives; *Figure 5.5 bottom right:* Courtesy of The Advertising Archives; *Figure 5.7:* Alessie, R. et al. (1997) 'Income and wealth over the life cycle: evidence from the panel data', *Review of Income and Wealth*, series 43, no. 1. Blackwell Publishing Limited.
Photographs: *Page 199:* Copyright © Epictura/Alamy; *Page 208:* Copyright © Carl Fox/Rex Features; *Page 200:* Debt Management Office; *Page 210:* By permission of Mellon Global Investments.

Chapter 6

Text: *Box 6.3:* 'Gap between the cost of renting and buying narrows' (2005) Abbey National plc; *Box 6.6:* Copyright © Financial Services Authority.
Figures: *Figure 6.1:* National Statistics Online www.statistics.gov.uk. Crown copyright material is reproduced under Class Licence Number C01W0000065 with the permission of the Controller of HMSO and the Queen's Printer for Scotland; *Figure 6.2:* English House Condition Survey, Department of the Environment. Crown copyright material is reproduced under Class Licence Number C01W0000065 with the permission of the Controller of HMSO and the Queen's Printer for Scotland; *Figure 6.3:*

National Statistics Online www.statistics.gov.uk. Crown copyright material is reproduced under Class Licence Number C01W0000065 with the permission of the Controller of HMSO and the Queen's Printer for Scotland; *Figure 6.6:* Lloyds TSB plc.

Photographs: *Page 225 top left:* Copyright © John Birdsall www. JohnBirdsall.co.uk; *Page 225 top right:* Copyright © Tim Graham/Alamy; *Page 225 bottom left:* Copyright © Martin Higginson; *Page 225 bottom right:* Copyright © John Birdsall www.JohnBirdsall.co.uk; *Page 241:* Copyright © Sally & Richard Greenhill; *Page 243:* Copyright © Toby Melville/PA/ Empics.

Chapter 7

Photographs: *Page 275:* Copyright © Kirsty Wigglesworth/PA/Empics; *Page 281:* Copyright © Hulton-Deutsch Collection/Corbis; *Page 294:* Copyright © Reuters/Toby Melville; *Page 309:* Copyright © Martin Godwin.

Cartoon: Page 273: Copyright © Roger Beale.

Chapter 8

Photographs: *Page 320:* Copyright © Rex Features; *Pages 328, 329, 331 centre and 343:* Copyright © John Birdsall www.JohnBirdsall.co.uk; *Page 331 left:* Copyright © Bubbles-Jennie Woodcock; *Page 331 right:* Copyright © Assunta Del Buono www.JohnBirdsall.co.uk; *Page 353 left:* Copyright © Garry Hunter/Stone/Getty Images; *Page 353 right:* Copyright © Robert Llewellyn/Corbis.

Chapter 9

Text: *Box 9.1:* Harvey, F. (2005) 'Big rise in the cost of storms over next 70 years forecast by insurers', *Financial Times*, 29 June 2005; *Box 9.6:* Sankey, K. (2004) 'Life: it's all in the genes', *Reinsurance Magazine*, 1 May 2004, Incisive Media.

Table: *Table 9.1:* 'UK Insurance – Key Facts' (2005) Association of British Insurers.

Photographs: *Page 369:* Copyright © John Bazemore/AP/Empics; *Page 377 left:* Courtesy of Mary Evans Picture Library; *Page 377 right:* Copyright © Patrick Barth/Rex Features; *Page 378 right:* Courtesy of The Advertising Archives; *Page 392 left:* Copyright © Stephanie Paschal/Rex Features; *Page 392 right:* Copyright © BAA plc, see: www.baa.com/ photolibrary.

Chapter 10

Text: *Box 10.1:* 'Agenda for the UK General Election' (2005) *Age Concern*. By permission of Age Concern.

Figures: *Figure 10.2:* Soule, A. et al. (eds) (2005) Focus on Older People, *Office of National Statistics*. Crown copyright material is reproduced under Class Licence Number C01W0000065 with the permission of the Controller of HMSO and the Queen's Printer for Scotland; *Figure 10.3:* National Statistics Omnibus Survey (2006) *Office of National Statistics*. Crown copyright material is reproduced under Class Licence Number C01W0000065 with the permission of the Controller of HMSO and the Queen's Printer for Scotland.

Photographs: *Page 412:* Copyright © TopFoto.co.uk; *Page 419 left:* Copyright © Nicholas Bailey/Rex Features; *Page 419 right:* Copyright © Tony Sapiano/Rex Features; *Page 432:* By kind permission of Domino's Pizza, UK.

Cover

Copyright © Big Cheese Photo LLC/Alamy.